Marx, Engels, and Marxisms

The Marx renaissance is underway on a global scale. Wherever the critique of capitalism re-emerges, there is an intellectual and political demand for new, critical engagements with Marxism. The peer-reviewed series Marx, Engels and Marxisms (edited by Marcello Musto & Terrell Carver, with Babak Amini, Francesca Antonini, Paula Rauhala & Kohei Saito as Assistant Editors) publishes monographs, edited volumes, critical editions, reprints of old texts, as well as translations of books already published in other languages. Our volumes come from a wide range of political perspectives, subject matters, academic disciplines and geographical areas, producing an eclectic and informative collection that appeals to a diverse and international audience. Our main areas of focus include: the oeuvre of Marx and Engels, Marxist authors and traditions of the 19th and 20th centuries, labour and social movements, Marxist analyses of contemporary issues, and reception of Marxism in the world.

More information about this series at
http://www.palgrave.com/gp/series/14812

Marcello Musto
Editor

Rethinking Alternatives with Marx

Economy, Ecology and Migration

palgrave
macmillan

Editor
Marcello Musto
Department of Sociology
York University
Toronto, ON, Canada

ISSN 2524-7123 ISSN 2524-7131 (electronic)
Marx, Engels, and Marxisms
ISBN 978-3-030-81763-3 ISBN 978-3-030-81764-0 (eBook)
https://doi.org/10.1007/978-3-030-81764-0

Cover illustration: "Marx in the USA", digital illustration. Joey Guidone/2021. Used with permission

This Palgrave Macmillan imprint is published by the registered company Springer Nature Switzerland AG
The registered company address is: Gewerbestrasse 11, 6330 Cham, Switzerland

Titles Published

1. Terrell Carver & Daniel Blank, *A Political History of the Editions of Marx and Engels's "German Ideology" Manuscripts*, 2014.
2. Terrell Carver & Daniel Blank, *Marx and Engels's "German Ideology" Manuscripts: Presentation and Analysis of the "Feuerbach chapter,"* 2014.
3. Alfonso Maurizio Iacono, *The History and Theory of Fetishism*, 2015.
4. Paresh Chattopadhyay, *Marx's Associated Mode of Production: A Critique of Marxism*, 2016.
5. Domenico Losurdo, *Class Struggle: A Political and Philosophical History*, 2016.
6. Frederick Harry Pitts, *Critiquing Capitalism Today: New Ways to Read Marx*, 2017.
7. Ranabir Samaddar, *Karl Marx and the Postcolonial Age*, 2017.
8. George Comninel, *Alienation and Emancipation in the Work of Karl Marx*, 2018.
9. Jean-Numa Ducange & Razmig Keucheyan (Eds.), *The End of the Democratic State: Nicos Poulantzas, a Marxism for the 21st Century*, 2018.
10. Robert X. Ware, *Marx on Emancipation and Socialist Goals: Retrieving Marx for the Future*, 2018.
11. Xavier LaFrance & Charles Post (Eds.), *Case Studies in the Origins of Capitalism*, 2018.

12. John Gregson, *Marxism, Ethics, and Politics: The Work of Alasdair MacIntyre*, 2018.
13. Vladimir Puzone & Luis Felipe Miguel (Eds.), *The Brazilian Left in the 21st Century: Conflict and Conciliation in Peripheral Capitalism*, 2019.
14. James Muldoon & Gaard Kets (Eds.), *The German Revolution and Political Theory*, 2019.
15. Michael Brie, *Rediscovering Lenin: Dialectics of Revolution and Metaphysics of Domination*, 2019.
16. August H. Nimtz, *Marxism versus Liberalism: Comparative Real-Time Political Analysis*, 2019.
17. Gustavo Moura de Cavalcanti Mello and Mauricio de Souza Sabadini (Eds.), *Financial Speculation and Fictitious Profits: A Marxist Analysis*, 2019.
18. Shaibal Gupta, Marcello Musto & Babak Amini (Eds), *Karl Marx's Life, Ideas, and Influences: A Critical Examination on the Bicentenary*, 2019.
19. Igor Shoikhedbrod, *Revisiting Marx's Critique of Liberalism: Rethinking Justice, Legality, and Rights*, 2019.
20. Juan Pablo Rodríguez, *Resisting Neoliberal Capitalism in Chile: The Possibility of Social Critique*, 2019.
21. Kaan Kangal, *Friedrich Engels and the Dialectics of Nature*, 2020.
22. Victor Wallis, *Socialist Practice: Histories and Theories*, 2020.
23. Alfonso Maurizio Iacono, *The Bourgeois and the Savage: A Marxian Critique of the Image of the Isolated Individual in Defoe, Turgot and Smith*, 2020.
24. Terrell Carver, *Engels before Marx*, 2020.
25. Jean-Numa Ducange, *Jules Guesde: The Birth of Socialism and Marxism in France*, 2020.
26. Antonio Oliva, Ivan Novara & Angel Oliva (Eds.), *Marx and Contemporary Critical Theory: The Philosophy of Real Abstraction*, 2020.
27. Francesco Biagi, *Henri Lefebvre's Critical Theory of Space*, 2020.
28. Stefano Petrucciani, *The Ideas of Karl Marx: A Critical Introduction*, 2020.
29. Terrell Carver, *The Life and Thought of Friedrich Engels, 30th Anniversary Edition*, 2020.
30. Giuseppe Vacca, *Alternative Modernities: Antonio Gramsci's Twentieth Century*, 2020

31. Kevin B. Anderson, Kieran Durkin & Heather Brown (Eds.), *Raya Dunayevskaya's Intersectional Marxism: Race, Gender, and the Dialectics of Liberation*, 2020.
32. Marco Di Maggio, *The Rise and Fall of Communist Parties in France and Italy*, 2020.
33. Ryuji Sasaki, *A New Introduction to Karl Marx: New Materialism, Critique of Political Economy, and the Concept of Metabolism*, 2020.
34. Kohei Saito (Ed.), *Reexamining Engels's Legacy in the 21st Century*, 2021.
35. Paresh Chattopadhyay, *Socialism in Marx's Capital: Towards a Dealienated World*, 2021.
36. Marcello Musto, *Karl Marx's Writings on Alienation*, 2021.
37. Michael Brie & Jörn Schütrumpf, *Rosa Luxemburg: A Revolutionary Marxist at the Limits of Marxism*, 2021.
38. Stefano Petrucciani, *Theodor W. Adorno's Philosophy, Society, and Aesthetics*, 2021.
39. Miguel Vedda, *Siegfried Kracauer, or, The Allegories of Improvisation: Critical Studies*, 2021.
40. Ronaldo Munck, *Rethinking Development: Marxist Perspectives*, 2021.
41. Jean-Numa Ducange & Elisa Marcobelli (Eds.), *Selected Writings of Jean Jaurès: On Socialism, Pacifism and Marxism*, 2021.
42. Elisa Marcobelli, *Internationalism Toward Diplomatic Crisis: The Second International and French, German and Italian Socialists*, 2021.
43. James Steinhoff, *Automation and Autonomy: Labour, Capital and Machines in the Artificial Intelligence Industry*, 2021.
44. Juan Dal Maso, *Hegemony and Class Struggle: Trotsky, Gramsci and Marxism*, 2021.

Titles Forthcoming

Gianfranco Ragona & Monica Quirico, *Frontier Socialism: Self-organisation and Anti-capitalism*
Vesa Oittinen, *Marx's Russian Moment*
Kolja Lindner, *Marx, Marxism and the Question of Eurocentrism*
Adriana Petra, *Intellectuals and Communist Culture: Itineraries, Problems and Debates in Post-war Argentina*
George C. Comninel, *The Feudal Foundations of Modern Europe*
Spencer A. Leonard, *Marx, the India Question, and the Crisis of Cosmopolitanism*
Joe Collins, *Applying Marx's Capital to the 21st century*
Levy del Aguila Marchena, *Communism, Political Power and Personal Freedom in Marx*
Jeong Seongjin, *Korean Capitalism in the 21st Century: Marxist Analysis and Alternatives*
Marcello Mustè, *Marxism and Philosophy of Praxis: An Italian Perspective from Labriola to Gramsci*
Satoshi Matsui, *Normative Theories of Liberalism and Socialism: Marxist Analysis of Values*
Shannon Brincat, *Dialectical Dialogues in Contemporary World Politics: A Meeting of Traditions in Global Comparative Philosophy*
Francesca Antonini, *Reassessing Marx's Eighteenth Brumaire: Dictatorship, State, and Revolution*
Thomas Kemple, *Capital After Classical Sociology: The Faustian Lives of Social Theory*
Tsuyoshi Yuki, *Socialism, Markets and the Critique of Money: The Theory of "Labour Note"*
V. Geetha, *Bhimrao Ramji Ambedkar and the Question of Socialism in India*

Xavier Vigna, *A Political History of Factories in France: The Workers' Insubordination of 1968*
Attila Melegh, *Anti-Migrant Populism in Eastern Europe and Hungary: A Marxist Analysis*
Marie-Cecile Bouju, *A Political History of the Publishing Houses of the French Communist Party*
Gustavo Moura de Cavalcanti Mello & Henrique Pereira Braga (Eds.), *Wealth and Poverty in Contemporary Brazilian Capitalism*
Peter McMylor, Graeme Kirkpatrick & Simin Fadaee (Eds.), *Marxism, Religion, and Emancipatory Politics*
Mauro Buccheri, *Radical Humanism for the Left: The Quest for Meaning in Late Capitalism*
Rémy Herrera, *Confronting Mainstream Economics to Overcome Capitalism*
Tamás Krausz, Eszter Bartha (Eds.), *Socialist Experiences in Eastern Europe: A Hungarian Perspective*
Martin Cortés, *Marxism, Time and Politics: On the Autonomy of the Political*
João Antonio de Paula, Huga da Gama Cerqueira, Eduardo da Motta e Albuquer & Leonardo de Deus, *Marxian Economics for the 21st Century: Revaluating Marx's Critique of Political Economy*
Zhi Li, *The Concept of the Individual in the Thought of Karl Marx*
Lelio Demichelis, *Marx, Alienation and Techno-capitalism*
Dong-Min Rieu, *A Mathematical Approach to Marxian Value Theory: Time, Money, and Labor Productivity*
Salvatore Prinzi, *Representation, Expression, and Institution: The Philosophy of Merleau-Ponty and Castoriadis*
Agon Hamza, *Slavoj Žižek and the Reconstruction of Marxism*
Kei Ehara (Ed.), *Japanese Discourse on the Marxian Theory of Finance*
Éric Aunoble, *French Views on the Russian Revolution*
Paolo Favilli, *Historiography and Marxism: Innovations in Mid-Century Italy*
Terrell Carver, Smail Rapic (Eds.), *Friedrich Engels for the 21st Century: Perspectives and Problems*
Patrizia Dogliani, *A Political History of the International Union of Socialist Youth*
Alexandros Chrysis, *The Marx of Communism: Setting Limits in the Realm of Communism*
Stephen Maher, *Corporate Capitalism and the Integral State: General Electric and a Century of American Power*
Paul Raekstad, *Karl Marx's Realist Critique of Capitalism: Freedom, Alienation, and Socialism*
Alexis Cukier, *Democratic Work: Radical Democracy and the Future of Labour*
Christoph Henning, *Theories of Alienation: From Rousseau to the Present*
Daniel Egan, *Capitalism, War, and Revolution: A Marxist Analysis*
Genevieve Ritchie, Sara Carpenter & Shahrzad Mojab (Eds.), *Marxism and Migration*

Emanuela Conversano, *Capital from Afar: Anthropology and Critique of Political Economy in the Late Marx*
Vincenzo Mele, *City and Modernity in George Simmel and Walter Benjamin: Fragments of Metropolis*
David Norman Smith, *Self-Emancipation: Marx's Unfinished Theory of the Working Class*
José Ricardo Villanueva Lira, *Marxism and the Origins of International Relations*
Bertel Nygaard, *Marxism, Labor Movements, and Historiography*
Fabio Perocco (Ed.), *Racism in and for the Welfare State*
Marcos Del Roio, *Gramsci and the Emancipation of the Subaltern Classes*
Marcelo Badaró, *The Working Class from Marx to Our Times*
Tomonaga Tairako, *A New Perspective on Marx's Philosophy and Political Economy*

About the Editor

Marcello Musto is Professor of Sociology at York University (Toronto—Canada). He is author of: *Another Marx: Early Manuscripts to the International* (Bloomsbury, 2018); *The Last Years of Karl Marx: An Intellectual Biography* (Stanford University Press, 2020); and *Travels of Karl Marx: Destinations, Encounters and Reflections* (Europa Editions, forthcoming 2022). Among his edited volumes there are: *Karl Marx's Grundrisse: Foundations of the Critique of Political Economy 150 Years Later* (Routledge, 2008); *Marx for Today* (Routledge, 2012); *Workers Unite! The International 150 Years Later* (Bloomsbury, 2014); *The International After 150 Years: Labour Versus Capital, Then and Now* (with George Comninel and Victor Wallis, Routledge, 2015); *Marx's Capital after 150 Years: Critique and Alternative to Capitalism* (Routledge, 2019); *Karl Marx's Life, Ideas, Influences: A Critical Examination on the Bicentenary* (with Shaibal Gupta and Babak Amini, Palgrave, 2019); *The Marx Revival: Key Concepts and New Interpretations* (Cambridge University Press, 2020); *Karl Marx's Writings on Alienation* (Palgrave, 2021); and *The Routledge Handbook of Marx's 'Capital': A Global History of Translation, Dissemination and Reception* (with Babak Amini, Routledge, forthcoming 2022). His articles appeared in many journals, including the *International Review of Social History, Contemporary Sociology, Science & Society, Critique, Socialism and Democracy, and Economic & Political Weekly*. His writings—available at http://www.marcellomusto.org—have been published worldwide in more than twenty languages. He is also the co-editor (with Terrell Carver) of the Series *Marx, Engels, Marxisms* (Palgrave) and the editor of the Series *Critiques and Alternatives to Capitalism* (Routledge).

Preface

Which Marx?

The return to Marx following the economic crisis of 2008 has been distinct from the renewed interest in his critique of economics. Many authors, in a whole series of newspapers, journals, books, and academic volumes, have observed how indispensable Marx's analysis has proved to be for an understanding of the contradictions and destructive mechanisms of capitalism.[1] In the last few years, however, there has also been a reconsideration of Marx as a political figure and theorist.

The publication of previously unknown manuscripts in the German MEGA^2 edition,[2] along with innovative interpretations of his work, have opened up new research horizons and demonstrated more clearly than in the past his capacity to examine the contradictions of capitalist society on a global scale and in spheres beyond the conflict between capital and labour.[3] It is no exaggeration to say that, of the great classics of political,

[1] For a global perspective of the reception of Marx's work throughout the world from 2000 to 2010, see the second part of the volume Marcello Musto (ed.), *Marx for Today* (New York: Routledge, 2012), entitled 'Marx's Global Reception Today', pp. 170–234.

[2] For an updated state of the art of this edition see Marcello Musto, 'New Profiles of Marx After the *Marx-Engels-Gesamtausgabe* (MEGA^2)', *Contemporary Sociology*, vol. 49 (2020), n. 4: 407–19.

[3] See in particular the recent Marcello Musto (ed.), *The Marx Revival: Key Concepts and New Interpretations* (Cambridge: Cambridge University Press, 2020).

economic and philosophical thought, Marx is the one whose profile has changed the most in the opening decades of the twenty-first century.

As it is well known, *Capital* remained unfinished because of the grinding poverty in which Marx lived for two decades and because of his constant ill-health connected to daily worries.[4] But *Capital* was not the only project that remained incomplete. Marx's merciless self-criticism increased the difficulties of more than one of his undertakings and the large amount of time that he spent on many projects he wanted to publish was due to the extreme rigor to which he subjected all his thinking. When Marx was young, he was known among his university friends for his meticulousness. There are stories that depict him as somebody who refused 'to write a sentence if he was unable to prove it in ten different ways'.[5] This is why the most prolific young scholar in the Hegelian Left still published less than many of the others. Marx's belief that his information was insufficient, and his judgements immature, prevented him from publishing writings that remained in the form of outlines or fragments. But this is also why his notes are extremely useful and should be considered an integral part of his oeuvre. Many of his ceaseless labours had extraordinary theoretical consequences for the future.

This does not mean that his incomplete texts can be given the same weight of those that were published. One should distinguish five types of writings: published works, their preparatory manuscripts, journalistic articles, letters, and notebooks of excerpts. But distinctions must also be made within these categories. Some of Marx's published texts should not be regarded as his final word on the issues at hand. For example, the *Manifesto of the Communist Party* was considered by Friedrich Engels and Marx as a historical document from their youth and not as the definitive text in which their main political conceptions were stated. Or it must be kept in mind that political propaganda writings and scientific writings are often not combinable. These kinds of errors are very frequent in the secondary literature on Marx. Not to mention the absence of the chronological dimension in many reconstructions of his thought.

[4] Marcello Musto, 'Introduction: The Unfinished Critique of *Capital*', in: Marcello Musto (ed.), *Marx's Capital After 150 Years: Critique and Alternative to Capitalism* (London: Routledge, 2019), pp. 1–35.

[5] See Paul Lafargue, in Hans Magnus Enzensberger (ed.), *Gespräche mit Marx und Engels* (Frankfurt: Suhrkamp, 1973), p. 32.

The texts from the 1840s cannot be quoted indiscriminately alongside those from the 1860s and 1870s, since they do not carry equal weight of scientific knowledge and political experience. Some manuscripts were written by Marx only for himself, while others were actual preparatory materials for books to be published. Some were revised and often updated by Marx, while others were abandoned by him without the possibility of updating them (in this category there is *Capital*, Volume III). Some journalistic articles contain considerations that can be considered as a completion of Marx's works. Others, however, were written quickly in order to raise money to pay the rent. Some letters include Marx's authentic views on the issues discussed. Others contain only a softened version, because they were addressed to people outside Marx's circle, with whom it was sometimes necessary to express himself diplomatically. Finally, there are the more than 200 notebooks containing summaries (and sometimes commentaries) of all the most important books read by Marx during the long-time span from 1838 to 1882. They are essential for an understanding of the genesis of his theory and of those elements he was unable to develop as he would have wished.

New Profiles of a Classic Who Has Still a Lot to Say

Recent research has refuted the various approaches that reduce Marx's conception of communist society to superior development of the productive forces. In particular, it has shown the importance he attached to the ecological question: on repeated occasions, he denounced the fact that expansion ofthe capitalistmode of production increases not only the theft of workers' labour but also the pillage of natural resources.[6] Another question in which Marx took a close interest was migration. He showed that the forced movement of labour generated by capitalism was a major component of bourgeois exploitation and that the key to fighting this was class solidarity among workers, regardless of their origins or any distinction between local and imported labour.

Furthermore, Marx undertook thorough investigations of societies outside Europe and expressed himself unambiguously against the ravages

[6] See for example Kohei Saito, *Karl Marx's Ecosocialism: Capital, Nature, and the Unfinished Critique of Political Economy* (New York: Monthly Review Press, 2017).

of colonialism. These considerations are all too obvious to anyone who has read Marx, despite the skepticism nowadays fashionable in certain academic quarters.

The first and preeminent key to understand the wider variety of geographical interests in Marx's research, during the last decade of his life, lies in his plan to provide a more ample account of the dynamics of the capitalistmode of production on a global scale. England had been the main field of observation of *Capital*, Volume I; after its publication, he wanted to expand the socio-economic investigations for the two volumes of *Capital* that remained to be written. It was for this reason that he decided to learn Russian in 1870 and was then constantly demanding books and statistics on Russia and the United States of America. He believed that the analysis of the economic transformations of these countries would have been very useful for an understanding of the possible forms in which capitalism may develop in different periods and contexts. This crucial element is underestimated in the secondary literature on the—nowadays trendy—subject 'Marx and Eurocentrism'.

Another key question for Marx's research into non-European societies was whether capitalism was a necessary prerequisite for the birth of communist society and at which level it had to develop internationally. The more pronounced multilinear conception, that Marx assumed in his final years,[7] led him to look more attentively at the historical specificities and unevenness of economic and political development in different countries and social contexts. Marx became highly skeptical about the transfer of interpretive categories between completely different historical and geographical contexts and, as he wrote, also realized that 'events of striking similarity, taking place in different historical contexts, lead to totally disparate results'.[8] This approach certainly increased the difficulties he faced in the already bumpy course of completing the unfinished volumes of *Capital* and contributed to the slow acceptance that his major work would remain incomplete. But it certainly opened up new revolutionary hopes.

Marx went deeply into many other issues which, though often underestimated, or even ignored, are acquiring crucial importance for the political

[7] See Marcello Musto, *The Last Years of Karl Marx, 1881–1883: An Intellectual Biography* (Stanford: Stanford University Press, 2020).

[8] Karl Marx, 'Letter to *Otechestvennye Zapiski*', MECW, vol. 24, p. 201.

agenda of our times. Among these are individual freedom in the economic and political sphere, gender emancipation, the critique of nationalism, and forms of collective ownership not controlled by the state. Thus, thirty years after the fall of the Berlin wall, it has become possible to read a Marx very unlike the dogmatic, economistic and Eurocentric theorist who was paraded around for so long. One can find in Marx's massive literary bequest several statements suggesting that the development of the productive forces is leading to dissolution of the capitalistmode of production. But it would be wrong to attribute to him any idea that the advent of socialism is a historical inevitability. Indeed, for Marx the possibility of transforming society depended on the working class and its capacity, through struggle, to bring about social upheavals that led to the birth of an alternative economic and political system.

Alternative to Capitalism

Across Europe, North America, and many other regions of the world, economic and political instability is now a persistent feature of contemporary social life. Globalization, financial crises, the ascendance of ecological issues, and the recent global pandemic, are just a few of the shocks and strains producing the tensions and contradictions of our time. For the first time since the end of the Cold War, there is a growing global consensus about the need to rethink the dominant organizing logic of contemporary society and develop new economic and political solutions.

In contrast to the equation of communism with dictatorship of the proletariat, espoused in the propaganda of 'actually existing socialism', it is necessary to look again at Marx's reflections on communist society. He once defined it as 'an association of free individuals'.[9] If communism aims to be a higher form of society, it must promote the conditions for 'the full and free development of every individual'.[10]

In *Capital*, Marx revealed the mendacious character of bourgeois ideology. Capitalism is not an organization of society in which human beings, protected by impartial legal norms capable of guaranteeing justice and equity, enjoy true freedom, and live in an accomplished democracy.

[9] Karl Marx, *Capital, Volume I* (London: Penguin, 1976), p. 171.

[10] Ibid., p. 739.

In reality, they are degraded into mere objects, whose primary function is to produce commodities and profit for others.

To overturn this state of affairs, it is not enough to modify the distribution of consumption goods. What is needed is radical change at the level of the productive assets of society: 'the producers can be free only when they are in possession of the means of production'.[11] The socialist model that Marx had in mind did not allow for a state of general poverty but looked to the achievement of greater collective wealth and greater satisfaction of needs.

This collective volume presents a Marx in many ways different from the one familiar from the dominant currents of twentieth-century Marxism. Its dual aim is contributing to a new critical discussion of some of the classical themes of Marx's thought and to develop a deeper analysis of certain questions to which relatively little attention has been paid until recently. The result is a collection that will prove indispensable for all specialists in the field and which suggests that Marx's analyses are arguably resonating even more strongly today than they did in his own time.

Toronto, Canada Marcello Musto

References

Enzensberger, Hans Magnus (ed.) (1973), *Gespräche mit Marx und Engels*, Frankfurt: Suhrkamp.

Marx, Karl (1976), *Capital, Volume I*, London: Penguin.

———. (1989a), 'Letter to *Otechestvennye Zapiski*', MECW, vol. 24, pp. 196–202.

———. (1989b), 'Preamble to the Programme of the French Workers Party', MECW, vol. 24, pp. 340–341.

Musto, Marcello (ed.) (2012), *Marx for Today*, New York: Routledge.

———. (2019), 'Introduction: The Unfinished Critique of *Capital*', in: Marcello Musto (ed.), *Marx's Capital After 150 Years: Critique and Alternative to Capitalism*, London: Routledge, pp. 1–35.

———. (2020a), 'New Profiles of Marx After the *Marx-Engels-Gesamtausgabe* (MEGA^2)', *Contemporary Sociology*, vol. 49, n. 4: 407–19.

———. (2020b), *The Last Years of Karl Marx, 1881–1883: An Intellectual Biography*, Stanford: Stanford University Press.

[11] Karl Marx, 'Preamble to the Programme of the French Workers Party', MECW, vol. 24, p. 340.

———. (ed.) (2020c), *The Marx Revival: Key Concepts and New Interpretations*, Cambridge: Cambridge University Press.
Saito, Kohei (2017), *Karl Marx's Ecosocialism: Capital, Nature, and the Unfinished Critique of Political Economy*, New York: Monthly Review Press.

Acknowledgements

This volume contains the proceedings of the international conference *Marx 201. Ripensare l'alternativa* [Marx 201: Rethinking Alternatives], an event co-organized with Professor Alfonso Maurizio Iacono, supported by University of Pisa, Tuscany Region, and York University, and held at University of Pisa, from May 8–10, 2019.

The three days of the conference were organized into nine sessions, with the participation of 25 scholars, from 13 countries. This book contains a selection of 13 papers that were presented in four sessions: "Capitalism", "Ecology", "Migration", and "Communism".

The editor would like to thank Ksenia Arapko for her editorial work during the preparation of the manuscript and the Index. The editor and publisher would like to thank the Faculty of Liberal Arts & Professional Studies, York University, Toronto, Canada, for the financial support it provided to this work.

This research was supported by the Social Sciences and Humanities Research Council of Canada.

Toronto
May 2021

Marcello Musto

Contents

Note on the Text

Marx's writings have been generally quoted from the 50-volume *Marx Engels Collected Works* (MECW), Moscow/London/New York: Progress Publishers/Lawrence and Wishart/International Publishers, 1975–2005, but sometimes the reader is referred to single works translated into English not included in MECW.

Texts that have not yet been translated into English are often referenced to the *Marx-Engels-Gesamtausgabe* ($MEGA^2$), Berlin: Dietz/Akademie/De Gruyter, 1975–..., of which 67 of the originally planned 114 volumes have so far appeared in print. In a few cases, authors have cited single editions of texts still not published in the MECW and the $MEGA^2$ or have cited Marx's still unpublished manuscripts according to their location in either the International Institute of Social History (IISH) of Amsterdam or the Russian State Archive of Socio-Political History (RGASPI) of Moscow, where they are kept.

As regards the secondary literature, quotations from books and articles not published in English have been translated for the present volume.

Notes on Contributors

Himani Bannerji is Professor Emeritus of Sociology at York University (Toronto—Canada). She is the author of *Thinking Through: Essays on Feminism, Marxism and Anti-Racism* (Women's Press, 1995), *The Dark Side of the Nation: Essays on Multiculturalism, Nationalism and Racism* (Canadian Scholars' Press, 2000), *Inventing Subjects: Studies in Hegemony, Patriarchy and Colonialism* (Anthem, 2001), *Demography and Democracy: Essays on Nationalism, Gender and Ideology* (Canadian Scholars' Press, 2011), and *The Ideological Condition: Selected Essays on History, Race and Gender* (Brill, 2020).

Pietro Basso is Associate Professor of Sociology at Ca' Foscari University (Venice—Italy). He is the author of *Modern Times, Ancient Hours: Working Lives in the Twenty-First Century* (Verso, 2003), and *Le racisme européen. Critique de la rationalité institutionnelle de l'oppression* [*European Racism. Critique of the Institutional Rationality of Oppression*] (Syllepse, 2016). Among his edited books there are *Razzismo di stato. Stati Uniti, Europa, Italia* [*State Racism: United States, Europe, Italy*] (Angeli, 2010), and *The Science and Passion of Communism: Selected Writings of Amadeo Bordiga 1912–1965* (Brill, 2020).

Michael Brie is Senior Fellow and President of the Scientific Advisory Board of the Rosa Luxemburg Foundation (Berlin—Germany). He is the author of *Rediscovering Lenin: Dialectics of Revolution and Metaphysics of Domination* (Palgrave Macmillan, 2019), and *Rosa Luxemburg:*

A Revolutionary Marxist at the Limits of Marxism (with Jörn Schütrumpf, Palgrave Macmillan, 2021). Among his edited books there are *Karl Polanyi in Dialogue: A Socialist Thinker of Our Times* (Black Rose Books, 2017), *Futuring. Perspektiven der Transformation im Kapitalismus über ihn hinaus* [*Futuring: Perspectives of Transformation in and Beyond Capitalism*] (Westfälisches Dampfboot, 2014), and *Karl Polanyi's Vision of a Socialist Transformation* (with Claus Thomasberger, Black Rose Books, 2018).

Gregory Claeys is Professor Emeritus of History at the University of London (London—UK). He is the author of *Dystopia: A Natural History* (Oxford, 2017), *Marx and Marxism* (Penguin Books, 2018), *Utopia: The History of an Idea* (Thames & Hudson, 2020), and *Utopianism for a Dying Planet* (Princeton University Press, forthcoming 2022). Among his edited books there are *The Cambridge Companion to Utopian Literature* (Cambridge University Press, 2010), and *The Cambridge History of Nineteenth-Century Political Thought* (with Gareth Stedman Jones, Cambridge University Press, 2011).

Silvia Federici is Emeritus Professor of Political Philosophy at Hofstra University (Hempstead—US). She is the author of *Caliban and the Witch: Women, the Body, and Primitive Accumulation* (Autonomedia, 2004), *Revolution at Point Zero: Housework, Reproduction, and Feminist Struggle* (PM Press, 2012), *The New York Wages for Housework Committee 1972–1977: Theory, History, Documents* (with Arlen Austin, Autonomedia, 2017), *Witches, Witch-Hunting, and Women* (PM Press, 2018), *Beyond the Periphery of the Skin: Rethinking, Remaking, Reclaiming the Body in Contemporary Capitalism* (PM Press, 2020), and *Patriarchy of the Wage: Notes on Marx, Gender, and Feminism* (PM Press, 2021).

Álvaro García Linera was Vice-President of Bolivia from 2006 to 2019. He is the author of *Forma valor y forma comunidad. Aproximación teórica–abstracta a los fundamentos civilizatorios que preceden al Ayllu Universal* [*Value–Form and Community–Form: Theoretical–Abstract Approach to the Civilizational Foundations that Precede the Universal Ayllu*] (Prometeo/CLACSO, 2010), *Plebeian Power: Collective Action and Indigenous, Working–Class and Popular Identities in Bolivia* (Brill, 2014), and *Democracia, Estado, Revolución: Antología de textos politicos* [*Democracy, State, Revolution: Anthology of Political Texts*] (Txalaparta, 2016).

Alfonso Maurizio Iacono is Professor of History of Philosophy at the University of Pisa (Pisa—Italy). His authored books include*L'evénément et l'observateur* [*The Event and the Observer*] (L'Harmattan, 1998), *Autonomia, potere, minorità* [*Autonomy, Power, Minority*] (Feltrinelli Milano, 2000), *Storia, verità, finzione* [*History, Truth, Fiction*] (Manifestolibri, 2006), *L'illusione e il sostituto* [*The Illusion and the Substitute*] (Bruno Mondadori, 2010), *Il sogno di una copia* [*The Dream of a Copy*] (Guerini Scientifica, 2016), *History and Theory of Fetishism* (Palgrave Macmillan, 2016), *Studi su Marx* [*Studies on Marx*] (ETS, 2018), and *The Bourgeois and the Savage* (Palgrave Macmillan, 2020).

Bob Jessop is Distinguished Professor of Sociology at Lancaster University (Lancaster—UK). His authored books include *The Future of the Capitalist State* (Polity, 2002), *State Power: A Strategic-Relational Approach* (Polity, 2007), *Towards a Cultural Political Economy* (with Ngai-Ling Sum, Edward Elgar, 2013), *The State: Past, Present, Future* (Polity, 2015), and *Putting Civil Society in Its Place* (Policy Press, 2020). Among his edited books there are *Transnational Capitalism and Fractions of Capital* (with Henk Overbeek, Routledge, 2018), and *The Pedagogy of Economic, Political, and Social Crises: Dynamics, Construals, and Lessons* (with Karim Kniou, Routledge, 2018).

Razmig Keucheyan is Professor of Sociology at the University of Bordeaux, and a member of the Emile Durkheim Center (Bordeaux—France). He is the author of *The Left Hemisphere: Mapping Critical Theory Today* (Verso, 2014), *Nature Is a Battlefield: Towards a Political Ecology* (Polity, 2016), and *Les Besoins artificiels: Comment sortir du consumérisme* [*Artificial Needs: How to Get Out of Consumerism*] (La Découverte, 2019). Among his edited books there are *The End of the Democratic State: Nicos Poulantzas, A Marxism for the 21st Century* (with Jean-Numa Ducange, Palgrave Macmillan, 2019).

Marcello Musto is Professor of Sociology at York University (Toronto—Canada). He is author of *Another Marx: Early Manuscripts to the International* (Bloomsbury, 2018), and *The Last Years of Karl Marx: An Intellectual Biography* (Stanford University Press, 2020). Among his edited books there are *The Marx Revival: Key Concepts and New Interpretations* (Cambridge University Press, 2020), and *Karl Marx's Writings on Alienation* (Palgrave Macmillan, 2021).

Kohei Saito is Associate Professor of Political Economy at Osaka City University (Osaka—Japan). He is the author of *Karl Marx's Ecosocialism: Capital, Nature, and the Unfinished Critique of Political Economy* (Monthly Review Press, 2017). He is the co-editor (with Teinosuke Otani and Timm Graßmann) of *Marx–Engels–Gesamtausgabe* (MEGA^2), vol. IV/18, *Exzerpte und Notizen: Februar 1864 bis Oktober 1868, November 1869, März, April, Juni 1870, Dezember 1872* [*Excerpts and Notes: February 1864 to October 1868, November 1869, March, April, June 1870, December 1872*] (De Gruyter, 2019), and *Reexamining Engels's Legacy in the 21st Century* (Palgrave Macmillan, 2021).

Ranabir Samaddar is Distinguished Chair in Migration and Forced Migration Studies, Calcutta Research Group (Kolkata—India). Among his books there are *Memory, Identity, Power: Politics in the Junglemahals, 1890–1950* (Orient Longman, 1998), *The Marginal Nation: Transborder Migration from Bangladesh to West Bengal* (Sage, 1999), *Karl Marx and the Postcolonial Age* (Palgrave Macmillan, 2017), and *The Postcolonial Age of Migration* (Routledge, 2020). Among his edited books there is *Beyond Kolkata: Rajarhat and the Dystopia of Urban Imagination* (with Ishita Dey and Suhit K. Sen, Routledge, 2014).

David Norman Smith is Professor of Sociology at the University of Kansas (Kansas—US). He is the author of *Marx's Capital Illustrated* (Haymarket, 2014), and *George Orwell Illustrated* (Haymarket, 2018). Among his edited books there are *Authority, Culture, and Communication: The Sociology of Ernest Manheim* (with Frank Baron and Charles Reitz, Synchron, 2015), and *Marx's World: Global Society and Capital Accumulation in Marx's Late Manuscripts* (Yale University Press, forthcoming 2022).

List of Figures

PART I

Capitalism, Gender and Social Relations

CHAPTER 1

The Factory and the Family as Spaces of Capital

Himani Bannerji

> The premises on which we begin are not arbitrary ones, not dogmas, but real premises from which abstraction can only be made in the imagination. They are the real individuals, their activities and material conditions under which they live, both those which they find already existing and those produced by their activities [...] The first premise of all human history is, of course, existence of living human individuals.[1]

1.1 Introduction

Peter Linebaugh and Marcus Rediker in their Conclusion to *The Many-Headed Hydra* show us that capital's realization process involves the creation and organization of what they call sites for systemic exploita-

[1] Karl Marx and Friedrich Engels, *The German Ideology*, *Part One* (New York: International Publishers, 1970), p. 42.

H. Bannerji (✉)
York University, Toronto, ON, Canada

M. Musto (ed.), *Rethinking Alternatives with Marx*, Marx, Engels, and Marxisms, https://doi.org/10.1007/978-3-030-81764-0_1

tion of labour for the production of commodities.[2] These sites or spaces are not flat surfaces but have extension and depth which allows us to better conceptualize the topography of capitalist society. In this view the overall form of capital is constituted through different spaces which have their own interspatial practical and expressive architecture. They consist of productive apparatuses and institutions with their pertinent social relations, activities and forms of consciousness. This three-dimensional social space is a coalescence of 'sensuous, human activities, practice' undertaken by subjects in time.[3] Thus capital's space is a combination of activities for the production of commodities and life. These are dynamic spaces consisting of activities performed by conscious social subjects and agents and mediated in and through the objects they produce.[4]

[2] Peter Linebaugh and Marcus Rediker, *The Many-Headed Hydra: Sailors, Slaves, Commoners, and the Hidden History of the Revolutionary Atlantic* (Boston: Beacon Press, 2000). Though in the main my use of the concept of 'space' derives from social historians of class, feminist and anti-racist historians and sociologists, it also resonates with the critical geographers' use of Henri Lefebvre's idea of production of space: '*Space* stands for simultaneity, the synchronic order of social reality; time, on the other hand, denotes the diachronic order and thus the historic process of social production. Society here signifies neither a spatial-temporal totality of "bodies" or "matter" nor a sum total of actions and practices. Central to Lefebvre's materialist theory are human beings in their corporeality and sensuousness, with their sensitivity and imagination, their thinking and their ideologies; human beings who enter into relationships with each other through their activity and their practice', Christian Schmid, 'Lefebvre's Theory of Production of Space: Towards a Three–Dimensional Dialectic', in: Kanishka Goonewardena, Stefan Kipfer, Richard Milgram, and Christian Schmid (eds.), *Space, Difference, Everyday Life: Reading Henri Lefebvre* (London: Routledge, 2008), p. 28. I concur with their view that social reality is inconceivable without the idea of space, and also that this space 'does not exist in itself, it is produced', ibid., p. 29. The approach of social analysis that I have synthesized from these influences shows that capital is constituted through inter-forming spaces.

[3] Marx and Engels, *German Ideology*, p. 121.

[4] There are different interpretations of the term 'mediation', see Raymond Williams, 'From Reflection to Mediation', in: Raymond Williams, *Marxism and Literature* (Oxford: Oxford University Press, 1977), pp. 95–100. I use this concept to mean 'an interaction between different forces' and a process in which their original content is changed', ibid., p. 98. Mediation thus means for me what the Frankfurt School suggests: 'all active relations between different kinds of being and consciousness are inevitably mediated, and this process is not a separable – a "medium" – but intrinsic to the properties of the related kinds', ibid.

Linebaugh and Rediker explore four typical sites/spaces of capital: 'the commons, the plantation, the ship, and the factory'.[5] One space of capital, however, that they leave out is that of the family, thereby presenting an incomplete picture. Here I need to clarify what I mean by family, which has meant different things in different usages. I use the concept of family somewhat similarly to Marx in *The German Ideology*. We need to be mindful of the fact that family is not a planned relational organization. Yet most people throughout history have experienced some form of human grouping similar to what we call family. But wherever it has gained a definition it has had a relationship to ownership of property producing stable living arrangements for the privileged.[6] Other than being an informal social arrangement, the family proper was sanctioned in classical and medieval times by both the church and the state. Certain patterns of behaviour with patriarchy at its centre and governing moral norms emerged and continued to exist, though mutating through different historical moments. Thus, as an institution the family became a supra-individual force. But throughout, well into the maturity of capitalism in the West, the family remained patriarchal and connected with property as well as a social arrangement for meeting sexual and social needs.[7]

Inattention to the family as a space of capital obscures its actively organized form of being an existential daily space inhabited by experiencing subjects and agents. This approach echoes the bourgeois common sense of the public and the private which divides social life into two segments, a productive wage-earning life and a domestic one. It parallels the conventionally held disconnection between economic production and generation and sustenance of human life. The spaces that Linebaugh and

[5] Linebaugh and Rediker, *Many-Headed Hydra*, p. 327.

[6] For lower classes of the classical period the word 'family' is not applicable, because it is defined as property of the patrician, who owned his wife, children, workers, and slaves, as his *famulus*. Socio-sexual elements latent in this family form, in which Marx found the nucleus of slavery, expanded to include broader sections of society.

[7] For this reason, in Karl Marx and Friedrich Engels, *The Communist Manifesto* (New York: Bantam Books, 1992), Marx and Engels advocate the abolition of the family as they find it. 'What foundation is the present family, the bourgeois family, based on? On capital, on private gain. In its completely developed form this family exists only among the bourgeoisie', ibid., p. 38. They emphasize the view that 'this state of the family (bourgeois) finds its complement in the practical absence of the family among the proletariat', ibid.

Rediker critically depict are *directly* connected to commodity production and expansion of capital. But a fuller understanding of capital requires an exploration of the taken-for-granted family space *indirectly* and vitally connected to capitalist production. Phenomenally speaking, these spaces appear as unconnected because we go *out* to 'work' and come *in* to the precincts of the family where we 'live', producing an impression of disconnection. A dualist perception then arises, originating from the organization of capital itself, and facilitates an empiricist outlook which treats what is apparent as being actual, excluding a deeper relational inquiry. This bifurcation, creating visibility and invisibility of social spaces, is how capital functions. The normalization of wage labour itself becomes a screen hiding even from ourselves what we are actually doing when we work for a wage, namely that we earn money in order to buy back as life necessities the commodities that have been produced. Thus commodities and objects of consumption are allocated to separate realities. The result is a de-contexted perception of our activities/productivities under different circumstances. Sociality is thus robbed of its constitutive integrity of different moments, and instead there appear two coexisting self-regulating spheres, namely the factory and the family, considered as adjacent to each other rather than being mutually in-forming.

The factory and the family are treated here metonymically in relation to capital's overall organization. Only in conceiving them as internally constitutive spaces can capital assume its *full mode* of production. Relieving 'space' of its connotation of a physically bounded area, a container for storage, as a mere form whose content is external to it, we need to speak of space environmentally and projectively, created in every sense to facilitate particular and intentional activities of its inhabitants, who are at once self and other driven. Depth and extension, for which I use the concept of space, allows us to foreground some aspects of the formation, while others no less vital are relegated to the side or at the bottom, at the foundational level. Seen thus, capital is a social architecture with characteristic practical and cognitive activities suited to different aspects of the capitalist mode of production while sustaining also a dynamic continuum. The conception of space adjusted to the view of social historians makes the ideas of space and society interchangeable. Capital is shown to be a space-time conjuncture, in which activities are always within necessary durations. This spatialized understanding of society highlights the fact of production of space through human activity, while showing both the producers and produced objects within the power of time.[8] The morphing quality of capital's social spaces, however, have a concrete dimension at each point of its formation. It is always being and becoming at once, and generating an excess in the process, which gives a sense of disjuncture, as well as one of unspent life energy. This energy and productivity display the potentiality latent within human capacities, and cannot become fully absorbed by capital either in what it produces or how it produces. This excess becomes a source of politics, and holds the potential for critique of capital because it marks a separation between life and activities of the producers and the goal of the capitalist. The 'convergence of multiple determinations' that concretize life and the production process of commodities does not have the same destination.[9] Though dominance and exploitation prevail, simultaneously disobedience thrives in rebellion against the exploitive process continually. It is impossible in the languages of social sciences to express the always-at-once kind of concreteness of this reality, and theorization only aggravates the problem by directing sequentiality, seriality and empiricism. The challenge of this paper is to critique such theorization by pointing out as best as possible the mutually formative nature of social spaces. For this purpose we inquire into the relations of the family and the factory in conferring upon capital the full social character of a mode of production.

Social historians and anthropologists tell us that the family in ancient and classical periods was itself an economic and social organization under the governance of patriarchy.[10] Evolving through clan and kinship, family was at the heart of property relations and determined production

[8] Marx has been criticized as being almost wholly focused on time in his analysis of capital (the labour theory of value), and not concerned with space.

[9] Karl Marx, *Grundrisse: Foundations of the Critique of Political Economy* (London: Penguin, 1973). He says: 'The concrete is concrete because it is the concentration of many determinations, hence the unity of the diverse. It appears in the process of thinking, therefore as a process of concentration, as a result, not as a point of departure, even though it is the point of departure in reality, and hence also the point of departure for observation (*Anschauung*) and conception', ibid., p. 101.

[10] See, for example, Henrietta Moore, *Feminism and Anthropology* (Cambridge: Polity Press, 1988); Leonore Davidoff and Catherine Hall, *Family Fortunes: Men and Women of the English Middle Class, 1780–1850* (London: Hutchinson, 1987); and Friedrich Engels, *The Origins of the Family, Private Property, and the State* (New York: International Publishers, 1972); as well as Eleanor Burke Leacock, 'Introduction', in: Friedrich Engels, *The Origins of the Family, Private Property, and the State* (New York: International Publishers, 1972), pp. 7–70.

and distribution through sexual and social division of labour. Eventually the larger functions of the patriarchal family form disappeared, but some of its biological/physical, social, and cultural dimensions remained. However, they were mutated and were absorbed into other modes of production.[11] During the medieval period, the non-aristocratic family served as a complex of household arrangements and performed crucial economic functions. The organization of life and labour in these households changed under imperatives of capitalist development. Now major economic activities were removed to spaces away from daily life and performed in a concentrated manner in larger 'public' spaces, while individual living was to be conducted within a 'private' space. But even in this truncated bourgeois form family continued to be implicated in the economic base, and was an evolving institution with necessary life practices. In bourgeois society, where family assumes its nuclear form, it still stands at the crossroads of the economy and personal life, that is, of the public and the private. This emerging family, the dynamic double of the factory, is not apart from capital, but simultaneously its creation and its opposition. It becomes a socio-legal institution with a particular set of practices, relations and modes of internal mediation to the workings of capital. This family form and the economy are considered to be imbedded in the civil society, and both appear as 'natural' conditions and activities.

The idea of civil society is generally associated with Antonio Gramsci. But in Marx, and in Hegel for that matter, the term functioned differently, less prominently culturally, but more as regards the family, economy and the relationship of both to nature. It should be noted that Hegel, other political philosophers of the time and Marx agree that the civil society is the home of the economy and family. But unlike them, Marx pulls the civil society, and therefore the family, into the arena of politics—of social and historical struggles. For Marx: 'The form of intercourse determined by the existing productive forces at all previous historical stages, and in turn determining these, is *civil society*. [It] has as its premises and basis the simple family and the multiple, and the tribe'.[12]

He further specifies that the civil society 'embraces the whole material intercourse of individuals within a definite stage of development of

[11] See Mary O'Brien, *Reproducing the World: Essays in Feminist Theory* (Boulder: Westview, 1989).

[12] Marx and Engels, *German Ideology*, p. 57, emphasis in original.

productive forces'.[13] In this view both the family and social production are rooted in the civil society. It is important to note that while Hegel placed civil society as a whole with its economic and familial form in the realm of nature, as some sort of a nether world below the pursuit of reason and politics, Marx saw its economic aspect as the political ground for social emancipation. But he did not impute a political role to the family in this process. Both the organization of capital and its conceptualization made only a part of the capitalist mode of production visible. For us however, Marx's placement of the family in the base of civil society allows us to see the family as integral to class struggle. In fact he tells us it is only with the birth of civil society that the notion of class can be properly deployed and class struggle can ensue:

> The word 'civil' society [...] emerged in the eighteenth century, when property relationships had already extricated themselves from the ancient and medieval communal society. Civil society as such only develops with the bourgeoisie; the social organization evolving directly out of production and commerce, which in all ages forms the basis of the state and the rest of the idealistic superstructure, has, however, always been designated by the same name.[14]

The family's link with the capitalist mode of production is thus more foundational then generally assumed, and therefore of greater political potential.

If one took Marx's idea of transformational knowledge seriously, and agreed with him that it could only begin with the study of 'real individuals, their activities and material conditions under which they live', one could not overstate the importance of the family or such existential social arrangements. Both in analysing social organization and developing a critical conceptual apparatus for it, family provides a key point of entry for understanding class as a social formation. This will be discussed later. But for the moment, the question is, why did the political character of the civil society escape the attention of European political philosophers until the arrival of Marx and Engels? And why did they themselves, who saw the importance of one aspect of the civil society, neglect the other? The answer to these questions lies in the very fact that the civil society as a

[13] Ibid.

[14] Ibid.

space for physical quotidian life seemed too crude a space for intellectual engagement. The family, characterized by bodily and manual activities, was also excluded from having any connection with political and rational qualities. In other words, the family and civil society thus understood was tainted with nature. It is true that the life of the mind could not be possible without corporeal existence, but nature and manual labour belonged to a lower level of society, and bodily functions implicated in them best kept out of sight. While Hegel, among other philosophers, considered life in civil society as a kind of Hades, radically unconnected with the Idea and history making, leaving that task to the intellectuals, Marx saw the matter differently. He noted that life as lived was 'totally neglected or else considered as a minor matter quite irrelevant to the course of history'. For these philosophers 'the real production of life seems to be primeval history, while the truly historical appears to be separated from ordinary life'.[15] And the consequence? 'With this the relation of man to nature is excluded from history and hence the antithesis of nature and history is created'.[16] This same antithesis exemplified by the factory and the family was unemphasized by Marx himself when he could not see the family as a site for class struggle and history making.

In the last quarter of the eighteenth century the social form of the factory, which stands in for capital, associated with largescale industrial production, emerged. As such, unlike the family, it was a new and highly visible space.[17] Its special architectonic practical, cognitive and regulatory features combined into a template for capitalist society at large. This template constantly crept into other existential spaces, those of other kinds of activities connected to the production of life rather than of commodities. It intruded into and shaped the very realm of culture. But our project here is to highlight the family space, make it visible and redeem it from the state of being the natural unconscious of society. Rather, it is the living substrate of the productive world, with complex and subtle formal and cognitive features far exceeding those of the factory. As an existential space the family has an elusive quality of life. Some parts of its composition are visible, and others lurk in the shadow, but they can

[15] Ibid., p. 59.

[16] Ibid.

[17] Eric Hobsbawm, *Industry and Empire: From 1750 to the Present Day* (Harmondsworth: Penguin, 1969).

be accessed inferentially. In spite of the encroachment of the factory form in various ways on it, the family, as well as being the supplier of human beings for the factory space's hunger for living labour, holds on to life.

1.2 Spaces of Capital: Mode of Production and Class

> The way in which men produce their means of subsistence depends first of all on the nature of the actual means of subsistence they find in existence and have to reproduce. This mode of production must not be considered simply as being the production of the physical existence of the individuals. Rather it is a definite form of activity of these individuals, a definite form of expressing their life, a definite *mode of life* on their part. As individuals express their life, so they are.[18]

The double relation of formativeness and opposition between the factory and the family is best inquired into by using Marx's concept of mode of production, with equal emphasis on the notions of both 'mode' and 'production'. The critical primacy I accord to the mode of production does not, however, signify abandonment of the importance of class as a critical concept in Marxist analysis. But initially, in order to problematize the relationship between these two spaces of capital, we need a concept of a larger scope than that of class, which mediates them. Strictly speaking, class should be used as a concept typical to capitalism, and becomes important from the eighteenth century onwards.[19] Its main emphasis lay on the economic relations particular to the capitalist mode of production, namely the fact of possession of most means of production by the few, with the many dispossessed of any productive property other than their labour. This situation, accomplished through both force and law and enabled by the emergence of the capitalist state, elaborated a judicial and penal system with rules governing property and social relations and specific divisions of labour.

[18] Marx and Engels, *German Ideology*, p. 42, emphasis in original.

[19] See Raymond Williams, *Key Words: A Vocabulary of Culture and Society* (London: Fontana Press, 1976), pp. 60–9. Also see Gary Day, *Class* (London: Routledge, 2007), pp. 6–14, and Chapter Six, 'The Twentieth Century', pp. 154–204; and Richard W. Miller, 'Social and Political Theory: Class, State, Revolution', in: Terrell Carver (ed.), *Cambridge Companion to Marx* (Cambridge: Cambridge University Press, 1991), pp. 55–105.

For Marx the mode of production is obviously the starting concept, emphasizing the very species nature of human beings as a capacity for production and the fact that this production is existentially and socially all-inclusive. In support of this, he continues to say, ‘What they are, therefore, coincides with their production, both with *what* they produce and with *how* they produce’.[20] Marx’s interest in the mode of production can be considered the ‘leading thread’ of his studies,[21] in particular of the capitalist mode. Sociality among humans arises from the social nature of their production, which they.

> carry on [as] they enter into definite relations that are indispensable and independent of their will; these relations correspond to a definite stage of development of their material powers of production. The sum total of these relations of production constitutes the economic structure of society – the real foundation, on which rise legal and political superstructures and to which correspond definite forms of social consciousness.[22]

These oft quoted lines have stigmatized Marx (and Engels) as economistic thinkers, and also as structuralists lacking a subject in history. They provide the basis for designating Marx not only as an economic determinist, but also as a dualist thinker who tries to bridge his base-superstructure distinction through a theory of ‘correspondence’. In my view, this long established critique of Marx occasionally has some plausibility, but not in the main. As a corrective we need to re-interpret Marx’s use of the notions of ‘economy’ and ‘economic’. Since in his usage these concepts do not hold strong and consistent associations with money, market, commodity production, wage labour, etc., they should be read differently. The notion of economy in Marx should not be read through the discourse of bourgeois political economy. The notion of economy in his writings holds much of how he uses it about non-capitalist modes of production, that is, the idea signals to how a society is organized to produce and allocate its resources. This is a social perception of the economy, rather than an economistic perception of the society. Economy here includes the entire scope of social existence in a given historical

[20] Ibid., emphasis in original.

[21] Karl Marx, *Contribution to the Critique of Political Economy*, in: Robert Tucker (ed.), *The Marx–Engels Reader* (New York: Norton & Co., 1972), p. 4.

[22] Ibid.

situation. It refers to a continuing complex reality produced conjointly through activities of production, consumption, distribution and exchange in a formative rhythmic composition. The idea of 'mode' here, then, should be interpreted in social and cultural terms, and even in terms of style and fashion, within which capital arises and socializes itself. It is in this regard we could turn to Marx, as he makes a determining connection between the general character of the social with the material life found in any given mode of production.[23] As there is no beginning of existence and producing at any ground zero, the social and the mode of production are not sequential. The same goes for the political and spiritual processes of life. This is what leads Marx to say:

> It is not the consciousness of men [qua individuals] that determines their existence [since they arrive into an always already there society], but on the contrary, their *social* existence that determines their consciousness.[24]

Let us place the concept of class against this background of a larger social existence, or mode of production, without which nothing could be said about capitalism or class. There is significant confusion about the concept of class, as its deployment in different contexts has generated much 'critical ambiguity'.[25] But notwithstanding that, at least two aspects of class are generally agreed upon: one, that the concept has an economic aspect; and also, a social one. Thus class is seen as an active economic force, but also as a set of social relations which rely upon divergent socio-cultural practices and ideas. The question arises here as to how these two aspects relate to each other, and why they are often seen as disconnected or antagonistic. The answer seems to lie in whether or not class is treated mainly as

[23] The idea of determination needs clarification. I do not use it in the sense of accusation of economic determination made about Marx. In my usage this term should be read in the sense of Marx's use of it in Karl Marx, *The Eighteenth Brumaire of Louis Bonaparte*, MECW, vol. 11, where he says: 'Men make their own history, but they do not make it just as they please: they do not make it under circumstances chosen by themselves, but under circumstances directly found, given and transmitted from the past', p. 103. What Marx says here explains the notion of determination, which means the placing of actions and ideas in the context of history, recognizing the influences on social and historical movements at any given point in time, as 'pressures exerted' by new and old formations. On determination, see Raymond Williams, 'Determination', in: *Marxism and Literature*, pp. 83–9.

[24] Marx, *Contribution to the Critique*, p. 12, emphasis added.

[25] Williams, *Key Words*, p. 65.

an economic category, without any particular social or historical content, other than the fact of ownership of social means of production by a few and lack of it for the majority. Class as an economic category does not provide us with the context of how things got to be this way. As a pure signifier of economic activity it is more of a rational abstraction which has to acquire a social content to become concretized. This means that class must become a concept of social formation which is orchestrated by a particular ensemble of social relations. This can only happen through the economic category being grounded in the overall mode of production. In capitalism this ground for class is a mixed one, consisting of feudal and emerging capitalist social organizations and forces of production. Class in capitalism, therefore, can never be a pure form locked in the process of commodity production. It must be considered as concept of social formation with multiple dimensions that can be substantially different, and even at odds with each other.

Just as class cannot be an unmixed single concept and reality, nor can the mode of production. A new mode does not signal the erasure of the old one. Thus the new mode of capitalist productionrelies on the continuation of aspects of the older mode. We can infer this from the following comment by Marx:

> No social order ever disappeared before all the productive forces for which there is room in it have been developed, and new higher relations of production never appear before the material conditions of existence have matured in the womb of the old society.[26]

Capital assumes the overall social form of capitalism by including in itself the old and the new in different historical and geographical locations. In its own turn it too puts its imprint on the social relations that go into the making of class and the social spaces of the factory and the family. Productive and existential mores which signify differences articulated to power enter into both the process of exploitation and the living of everyday life. The relations and ideas of difference, coded as gender, race, caste, and so on, flesh out the social relations and provide substance to capitalism. The notion of class, therefore, in its modern usage holds in itself current capitalist relations of power and property, but also brings into it social status

[26] Marx, *Contribution to the Critique*, p. 12.

and cultural dimensions which pre-existed capitalism. Though the hierarchical differentiation found in feudalism may not exactly be called 'class' in our sense, yet these class-like forms influence the common sense and conduct of class in our times. Capital and class become actually existing capitalism through a process of socialization conferred upon them by the mixed nature of the mode of production. Class formation in capitalism interpellates within itself whatever power-scripted kinds of difference are at hand.

It helps to capture the operative relations between the direct space of capitalist production and the indirect ones that come into it. Beginning our exploration from the mode of production, the latter generate the materiality of daily activities and cultures of the society as a whole with its multidimentionality. These mediatory relations take class beyond an economic category to becoming a social formation. This mediation introduces diverse and anterior social features into the new ones, for example those of feudalism into capitalism. The family contains more of these precapitalist aspects with a qualitative difference from those productive forces developed in the factory. Guided by the goal of life production, they rely on manual and affective activities; their cultural life is the opposite of the culture of exploitation. These differences are necessary, however, for capital to function, as it needs healthy living labour.

The difference between the factory and the family is most prominent in their use of time.[27] The use and quality of time between them are antithetical. In the factory, ruled by the logic of production, time is abstracted and averaged. The practicalization of socially necessary labour time requires serialization and speed. Motion in time is quantified and sets the basis for exchange value. Time in the family is that of living, involving human needs. Both spaces are produced through activities in time of a radically different nature. Naturally, this life in time is experienced by and physically impacts social subjects differently. One is that of depletion and the other of renewal in all senses. Factories convert human capacities into labour power for exchange value, while the family converts exchange value manifested as a wage into use value. The time of wage labour comes into direct confrontation with lived time. In the chapters on labour process and the working day in *Capital*, Marx discusses precisely these issues and

[27] See E. P. Thompson, 'Time, Work–Discipline and Industrial Capitalism', in: *Customs in Common* (London: Penguin, 1993), pp. 352–403.

discloses how this lived time is the *sine qua non* of human embodiment and all this entails.[28] It is the human body's capacity to labour that sets the limit of the working day, the ultimate extent of exploitation of labour, reaching which limit mechanization arises.

With all their opposition, productive time and existential time cooperate and maintain an integral relationship between them. This makes the time of production of supreme importance to people, because human capacities themselves must be sold in the market. Life itself must be commoditized as labour power, but it is not detachable from the body. The family form, signifying a space of existence, to the extent it can cleaves onto qualitative time necessary for regeneration and sustenance, tries to meet human needs through sensuous individual interaction. Thus the social space of capital is textured with these opposite time-based activities and contains multiple planes or spaces of existence within a general formation or mode. These planes are not vertically stacked up or horizontally adjacent, but rather metaphorically comparable to a cubistic shape, in which each component section is three-dimensional and juxtaposed in such a way as to form simultaneously an equally three-dimensional whole.[29]

This particular spatial composition is visible if existence of people, as Marx advocates, becomes the point of departure for the inquiry. It is from the spatial perspective of production of life that the best view of commodity production can be had—though this entry point is 'hidden' from a theoretical vantage point. From the bourgeois standpoint capital is a life-saver and the beating heart of the world. What we need to do is reverse the standpoint, enter the internal life space of capital, rather than begin with theorization. Thus existence must take, as it is immutably the final aim for all modes of production. It is only in capitalism that this reality is pushed out of view and life is subsumed within the commodity form, giving rise to the bourgeois interiorization and devaluation of the family. This simultaneously sustains bourgeois rule and creates an economistic ideological reading habit. This fact is discussed by Marx in the first chapter of *Capital, Volume I* while discussing commodity

[28] Karl Marx, *Capital, Volume I* (Moscow: Progress Publishers, 1887), Chapter VII, pp. 173–82, and Chapter X, pp. 222–86.

[29] John Berger, *Success and Failure of Picasso* (Harmondsworth: Penguin, 1965).

fetishism.[30] What we discover with his help is that hiding in plain sight, economic production for profit feeds on the production of life, and goes on until the truth is bared through constant struggles.

Our critique, developed from Marx, provides a non-economistic, therefore non-ideological way of thinking about the social as complex form. The notion of form, as with class, is crucial here, and gathers content from reality. This content, with multiple socio-historical relations, productive forces, socio-sexual division of labourand forms of consciousness, intricately mediates and sustains a recognizable and reproducible capitalist mode. But content is susceptible to social changes which shift the form accordingly. In the long formative duration of any mode of production response and flexibility are key. While there is a relative autonomy in the ways in which the details of the formative content of the mode interact, the form still has its developmental path as capitalism. It generates, develops, or even cancels certain parts of the content to balance the internal and external relational contradictions that compose it.[31] Thus the dominant, residual and emergent elements of capital must be heeded in their mediatory and determining functions.[32]

If we concede that capital is more than an economic formation, then we can counter an ideological manner of thinking whereby capital becomes a one-dimensional phenomenon. The absurdity of conceiving capital as a viable self-standing economy, simply a functioning calculus producing and renewing itself in a social vacuum, becomes apparent. In fact, far from being only an economic process, capitalism reaches its full form when it is most extensively mediated, that is, social. But the social mediation is so complex that the complexity itself can make the producer disappear from production and substitute the commodity as a self-reproducing object, while the dependent nature of its existence is there for all to see. Put simply, the more social and expansive capitalism becomes, the more it gives the impression of the primacy of the economic.

[30] Marx, *Capital, Volume I*, pp. 76–87.

[31] These are the overdeterminations that Marx mentions in *The Eighteenth Brumaire of Louis Bonaparte*, *Grundrisse*, and other texts.

[32] See Williams, *Marxism and Literature*, pp. 121–7.

1.3 On Transition

What makes the mode of production so complex yet sustainable is the way in which class introduces and mediates the actualizing relations and forms from society at large. Class, as we know, itself is a social formation, not only an economic category. Thus the family and the factory cannot be kept apart. To be a social reality economy must be socialized, human existence cease to be seen as its adjunct.

In order to provide an example of what I have been saying, we now turn to Britain's transition from feudalism to capitalism. This period spans approximately from the mid-seventeenth century to the end of the nineteenth; the hundred years from 1740–1848 are particularly important, by which time English capitalism had reached a mature condition. This period witnesses the waning of one mode of production and the rise of another.[33] This allows a clear visibility of the twin rise of the bourgeois familyand the factory. These two spaces emerge through the mutation of medieval common households to the nuclear family and manufactories into factories. Capital expanded and consolidated during this time, but its path was not linear nor smooth as it had to come to terms with feudal productive forces and their cultural activities and sociality. Through their gradual morphing emerged new ways of living, institutions and cultural productions. With all its changes and gradualism, one aspect of capital continued, in England and abroad, that of violence. As Marx and numerous others have written, capital grew from and thrived on dispossession of the social majority, mainly peasants, small artisans, and the rural poor. The so-called primitive accumulation[34] within Britain itself displayed a determined brute force with which the commons were encroached and property of peasants and small producers seized by moneyed classes. They retained their gain through equally brutal property laws of the rising bourgeois state. This is how capital was birthed, 'dripping from head to foot, from every pore, with blood and dirt'.[35] This monstrous child continued to be nourished on a constant diet of direct force and exploitation of labour, colonization, and slavery. The turbulence and chaos of the transition were facilitated by the violence of

[33] In Marx, *Communist Manifesto*, we see a potted history of this change.

[34] For how Marx uses this concept see Marx, *Capital, Volume I*, Chapter XXV, pp. 574–666, Chapter XXVII, pp. 671–85, and Chapter XXVIII, pp. 686–93.

[35] Ibid., p. 712.

the long war of the Puritan revolution. This was indeed a world 'turned upside down',[36] and cleared much of the ground for capital's takeover and the rise of the bourgeois state. With the birth of the monster child was also born 'free' wage labour, subject to all manner of violence in its efforts to survive. In this existential crisis for the majority whatever living arrangements emerged came under the rubric of the family. Torn apart from settled households and communities and thrust into precarious life and work, they were subjected to homelessness and hunger.

It is at this juncture that class, in Marxist terms, appeared.[37] The still solvent aristocracy, expanding gentry and emergent capitalists did well, and eventually coalesced in their economic interests as the bourgeoisie, while the majority of the 'freed' population became the proletariat, who had nothing but their labour to sell.[38] Initially neither the modern family nor the industrial factory had emerged. They matured during this interim century. New spaces took shape where large manufacturing concerns made demand for wage labour, and importantly these concerns grew in the countryside. The supply for this demand was, of course, never scarce.[39] Alongside this desperate and disordered life of the majority of 'free' people, the nuclear bourgeois familyarose, with its distinct practices and ideology, and eventually became a social and legal institution. The bourgeoisie as a class, however, retained some of the feudal attributes

[36] Christopher Hill, *The World Turned Upside Down: Radical Ideas During the English Revolution* (London: Temples Smith, 1972); and see also Christopher Hill, *The Century of Revolution, 1603–1714* (New York: Norton, 1961).

[37] See Marx and Engels, *Communist Manifesto*. The modern bourgeois society 'has simplified a complicated arrangement of society into various orders, a manifold gradation of social ranks [but it] has not done away with class and antagonisms. It has but established new classes [...] two great classes directly facing each other: the bourgeoisie and proletariat', ibid., p. 18.

[38] For his analytical purposes Marx simplifies into two distinct classes of the proletariat and the bourgeoisie. This binary notion has become commonplace, though in discussions on class in capitalism we speak of middle or auxiliary classes as well. The word 'proletariat' etymologically refers to those who have nothing but themselves and their children to be employed by landed proprietors. With Marx some of the absolute dispossession found in classical societies is retained, while instead of bonding themselves the dispossessed keep a distance between themselves and their labour power. This is their basic distinction from slaves.

[39] See Himani Bannerji, 'Towards a Communist Revolution: Gender and Class in *Capital*, Volume I', in: Marcello Musto (ed.), *Marx's Capital After 150 Years: Critique and Alternative to Capitalism* (London: Routledge, 2019), pp. 145–66.

of rank or status, and absorbed in their family form some of the décor and life style of the aristocracy. But the organization of their familial spaces and comportment within them were significantly different from the aristorcrats. These families of capitalists and their auxiliaries, the middle classes, were modelled in christian (both Anglican and Puritan) patriarchal values and sentiments.

The familial spaces of the working class/proletariat were formed in ad hoc manner as mere shelters with minimum life amenities. These spaces constantly expanded and shifted by a migratory population until some stability was introduced with the rise of industrial towns replete with slums. The actual and the potential working classes, therefore, did not have families in the sense of the bourgeoisie and the middle classes. At best they became objects of charity of the church and the middle classes, also of social reform. Eventually the state appointed social workers to keep tab on them. Though much has been written on the English working class, little material exists within that corpus that speaks of families—but rather to the lack of them.[40] Though ideologically annexed by the bourgeois/nuclear family which gained a hegemonic 'normalcy', the working class was not able to afford nor feel identified with this institution. The majority of the so-called families were no more than an aggregation of people for minimum life requirements. Life needs of the bourgeoisie or the middle classes, on the other hand, were not only met, but embellished with medicine, education and culture.

The rise of capitalism precipitated a massive crisis in the biological and social life of the displaced and unsettled. This resulted in massive child labourand overwhelming presence of women working in manufacturing concerns. No party was willing to take responsibility for this situation, leaving the poor to fend for themselves. Neither the capitalist, the state, nor the church were ready to take any effective steps. As long as the supply of labour could be guaranteed there were evasions and justification of this state of affairs.[41] Women of working-class families, according to patriarchal religious common sense, were left in charge of

[40] See Friedrich Engels, *The Condition of the Working Class in England* (Oxford: Blackwell, 1971); Henry Mayhew, *London Labour and the London Poor* (New York: Dover Publications, 1968); and Gareth Stedman Jones, *Outcast London: A Study of the Relationship Between Classes in Victorian Society* (Oxford: Clarendon Press, 1971).

[41] Thomas Robert Malthus, *An Essay on the Principle of Population* (London: J. Johnson, 1798).

the renewal and maintenance of existence. This was an impossible proposition because even middle class women, supported by the income of the head of the family, were unable to do so. Women's responsibility was further intensified by an association of women with nature, as they were mainly biologically identified and also associated with manual labour.[42] Such an arrangement was doomed to fail. Thus life became the responsibility of (female) individuals, while production of capital was a collective and systemic compulsion. 'The woman question' which evolved during this era, we can discern, was in actuality the child question or the family question.[43] It should also be noted that middle and upper class families employed women of the lower classes to work in their households in various capacities, thus lightening their labour. Poor women bore the double burden of exploitation at work and expectations to take care of their own homes and children.[44]

Association of women with family, implicitly with nature, not only legitimized the neglect of women, but created an environment of degradation for those who were perceived mainly in bodily terms. Gender devalued women's labour even more than that of male manual workers. In the name of nature and the holy family, women were pushed out of the developing industrial labour forceby the state, social reformers, and male co-workers, and thus 'freed' from commodity production to make a 'home' on the low income of 'family wage' paid to the male 'head of the family'. But working-class women, whose families lived under the constant threat of unemployment, could not be stay-at-home mothers, wives, and homemakers.

They continued to work in overwhelming numbers, with very few avenues for joining a skilled and well-paid labour force. Doomed to work as domestics, nannies, cooks, and in other 'feminine' activities, including wetnursing/breast feeding,[45] and prostitution, their hard and

[42] See Jeff Hearn, 'Gender: Biology, Nature, and Capitalism', in: *Cambridge Companion to Marx*, pp. 222–34.

[43] See Judith Walkowitz, *Prostitution and Victorian Society* (Cambridge: Cambridge University Press, 1980); Ivey Pinchbeck and Margaret Hewitt, *Children in English Society* (London: Routledge and Kegan Paul, 1973); and Philippe Ariés, *Centuries of Childhood: A Social History of Family Life* (London: Jonathan Cape, 1962).

[44] Juliet Mitchell and Ann Oakley (eds.), *Rights and Wrongs of Women* (Harmondsworth: Penguin, 1976).

[45] Depicted by George Moore in the 1894 novel *Esther Waters*.

necessary labour was seriously devalued as natural and manual. Nuclearized and isolated, deprived of the facility of forming a community of related households as before, working-class families, open to capital's predations, the state's regulation, and moral exhortation from religious and secular reformers, had some resemblance to prisons.[46]

This poor family was the catchment pool for factory labour. But for the people themselves it was their place of birth and existence. They were not born as labourers. Here a comment on 'labour' is necessary. Though the term pre-existed capitalism and Marx himself used it in the wider sense of expression of human capacity to produce, this word came to signify wage labour in common parlance. Therefore families came to be seen as places whose main function was to generate and renew that. But we have to question this customary view because in its use 'labour' in capitalism consisted of a selective and limited articulation from a large range of human capacities, most of which are of no importance from the point of view of capitalist production. The creative or expressive dimension of human capacities is absent in this deployment.[47] Furthermore, the English language usage of 'labour' resonates with the Biblical association of pain and punishment, without any connotation of creativity and aesthetic pleasure. Implicit in this thinking is the idea that just as factories are constructed to produce commodities, so the activities in the family are directed to produce 'labour' for commodification. But families are not in reality factory farms for the production and reproduction of labour, rather, shared spaces where people, rich or poor, live. This is where, however limitedly, human capacities develop. This is what people

[46] The repressive nature of the family form, particularly for women, was noted by political thinkers such Charles Fourier as well as by Marx and Engels and others who followed them. In *The Communist Manifesto*, and other texts, Marx and Engels advocated the abolition of the (bourgeois) family. They state: 'The bourgeois clap-trap about the family and education, about the hallowed co-relation of parent and child, becomes all the more disgusting, the more, by the absence of modern industry all family ties among the proletarians are torn asunder and their children transformed into simple articles of commerce and instruments of labour', ibid., p. 39. The same sentiment is expressed at length and in a more reasoned manner by Engels in *The Origins of the Family*.

[47] Regarding alienation of labour Marx says the following: 'The alienation of the worker in his product means not only that his labour becomes an object, an external existence, but that it exists outside him, and that it becomes a power on its own confronting him. It means that the life which he has conferred on the object confronts him as something hostile and alien', Karl Marx, *The Economic and Philosophic Manuscripts of 1844* (New York: International Publishers, 1964), p. 108.

need for existing, which cannot but be done socially. This is what goes on under the rubric of the family. The fact that people labour for wages means this is the only way they have of accessing their means of consumption. This is the fate of people who are dispossessed and live in a market society.

It is important to note that people have and could have gone on producing their life through many historical stages without capitalism, but capitalism could not function without human energies or capacities that they bring to the site of capital.[48] To lose sight of this vital fact would lead us to a false conclusion about capital and the roles human existence and the family play in it, with serious political consequences. This devaluation of life and human capacities develops from the standpoint of capital, which relies on quantity rather than quality. Thus as familial activities cannot be measured, they are seen as of no value. As much of this life sustaining activity is carried on by women, the devaluation is further deepened. When women do join the labour forcein whatever capacity, they earn less than men. Thus the family, a space of daily existence, continues to exist as a space in capital's lower depth with a pseudo-naturalness built into it. Concealed by its ideologically spatial location and a commonsensical association with nature, family is relegated to a zone outside of politics and history. But this family, through a Marxist scrutiny, is revealed to be the inside of the outside of capitalism. It is not its institutional status, but as a social organization for renewing human existence, that the family becomes a more powerful institution than the factory.

1.4 Conclusion

By now it is clear that spatialization of capital is none other than its socialization. From being an abstract economic relation capital becomes a concrete formation through mediations of class, which is itself a complex of social and economic relations. Society's relational and ideational composition is to be found everywhere in capitalist production. Thus if any of these constitutive social elements were to be significantly disturbed or erased, capital formation would be seriously challenged. It cannot but

[48] However, one has to remember certain projects undertaken by capital to reproduce human labour: slavery, bonded and indenture labour, as well as Nazi concentration camps, were such attempts.

depend on social and historical exigencies and contingencies which flesh it out as an operational form.

It is only in its logic that capital can ever be an asocial, one-dimensional economic form, but in reality it is inherently social and spatially uneven. This unevenness derives from pre-capitalist history as well as capital's needs for nature both in productive human energy and raw materials as means of production. Thus natural and feudal economies with low level productive forces can be articulated to capital's project without compromising its fundamental rationality of exploitation of labour, whether through wage labour or slavery. Considering cost efficiency, there is little effort to expand on the productive forces or to raise the standard of living of workers until absolutely necessary due to loss of market through competition. Therefore if work can be done manually, 'naturally', under the most life depleting conditions, that will be the path taken. Thus capital has always been an agent degradation and underdevelopment in the spaces that it penetrates locally or globally.[49]

All modes of production, as noted, centrally depend on nature in many ways. The capitalist mode is no exception. All of capital's rationality and inventiveness can only be set in motion by relying on nature, including human activities, for producing objects for the market. But nature is perverted in the way capital uses it. Human capacities which are natural but cultivated through and along the productive forces are subjected through exploitation to unnatural and alienating activities for profit. Though other modes of production also relied on human capacity and natural resources, they did so, as in feudalism, through external compulsion of production and appropriation, but not systemically as in capitalism. Capital is unique in that it is able to hide the fact of its own extortive exploitation within the very process of production itself.

From its inception capital's development always continues through the extension of primitive accumulation. People are stripped to bare life until they have no choice but to sell their energies and capacities, that is,

[49] Capital's character as uneven development has been noted by Marx himself, as well as scholars of development studies and critical geography. See, for example, Walter Rodney, *How Europe Underdeveloped Africa* (Washington: Howard University Press, 1974); Amiya Bagchi, *Political Economy of Underdevelopment* (Cambridge: Cambridge University Press, 1982); and Neil Smith, *Uneven Development: Nature, Capital, and the Production of Space* (Oxford: Blackwell, 1984). Both within a nation state and internationally, capital combines pre-capitalist pre-industrial forms of labour and society. For that reason, a pure form of capitalist development is impossible.

practically themselves. Capital subjects the masses to a man-made 'natural' scarcity, thus plunging them into an artificial state of nature. It subjugates people by force or law to dependency, and the economy as a systemic whole goes completely out of their control as individuals. It is not their well-being that stops capital short of extinction of humanity and nature, but its constant need for labour and consumption. Thus a fundamental antagonism between human existence and capital produces alienation. The ultimate political consequence of this alienation is an ongoing conscious or unconscious struggle between existence and capital. This predator–prey relation between humanity qua humanity and capital is the basic content of class struggle.

This struggle can be returned to the language of time. Capital's relationship to time is like no other mode of production. It directly harnesses and reshapes time, once seen as god's prerogative, in its labour process seeking an exponential rapidity in commodity production. Thus commodities, starting with wage labour itself, are congealed labour units of time. This time is not existential and experiential, but instrumental for the measurement of the rate of exchange value and profit. The time of the factory faces the time of life, which involves birth, growth of human beings and ultimately their death. Capital cannot fully exhaust what is human, which retains its humanity, its sensuous communicative and productive capacities even in the grip of capital. There is an excess of energies and capacities in humanity which is a collective resource that evades capital's domination and enables people to break through the disciplinary and punitive measures of capital and the capitalist state. It is this collectivity born of identification with others in similar conditions, a kind of sharing and mutual recognition, that we call class and class consciousness. And it is from this that class struggle flows. Their struggle is not only for higher wages and better working conditions, but also for full control over their life and time, always refusing to be no more than 'hands' for capital.

This returns us to the topic of civil society, which Marx called in *German Ideology* the theatre of history. In this space class and family are fused inseparably. The traits that mark the social relations simultaneously form class and family. This is where from social customs and values the relative worth of labour by different groups of people arises, such as of women and racialized people. Because such traits are found in society in general, they find their way in class formation. Venues for open and hidden struggles of classes are found to begin within this space.[50] This situation compels us simultaneously to broaden our understanding of class and the nature of class struggle, taking in the entire mode of production. Thus social movements aimed at constitutive social differences of power are actually and potentially ways to conduct class struggle for the revolutionary overthrow of capitalism. Class in itself as an economic rationality and fact of property has no separate content of social protocol of its own, though poverty and misery, along with wealth and accumulation, usually accompany the proletariat and the bourgeoisie. Even so, when workers are affluent and share the cultural values and politics of the ruling classes, they cannot escape that precarious relation which denies them the ownership of means of production. Under capitalism in everything social that we do or live in, we find ourselves *in* class. Not only the factory, the symbol of capitalist production, but also the family, the symbol of daily existence, can be/is the space of revolutionary struggle. Our hope relies on that, and the fact that class in all its aspects is an antagonistic relation and therefore inevitably runs into fatal crises. When such a critical moment is reached capital's very existence totters on the brink of destruction. In such moments a decisive choice has to be made between what Rosa Luxembourg called socialism or barbarism. At this long moment of struggle we are still waiting for the outcome.

References

Ariés, Philippe (1962), *Centuries of Childhood: A Social History of Family Life*, London: Jonathan Cape.

Bagchi, Amiya (1982), *Political Economy of Underdevelopment*, Cambridge: Cambridge University Press.

Bannerji, Himani (2019), 'Towards a Communist Revolution: Gender and Class, in *Capital*, Volume I', in: Marcello Musto (ed.), *Marx's Capital After 150 Years: Critique and Alternative to Capitalism*, London: Routledge, pp. 145–66.

Berger, John (1965), *Success and Failure of Picasso*, Harmondsworth: Penguin.

[50] Marx and Engels, *Communist Manifesto*, p. 18. See also Harry Braverman, *Labour and Monopoly Capital: The Degradation of Work in the Twentieth Century* (New York: Monthly Review Press, 1974), where he talks about the many ways in which workers sabotage capital through absenteeism, machine breaking, and other forms of daily resistance.

Braverman, Harry (1974), *Labour and Monopoly Capital: The Degradation of Work in the Twentieth Century*, New York: Monthly Review Press.

Davidoff, Leonore, and Hall, Catherine (1987), *Family Fortunes: Men and Women of the English Middle Class, 1780–1850*, London: Hutchinson.

Day, Gary (2007), *Class*, London: Routledge.

Engels, Friedrich (1971), *The Condition of the Working Class in England*, Oxford: Blackwell.

———. (1972), *The Origins of the Family, Private Property, and the State*, New York: International Publishers.

Hearn, Jeff (1991), 'Gender: Biology, Nature, and Capitalism', in: Terrell Carver (ed.), *Cambridge Companion to Marx*, Cambridge: Cambridge University Press, pp. 222–34.

Hill, Christopher (1961), *The Century of Revolution, 1603–1714*, New York: Norton.

———. (1972), *The World Turned Upside Down: Radical Ideas During the English Revolution*, New York: Viking Press.

Hobsbawm, Eric (1969), *Industry and Empire: From 1750 to the Present Day*, Harmondsworth: Penguin.

Leacock, Eleanor Burke (1972), 'Introduction', in: Friedrich Engels, *The Origins of the Family, Private Property, and the State*, New York: International Publishers, pp. 7–70.

Linebaugh, Peter, and Rediker, Marcus (2000), *The Many-Headed Hydra: Sailors, Slaves, Commoners, and the Hidden History of the Revolutionary Atlantic*, Boston: Beacon Press.

Malthus, Thomas Robert (1798), *An Essay on the Principle of Population*, London: J. Johnson.

Marx, Karl (1887), *Capital, Volume I*, Moscow: Progress Publishers.

———. (1964), *The Economic and Philosophic Manuscripts of 1844*, New York: International Publishers.

———. (1972), *Contribution to the Critique of Political Economy*, in: Robert Tucker (ed.), *The Marx–Engels Reader*, New York: Norton & Co.

———. (1973), *Grundrisse: Foundations of the Critique of Political Economy*, London: Penguin.

———. (1979), *The Eighteenth Brumaire of Louis Bonaparte*, MECW, vol. 11, pp. 19–197.

Marx, Karl, and Engels, Friedrich (1992), *The Communist Manifesto*, New York: Bantam Books.

Mayhew, Henry (1968), *London Labour and the London Poor*, New York: Dover Publications.

Miller, Richard (1991), 'Social and Political Theory: Class, State, Revolution', in: Terrell Carver (ed.), *Cambridge Companion to Marx*, Cambridge: Cambridge University Press, pp. 55–105.

Mitchell, Juliet, and Oakley, Ann (eds.) (1976), *Rights and Wrongs of Women*, Harmondsworth: Penguin.
Moore, Henrietta (1988), *Feminism and Anthropology*, Cambridge: Polity Press.
O'Brien, Mary (1989), *Reproducing the World: Essays in Feminist Theory*, Boulder: Westview.
Pinchbeck, Ivey, and Hewitt, Margaret (1973), *Children in English Society*, London: Routledge and Kegan Paul.
Rodney, Walter (1974), *How Europe Underdeveloped Africa*, Washington: Howard University Press.
Schmid, Christian (2008), 'Lefebvre's Theory of Production of Space: Towards a Three-Dimensional Dialectic', in: Kanishka Goonewardena, Stefan Kipfer, Richard Milgram, and Christian Schmid (eds.), *Space, Difference, Everyday Life: Reading Henri Lefebvre*, London: Routledge, pp. 27–45.
Smith, Neil (1984), *Uneven Development: Nature, Capital, and the Production of Space*, Oxford: Blackwell.
Stedman Jones, Gareth (1971), *Outcast London: A Study of the Relationship Between Classes in Victorian Society*, Oxford: Clarendon Press.
Thompson, E. P. (1993), 'Time, Work–Discipline and Industrial Capitalism', in: E. P. Thompson, *Customs in Common*, London: Penguin, pp. 352–403.
Walkowitz, Judith (1980), *Prostitution and Victorian Society*, Cambridge: Cambridge University Press.
Williams, Raymond (1976), *Key Words: A Vocabulary of Culture and Society*, London: Fontana Press.
———. (1977), *Marxism and Literature*, Oxford: Oxford University Press.
———. (1977), 'Determination', in: Raymond Williams, *Marxism and Literature*, Oxford: Oxford University Press, pp. 83–9.
———. (1977), 'From Reflection to Mediation', in: Raymond Williams, *Marxism and Literature*, Oxford: Oxford University Press, pp. 95–100.

CHAPTER 2

Marx on Gender, Race, and Social Reproduction: A Feminist Perspective

Silvia Federici

2.1 For a Feminist Reconstruction of Marx's Critique of Capitalism

Rethinking Marx's treatment of 'gender' relations confronts us with a paradox. On one side, Marx's approach to 'gender', as discussed in his major works, is at best wanting. Whether by gender we refer to male–female relations and the rules by which they are constructed, or to the history and origins of the sexual division of labour and patriarchal domination in capitalism, in vain we turn to Marx for an analysis of these issues. With the exception of scattered remarks in his early works, and a discussion of female industrial employment in *Capital* Vol. 1, much of Marx's political theory is written from a male viewpoint, that of the working man, in whose name the First International was formed. On the other end, Marx's work has greatly contributed to the development of feminist theory as feminists have taken Marx to places where he was unable or unwilling to go. This has been more than an exercise in filling the gender gaps in Marx's work. Investigating the consequences of Marx's omissions

S. Federici (✉)
Hofstra University, Hempstead, NY, USA

M. Musto (ed.), *Rethinking Alternatives with Marx*, Marx, Engels, and Marxisms, https://doi.org/10.1007/978-3-030-81764-0_2

has inevitably forced a rethinking of the nature and history of the capitalist system and what constitutes an anti-capitalist struggle. It is the objective of this article to demonstrate that this feminist rethinking is a necessary condition for a reconstructed Marxism to be a guidance for the struggles of our time.

To make this case several steps are necessary. First, we have to question the argument, often put forward by feminists as well, that Marx's 'under-theorization' of gender relations is a minor omission in the general economy of his work. It would be absurd, it is argued, to expect from Marx the treatment of a subject that was outside the main scope of his analysis. It is also said that what matters in Marx, more than any statement he made on the question of gender, is his methodology, and stress is placed on his denunciations of patriarchal rule in several of his early works, although it is also acknowledged that Marx was a Victorian man, sharing the male biases of his age, making him blind to the activities in which women were engaged other than industrial work.

There is some truth in each of these arguments. But the conclusion proposed must be rejected. It assumes that Marx's exclusion from his political analysis of issues relating to gender, patriarchal rule, and reproduction did not affect his understanding of the functioning of capitalism and the struggle against it. And it assumes that the logic driving capitalist development and the 'class struggle' can be fully comprehended even when the analysis is oblivious to some of the activities that most matter in our lives and without which life itself cannot be sustained.

Contrary to this assumption, we must recognize, that Marx's approach to 'gender' had an impact on his work and does reveal limits, in his otherwise powerful social/political theory, that cannot be ignored. Gender blindness affected his concept of what constitutes work and who qualifies as a productive worker and as a revolutionary subject in capitalist society. It also led him to underestimate the power of the capitalist class to neutralize class insurgency through the construction of labour hierarchies that have not only divided workers, but redirected class antagonism towards antagonism within the working class. In all these respects, there is a direct connection between Marx's treatment of gender and his treatment of race. While he wrote quite extensively on slavery and slave labour, and 'was well aware of the centrality of race under capitalism',[1] he did not address racialization as a structural element of capitalist exploitation, nor ever departed from his conviction that the destiny of the struggle against capitalist exploitation is decided on the terrain of industrial work and by waged industrial workers. Underlying Marx's treatment of gender and race there is a common underplaying of the existence, in the history of capitalism, of different labour regimes. Thus, while this article centres on Marx's view of 'gender', it also considers how gender and race intersects in his work and in the recurrent processes of 'primitive accumulation' that have structured the history of capitalist development to the present.

The point of this exercise is not to fault Marx, nor deny the foundational character of his work for an understanding of the capitalist system and the possibility of its demise. Rather, it is to consider how rethinking his work from the viewpoint of those whose task has been the daily reproduction of life alters our understanding of both the capitalist system and the efforts to build a world beyond it. This is the path that, since the 1970s, many feminists have taken, using Marx to go beyond Marx, broadening his concept of work, of revolutionary subjects, and capitalist exploitation, and shifting the centre of gravity of the analysis from 'production' to 'reproduction'. Focusing on social reproductionhas not meant, however, privileging a different or complementary 'sector' of the capitalist organization of work, but looking at capitalism and the struggle against it from the viewpoint of the 'whole individual', the whole worker, rejecting the separations and mutilations that capitalism has created in our lives. From this viewpoint, a different conception of what is an anti-capitalist struggle and what shapes a revolutionary subjectivity has become possible that acknowledges, but also subverts the divisions capitalism has created within the proletariat, broadening the terrain of confrontation beyond a narrowly intended labour-capital relationand calling for a plurality of movements, corresponding to the plurality of labour regimes to which capitalism has submitted those that it has brought under its rule.

[1] See Keeanga-Yamahtta Taylor, *From Black Lives Matter to Black Liberation* (Chicago: Haymarket Books, 2014), p. 206. See also John Bellamy Foster, Hannah Holleman, and Brett Clark, 'Marx and Slavery', *Monthly Review*, vol. 72 (2020), n. 3: 96–117.

2.2 Marx on the 'Gender' Question

Feminists who stress Marx's continuous interest in gender issues point to his several denunciations of patriarchal relations in his early work.[2] In the *Economic and Philosophic Manuscripts of 1844*, for instance, echoing Fourier, he argued that the man-woman relation is a measure of social progress, as it tells us the extent to which 'the human essence has become nature to man'.[3] In *The German Ideology*, authored with Frederick Engels, he spoke of the 'slavery latent in the family', noting that within it the father can dispose of the labour of his wife and children.[4] Then, in his translation of Jacques Peuchet's essay *On suicide* he showed the destructive consequences of bourgeois morality on women's lives, leading them often to suicide.[5] Again, in the *Communist Manifesto* he derided the bourgeois familyas built on adultery and treating women like 'an instrument of production'.[6] Yet, what these texts demonstrate is that Marx condemned the subjection of women to patriarchal rule, but he did not consider it a key aspect of the capitalist organization of production, requiring an investigation of its history and function, nor was he concerned that sexism would be an obstacle to the unification of the working class. As he and Engels put it in the *Communist Manifesto*: 'Differences of age and sex no longer have any distinctive validity for the working class. All are instruments of labor'.[7]

Gender enters Marx's work with women's entrance into the factories during the industrial revolution. His description, in *Capital, Volume I*, of the cruelty of the capitalist exploitation of female and child labour, is powerful, driven by moral outrage and rich in details, but is also quite reductive. As Verónica Gago put it, 'Difference in Marx's and Engels'

[2] See Heather A. Brown, 'The Early Writings on Gender and the Family', in: Heather A. Brown, *Marx on Gender and the Family: A Critical Study* (Leiden: Brill, 2012), pp. 11ff.

[3] Karl Marx, *The Economic and Philosophic Manuscripts of 1844* (New York: International Publishers, 1976), p. 134.

[4] Karl Marx and Friedrich Engels, *The German Ideology* (Moscow: Progress Publishers, 1968), p. 44.

[5] Karl Marx, 'Peuchet on Suicide', in: Erica C. Plaut and Kevin Anderson (eds.), *Marx on Suicide* (Evanston: Northwestern University Press, 1999).

[6] Karl Marx and Friedrich Engels, *Manifesto of the Communist Party*, in: Dirk J. Struik (ed.), *The Birth of the Communist Manifesto* (New York: International Publishers, 1975), p. 108.

[7] Marx and Engels, *Manifesto of the Communist Party*, p. 97.

[analysis of gender on the shop floor] is reduced to a question of costs. Age and sex are variables that make labour cheaper, but they are without social significance'; 'the incorporation of difference is carried out under the sign of its cancellation'.[8] And it is a victimizing account, failing to do justice to women's capacity for resistance, or acknowledging the independence they gained by being wage earners, stressing, instead, the negative effects, on their character, of the promiscuous conditions of factory work. Marx's analysis of slave labour is also gender neutral, although enslaved women suffered a more brutal treatment than men, being subjected to constant sexual assaults and the unspeakable pain of seeing their children taken away and sold at auctions, often being forcibly inseminated so that they could breed more slaves.

In *Capital,* as in earlier works, Marx acknowledges the existence of patriarchal relations, but he does not tell us what makes them possible. He refers to the patriarchal character of the 'put-out system', arguing that here the father was the exploiter of his wife's and daughters' work.[9] He further laments that industrialization has turned proletarian men into slave-dealers, enabling them to sell their wives and children to the capitalists.[10] Yet, while he dedicated much work to studying the history of social categories, he did not investigate the origin of male domination in capitalism, a remarkable omission, especially considering that he had come of age in Germany, a country that, for more than two centuries, had led Europe in an unprecedented persecution of women under the guise of witch-hunting.[11] More surprisingly, in this context, Marx did

[8] Verónica Gago, *Feminist International: How to Change Everything* (New York: Verso, 2020), p. 123.

[9] Karl Marx, *Capital, Volume I* (London: Penguin, 1976), p. 620.

[10] Ibid., p. 519: 'Previously the worker sold his own labor power, which he disposed of as a free agent [...] Now he sells wife and child'.

[11] The Witch Trials of Trier, in the years from 1581 to 1593, were perhaps the biggest witch trials in European history. They lead to the death of about 368 people, and 'were perhaps the biggest mass execution in Europe in peace time. This counts only those executed within the city itself; the number of those executed in all the witch hunts within the diocese was even larger. The exact number of executions has never been established; a total of 1000 has been suggested but not confirmed', Wikipedia, 'Trier Witch Trials', *Wikipedia*, n.d., https://en.wikipedia.org/wiki/Trier_witch_trials, accessed on 3 January 2021. On the Trier witch trials, see H. C. Erik Midelfort, *Witch Hunting in Southwestern Germany 1562–1684: The Social and Intellectual Foundations* (Stanford: Stanford University Press, 1972).

not acknowledge male factory workers' hostility to women's industrial employment and its effects on organizing and solidarity building, as he did with regard to English workers' antagonism towards the Irish.

Had Marx examined the historical roots and genealogy of patriarchy in capitalist society he could have explained why, in England's factories, women's labour, like that of children, was of lesser cost, lesser value than that of men. He would have recognized that, unlike men, expropriated women did not enter capitalism as possessors of their labour-power, being subjected to a far more radical dispossession extending to their body, their sexuality and their legal identity. It is this radical devaluation, to which they were subjected also through the orchestration of two centuries of witch-hunting. This helps us explain why proletarian men in the put-out system could appropriate their wives' and daughters' labours and, with industrial development, for a time, sell them to the factories.

So different was the inclusion of women into capitalist society that in Marx's time, married women in England, like children, had no legal rights, and they had to be represented in the courts by men of their family or a tutor. Above all, they had no right to their wages or any other income they earned.[12] The unfree status of women was such, that, as late as the mid-nineteenth century, 'sales of wives' were still practised in the working class, with the husband carrying his wife to the market, at times wearing a halter around her neck, as a cheap way to divorce.[13] The practice, E. P. Thompson tells us, by the mid-nineteenth century was in decline, frowned upon by the urban middle classes.[14] But that it survived so long tells us of the depth of degradation that women suffered in Europe, and the inequality that characterized male–female relations also in the working class. Sales of wives were not casual affairs, but highly ritualized ones,

[12] This ended with the passing of the Married Women's Property Act 1870, which for the first time in British history enabled women to keep their earnings, for their separate use, independent of any husband to whom they may be married. See Wikipedia, 'Married Women's Property Act 1870', *Wikipedia*, n.d., https://en.wikipedia.org/wiki/Married_Women%27s_Property_Act_1870, accessed on 3 January 2021.

[13] Carole Pateman, *The Sexual Contract* (Stanford: Stanford University Press, 1988), writes that 'popular belief seems to have been that the sale was valid only if the halter were in place; she also comments on the symbolism of the halter, noting it was part of livestock sales, and that the practice indicates that the wife was considered a property of the husband', pp. 121–2.

[14] E. P. Thompson, 'The Sale of Wives', in: E. P. Thompson (ed.), *Customs in Common: Studies in Traditional Popular Culture* (New York: The New Press, 1991), pp. 410–1.

performed publicly, in the market place,[15] by workers from many trades, and we are left to speculate why no mention of it is found in Marx.

References to gender relations are also absent in Marx's analysis of the activities catering to the reproduction of labour-power. As Leopoldina Fortunati has pointed out, in *The Arcane of Reproduction*, domestic/reproductive activities—domestic work, childcare, sexual work, procreation—are barely mentioned in his major works, except to register their absence in the life of the proletariat, due to women's day-long employment in industrial work. As she puts it: 'Marx managed to see housework only when capital destroyed it, and saw it only through government reports'.[16] Throughout *Capital,* Marx affirms that labour-power must be constantly reproduced, being daily consumed in the labour process. He also describes this reproduction as productive consumption, as necessary to capital accumulation as the cleaning of the machines, 'insofar as it is the production and reproduction of the capitalist's most indispensable means of production: the worker'.[17] However, he insistently tells us that it is accomplished only through the market, with workers purchasing the necessities of life their wages can buy. No labour, other than that required to produce the 'means of subsistence' to be bought on the market, is considered by Marx necessary to the reproduction of the worker's labour-power. At no point does he recognize that reproducing labour-power requires some domestic work—to prepare food, wash and mend clothes, clean, raise children. He also ignores that some of the most important commodities for the reproduction of labour-power in Europe, those that fuelled the Industrial Revolution—coffee, sugar, tobacco, cotton—were produced by slave labour in the American plantations.

Even when referring to the procreation of new workers, Marx never mentions women's labour, and never hints to the fact that women and

[15] Thompson, 'The Sale of Wives', p. 417.

[16] Leopoldina Fortunati, *The Arcane of Reproduction: Housework, Prostitution, Labor, and Capital* (Brooklyn: Autonomedia, 1995), p. 169.

[17] Marx, *Capital, Volume I*, pp. 717–8. Marx writes that: 'The individual consumption of the worker, whether it occurs inside or outside the workshop, inside or outside the labour process, remains an aspect of the production and reproduction of capital, just as the cleaning of machinery does, whether it is done during the labor process, or when intervals in that process permit. The fact that the worker performs acts of individual consumption in his own interest, and not to please the capitalist, is entirely irrelevant to the matter', p. 717.

men may have had different and even conflicting interests with regard to it. He thus speaks of the 'natural increase of population',[18] and only considers the rise and fall of wages as a factor in the determination of family size, overlooking the fact that childbirth was in England, at the time, one of the main causes of women's mortality and, on account of their poverty, proletarian women dreaded any new pregnancy, engaging in daily struggles to avoid sexual relations with their husbands or convince them to practice 'coitus interruptus'.

For an unmarried woman a pregnancy was even a bigger threat, as it could mean a loss of employment and social ostracism. Abortion would not be possible, except at a considerable risk, having been banned in the United Kingdom since the passing of an act of law in 1803 that made terminating a pregnancy after quickening a capital crime to be punish with death; this was followed by a further act, in 1836, that made it a crime to terminate a pregnancy at all times, punishable with a maximum of life transportation.[19] How unwelcome pregnancies were among proletarians, women in particular, is also proven by the high number of abandoned children, especially in London, a phenomenon otherwise typical, in the nineteenth century, of many European cities, where even today, in some we can see the sites where they would be abandoned.

Marx well understood that capitalism cannot expand without accumulating more workers, also to function as a reserve army. He often returned to this topic, introducing the idea that 'every particular historical mode of production has its own special laws of population', thus powerfully de-naturalizing the most 'natural' activity on earth, that of procreating new human beings.[20] Yet, he never mentioned women in this context, not even when acknowledging the existence of a breeding industry, organized in states like Virginia, in the early nineteenth century, after England banned the slave trade, whereby enslaved women were subjected to systematic rape, as part of the slave owners' efforts to avoid the cost of transporting enslaved people from Africa.

[18] Ibid., pp. 788, 794.

[19] R. Sauer, 'Infanticide and Abortion in Nineteenth Century Britain', *Population Studies: A Journal of Demography*, vol. 32 (1978), n. 1: 85–6.

[20] Marx, *Capital, Volume I*, 'An abstract law of population' he added 'exists only for plants and animals. And even then only in the absence of any historical intervention by man', p. 784.

The history of this peculiar aspect of capitalist production is now often forgotten; yet it is one of the most revealing examples of the utter inhumanity of the capitalist system. Dorothy Roberts' classic work, *Killing the Black Body, Race, Reproduction, and the Meaning of Liberty* shows how slave breeding is an iconic example of the way in which black women have been denied maternity and have experience in their very bodies, more than any other population, what atrocities have been necessary to turn human blood into gold.[21] Marx saw the horrors of industrial workbut he was blind to the horrors of the capitalist exploitation of women's reproductive capacity which, especially in the case of the breeding industry, is an iconic example of capitalism's mercenary logic and unlimited violation of the female body.

This is why, when it comes to proletarian women and especially afro-descendant women, Marx's theory must always be 'stretched' (to use Fanon's words),[22] especially when dealing with such issues as the right to abortion and the right to have the children one wants, around which millions of women (as we saw recently in Argentina) continue to mobilize. Symptomatic of Marx's inability to address 'gender issues' is also his moralizing attitude towards sex work, which in *Capital* appears not as a form of reproductive labour but as an object of censure, though it was a source of income for thousands of proletarian women, 'milliners, shop girls, domestic servants, and women employed in factories or working in agricultural gangs', according to an 1870 account by a member of the Royal College of Surgeons.[23]

Why was Marx obviously reluctant to address the specific character of women's oppression and exploitation in capitalist society? A common answer is that he undertheorized housework because very little domestic work was performed in the industrial districts, the focus of his analysis, and like most men of his time, he saw domestic reproductive activities as

[21] Dorothy Roberts, 'Reproduction in Bondage', in: Dorothy Roberts (ed.), *Killing the Black Body: Race, Reproduction, and the Meaning of Liberty* (New York: Vintage Books, 2017), pp. 24–8.

[22] Frantz Fanon, *The Wretched of the Earth* (New York: Grove Press, 1963): 'When you examine at close quarters the colonial context it is clear that what parcels out the world is to begin with the fact of belonging or not belonging to a given race, a given species [...] This is why Marxist analysis should always be slightly stretched every time we have to do with the colonial problem', p. 40.

[23] William Acton, *Prostitution* (New York: Praeger, 1969).

a natural resource, not different, as far as their capitalist function, from the raw materials required by industrial work. Another possible reason is that, being unpaid, reproductive work was not easily calculable, although Marx knew that labour-time, the essence of value, is a relational entity and does not consist of any specific amount of time. We can also surmise that being, for the most part, irreducible to industrialization, domestic work was of scarce interest for Marx, who was enthralled by the possibility—which industry promised—of reducing necessary work and placing work itself on a more rational basis. Not last, as with enslaved labour, he likely presumed that domestic work would soon be a thing of the past, replaced by more socially and technologically advanced forms of production.

Be this as it may, more important than the reasons for Marx's underplay of gender differences, for the purpose of this article, are its consequences. Politically, the main have been his inability to see that *women's rights were also labor rights*,[24] and inability to appreciate the significance of the contemporary feminist organizations which he generally saw as bourgeois initiatives, occasionally advising women to abstain from them. He also overestimated the equalizing effects of women's industrial employment. As for later generations of leftists, for Marx and Engels as well, it is through participation in industrial work that the inequality between women and men can be overcome.[25] That women are differently embodied subjects, have different experiences from men, with regard to sexuality, procreation, child-raising, that these differences have historically been mystified, exploited, used in ways that have instigated male violence against women even of their own class and that, in capitalism, all activities pertaining to 'women's labor' have been socially devalued, is something Marx did not confront neither theoretically nor politically.

Thus, he did not take a position against workers and labour unions mobilization for a 'family wage', that called for women to be sent back to the home, nor did he comment on the reform of industrial work and proletarian family that was already unfolding in the 1860s, which (together with colonial expansion) put an end to the revolutionary season,

[24] This is a theme in Fortunati, *The Arcane of Reproduction.*

[25] As he wrote, 'large-scale industry by assigning an important part in socially organized processes of production, outside the sphere of the domestic economy, to women, young person and children of both sexes, does nevertheless create a new economic foundation for a higher form of the family and of the relation between the sexes', Marx, *Capital, Volume I*, pp. 620–1.

in England first and then in much of Europe, reconstituting a new form of patriarchy that can be properly defined as the 'patriarchy of the wage'.[26]

2.3 Marx on the Question of Slave Labour and 'Race'

There is a strong connection, in this context, though a difference as well, between Marx's relation to gender and his approach to the question of 'race'. While he was silent on reproductive activities, throughout his work Marx gave constant attention, theoretically and politically, to slavery and slave labour. As he was working on *Capital*, in the Unites States the civil war was raging, soon centring on the question of the 'emancipation'. Marx believed the outcome would be of world historical importance, wrote many articles on the subject for the *New York Tribune*. And in 1963, on behalf of the First International, he wrote to President Lincoln to congratulate him on the Emancipation Declaration, stating that [slavery] 'this barrier to progress has been swept off by the red sea of the civil war'.[27] He was very aware that as long as slavery existed it would be difficult for any worker to succeed in their struggle[28] and that slavery in the American colonies was not a vestigial remnant of a pre-capitalist world but as an essential aspect of capital accumulation.

[26] On this subject, see Silvia Federici, 'Revolution Begins at Home', in: Marcello Musto (ed.), *Marx's Capital After 150 Years* (New York: Routledge, 2019), pp. 125–44.

[27] Karl Marx, 'To Abraham Lincoln, President of the United States of America', MECW, vol. 20, p. 20. The full quote runs as follows: 'While the working men, the true political power of the North, allowed slavery to defile their own republic, while before the Negro, mastered and sold without his concurrence, they boasted it the highest prerogative of the white-skinned labourer to sell himself and chose his ow master, they were unable to attain the true freedom of labour [...] but this barrier to progress has been swept off by the red of civil war', ibid.

[28] 'In the United States of America, every independent workers' movement was paralysed as long as slavery disfigured a part of the republic. Labor in the white skin cannot emancipate itself' he famously wrote 'where it is branded in a black skin', adding that 'However, a new life immediately arose from the death of slavery. The first fruit of the American Civil War was the eight hours' agitation, which ran from the Atlantic to the Pacific, from New England to California with the seven-league boots of the locomotive', Marx, *Capital, Volume I*, p. 414.

> Direct slavery is as much the pivot upon which our present-day industrialism turns as are machinery, credit, etc. Without slavery there would be no cotton, without cotton there would be no modern industry. It is slavery which has given value to the colonies, it is the colonies which have created world trade, and world trade is the necessary condition for large-scale machine industry. Consequently, prior to the slave trade, the colonies sent few products to the Old World and did not noticeably change the face of the world. Slavery is therefore and economic category of paramount importance.[29]

Comparison with slave labour in all its historical incarnations, in Greece, Rome, and above all as organized in the American plantation economies, is a constant theme in *Capital*, called on to illustrate the conditions of capital development and, at the same time, the specificity of waged work. As Biko Agozino has pointed out, slavery and slave labour are not only an important presence in Marx's main works, but constitute the backdrop against which all other forms of exploitation, children's, women's, industrial workers', are analysed.[30]

Nevertheless, Marx never departed from an exclusionary concept of class and, as Karl Heinz Roth and Marcel van der Linden have pointed out, he excluded slave labour or from his calculation of the labour contributing to the creation of value, defining slaves as fixed capital, rather than providers of surplus labour.[31] One possible reason is that 'Marx considered slavery a historically backward mode of exploitation that would soon be a thing of the past'.[32] He was convinced, in fact, that slave

[29] Karl Marx to Vasilyevich Annenkov, 28 December 1846, MECW, vol. 38, pp. 101–2. Strangely enough, however, the sequel to this much quoted statement suggests that slavery had a beneficial effect on not only American society but far beyond it. 'Without slavery, North America, the most progressive nation, would be transformed into a patriarchal country. Only wipe North America off the map and you will get anarchy, the complete decay of trade and modern civilization. But to do away with slavery would be to wipe America off the map', ibid., p. 102.

[30] See Biko Agozino 'The Africana Paradigm: The Debts of Karl Marx to the People of African Descent in *Capital*', *Review of African Political Economy*, vol. 41 (2014), n. 140: 172–84.

[31] Karl Heinz Roth and Marcel van der Linden, 'Results and Prospects', in: Karl Heinz Roth and Marcel van der Linden (eds.), *Beyond Marx: Theorizing the Global Labour Relations* (Leiden: Brill), pp. 445–85. See especially the section titled 'Karl Marx and the Problem of Slave Labour', p. 470.

[32] Karl Heinz Roth and Marcel van der Linden, 'Results and Prospects', p. 468.

labour was more expensive and less productive than free labour, since not facing competition and being guaranteed in their survival, enslaved workers had no incentive to work, which they made clear by constantly breaking their tools, so that slave owners gave them outdated technological equipment, expecting it would be soon put of use.[33] The low productivity of slave labour was a common assumption at his time, also among abolitionists, who used it as an argument in support of the abolition of slavery. Marx brought new arguments to it, in part evocative of his views concerning the inferior quality of women's industrial work. The advantage of slave labour was his low cost, but not having to fend for their survival, not having to make choices about how to use a wage, enslaved workers could not develop the versatility and self-activity of free labour, always needing 'direct compulsion' to be activated. Comparing the free worker to the enslaved worker, Marx thus wrote that the formers' labour:

> becomes more productive because more intensive, since the slave works only under the spur of external fear, but not for *his existence* which is *guaranteed* even though it does not belong to him. The free worker, however, is impelled by his wants. The consciousness [...] of free self-determination, of liberty, makes a better worker [...] as does the related feeling of *responsibility*.[34]

And again:

> For the free worker [...] the *value of his labour-power* and the average wage *corresponding to it*, does not appear to him as something predestined, as something independent of his labour and determined by the mere needs of his existence [...] In the case of the slave, great physical strength or a special talent may enhance his value to a *purchaser*, but this is of no concern to him. It is otherwise with the free workers who is the owner of *his labour power*.[35]

[33] Marx, *Capital, Volume I*, pp. 303–4, n. 18. Marx quotes here Frederick Law Olmstead, *A Journey to the Seaboard Slave States* (1856), who wrote: 'I am here shown tools that no man in his senses, with us, would allow a labourer, for whom he was paying wages, to be encumbered with'.

[34] Ibid., p. 1031, italics in original.

[35] Ibid., p. 1032. Along the same line, Marx favorably compares the 'versatility' of free labor, with the 'utterly monotonous and traditional nature of slave labor', due to the indifference of the enslaved workers to the content of their work', p. 1034.

It is possibly because of his belief in the lesser productivity of the slaves, that Marx did not anticipate that the end of slavery would not be the end of racialize labour hierarchies, but would, instead, witness the rise of a new type of racism, more structured, more organized, and institutionalized.[36] He did not anticipate that (in E. B. Du Bois' words) race, 'the color line' would be the twentieth-century's problem,[37] and that the descendants of the slaves would become a revolutionary force in the United States, while the mostly white wage labourers would increasingly turn their solidarity into a defence of privilege, and support not only institutionalized racism but a seemingly endless process of imperial expansion.

A factor limiting Marx's anticipation of the future of the 'class struggle' is his conception of the determinants of class consciousness and revolutionary subjectivity, that focuses almost exclusively on the relations structuring the labour process. Thus, in his assessment of the formation of the subjectivity of the slaves, he only considered their life as workers, to the exclusion of the time of their own reproduction—the time when, 'from sundown to sunup', the master would be asleep, work would be over and, for a brief time, they would regain some control over their lives—the time for talks, for music, for reviving the rituals brought from Africa, and the time, as well, to plan escapes or to help those who had succeeded and now lived as maroons, but still dependent, often coming back at night, on those who had remained at the plantation.[38] This time was especially crucial for women, who often used it to go find their

[36] As George Rawick has argued, with the end of slavery a new page in the history of racism has been opened, since racism has been systematically reorganized to replace slavery as a means to control black people once slavery was dismantled. This is why racism in the U.S. has been so pervasive, shaping every institution and social relation, and has proven so difficult to eradicate. George Rawick, 'Racism and Slavery', in: George Rawick (ed.), *From Sundown to Sunup: The Making of the Black Community* (Westport: Greenwood Publishing, 1972), pp. 142–7. For this reason, we cannot accept the argument of Marxists who believe that being founded on the exploitation of labor, capitalism is essentially color blind. This, however, is to operate an unwarranted separation between capitalism as an abstract system and its historical embodiment. Capitalism, however, is not an abstraction, but a system consolidated under very specific historical conditions that have marked it, have directed its choices, and determined the forms of its development. Three centuries of slavery have sedimented institutions, created subjectivities, produced a powerful system of means of control and repression.

[37] W. E. B. Du Bois, *The Soul of Black Folks* (New York: Dover Publications, 1903).

[38] Rawick, *From Sundown to Sunup*, p. 110.

children who may have been sold to a nearby slave owner, travelling in the dark, at the risk of terrible punishments, if discovered.[39] As it has often been recognized, this other side of the lives of the enslaved is what allowed for their pain to become productive, to generate culture, to sustain the passive resistance that broke the tools, to give the courage to revolt.

This was a world surely unknown to Marx. Yet, his omission of those moments when the enslaved experienced something of an 'outside' to slavery, evoques his tendency to bring to the centre stage only issues connected with the processes and conflicts inherent to the work relation. This is one reason why black radicals have often found it difficult to come to terms with Marx. As Cedric Robinson has argued, in *Black Marxism,* while criticizing Marx for overlooking the subjectivity of the enslaved,

> Marx had not realized fully that the cargoes of laborers also contained African cultures, critical mixes and admixtures of language and thought, of cosmology and metaphysics, of habits, beliefs, and morality. These were the actual terms of their humanity. These cargoes, then, did not consist of intellectually isolates or deculturated Blacks - men, women, and children separated from their previous universe. African labor brought the past with it, a past that had produced it and settled on it the first elements of consciousness and comprehension.[40]

The underestimation of the importance of subjective factors, particularly as determinants of a revolutionary potential, is particularly evident in Marx's treatment of women who, enslaved or free, are absent, as subjects with specific concerns and dispositions, in his conceptualization of the revolutionary process. Unlike, many of his contemporary, even within the workers' movement, Marx always defended women's right to be treated equally with men. Thus, in his Preamble to the 'Programme of the Parti Ouvrier' of 1880, he wrote that 'the emancipation of the productive class

[39] As bell hooks reports, a reference to these night journeys enslaved women took to visit their children is to be found in Frederick Douglas 1845 slave narrative. See bell hooks, *Yearning, Race, Gender, and Cultural Politics* (Boston: South End Press, 1990), p. 44.

[40] Cedric J. Robinson, *Black Marxism: The Making of the Black Radical Tradition* (Chapel Hill: North Carolina University Press, 2000), p. 121.

is that of all human beings without distinction of sex or race'.[41] What is missing, however, in his work is a recognition of the specific ways in which women were exploited in capitalism, of the misogynous treatment to which they were subjected also by men of their own class, and the specific ways in which they struggled against it.

2.4 Feminist Reconstructions

Considering the absence in Marx's work of a serious analysis of gender-based activities and relations, it is remarkable and evidence of the power of Marx's critique of capitalist political economy that generations of feminists have been inspired by it and taken it as a foundational element of a feminist anti-capitalist perspective.

Incorporation of Marx's work into a feminist framework has taken different forms, but despite the differences, and in some cases incompatibilities, one common denominator has been the recognition of the importance, for feminist theory, of his historical materialist method which identifies the production of everyday life and social struggle as the engine of historical becoming and the key elements in the production of human nature, thus ruling out any fixed conception of what it means to be human. The possibility of debunking essentializing view of femininity—always invoked to convince women to accept a subordinate social role—has been undoubtedly the main reason why many feminists have turned to Marx.

However, even more important, from the viewpoint of the restructuring of Marxism, has been the feminist discovery that Marx's theory can provide the key to understand the specific character and roots of patriarchal rule in capitalism. A crucial element, in this context, has been Marx's analysis of the production of labour-power, which in the 1970s inspired feminists like Mariarosa Dalla Costa, Leopoldina Fortunati, and Selma James to redefine domestic work and the function of the nuclear family, respectively as the activity and the centre for the reproduction of the workforce.[42]

[41] Quoted by Brown, *Marx On Gender and the Family*, p. 216. See also Marcello Musto, *The Last Years of Karl Marx: An Intellectual Biography* (Stanford: Stanford University Press, 2020), p. 45.

[42] See in particular Mariarosa Dalla Costa, 'Women and the Subversion of the Community', in: Mariarosa Dalla Costa and Selma James (eds.), *The Power of Women and the*

Finding that this much despised work, always taken for granted and dismissed by socialists as a pre-capitalist heritage, has been one of the pillars of the capitalist organization of work has produced a political and theoretical revolution, triggering a re-examination of not only the Marxian conception of work, but the nature of the wage relation and the function of patriarchy in capitalism. It has helped feminists to establish that the wage is a highly political instrument, in that it not only mystifies the exchange between waged workers and capital as a contract among equals, but conceals and naturalizes the unpaid labourrequired for the reproduction of waged workers. In addition, the wage has given waged workers powers over the unwaged; it has allowed the capitalist class to delegate to men the supervision and disciplining of women's reproductive work in a reconstituted patriarchal regime that can be defined as the 'patriarchy of the wage'.[43] Much domestic violence has been rooted in this system and, as feminists have recognized, for this very reason it has historically been tolerated by the state, in the same way as inflicting physical punishments on children has been tolerated and even encouraged to prepare them to become future workers, and in the same way as violence against black and brown people has been tolerated to contain their revolt.

Discovering the centrality of women's unpaid labourin the home for the production of the workforce has not only resolved the vexed question of the relation between gender and class, and uncovered the capitalist function of the nuclear family. It has redefined class, and deepened our understanding of class antagonism at the roots of capitalist society. It has confirmed that as house-workers, maids, sex workers, women did not have to join men in the factories to be part of the working class and make an anti-capitalist struggle, and that this struggle had often to be waged first against the men of one's family since, through the male wage and the marriage contract, capitalism has empowered men to supervise and command women's unpaid work. Ironically, then, the feminist appropriation of the Marxian analysis of the reproduction of labour-power, in a

Subversion of the Community (Bristol: Falling Wall Press, 1975), pp. 21–56; Selma James, *Sex, Race, and Class* (Bristol: Falling Wall Press, 1975); and Leopoldina, *The Arcane of Reproduction.*

43 See Silvia Federici, 'The Accumulation of Labor and the Degradation of Women: Constructing "Difference" in the "Transition to Capitalism"', in: Silvia Federici (ed.), *Caliban and the Witch: Women, the Body, and Primitive Accumulation* (Brooklyn: Autonomedia, 2004), pp. 97ff.; and Silvia Federici, *Marxism, Feminism, and the Patriarchy of the Wage* (Oakland: PM Press, 2021, forthcoming).

way consecrating Marx's importance for feminism, has also provided the conclusive evidence that Marx had to be turned upside down, and that women's struggle had to focus precisely on that part of the 'social factory' that had been excluded from his work.[44]

Shifting the centre of gravity from 'production' to 'reproduction'—reinterpreted as production of the workforce—has not meant, however, to abandon Marx's theory of value creation and capital valorization. It has instead highlighted the fact that Marx's identification of the valorization process with the production of commodities and of the productive worker with the waged industrial worker has precluded a full understanding of who is the working class, what is the production of value, in what sites it occurs, and what are the conditions of its production. In this sense, speaking of shifting the focus of analysis from production to reproduction is not performing a sectorial change or replicating an exclusionary conception of the producers of capitalism. It is to broaden the horizon from which we look at capitalist accumulation, to include a world of activities that have been excluded from it by the traditional male left, and by Marx himself and, in this way, to multiply the subjects and sites of struggle against capitalism and the visions of the world to be constructed once the expropriators have themselves been expropriated. It is also to make visible that 'embodiment' is an essential, irreducible aspect of every labouring practice.

In the 1970s, feminist analysis of reproduction focused primarily on the question of domestic work and sex work. Since then, the concept has expanded. Especially in the global South, feminists have argued that 'reproduction' must be defined in such a way as to take into account all the struggles involved in the preservation of the conditions of our lives, such as the fight against land privatization, against the destruction of our ecosystems, against deforestation, the poisoning of the soil and cropland, the genetic engineering and commodification of seeds.[45] As

[44] On this subject, see Silvia Federici, 'Wages Against Housework', in: Silvia Federici, *Revolution at Point Zero: Housework, Reproduction, and Feminist Struggle* (Oakland: PM Press, 2020), pp. 11–8; and Silvia Federici, 'Introduction', in: Silvia Federici and Arlen Austin (eds.), *The New York Wages For Housework Committee 1972–1977: History, Theory, Documents* (Brooklyn: Autonomedia, 2017), pp. 202–10.

[45] In this context, see the powerful work of Gago, *Feminist International*, especially Chapters 2 'Violence: Is There a War On and Against Women's Bodies?', pp. 56–83, and Chapter 3 'Body–Territory: The Body as Battlefield', pp. 84–114. Gago insists on not reducing 'social reproduction' to a partial, sectorial aspect of capitalist organization

Michelle Murphy, among others, has put it: 'reproduction is not reducible to bodies and labor', or even childbirth and child-raising, but must extend to include the natural world, now under siege from multiple threats all, however, reducible to the subordination to the profit motive of the activities and resources most necessary for our lives and the lives of our ecosystems.[46]

A further factor in the redefinition/ extension of the concept of 'reproduction' have been the precarization of labour and collapse of the male wage, beginning in the 1980s, due to the restructuring of the world economy and the rise of 'neo-liberalism', and the massive recruitment of women into waged labour. As more women have begun to work outside the home and many reproductive activities have been commercialized, the distinction between production and reproduction has begun to blur, and the latter has become the terrain for new forms of exploitation and capital accumulation. Indeed, reproductive activities are today exploited both as unpaid labour, catering to the reproduction of the new generations of workers, and as direct sources of profit through the marketization and financialization of reproduction, insofar as their performance increasingly depends on the use of financial instruments (like credit cards) that turn reproductive activities into direct processes of value-creation. The rise of a paid domestic workers' movements, fighting for classic labour rights, has also contributed to bridge two spheres of work and two population of workers that capitalism throughout its history has striven to separate.[47] Thus, studies of contemporary forms of social reproductionincreasingly focus on waged work performed outside the home: nursing, education, retailing, and so forth.

All these developments are important as they enable us to recognize that (a) capitalism has not only built its power through the exploitation of waged work and the factory system or through the privatization of land and other resources, but has reached far deeper into our lives, our bodies, our reciprocal relations. Therefore, the sites and subjects of the 'class struggle' are not limited to the world of smokestacks and offices,

of work, but viewing it instead as a perspective from which to redefine every aspect of capitalist society.

[46] Michelle Murphy, 'Reproduction', in: Shahrzad Mojab (ed.), *Marxism and Feminism* (London: Zed Books, 2015), pp. 287–304.

[47] See Silvia Federici, 'We Have Seen Other Countries and Have Another Culture', in: *Revolution at Point Zero*, pp. 167–80.

for every aspect of our life is a terrain of struggle. (b) This lays the foundation for a theory of the 'class struggle' that is not vertically constructed or built on a homogeneous conception of the 'worker' and the 'revolutionary subject', and does not presumes that the nature of capitalism can by understood from one unique standpoint, as capitalist development has been the development of hierarchies, inequalities, generating profoundly different experiences that can only be expressed and overcome through a politics of cooperation between different social movements, unconceivable in organizational structures that always privileged those assumed to be the most 'productive'.

It is worth repeating that by broadening the concept of reproduction, to include all the sites and subjects that today are engaged in resistance to the expansion of capitalist relations, we also learn to appreciate the multiplicity of visions of the world that is to be built, beyond capitalism. Here too a distance must be taken from the Marxian and Marxist conceptions of the future communist society, insofar as they suggest enrichment through a process of universal exchange, whose material foundation is to be provided by the global reach of industrialization. This is a topic that exceeds the aim of this article. Suffice to say that in a world where 'no contact people' are still fighting, perhaps their last battle on earth, not to be 'discovered', and where many indigenous communities insist that they do not want to be 'developed', we have to be concerned with any universalizing, world historical view of the postcapitalist society, such as Marx and Engels proposes, for instance, in *The German Ideology*. More humbly, we must appreciate the diversity of histories, cultural trajectories and struggles, and the sentiment of those who, like the Zapatistas, argue that when it comes to the goals of an anti-capitalist struggle our slogan must be 'One No, and Many Yesses'. That is: one absolute refusal of every form of social injustice and, at the same time, the acceptance of the multiple ways in which the *buen vivir*, the good life can be imagined and realized.

Thus, hand in hand, with a feminist recuperation of important aspects of Marx's theoretical and political perspective, we need a new critique of the Marxian drive to homogenize not only the subjects and forms of capitalist exploitation, but the subjects and terrains of the struggle against it and the vision of the new world to be constructed.

References

Acton, William (1969), *Prostitution*, New York: Praeger.

Agozino, Biko (2014), 'The Africana Paradigm: The Debts of Karl Marx to the People of African Descent in *Capital*', *Review of African Political Economy*, vol. 41, n. 140: 172–84.

Brown, Heather A. (2012), *Marx on Gender and the Family: A Critical Study*, Leiden: Brill.

———. (2012), 'The Early Writings on Gender and the Family', in: Heather A. Brown (ed.), *Marx on Gender and the Family: A Critical Study*, Leiden: Brill, pp. 11–51.

Dalla Costa, Mariarosa (1975), 'Women and the Subversion of the Community', in: Mariarosa Dalla Costa and Selma James (eds.), *The Power of Women and the Subversion of the Community*, Bristol: Falling Wall Press, pp. 21–56.

Du Bois, W. E. B. (1903), *The Soul of Black Folks*, New York: Dover Publications.

Fanon, Frantz (1963), *The Wretched of the Earth*, New York: Grove Press.

Federici, Silvia (2004), *Caliban and the Witch: Women, the Body, and Primitive Accumulation*, Brooklyn: Autonomedia.

———. (2004), 'The Accumulation of Labor and the Degradation of Women: Constructing "Difference" in the "Transition to Capitalism"', in: Silvia Federici (ed.), *Caliban and the Witch: Women, the Body, and Primitive Accumulation*, Brooklyn: Autonomedia, pp. 61–132.

———. (2017), 'Introduction', in: Silvia Federici and Arlen Austin (eds.), *The New York Wages For Housework Committee 1972–1977: History, Theory, Documents*, Brooklyn: Autonomedia, pp. 202–10.

———. (2019), 'Revolution Begins at Home', in: Marcello Musto (ed.), *Marx's Capital After 150 Years*, New York: Routledge, pp. 125–44.

———. (2020), 'Wages Against Housework', in: Silvia Federici (ed.), *Revolution at Point Zero: Housework, Reproduction, and Feminist Struggle*, Oakland: PM Press, pp. 11–8.

———. (2020), 'We Have Seen Other Countries and Have Another Culture', in: Silvia Federici (ed.), *Revolution at Point Zero: Housework, Reproduction, and Feminist Struggle*, Oakland: PM Press, pp. 167–80.

———. (2021, forthcoming), *Marxism, Feminism, and the Patriarchy of the Wage*, Oakland: PM Press.

Fortunati, Leopoldina (1995), *The Arcane of Reproduction: Housework, Prostitution, Labor, and Capital*, Brooklyn: Autonomedia.

Foster, John Bellamy, Holleman, Hannah, and Clark, Brett (2020), 'Marx and Slavery', *Monthly Review*, vol. 72, n. 3: 96–117.

Gago, Verónica (2020), *Feminist International: How to Change Everything*, New York: Verso.

———. (2020), 'Violence: Is There a War On and Against Women's Bodies?', in: Verónica Gago (ed.), *Feminist International: How to Change Everything*, New York: Verso, pp. 56–83.

———. (2020), 'Body–Territory: The Body as Battlefield', in: Verónica Gago (ed.), *Feminist International: How to Change Everything*, New York: Verso, pp. 84–114.

hooks, bell (1990), *Yearning, Race, Gender, and Cultural Politics*, Boston: South End Press.

James, Selma (1975), *Sex, Race, and Class*, Bristol: Falling Wall Press.

Marx, Karl (1976), *The Economic and Philosophic Manuscripts of 1844*, New York: International Publishers.

———. (1976), *Capital, Volume I*, London: Penguin.

———. (1985), 'To Abraham Lincoln, President of the United States of America', MECW, vol. 20, pp. 19–21.

———. (1999), 'Peuchet on Suicide', in: Erica C. Plaut and Kevin Anderson (eds.), *Marx on Suicide*, Evanston: Northwestern University Press.

Marx, Karl, and Engels, Friedrich (1968), *The German Ideology*, Moscow: Progress Publishers.

———. (1975), *Manifesto of the Communist Party*, in: Dirk J. Struik (ed.), *The Birth of the Communist Manifesto*, New York: International Publishers, pp. 85–126.

———. (1982), *Letters 1844–51*, MECW, vol. 38.

Midelfort, H. C. Erik (1972), *Witch Hunting in Southwestern Germany 1562–1684: The Social and Intellectual Foundations*, Stanford: Stanford University Press.

Murphy, Michelle (2015), 'Reproduction', in: Shahrzad Mojab (ed.), *Marxism and Feminism,* London: Zed Books, pp. 287–304.

Musto, Marcello (ed.) (2019), *Marx's Capital After 150 Years: Critique and Alternative to Capitalism*, New York: Routledge.

———. (2020), *The Last Years of Karl Marx: An Intellectual Biography*, Stanford: Stanford University Press.

Pateman, Carole (1988), *The Sexual Contract*, Stanford: Stanford University Press.

Rawick, George (1972), 'Racism and Slavery', in: George Rawick (ed.), *From Sundown to Sunup: The Making of the Black Community*, Westport: Greenwood Publishing, pp. 142–7.

Roberts, Dorothy (2017), 'Reproduction in Bondage', in: Dorothy Roberts (ed.), *Killing the Black Body: Race, Reproduction, and the Meaning of Liberty*, New York: Vintage Books, pp. 22–55.

Robinson, Cedric J. (2000), *Black Marxism: The Making of the Black Radical Tradition*, Chapel Hill: North Carolina University Press.

Sauer, R. (1978), 'Infanticide and Abortion in Nineteenth Century Britain', *Population Studies: A Journal of Demography*, vol. 32, n. 1: 81–93.

Taylor, Keeanga-Yamahtta (2014), *From Black Lives Matter to Black Liberation*, Chicago: Haymarket Books.

Thompson, E. P. (1991), 'The Sale of Wives', in: E. P. Thompson (ed.), *Customs in Common: Studies in Traditional Popular Culture*, New York: The New Press, pp. 404–66.

Roth, Karl Heinz, and van der Linden, Marcel (2014), 'Results and Prospects', in: Karl Heinz Roth and Marcel van der Linden (eds.), *Beyond Marx: Theorizing the Global Labour Relations*, Leiden: Brill, pp. 445–85.

Wikipedia (n.d.), 'Trier Witch Trials', *Wikipedia*, https://en.wikipedia.org/wiki/Trier_witch_trials. Accessed on 3 January 2021.

———. (n.d.), 'Married Women's Property Act 1870', *Wikipedia*, https://en.wikipedia.org/wiki/Married_Women%27s_Property_Act_1870. Accessed on 3 January 2021.

CHAPTER 3

Capital as a Social Relation: Form Analysis and Class Struggle

Bob Jessop

3.1 The Capitalist Mode of Production

Marx rarely used the word *capitalism* (as opposed to *capitalist*). He developed a critique of bourgeois (*bürgerliche*) society, the bourgeois form of production, relations of bourgeois production, the mode of production based on capital, and, after 1860, the capitalist mode of production (CMP).[1] He also analysed social formations dominated by the CMP. This said, to simplify my presentation, I sometimes use 'capitalism' to refer to the first two analytically distinct, but empirically interconnected, sets of social relations—bourgeois production and bourgeois social formations. It is nonetheless important to remember his focus on the capitalist mode of production when considering alternatives because they can either be aimed at reforming capitalism or replacing it in the medium- to long-term. I address strategies to pursue alternatives to bourgeois formations in the last part of my contribution.

[1] Sumio Shigeta, 'Zur Herkunft und Verbreitung des Begriffs »Kapitalismus«', *Beiträge zur Marx-Engels-Forschung. Neue Folge*, vol. 2004: 87–4.

B. Jessop (✉)
Lancaster University, Lancaster, UK

M. Musto (ed.), *Rethinking Alternatives with Marx*, Marx, Engels, and Marxisms, https://doi.org/10.1007/978-3-030-81764-0_3

The CMP is a historically specific instantiation of a mode of production. As a rational abstraction, which fixes the generic features of a social category, a mode of production comprises a form of organization of material production and distribution—and their concomitant social preconditions—that is reproducible for an extended period of time. It comprises (1) the forces of production and their associated technical relations of production and (2) the social relations of production. The latter are historically specific patterns of control over the deployment of means of production, especially ownership of the means of production, control over the labour process, the distribution of the product, and the appropriation of surplus labour. With rare exceptions, Marx insisted on the primacy of the social relations of production over the forces of production. In this sense, he was not a technological determinist and did not rely on technological change to supersede capitalism. This required changes in the social relations of production and their external conditions, which, in turn, required a change of social consciousness.

Regarding the CMP, for example, Marx emphasized that 'capital is not a thing, but a social relation between persons, mediated through the instrumentality of things'.[2] Even these 'things' embody or selectively structure social relations. For example, Marx noted the formal and substantive adequacy of 'machinofacture', as opposed to simple or complex cooperation within 'manufacture', to capitalist control over the labour process. For, whereas capital can secure nominal control over labour-power in the manufacturing division of labour, machinofacture enables capital to achieve its real subsumption because the worker becomes an appendage to the machine and it is easier to extract surplus labour. In *Capital I*, he wrote: '[m]odern industry had therefore itself to take in hand the machine, its characteristic instrument of production, and to construct machines by machines. It was not till it did this, that it built up for itself a fitting technical foundation, and stood on its own feet'.[3] Recognition that capital is a social relation is the key not only to describing, explaining, and critiquing the capitalist labour process and

[2] Karl Marx, *Capital, Volume I*, MECW, vol. 35, p. 753.

[3] Ibid., p. 387.

distribution of revenues but also to understanding the specifically bourgeois form of law and political sovereignty.[4] This in turn is the key to projecting alternatives.

Marx's emerging account of the CMP and bourgeois society began with his critical engagement with Hegel's *Philosophy of Law* (1843–1844) and his critique of Proudhon in 1844 and 1847.[5] His critique of Hegel noted the institutional separation of civil society (dominated by private property, market forces, and crass materialism) and the state, which, for Hegel, represented the general interest of society as a whole. Here Marx argued that the state could not achieve this while private property existed. Accordingly, the general interest was illusory. As he and Engels noted in *The German Ideology*, '[t]he ideas of the ruling class are in every epoch the ruling ideas: i.e. the class which is the ruling *material* force of society is at the same time its ruling *intellectual* force'.[6] The separation of civil society and state was a recurrent theme in Marx's work for four decades. For example, in his *First Draft of the Civil War in France* (1871), Marx argued that the abolition of this separation and the formation of the Paris Commune was '*the political form of the social emancipation*, of the liberation of labour from the usurpation of the (slaveholding) monopolists of the means of labour, created by the labourers themselves or forming the gift of nature'.[7]

Marx viewed the state as an alienated form of political organization based on the separation of rulers and ruled. In bourgeois society, this alienation rests on separation of (1) the 'public sphere', with the state at its centre, where politics is allegedly oriented to the collective interest; and (2) 'civil society', dominated by private property and individual self-interest and, in the CMP, wage-labour. A modern state can represent only

[4] Karl Marx, *Capital, Volume III*, MECW, vol. 37, pp. 777–8.

[5] See also Karl Marx, *Contribution to the Critique of Hegel's Philosophy of Law*, MECW, vol. 3, pp. 3–129. On Proudhon, see Karl Marx and Friedrich Engels, *The Holy Family*, MECW, vol. 4, pp. 23–55; and Karl Marx, *The Poverty of Philosophy*, MECW, vol. 6, pp. 105–215.

[6] Karl Marx and Friedrich Engels, *The German Ideology*, MECW, vol. 5, p. 59. Cf. Karl Marx and Friedrich Engels, *The Manifesto of the Communist Party*, MECW, vol. 6, 'The ruling ideas of each age have ever been the ideas of its ruling class', p. 503.

[7] Karl Marx, *Drafts of The Civil War in France*, MECW, vol. 22, p. 490, italics in original.

an 'illusory' community of interest that obscures the continuing antagonisms, crass materialism and egoistic conflicts of 'civil society'. This can take different forms, depending which fraction of capital is dominant, until the class struggle intensifies, leading the fractions to merge in the Party of Order to oppose proletarian attempts to build a social republic.[8]

His critique of Proudhon focused on the Frenchman's account of property, which failed to distinguish its specifically capitalist form and its consequences for bourgeois societies. By 1859, after several false starts, Marx had decided on the eventual starting point of his critique of the CMP (*Contribution to the Critique of Political Economy*; followed by *Capital, Volume I*, 1867). In both texts, Marx first remarks that, in societies dominated by the capitalist mode of production, 'the wealth of bourgeois society, at first sight, presents itself as an immense accumulation of commodities, its unit being a single commodity. Every commodity, however, has a twofold aspect—*use-value* and *exchange-value*'.[9] He therefore began his critique with the value formof the commodity.

This starting point can be contrasted with two others. First, despite the *Manifesto's* opening remarks (1976), Marx did not begin with class struggle in general or its specifically bourgeois form. Indeed, he disavowed having discovered classes in existence or class struggle as an explanatory principle—it was already well-established in observers of his epoch.[10] Yet a 'class-theoretical' approach remains popular—and vital—in analysing bourgeois societies. Indeed, Marx stressed the primacy of class struggle (especially political struggle) and its discursive, organizational, and strategic features in shaping history (see especially the *Eighteenth Brumaire*). Second, while Marx explored the self-valorization of capital and identified many laws that were immanent in the CMP, he did not treat them as if they somehow operate autonomously from social agents, who would then be considered as alienated *Träger* (bearers) of capital's self-valorizing logic.

Marx's value-form-analytical approach provides a way to integrate both class-theoretical and capital-theoretical analyses. For, as he developed his

[8] Ibid., p. 549.

[9] Karl Marx, *Contribution to the Critique of Political Economy*, MECW, vol. 29, p. 269. Cf. *Capital, Volume I*, p. 45.

[10] Karl Marx, 'Karl Marx to Joseph Weydemeyer, 5 March 1852', MECW, vol. 39, pp. 62–5.

analysis of different forms of the capital relation, he also elaborated the formal and institutional framework of the CMP. This shapes:

1. The forms and stakes of class struggle in bourgeois societies, as opposed to pre-capitalist economic formations, at different scales from local to global. The fictitious commodificationof labour-power, the fact that capital is a social relation, and the fetishized separation of the economic, political, and ideological spheres are crucial here (as I show later); and
2. The forms and stakes of competition in bourgeois societies around differential accumulation over the course of different economic cycles, i.e., the competition between individual capitals, class fractions, and so on to gain above-average rates of profit, interest, rent or, in downturns or recessions, avoid above-average losses. Within this framework, and excluding extra-economic coercion, competition occurs around innovations that reduce socially necessary labour time and turnover time, and, increasingly, the naturally necessary time (prior to social intervention) required to reproduce nature's inputs (e.g., through innovations in plant breeding, animal husbandry and agriculture).
3. Extra-economic intervention varies with the type of state, political regime, and balance of forces. The market mechanism cannot secure all conditions of capitalist reproduction (even ignoring labour process) and extra-economic intervention in needed. This is mediated through the institutional forms that occur around the general illusory interest.

In all three respects, Marx was no teleological theorist. *Capital* discussed class struggle mainly in terms of the struggle between capital and labour *within* the CMP and *within* bourgeois societies rather than its potential role in the revolutionary overthrow of capitalism. Its outcome was not guaranteed (stalemate or 'the common ruin of the contending classes' were also possible).[11] Likewise, the emerging laws of capital accumulation do not determine how and when capitalism would eventually collapse or be overthrown (although Marx expected this to occur). Capital was

[11] Marx and Engels, *Manifesto*, p. 482.

more concerned to examine the genesis, historical form, overall articulation, and crisis tendencies of the CMP. And the form-determined circuit of capital entails the *abstract* possibility of crisis but cannot explain the manner in which they are realized.

This indicates the scope for a synthesis of all three interpretations of Marx's work. It provides the means to analyse the historically specific forms of class struggle within bourgeois societies, how it both reproduces and transforms capitalism, how it shapes the specific manifestations and interaction of the various laws that characterize the CMP in so far as its forms are reproduced.

3.2 The Historical Specificity of the CMP

For Marx, the historical specificity of the CMP was based on the commodification (real or fictitious) of all the inputs into the CMP. First, all goods and services are produced as commodities in anticipation of monetary profit rather than for immediate consumption by their producers. Second, crucially, labour-power (the capacity to work) acquires the form of a commodity bought and sold in the labour market. This is reflected in the fact that commodified labour-power has a price (the wage). But it is not itself produced within competitive capitalist relations of production that reduce the socially necessary labour-time involved in its reproduction. This is an accomplishment of civil society and the state—reflected in the role of domestic labour, schooling, philanthropy, and welfare. There is always a necessary historical and moral element to the wage.[12] This would have been explored in a planned book on wage-labour, which would have taken the proletariat as an active subject in the CMP.[13] Third, labour-power is the sole source of the total surplus-value available for reinvestment or redistribution in such forms as profits of enterprise, interest, and rent). What determines the value of commodities? It is the socially necessary amount of labour-time embodied in a commodity. This is the amount of labour-power measured in time that a typical (standardized, mass-produced) commodity requires for its

[12] Marx, *Capital, Volume I*, p. 181.

[13] See for a proposed draft, Michael A. Lebowitz, *Beyond Capital: Marx's Political Economy of the Working Class* (Houndmills: Palgrave Macmillan, 2003).

production with typical qualities. This is set in competition among individual capitals producing the same commodity, aiming at the greatest efficiency. Competition drives innovation in the organization and control over the labour process, in methods of production, transportation, distribution, etc. Thus, socially necessary labour-time is continually redefined. However, whether labour-power does generate surplus-value depends on capital's ability to control workers in the labour process. This is the main site of economic class struggle.

Marx also analysed money as a special commodity in Volume I. In short, money is not a thing, it is a fetishized social relation. Apart from bullion, which does have a real cost of production, money is another fictitious commodity. Money is a not a single social relation but a complex and contradictory set of social relations. especially in the form of capitalist credit, money as capital, and, indeed, fictive capital (e.g. government bonds, derivatives). In capitalist social formations one needs to study three *inter-related* moments of the money, credit, and capital forms: the functions of money; the hierarchy of money forms; tensions between 'national currencies' and world money.[14]

Likewise, Marx added land as another special commodity in volume III, where he addressed the forms in which surplus-value was distributed between fractions of capital (with capitalist landowners being one fraction). He considered private property in 'land' (nature) as another fictitious commodity, one that generates rents. Land is a free gift of nature but can be improved. Marx read widely in geology, agronomy, chemistry, animal husbandry, plant breeding, etc., to understand land as a source of absolute, relative, and differential rent. The capitalist form of landed property is historically unique: it is a pure economic form, free from lordship and servitude. Rent derives from the monopoly of landed property: it is the price of access to this third special commodity. Marx integrated land into his analysis of the 'metabolic rift', his most key contribution to critique of political ecology.[15]

[14] Marx, *Capital, Volume I*, pp. 97–166.

[15] On the metabolic rift, see John Bellamy Foster, *Marx's Ecology* (New York: Monthly Review Press, 2000).

> If in the fully developed bourgeois system each economic relationship presupposes the other in a bourgeois-economic form, and everything posited is thus also a premiss, *that is the case with every organic system*. This organic system itself has its premisses as a totality, and its development into a totality consists precisely in subordinating all elements of society to itself, or in creating out of it the organs it still lacks. This is historically how it becomes a totality. It's becoming this totality constitutes a moment of its process, of its development.[16]

He also identified many other forms of the commodity and capital relation, within the circuits of capital and bourgeois society (e.g. the legal form, the form of sovereignty). In this context, he explored the organic interconnection of these and other specifically bourgeois forms and their embedding in a bourgeois society as capitalism develops.

For Marx, these forms are not reproduced quasi-automatically. They are reproduced in various ways, whether this occurs through continuing commodity fetishism, reification of the institutional separation of the economic and political spheres, the inevitable 'statolatrous' fetishization of the autonomy of the state and its role in promoting the 'general' (but illusory) interest of society, false consciousness, and so on.

On the contrary, without class struggle to reproduce these forms and secure an appropriate balance of forces, continuing (if frequently crisis-prone and discontinuous) capital accumulation is impossible. This concerns not only capital's ability to dominate wage labour in the economy but also, because capital accumulation has important extra-economic conditions and because workers try to extend their resistance beyond the factory gates and labour market into the wider society. This is why Marx stressed the primacy of political struggle. Three examples from Marx are, first, political Chartism in the United Kingdom (1838–1857), which was a proletarian movement that mobilized external pressure on the state to enfranchise workers; second, agitation for the legalization of trade union activities; and, third, demands to limit factory working hours.[17] To fully understand political class struggle, we must look beyond *Capital I* and the preparatory manuscripts for *Capital II* and *III*. These texts focus

[16] Karl Marx, *The Economic Manuscripts of 1857–58*, MECW, vol. 28, p. 208.

[17] For example, Karl Marx, 'The Chartists', MECW, vol. 11, pp. 333–41; Marx, *Capital, Volume I*, pp. 458, 634, 728–30; and Marx, *The Economic Manuscripts of 1857–58*, pp. 283–302, respectively.

on the interests of capital and treat workers mainly as its victims, whose struggles are essentially reactions to capitalist offensives. Marx did not write a promised book (one of three 'missing books' belonging to the planned six volume work on *Capital*) on labour. This would have treated the proletariat, as Michael Lebowitz observed in *Beyond Capital* (2003), as an *active* economic and political subject, whose resistance shapes capital accumulation and also seeks to overthrow the capital-labour relation.[18]

For example, he identified a 'comprehensive contradiction' in bourgeois democratic constitutions. This results from the institutional separation of the economic and political spheres noted in his critique of Hegel. Thus, in *The Class Struggles in France*, he wrote:

> The classes whose social slavery the constitution is to perpetuate, proletariat, peasantry, petty bourgeoisie, it puts in possession of *political power* through *universal suffrage*. And from the class whose old *social power* it sanctions, the bourgeoisie, it withdraws the *political guarantees* of this power. [...] From the [former] it demands that they should not go forward *from political to social emancipation*; from the [latter it demands] that they should not go back *from social to political restoration*.[19]

From the standpoint of the bourgeoisie, solving this contradiction requires that subaltern economic struggles are limited to economic-corporate struggles over wages, the length and intensity of the working day, working conditions, the introduction of new techniques of production and distribution, the social wage, etc., and that subaltern political struggles are confined within the limits of electoral competition based on universal franchise, individual citizenship, and efforts to define the (illusory) general interest. Where subaltern classes resort to general strikes to challenge state poweror use state powerto advance social emancipation, this challenges bourgeois hegemony and prompts efforts by the bourgeoisie to concerted economic and political action to challenge the rule of capital. Yet the bourgeoisie is less inclined to respect these fetishized institutional divisions and deploys both economic and political power to advance its particular or general interests.

[18] Lebowitz, *Beyond Marx's Capital*.

[19] Karl Marx, *The Class Struggles in France, 1848 to 1850*, MECW, vol. 10, p. 79, italics added.

This suggests that there are three kinds of class struggle in capitalist social formations: (1) struggles to secure advantage within distinct, but reified or fetishized, social forms, including the economic and political spheres; (2) struggles outside these forms that modify the balance of forces in the first type of struggle, for example, within or beyond the interstices of civil society (as Gramsci rather than Hegel or Marx would define it); (3) struggles to reproduce these forms in the face of efforts to overturn or replace them, which normally depends on 'hegemony protected by the armour of coercion'[20] but may, in exceptional conditions, involve an 'open war of class struggle'.

I now turn to the relations among social forms, class struggle, and the logic of capital. The ability to identify laws of capital accumulation depends on the tendential reproduction of the social forms in which they emerge and work their effects. Where the forms break down, the laws also break down. Thus, as Gramsci put it, more explicitly than Marx, economic laws (necessities, 'automatism', *regolarità*) should be understood as tendencies. Indeed, they are always doubly tendential. Thus, commenting on Ricardo's discoveries of laws of tendency, Gramsci wrote:

> these are laws of tendency which are not laws in the naturalistic sense or that of speculative determinism, but in a 'historicist' sense, valid, that is, to the extent that there exists the 'determined market' (mercato determinato) or in other words an environment which is organically alive and interconnected in its movements of development.[21]

In short, an integral analysis of the CMP and bourgeois social formations requires moving beyond one-sided analyses of the capital relation. Class struggle is one-sided if it fails to answer the critical question: this is not what kind of labour creates *value* but what kind of labour creates *surplus value*. And this requires an examination of the historical specificity of the CMP.

A focus on the logic of capital as if it were a self-reproducing totality fails because it does not recognize that the laws of capital accumulation are realized only to the extent that the forms and institutions in which they emerge depend on continuing class struggle to reproduce these forms.

[20] Antonio Gramsci, *Selections from the Prison Notebooks* (London: Lawrence & Wishart, 1971), p. 263.

[21] Ibid., p. 401.

And a focus on forms without examining how they embody multiple structural contradictions and generate associated strategic dilemmas, that can be approached in different ways by different sets of actors, leaves us with empty formulae without substantive content. Marx combined all three perspectives in his critique of capital's political economy and, if he had realized his 'six book plan' for *Capital* (or something like it), would have taken this analysis beyond capital, labour, and land to include the state, foreign trade, and the world market in a much more comprehensive analysis than can be discerned by reading *Capital* alone.

3.3 Form Analysis

The basic premise of a form analysis of capitalist social formations is that a given economic formation or broader social formation is dominated by the social forms of the capital relation and its associated forms of life. If so, then the analysis should investigate three interrelated aspects: (1) the historical and/or formal constitution of the socio-economic relations under examination considered as a complex institutional ensemble with a spatio-temporally specific pattern of 'structurally-inscribed strategic selectivity'[22]; (2) the historical and substantive organization and configuration of relevant social forces in specific conjunctures and their strategies, including their capacity to reflect on and respond to the strategic selectivities inscribed in specific ensembles of social relations and the relevant social configuration as a whole; and (3) the interaction of these forces on this strategically selective terrain and/or at a distance therefrom as they pursue immediate goals or seek to alter the balance of forces and/or to transform the current conjuncture and its basic strategic selectivities.

In adopting this approach, it is important to reject a general theory of economy and its development in favour of form-analytical historical analyses of the agency-mediated expanded reproduction (or transformation) of the capital relation. For the historical and formal constitution of a social order is not pre-given but results from past struggles and is also reproduced (or transformed) in and through struggle. Nor should we treat the balance of forces as fixed but explore instead how it is modified through shifts in the strategic-relational terrain of the state, economy, and wider social formation as well as by changes in organization, strategy, and

22 Bob Jessop, *State Theory: Putting the Capitalist State in its Place* (Cambridge: Polity, 1990), pp. 9–10 and seriatim.

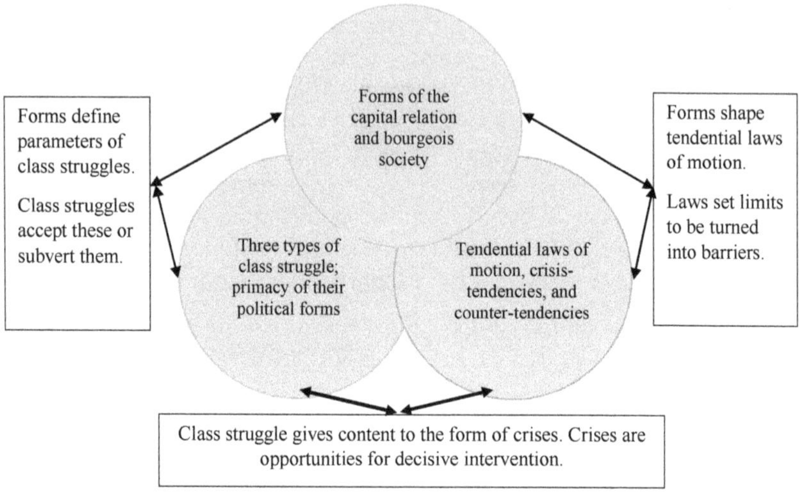

Fig. 3.1 How forms, struggles, and laws interact

tactics (see Fig. 3.1). Nonetheless, where this necessary basic premise is absent, other approaches are appropriate and, indeed, mandatory, if one is to avoid a capital-centric analysis. In this context, historical, institutional, configurational, or agency-centred approaches are especially useful.

Marxian form analysis is (implicitly) oriented *in the first instance* to questions of structuration. It involves the study of specific modes of organizing social life, their articulation in a distinctive social formation (an ensemble of structural forms typical of a given mode of societalization), and their associated configuration of 'forms of life'. Thus, a *social form* is a specific mode of organization of a social content. Form analysis rests on the separation of form and content insofar as the same 'content' can assume different forms and, within limits, the same form may include different contents. For example, while Marx asks why wealth in capitalism 'presents itself as an immense accumulation of commodities'[23]; Pashukanis asks why political class domination in capitalist social formations takes the form of official state domination.[24] Forms are associated

[23] Marx, *Capital, Volume I*, p. 45.

[24] Evgeny B. Pashukanis, *A General Theory of Law and Marxism* (London: Transaction Books, 2002), p. 139.

with specific logics of action, which may (or may not) be realized; and, in this sense, form analysis must be complemented by analysis of social action in order to understand the relationship of form and content. This said, form analysis does not reify forms as ontologically prior to social relations but considers how social action is involved in reproducing fetishized forms of social relations and the contradictions and antagonisms with which they are associated. Thus, a key part of a critical form analysis is to explore the genealogy of specific social forms, their manner in which they are combined in specific social formations, and the critical role of social agents in reproducing the dominance (and naturalization) of these forms.

Form analysis is not a via *media* and is not appropriate in all cases. Forms are not ontologically prior to content and one can neither explain the logic of capital through form analysis alone nor derive the character of class struggles therefrom. Form analysis studies forms as modes of organizing social life. It would be useful to combine the analysis of structural forms with analysis of forms of life to do justice to the complexities of the social world. This would provide a good basis for analysing the 'social formation' as an ensemble of social forms and its accompanying 'society' as an ensemble of forms of life. Indeed, developing a broad form-analytic argument, we can hypothesize that, the more that social forms and forms of life in different domains are mutually supportive, complementary, and reinforcing, the greater the underlying stability of a social formation. This approach begins with the dominance of specific social forms such as the commodity form, money form, wage form, capital form, legal form, state form, tax form, and so forth, and seeks to explain both the logic of capital accumulation and the nature of class relations in terms of the strategic-relational character of these forms. This in turn has implications for thinking about the relations among reform, rearticulations, counterformation, and transformation (see below).

Marx initiated such an analysis of the capitalist mode of production with the commodity and then unfolded its other forms, including the price form, wage form, money form, capital form, credit form, and so on. In each case he identified its inherent contradictions and the social dynamic entailed in these contradictions. He also discusses the formal adequacy of these forms. The case of machinofacture was discussed above. Marx likewise analysed money as the adequate form (or medium) of expression of value in exchange in contrast to ad hoc barter relations and, in addition, as the most adequate form of capital in its guise as money capital available for investment in any activity as opposed to particular assets that must be valorized according to specific temporalities in specific places.[25]

Marx also offered some hints about bourgeois legal and state forms, especially in his early critique of Hegel's philosophy of right and his later comments on the *Civil War in France*. For Marx, the *form* of the modern (capitalist) state is distinguished above all by its institutional separation from the economy. The former is the world of the *citoyen* and national interest, the latter of the *bourgeois* and the primacy of private profit. He adds that the modern representative state based on rational bureaucracy and universal suffrage is formally adequate to capitalist social formations. This state form corresponds to the value form of the CMP and provides a suitable extra-economic support for it. The freedom of economic agents to engage in exchange (belied by factory despotism in the labour process) is matched by the freedom of individual citizens (belied by the state's subordination to the logic of capital). The absence of direct control by the capitalist class over the state means, however, that the development of state projects and policies that favour capital is subject to complex mediations. This means that the normal (or bourgeois democratic) form of capitalist state serves both to promote the interests of capital and to disguise this, rendering capitalist political domination relatively intransparent.

The *real barrier* (*Schranke*) of capitalist production is capital *itself*.[26] Since capital represents the general form of wealth—money—it has a boundless and measureless urge to exceed its own limits. Every boundary (*Grenze*) is and must be a barrier (*Schranke*) for it.[27] The quantitative border to surplus-value appears to it only as a natural barrier, as a necessity, which it constantly tries to overcome and beyond which it constantly tries to go.[28]

Capital and its self-expansion appear as the starting and the closing point, the motive and the purpose of production; that production is

[25] Marx, *Capital, Volume I*, pp. 92, 122–3, 159–63.

[26] *Marx, Capital, Volume III*, p. 256.

[27] Marx, *Economic Manuscripts of 1857–58*, p. 259.

[28] Ibid., p. 260.

only production for *capital* and not vice versa, the means of production are not mere means for a constant expansion of the living process of the *society* of producers. The limits within which the preservation and self-expansion of the value of capital resting on the expropriationand pauperization of the great mass of producers can alone move—these limits come continually into conflict with the methods of production employed by capital for its purposes, which drive towards unlimited extension of production, towards production as an end in itself, towards unconditional development of the social productivity of labour.[29]

3.4 Class-Analysis (Classes and Class Struggle)

The limits to capital become evident in part through human consciousness that bring its barriers to the surface. Workers become aware that they are alienated in the relations of production, circulation, and distribution. In short, it is conscious human beings who recognize that capital is its own barrier, who are the limit to capital.[30] This raises the question of how class struggle fits into this analysis.

Marx analyses classes at different levels of abstraction and in different kinds of bourgeois social formation. For example, the relation between capital and labour is explored at the level of the capital-labour relation, the economic relations between capitalists and workers, and the political and ideological relations between bourgeoisie and proletariat. The *Manifesto* predicted that the logic of capital accumulation would simplify the class struggle as the proletariat grew and intermediate classes disappeared. *Capital* is concerned with the economic logic of the capital-labour relation and the distribution of revenues between landowners, capitalists (including finance as well as industry and merchant capital), and workers. And Marx's *political writings* concern contemporary political conjunctures in which class relations develop in a complex and changing economic and political terrain and subject to a political logic shaped by the prevailing state form(s).

[29] Marx, *Capital, Volume III*, p. 249.

[30] Michael A. Lebowitz, *Following Marx: Method, Critique, and Crisis* (Leiden: Brill, 2009), p. 127.

Capital is analysed at different levels of abstraction to reveal the emergent economic laws of motion of modern society: exploitation, accumulation, tendency of the rate of profit to fall, the equalization of profit rates, the equalization of interest rates, are explored in terms of capital in general, particular capitals, and fractions of capital.

The self-valorization of capital can occur where most of the key inputs into capitalist production take the form of (real or fictitious) commodities; there is effective control over labour-power within the labour process; the environment is sufficiently stable to enable capitals to systematically orient their activities to opportunities for profit; and profits can be realized and reinvested. None of this requires that all social relations have been subsumed under the commodity form and entirely subordinated to market forces. Indeed, there is wide variation in how far capitalist market forces (and the associated logic of profit-seeking) come to dominate the overall organization and dynamics of social formations. This raises questions about the conditions under which accumulation can become the dominant principle of societal organization (or societalization). This implies in turn that there is ample scope for conflict over societal projects that privilege quite other organizational principles as well as for conflict over rival projects based on the same principle.

The organization of a social formation under the dominance of profit-oriented, market-mediated differential accumulation as the axial principle of social organization) involves far more than continuing accumulation. Market exchange and capital accumulation can also occur in theocracies, national security states, new nations, revolutionary situations or state socialist societies. What bourgeois societalization involves in addition to the mere fact of commodity production and exchange is the relative subordination of an entire social order to the logic and reproduction requirements of capital accumulation. This could be described as the recognition that 'a market economy can exist only in a market society'[31]; as the development of an 'historic bloc' between the economic base, juridico-political superstructure and forms of consciousness; or as the rise of a 'bourgeois civilization'.

[31] Karl Polanyi, *The Great Transformation: The Political and Economic Origins of Our Time* (Boston: Beacon Press, 2001), p. 74.

3.5 Alternatives to Capitalist Formations

A key question follows from this review of Marx's analysis of the capitalist mode of production and bourgeois social formations. If it is no longer feasible, if it ever was, to attempt to smash capitalism through a revolutionary seizure of power when capitalism enters crisis or is overthrown by violence and to build socialism and/or communism from the foundations up, we must accept, as Erik Olin Wright argues, that:

> system-level rupture doesn't work as a strategy for social emancipation. This doesn't imply rejecting the idea of an emancipatory alternative to capitalism, organized around qualitatively different principles, as the fundamental goal of social transformation; what it questions is the plausibility of a strategy that attempts to destroy in a ruptural manner the dominance of capitalism.[32]

The prospects of subordinate classes and strata moving from political emancipation to social emancipation pose the problem of how to distinguish among changes that:

1. modify a specific, extant form of bourgeois social relations to preserve or enhance its operation, such as redesigning markets to enhance their efficiency in the realization of profit-oriented, market-mediated accumulation;
2. modify the articulation among existing forms to preserve or enhance their contribution to the reproduction of the dominant social order organized under a bourgeois principle of societalization, such as a shift from the liberal state to the interventionist state to manage new crisis tendencies linked to the development of profit-oriented, market-mediated accumulation;
3. subvert the primary aspect of dominant social forms, and, in so doing, subvert the dominant social forms themselves; an example would be to successfully challenge the primacy of the exchange-value moment in the different expressions of the value-form; and
4. introduce new forms and articulate them in new ways to pursue to emancipatory aspirations and effects.

[32] Erik Olin Wright, *How to Be an Anticapitalist in the 21st Century* (London: Verso, 2019), pp. 41–2.

These four types can be called *reform*, *re-articulation*, *counterformation*, and *transformation* respectively. The last three can also be linked to Wright's distinction between taming capitalism, dismantling and resisting it, and escaping it respectively.[33] We can ask how these four transition processes may relate to each other, whether positively (reinforcing each other to bring about transition) or negatively (such that reform blocks re-articulation and/or re-articulation blocks counterformation and transformation).[34] Re-articulation may also involve pro-capitalist as well as anti-capitalist reforms. In contrast, counterformation and transformation typically involve subversive and emancipatory reforms that 'introduce in one way or another egalitarian, democratic and solidaristic values and principles into the operation of capitalism'.[35] These are not just technical processes but are mediated through shifts in the balance of forces and, perhaps, open contestation and struggle. Likewise, they are not just issues for scholarly observation in form analysis but also issues that people face in real life, especially those social movements that are committed to social transformation or its prevention.

To effect a transformation of the capitalist mode of production, the priority is counterformation and transformation to alter the primacy of capitalist forms rather than relying on smashing capitalism in a ruptural moment. As Wright notes, this involves combining taming, dismantling, resisting, and escaping strategies in a way that erodes capitalism in symbiotic and interstitial ways. Rather than ruptural transformation based on marked discontinuities in capitalist reproduction, symbiotic transformation builds on reforms that sustain capitalism but also enable emancipatory changes, and interstitial transformation works within the niches of the capitalist system to bring about gradual transformation and social emancipation.[36]

This requires class and other collective struggles focused on contemporary dominant forms—including financialization, the platform economy,

[33] Ibid., pp. 37–59.

[34] Bob Jessop, 'Reform, Umformierung, Gegenformierung, Neuformierung und Transformation', in: Michael Brie (ed.), *Futuring: Perspektiven einer Transformation im Kapitalismus über ihn hinaus* (Berlin: Dietz Verlag, 2014), pp. 127–60.

[35] Wright, *Anticapitalist*, p. 46. Wright adds that 'Such reforms may also help stabilize capitalism—indeed, this is partially what makes them possible—but they do so in ways that also make the system as a whole function in a less purely capitalistic way', ibid.

[36] Ibid., pp. 55, 59.

and digital capitalism—by promoting social cooperation and peer-to-peer production and enhancing social networks and solidarity as alternatives to market exchange and command. A key role here is played by solidaristic, reciprocal, mutual social innovation strategies in forms of social innovation. The latter can be defined as 'ethical and socio-political agency working towards a more inclusive democracy and a socially as well as ecologically sustainable society and economy'.[37] It has three interconnected core principles: 'it meets genuine needs neglected or exacerbated by the state/market apparatus; it creates new forms of eco-social/institutional relations and polities; and it collectively empowers people (especially marginalized people) to act—not only within the existent systems and modes of governance, but also towards transforming them'.[38] In contrast to a taming strategy, social innovation should not be seen as solving bourgeois problems within the margins of the free-market economy and the bourgeois state. Instead, it should serve to generate counter-hegemonic modes of human, cultural and economic development that emphasize the ethics of solidarity, conviviality and socio-ecological sustainability.[39] In other words, it should challenge the role of market forces and hierarchical command and promote cooperative networks and social solidarity.

> One way to challenge capitalism is to build more democratic, egalitarian, participatory economic relations where possible in the spaces and cracks within this complex system. The idea of eroding capitalism imagines that these alternatives have the potential, in the long run, to become sufficiently prominent in the lives of individuals and communities that capitalism could eventually be displaced from its dominant role in the system. [...] Eventually, the cumulative effect of this interplay between changes from above and initiatives from below may reach a point where the socialist relations created within the economic ecosystem become sufficiently prominent in the lives of individuals and communities that capitalism can no longer be said to be dominant.[40]

[37] Frank Moulaert and Diana MacCallum, *Advanced Introduction to Social Innovation* (Cheltenham: Edward Elgar, 2019), p. xi.

[38] Ibid., p. 4.

[39] Ibid., pp. 34–5.

[40] Wright, *Anticapitalist*, pp. 60, 62.

The focus in pursuing erosion is to promote social relations of productionthat do not promote exchange-values but cooperatively produce use-values distributed through cooperative principles of network partnership and solidarity. This has become easier with digital technologies that enable communication and social cooperation to be scaled up. The ambition would not be to reduce socially necessary labour-time to increase surplus labour-time but to allow free time and general intellect to flourish.[41] The measure of freedom in a postcapitalist society would be to maximize free time for creative learning and experimentation for all. In this way the general intellect would be liberated to generate collective knowledge to serve the public interest rather than private profit. In capitalist relations of production, conversely, science becomes a business pursued for profit. A key contribution to this purpose would be a universal basic income that frees people to choose how to spend their time in waged labour for a capitalist enterprise or other productive work (e.g., in cooperative organizations) and to participate in democratic decision-making in a myriad of cooperative bottom-linked ways.[42]

In addition to eroding the dominance of the wage form and its role in reproducing labour-power as a fictitious commodity, anti-capitalist strategy should also focus on marginalizing and eventually eroding the role of the three other fictitious commodities that dominate capitalist relations of production. These are money as interest-generating capital; land (broadly understood as private ownership of nature) as a monopolistic source of rents; and intellectual property rights as sources of royalties and licence income.[43] This would require cooperative banking, forms of collective ownership of the land as a commons, and common forms of intellectual property such as Copyleft, Patentleft, Creative Commons licenses, and BiOS (Biological Open Source) licenses.[44] Each

[41] On the general intellect and free time, see Karl Marx, *Economic Manuscripts of 1857–58*, MECW, vol. 29, pp. 92–7.

[42] Moulaert and MacCallum, *Social Innovation*, p. 84; and Wright, *Anticapitalist*, p. 75.

[43] Polanyi, *The Great Transformation*, passim, on labour-power, money, and land. On intellectual property rights, see Bob Jessop, 'Knowledge as a Fictitious Commodity: Insights and Limits of a Polanyian Analysis', in: Ayşe Buğra and Kaan Ağartan (eds.), *Reading Karl Polanyi for the 21st Century: Market Economy as a Political Project* (Basingstoke: Palgrave, 2007), pp. 115–34.

[44] On alternative forms of intellectual property, see Wright, *Anticapitalist*, p. 91.

of these innovations would promote the expansion of the commons as a collectively managed resource in opposition to private ownership.[45]

The principle of social cooperation was realized by the Commune which reserved all matters of social life to its control and executed all public functions: policing, administration, judiciary, etc.[46] Throughout France, 'the standing army replaced by the popular militias, the army of state parasites removed, the clerical hierarchy displaced by the schoolmaster, the state judges transformed into Communal organs, the suffrage for the National representation not a matter of sleight of hand for an all-powerful government, but the deliberate expression of organized communes, the state functions reduced to a few functions for general national purposes'.[47]

The short-lived and brutally oppressed example of the Paris Commune and the spread of communal forms elsewhere in France illustrate Marx's attempt to deal with the question of alternatives to bourgeois social formations and to highlight the primacy of political struggle in subverting bourgeois economic and political forms. The further development of the world market and the attempt to complete it in the neoliberal epoch suggest that national solutions like the Commune are inadequate. As Marx and Engels argued in the *Manifesto*, class struggle may take the form of a national contest: '[t]he proletariat of each country must, of course, first of all settle matters with its own bourgeoisie'.[48] But they held that the struggle will be globally substantive in impact as the world market becomes more integrated and tends to unify proletarian struggles. The limits to this thesis are seen in the continuing rivalry of national varieties of capitalism as well as the rise of transnational financial and industrial capitals. But the development of a planetary environmental crisis shows that global action is required to address planetary problems and reveals how far class struggle narrowly conceived cannot be an adequate basis for global transformation.

[45] On commons as systems of social relations and their governance, see Massimo De Angelis, *Omnia Sunt Communia: On the Commons and the Transformation to Postcapitalism* (London: Zed, 2017); and Guido Ruivenkamp and Andy Hilton (eds.), *Perspectives on Commoning: Autonomist Principles and Practices* (London: Zed Books, 2017).

[46] Marx, *Drafts of The Civil War in France*, p. 537.

[47] Ibid., p. 490.

[48] Marx and Engels, *Manifesto*, p. 495.

Returning to the semiotic aspect of form analysis, emancipatory transformation requires a new semantics, a new common sense, and new conceptions of individuality and sociality. An opportunity for such discursive articulation is revealed in the current problems of global accumulation. When capitalists themselves are worried about global events, this suggests discursive openings for counter-hegemonic strategies. The world market crisis, climate change, and the global Covid-19 pandemic are key vulnerabilities in this regard for counter-mobilization among a wide range of social forces. They indicate the need to develop social alliances that encompass many movements against oppression, exploitation and crisis tendencies and to develop a radical 'green new deal' based on asserting solidaristic control over natural resources, reliance on solar, tidal, and wind energy, renewable and sustainable production, social redistribution, and so forth. By eventually replacing the structural forms of the capital relation in this way, capitalist laws of motion will also be dethroned. This depends on a global mobilization of social forces behind an alternative hegemonic project based on networks and solidarity and a reflexive concern with collective adaptation as fresh problems emerge.[49]

This requires new forms of governance that depend on collective networks and solidarity rather than profit-oriented market forces and hierarchical command structures. These must reject fatalism, cynicism, stoicism, and opportunism and rely on decentralized collective action that accepts the possibility of failure and learns from it.[50] We can envisage this as promoting bottom-linked governance rather than top-down leadership. Bottom-linked governance does not mean 'bottom-led' governance but reliance on multi-scalar social innovative movements connected to grass-roots mobilization. This reflects the worry that many new socially innovative initiatives are highly necessary to social emancipation but that their governance, as well as that of the relevant supportive as well as re-democratizing state institutions, should be developed interactively.[51] Small as the building blocks are for transformation, it micro-politics within and across initiatives, civil society organizations and trans-local

[49] For a detailed theoretical account of this strategic orientation, see Bob Jessop, *Putting Civil Society in its Place: Governance, Metagovernance, and Subjectivities* (Bristol: Policy Press, 2020).

[50] Ibid.

[51] Moulaert and MacCallum, *Social Innovation*, p. 94.

networks are central to re-constructing democracy through bottom-linked governance.[52] It prioritizes the renewal of solidarity, mutual aid and ethics in interpersonal relations, community life, public action and policy and the possibility of spontaneous care among human beings.[53]

By way of conclusion, let me cite Erik Olin Wright's central argument on anti-capitalist strategies:

> [F]irst, another world is indeed possible. Second, it could improve the conditions for human flourishing for most people. Third, elements of this new world are already being created in the world as it is. And finally, there are ways to move from here to there. Anticapitalism is possible not simply as a moral stance toward the harms and injustices in the world in which we live, but as a practical stance toward building an alternative for greater human flourishing.[54]

References

De Angelis, Massimo (2017), *Omnia Sunt Communia: On the Commons and the Transformation to Postcapitalism*, London: Zed Books.

Foster, John Bellamy (2000), *Marx's Ecology*, New York: Monthly Review Press.

Gramsci, Antonio (1971), *Selections from the Prison Notebooks*, London: Lawrence & Wishart.

Jessop, Bob (1990), *State Theory: Putting the Capitalist State in its Place*, Cambridge: Polity.

———. (2007), 'Knowledge as a Fictitious Commodity: Insights and Limits of a Polanyian Analysis', in: Ayşe Buğra and Kaan Ağartan (eds.), *Reading Karl Polanyi for the 21st Century: Market Economy as a Political Project*, Basingstoke: Palgrave, pp. 115–34.

———. (2014), 'Reform, Umformierung, Gegenformierung, Neuformierung und Transformation', in: Michael Brie (ed.), *Futuring: Perspektiven einer Transformation im Kapitalismus über ihn hinaus*, Berlin: Dietz Verlag, pp. 127–60.

———. (2020), *Putting Civil Society in its Place: Governance, Metagovernance, and Subjectivities*, Bristol: Policy Press.

[52] Ibid., p. 119.

[53] Ibid., p. xii. On the principles and practices of mutual aid as opposed to charities, not-for-profit organizations, and formal organizations, see Dean Spade, *Mutual Aid: Building Solidarity During This Crisis (and the Next)* (London: Verso, 2020).

[54] Wright, *Anticapitalist*, p. 3.

Lebowitz, Michael A. (2003), *Beyond Capital: Marx's Political Economy of the Working Class*, Houndmills: Palgrave Macmillan.

———. (2009), *Following Marx: Method, Critique, and Crisis*, Leiden: Brill.

Marx, Karl (1975), *Contribution to the Critique of Hegel's Philosophy of Law*, MECW, vol. 3, pp. 3–129.

———. (1976), *The Poverty of Philosophy*, MECW, vol. 6, pp. 105–215.

———. (1978), *The Class Struggles in France, 1848 to 1850*, MECW, vol. 10, pp. 45–145.

———. (1979), *The Eighteenth Brumaire of Louis Bonaparte*, MECW, vol. 11, pp. 99–197.

———. (1979), 'The Chartists', MECW, vol. 11, pp. 333–41.

———. (1986), *The Civil War in France: Address of the General Council of the International Working Men's Association*, MECW, vol. 22, pp. 307–59.

———. (1986), *Drafts of The Civil War in France*, MECW, vol. 22, pp. 435–551.

———. (1986), *Economic Manuscripts of 1857–58*, MECW, vol. 28.

———. (1987), *Economic Manuscripts of 1857–58*, MECW, vol. 29, pp. 5–417.

———. (1987), *A Contribution to the Critique of Political Economy*, MECW, vol. 29, pp. 257–417.

———. (1989), *Critique of the Gotha Programme*, MECW, vol. 24, pp. 75–99.

———. (1996), *Capital, Volume I*, MECW, vol. 35.

———. (1998), *Capital, Volume III*, MECW, vol. 37.

Marx, Karl, and Engels, Friedrich (1975), *The German Ideology*, MECW, vol. 5, pp. 19–539.

———. (1975), *The Holy Family*, MECW, vol. 4, pp. 5–211.

———. (1976), *Manifesto of the Communist Party*, MECW, vol. 6, pp. 477–519.

———. (1984), *Letters 1852–55*, MECW, vol. 39.

Moulaert, Frank, and MacCallum, Diana (2019), *Advanced Introduction to Social Innovation*, Cheltenham, UK: Edward Elgar.

Pashukanis, Evgeny B. (2002), *A General Theory of Law and Marxism*, London: Transaction Books.

Polanyi, Karl (2001), *The Great Transformation: The Political and Economic Origins of Our Time*, Boston: Beacon Press.

Ruivenkamp, Guido, and Hilton, Andy (eds.) (2017), *Perspectives on Commoning: Autonomist Principles and Practices*, London: Zed Books.

Shigeta, Sumio (2004), 'Zur Herkunft und Verbreitung des Begriffs »Kapitalismus«', *Beiträge zur Marx-Engels-Forschung. Neue Folge*, vol. 2004: 87–94.

Spade, Dean (2020), *Mutual Aid: Building Solidarity During This Crisis (and the Next)*, London: Verso.

Wright, Erik Olin (2019), *How to Be an Anticapitalist in the 21st Century*, London: Verso.

CHAPTER 4

Commodity and the Postmodern Spectacle

Alfonso Maurizio Iacono

4.1 The Dancing Tables

Gustave Flaubert started writing his masterpiece *Bouvard et Pécuchet* in 1872 and continued until he died. In one of the passages in his book, he talks about the so-called *dancing tables*, which during that period were very popular all over the world, evoking spirits and ghosts. Shortly before this, in 1867, Karl Marx had published *Capital*, *Volume I*, in which the *dancing tables* had already entered the scene to present the concept of commodity and its fetich character.

In Derrida's *Spectres of Marx*, written after the fall of the Berlin wall and in controversy with Fukuyama's book about the end of History, he points out that when Marx talks about commodity fetishism in his book *Capital*, he refers to the dancing tables of a séance. When giving the example of the table, he uses the term *auftritt* which means *enters the*

This chapter has been translated into English by Leigh-Ann Mazzoncini.

A. M. Iacono (✉)
University of Pisa, Pisa, Italy

M. Musto (ed.), *Rethinking Alternatives with Marx*, Marx, Engels, and Marxisms, https://doi.org/10.1007/978-3-030-81764-0_4

scene. According to him a table is simply a wooden table when it has use-value and can change and transform itself, but it is still remains simply wood.

'It is quite different' Derrida writes, 'when it becomes a commodity, when the curtain goes up on the market and the table plays actor and character at the same time, when the commodity-table, says Marx, comes on stage (*auftritt*), begins to walk around and to put itself forward as a market value. Coup de theatre: the ordinary, sensuous thing is transfigured (*verwandelt sich*), it becomes someone, it assumes a figure'.[1]

Marx states that commodity becomes a sensuously supersensible thing (*sinnliche übersinnilichen Ding*).[2] Derrida plays on the spectral aspect of the commodity, but the idea of something supersensible which is also sensuous, more than something spectral it seems to lead to a body or a face that is deceiving, by presenting and hiding at the same time an alterity. Just like an actor who portrays both himself and a fictitious character at the same time.

Derrida continues: 'Marx must have recourse to theatrical language and must describe the apparition of the commodity as a stage entrance (*auftritt*). And he must describe the table become commodity as a table that turns, to be sure, during a spiritualist séance, but also as a ghostly silhouette, the figuration of an actor or a dancer'.[3] Derrida brings together the image of the ghost, which is theatricality, highly legitimized by Shakespeare in *Hamlet*. The image of the ghost recalls the topic of the *simulacrum*, meaning an image that has no reference (it is not the copy of the original).[4]

However, when Marx refers to the table as a commodity which is 'sensuously supersensible', placing the emphasis on the adverb 'sensuously', he emphasizes materiality, that is, a referent that is not an original, but something that has to have a physical dimension. It is not a ghost nor

[1] Jacques Derrida, *Spectres of Marx* (London: Routledge, 1994), p. 188.

[2] Karl Marx, *Capital, Volume I*, MECW, vol. 35. *Sinnliche übersinnilichen Ding* is translated as 'something transcendent'. Ben Fowkes translates this as 'transcends sensuousness', cf. Karl Marx, *Capital, Volume I* (London: Penguin Books, 1990), p. 163.

[3] Ibid., p. 189.

[4] Cf. Gilles Deleuze, 'The Simulacrum and Ancient Philosophy', in: Gilles Deleuze (ed.), *The Logic of Sense* (London: The Athlone Press, 1990); Jean Baudrillard, *Simulacra and Simulation* (Los Angeles: Semiotext[e], 1983); and Guy Debord, *The Society of the Spectacle* (Detroit: Black & Red, 2013).

a simulacrum but an image of a table, that although it does not have a physical form which is its exchange-value, it is made of matter (for example silicon which is used to produce the pixels of a virtual table). It is *supersensible* because the table has an exchange-value which is its representation of the use-value, exceeding reality while representing it.[5] This *excess* is both the visible and invisible: the exchange is visible as the result of *social* labour, of the cooperation among men, of a collective process, it remains invisible. In commodity the immateriality of human and social relationships is presented as an exchange of relationships. An object is considered a commodity specifically because it is *sensuously super-sensitive*. A representation that exceeds is something more than a mere copy. Being the exchange-value of the commodity-table is something more than its use-value. It exceeds the value of use until it becomes a medium, a support (like wood is a support for the table). But despite this, one cannot imagine an exchange-value with the absence of a use-value. Even when we go to buy butter at the supermarket the colours and shape of the packaging may catch your eye, but the butter for its use-value should remain simply as it is: an edible delight which is the product of historical-social knowledge and social-cooperative labour. When we taste it and use it we forget all about the (historical-social) knowledge and the (social-cooperative) labour which is incorporated in it. The immaterial relationship of exchange which makes us buy and use a product with the representational excess causing the oblivion of its history and replacing it by putting it on show at the supermarket in an aesthetic dimension. It is important that an object has an aesthetic power, yet the so-called *Real socialisms* did not understand this. The postmodernism on the other hand took it upon itself to make this excessive representation not only aesthetic but also self-serving.

The use-value remains the referent for the exchange-value. It cannot be eliminated. Even money, the general equivalent thanks to which the exchange can happen, cannot lose its use-value which is of course its *sensuously supersensible* ability to be a general equivalent for all possible exchange-values. However, the exchange can be transformed from the result of social labour into the property of the object, into something fetish.

[5] Cf. Richard Wollheim, 'Walter Pater as a Critic of the Arts', in: Richard Wollheim (ed.), *On Art and the Mind* (Cambridge: Harvard University Press, 1974), pp. 155–76.

Marx writes: ‘As a general rule, articles of utility become commodities, only because they are products of the labour of private individuals or groups of individuals who carry on their work independently of each other. The sum total of the labour of all these private individuals forms the aggregate labour of society. Since the producers do not come into social contact with each other until they exchange their products, the specific social character of each producer’s labour does not show itself except in the act of exchange. In other words, the labour of the individual asserts itself as a part of the labour of society, only by means of the relations which the act of exchange establishes directly between the products, and indirectly, through them, between the producers. To the latter, therefore, the relations connecting then labour of one individual with that the rest appear, not as direct social relations between individuals at works, but as what they are, material relations between persons and social relations between things’.[6]

Social relationships *appear as what they really are*. Relationships of objects among people and social relationships among objects. The commodities therefore hide nothing, there is no world which appears upside down, there is no essence hidden behind the deceptive appearance, but there is also no simulacrum, a copy without an original, a representation without a referent. The use-value has not disappeared, it has become slave to the exchange-value and, as such, has separated itself from the labouring process that produced it and which is the result of *cooperation*; what Marx calls the faculty of the human species and for this precise reason has become the most powerful means in capitalist exploitation. This being the exchange-value, it has entered the scene in shops, in universal exhibitions, in large warehouses, supermarkets, and in malls. Cooperation disappears as the social force of labour and reappears as non-labour, in voluntary work, in corporate forms that base their union against the other, the enemy, the villain. The problem of the re-appropriation of cooperative labour arises against this concealment.

The postmodernism believed in the simulacrum, in the copy without the original, in the representation without the referent, self-referencing, and the narcissism of the appearance. It was maybe the necessary answer to the aporias of modernism, but from a cooperative and social labourpoint of view. The fact that we have moved from the centrality

[6] Karl Marx, *Capital, Volume I*, MECW, vol. 35, pp. 83–4.

of the despotism of the factory to the breaking up of corporate despotism certainly changes the political substance of the struggle against its exploitation and organization, but not the fact that cooperation remains the fundamental form of labour and production. Technological changes can change the forms and ways of cooperation, but they cannot cancel it. Only in a society based on profit, exploitation, and individualism does the problem of the conflict between man and technology, and the dismissal of the workforce replaced by machines arise.

Commodity is not a simulacrum, instead it is an actress who enters the scene, and as such she tries to cancel the actor (the labour imbedded in it) with the character (object-commodity) portrayed and therefore the spectators unwillingly and temporarily suspend their disbelief. Coleridge had the same intent with his poetry, only that it was involuntary and permanent. During the era of the apparent end of the grand narratives, which, according to Lyotard, characterizes the postmodern condition, goods, to use Vico's words, are *real stories*, that is, in showing themselves seductive and captivating, as the myths do, they tell us something true and they appear as what they are, exactly like the characters on stage; that is, both actors and characters who, unlike those of Pirandello, do not seek the author, but rather want to hide and forget him.

The use-value therefore refers to the cooperation, while on the other hand the commodity, the exchange-value, refers to the scene and the show. The cooperation is made up of actors that interact with one another. The show is made up of spectators who are alone even when they are in the company of others because they are always in the crowd in the dark. The fetish exchange between persons and things corresponds to the exchange between the cooperation and the show.

Within the cooperation, people operate actively, during the show they assist passively. Politics reduced to being a show is the result of the fetish confusion between objects and people. Of course, this a just simplified outline. It is clear that there are kinds of shows where the spectator is active or where one can be an actor and spectator at the same time, but the dominant tendency in the capitalist system, where the commodity enters the scene, is the condition of the prisoner in Plato's cave: the spectator is isolated and chained. The ideal situation for the modern audience is to be isolated in the crowd and in the dark.

Let us take into consideration the spectator at the cinema. As it has been observed: 'Cinema has always been associated with an audience: The new media context allows for the construction of imagined audiences, even when spectators find themselves alone in front of a computer or tablet screen'.[7]

The audience implies the solitude of the crowd. Inside the cinema the spectators are altogether but alone. This is the same for those that watch a film on a computer or tablet, they are alone even if they are connected. But with these new devices 'How then can we be sure we are watching cinema, when we are no longer occupying the darkened theatre?'[8] The answer is that even though the experience shared with the new devices is so far from that of the classic experience in the cinema 'thanks to the presence of an imagined public, we can once again merge with a community, even if we are engaged in individual viewing'.[9]

This remedy is possible because even at the cinema where we are individual viewers, we are alone among others. However, being alone in the midst of others (even imaginary others) is neither community, congregation, or cooperation, it instead regards isolated individuals in the crowd who, starting from the fifteenth-century invention of the painting and linear perspective, have become the spectators of those Albertian windows which later became the theatre of Palladio—the cinema, the television, the computer, the tablet, the smartphone.

Therefore, it is of utmost importance that there is a conceptual difference between public (audience), community, congregation, and cooperation. Commodity seeks a public, but the result is a cooperation. The contradictions between exchange value and use-value, between commodity and labour live in the antinomy between *audience* and cooperation, between spectators who are unable to become actors and actors who do not want to be spectators.

4.2 The Immateriality of Value

David Harvey underlines two characteristics about value: being in motion and being immaterial. Capital flows are compared to the water cycle. Being immaterial refers to its definition as *socially necessary labour time*.

[7] Francesco Casetti, *The Lumière Galaxy: 7 Key Words for the Cinema to Come* (New York: Columbia University Press, 2015), p. 73.

[8] Ibid.

[9] Ibid.

This implies forms of social relationships that cannot be empirically measured.

'Historical materialism' Harvey writes, 'recognises the importance of immaterial but objective powers of this sort. We typically appeal to them to account for the collapse of the Berlin Wall, the election of Donald Trump, feelings of national identity or the desire of indigenous populations to live according to their own cultural norms. We describe features such as power, influence, belief, status, loyalty, and social solidarity in immaterial terms. Value, for Marx, is exactly such a concept'.[10]

Harvey cites a passage from Marx's *Grundrisse* to sustain his theory: 'it then again occurs to them that capital is in one respect *value*, i.e., something *immaterial*, indifferent to its physical consistency'.[11] In this case the immateriality is specified by the fact that the *value* is uninterested in the matter. In other words, it is safe to say that the *value* as an *exchange value* is immaterial because it is uninterested in the *use-value*. The unconcern of the exchange-value regarding the use-value does not mean at all that the exchange-value loses its material dimension, instead it means that it arises abstractly in relation to any possible use-value. All the same, it cannot help but have a relationship with a use-value. Basically, the exchange-value never loses its referent which is the use-value, even if the latter can vary. The immaterial is defined as that which keeps a relationship with what is material and does not disappear in the mists of the spirit.

It is true, as Harvey says, that realities such as power or belief are immaterial, but it is also true that they exist only when they are defined in a material way. Power and belief are in the same situation as Plato's triangle which can be thought of as an idea, but which can only be represented as *that* triangle that someone draws on a piece of paper. It is true that, as Bateson says, information which is immaterial depends on the difference that exists between the white colour of the paper and the blue of the ink, but, precisely, the immaterial idea of the *difference*, which gives us

[10] David Harvey, *Marx, Capital, and the Madness of Economic Reason* (Oxford: Oxford University Press, 2018), p. 5.

[11] Karl Marx, *Economic Manuscripts of 1857–61*, MECW, vol. 28, p. 235. Marx quotes Jean-Baptiste Say's *Traité d'économie politique*, vol. II, 'Le *capital est toujours d'une essence immaterielle,* puisque ce n'est pas la matiere qui fait le capital, mais la *valeur de* cette matiere, valeur qui n'a rien de corporel' ['*Capital is always immaterial by nature*, since it is not matter which makes capital, but the value of that matter, value which has nothing corporeal about it'].

information, is ensured by the paper and ink which are material. To represent Power, it is always *that* power with material supports (the throne, the crown, the tiara). To represent belief, it is *that* belief equipped with material supports (voice, language, writing, and recording).

From this point of view, commodity as an exchange value becomes fetish when what is material and immaterial exchange roles and social relationships become objectified in things. It is no longer the immaterial exchange-value that has the material use-value as its referent, but it is the material use-value that represents the immaterial exchange-value. The commodity appropriates the social relationships that produced it and enters the scene.

4.3 Postmodernism and the Bonaventura Hotel in Los Angeles

Jameson's writes in referral to the Bonaventura Hotel in Los Angeles as an expression of postmodernism: 'I believe that, with a certain number of other characteristic postmodern buildings, such as the Beaubourg in Paris or the Eaton Centre in Toronto, the Bonaventure aspires to being a total space, a complete world, a kind of miniature city; to this new total space, meanwhile, corresponds a new collective practice, a new mode in which individuals move and congregate, something like the practice of a new and historically original kind of hypercrowd.'[12] Jameson observes that the building seems to be self-enclosed, self-referential, and self-operating: 'it does not wish to be a part of the city but rather its equivalent and replacement or substitute'.[13] This produces a paradoxical effect: the marketing aspect is almost hidden by the aesthetic one.

The exchange-value becomes the use-value, but not entirely as this is impossible: it is a hotel and as such it must be functional. Its use-value, being a building made of metal, glass, and concrete, wants to eliminate its exchange-value, stealing its aesthetic and desirable value, but it cannot do so entirely. Desire overrides need, but it cannot cancel it. Postmodernism has strongly emphasized this trend which aims for the impossible.

[12] Fredric Jameson, *Postmodernism, or, the Cultural Logic of Late Capitalism* (Durham: Duke University Press, 1991), p. 40.

[13] Ibid.

From this scenario Jameson reaches the conclusion that 'all modern culture [...] tends to turn upon itself and designate its own cultural production as its content'.[14] This is made possible due to the loss of *depth* in contemporary culture and the tendency of the exchange-value to erase the memory of the use-value. But can the use-value be *completely* erased? In art perhaps yes, but not in economic and social life. The topic of the *simulacrum* is proposed again. Jameson says that contemporary art favours *pastiche*, therefore it loses depth.

Pastiche implies the loss of history at the same moment it becomes an imitation of ironically juxtaposed texts or images or music. According to Jameson, *pastiche* corresponds to the *simulacrum* (cf. Deleuze, Baudrillard and before that Debord), that is the copy of an original that has never existed (Platone). Jameson writes that: 'The culture of the simulacrum comes to life in a society where exchange-value has been generalized to the point at which the very memory of use-value is effaced, a society of which Guy Debord has observed, in an extraordinary phrase, that in it "the image has become the final form of commodity reification" (*The Society of the Spectacle*)'.[15]

However, if Marx believes that everything is as it seems, then the ideology and the false consciousness are not part of the dichotomy essence-appearance. This does not mean assimilating Marx in postmodern *pastiche*, but to find another idea of depth which is probably what Merleau-Ponty sought in Cézanne with his Montagne St.-Victoire, where representation exceeds what is represented by representing it. Excess does not at all mean that the referent disappears, it just means that the correspondence between the representation and what is being represented fades away until the real Mountain is only a support for the painted Mountain, like a use-value that transforms into a medium for the exchange-value. We need to look for the exchange-value within the use-value, the same way as the invisible needs to be found within the visible, the cooperation in a show that transforms itself in a way that all the actors become spectators and all the spectators become actors.

[14] Ibid., p. 42.

[15] Ibid., p. 18. Jameson presents 5 models of depth (see pp. 11–2): 1. Inside-outside (The Scream by Munch); 2. Essence-appearance (ideology, false consciousness); 3. Latent-Manifest (or dismissal [target of *La volonté de savoir* by Foucault; Translated as *Introduction*]); 4. Authenticity-inauthenticity (repossession-alienation), and; 5. Signifier-Signified (depth: perspective in art).

In the paragraph on 'The character of fetish and its arcane' of *Capital, Volume I*, Marx points out that the most suitable analogy for understanding the fetishism of commodities is not the dark room, which he had already evoked with Engels in *The German Ideology*, but instead religion: a phantasmagorical form which does not reverse the image, but precisely by representation, *it exceeds* what is being represented by representing it.[16] What exceeds does not reverse itself but distorts itself, finding resemblance in the difference.[17]

As Vico did with the myths, these are 'real stories': different forms of representation within which the truth is found. The gods of the *Iliad* and the *Odyssey* are deformations of men, and precisely for this reason they tell truths about men. In Marx, the idea of depth is not based on the dichotomy essence-appearance that is why 'things are as they seem'. It is a mistake to apply the status of falsity to fetishism of commodities with appearance-false and essence-true. The truth is in the weavings of the appearance, the invisible that is found in the visible. Paul Klee wrote *Making Visible*: what is not visible becomes visible, but only within what is visible and not at its expense. Depth is not far away; it is in the relations that are simultaneously intertwined on all dimensions. There is not only one point of view. This is what Paul Cèzanne wanted to say and what others like Giacometti, Delaunay, and Merleau-Ponty understood.

As Mr. Palomar states: 'It is only after you have come to know the surface of things [...] that you venture to seek what is underneath. But the surface is inexhaustible'.[18] This is why depth lies not far off in another place, not beyond what appears, but as Cèzanne did with his Mountain, in the textures of the surface, because it is true that what is invisible lies in the net of what is visible, as does the Marxian exploitation in the plots of the commodity and its visibility. And we, as a spectator, spellbound by the show, confusing deception with illusion and abandoning the webs of truth that exist in the latter, we forget about it every time we go to buy a commodity.

[16] Cf. Richard Wollheim, 'Walter Pater as a Critic of the Arts', p. 176.

[17] Cf. Maurice Merleau-Ponty, *The Primacy of Perception: And Other Essays on Phenomenological Psychology, the Philosophy of Art, History and Politics* (Evanston: Northwestern University Press, 1964), pp. 159–90; Maurice Merleau-Ponty, *Notes de cours 1959–61* (Paris: Gallimard, 1996); and Martin Heidegger, *Identity and Difference* (Chicago: University of Chicago Press, 2002).

[18] Italo Calvino, *Mr. Palomar* (London: Vintage Random House, 1999), p. 51.

With TINA ('There is no alternative'), Neoliberalism has managed to take away the future that is not the present and, with technological changes and above all with the change in the organization of labour, the meaning of the cooperative force of labour has disappeared. The breaking up of companies, microphysics of their despotic power, the self-ideology of the individual entrepreneur, the application of the business model in schools, universities, health systems, and institutions, the dismantling of the welfare state, the imposition of short-term employment accompanied by the aesthetic sense of a life that wants to stop time as it has no future or past under the illusion that the present identifies itself with eternity. All of this, borrowed and modified by Mark Fisher from others, has been used to define *capitalist realism*, bringing to postmodern neoliberalism the extreme consequences which Marx had already emphasized when speaking of the bourgeois individual of the eighteenth century, describing him as one who tends to consider and treat society as a means to his private ends. A vision that favours few and punishes many and which, behind an image of freedom as the breaking of ties (historically necessary to break the ties from the past), leads to exploitation, inequalities, leaving that cooperative force behind the scenes, which from the faculty of the human species has become the most effective means of exploitation.

In the 1980s when people started talking about globalization it spread and become a dominant vision of the world. The vision gave room to the lowering of wages, the return of occult forms of slavery, the redeployment of production all over the world of production, wars fought in the name of humanity, idolatry and the omnipotence of the so-called managers, banking speculations, the weakening of moral values in the name of efficiency and realism, the savage private occupation of all that was public, and finally the end of social responsibility. There was even room for job precariousness that went from an unpleasant transitory phase of existence to a silent permanent condition. An aggressive right wing basically imposed the idea of precariousness as a permanent condition of work and a washed-out left wing ashamed of itself, in search of a servile entrepreneurial and managerial acknowledgment accepted it by calling it *flexibility*. What is flexibility? In theory it is a wonderful thing: the chance to change your job when you want and not feel the pressure of being a prisoner of daily routines and behaviours; freed from a fixed job that conditions you for life, being free to choose. A Wonderful world! However, flexibility has a dark side to it too, job precariousness: having to change one's job according to market fluctuations; to be conditioned for one's entire life by the lack of a stable job; not having a choice. *Precariousness* is not just job insecurity and insecurity about the future, but as time passes it tends to kill one's pride and dignity, blackmailed to the point that will is dispersed and one's autonomy dissolves.

The real problem is the fact that the *precariousness* from a transitory condition of existence has become, as already mentioned, a permanent condition in a world where every hope for the future, but also the anger for the present that is offending dignity and pride, are unable to find neither space nor collective values. Every critical sense remains private and dissolves in the self-deception induced by the swaying of the mass media between the false euphoria produced by advertising a world that does not exist, and the spectacle of corruption, immorality, and selfishness that we witness every day, watching it on TV as if from a keyhole: remaining in silence on the other side. The rise in inequalities and the successful rhetoric on precariousness represent the other side of cooperation, where a characteristic faculty of the human species becomes the most effective tool for the exploitation of men by men.

This is why it is important that both women and men reclaim the cooperative organization of labour; it is as if they are characters in a theatrical game where the authors have been hidden, then found and, having found them, in the end the characters realize that the authors are themselves. They could thus discover that, being together and cooperating with each other, like jazz musicians do, that being together is enriched by the individual differences of each one, they are no longer passive spectators, prisoners in a cave, isolated and connected, but they are themselves the authors of a drama which themes are equality and dignity.

But before getting to this it is necessary to start from Flaubert and his last masterpiece. *Bouvard* was in disbelief about the Dancing tables that had entered the scene, 'However' Flaubert writes, 'all over Europe, America, Australia and the Indies, millions of mortals passed their lives in making tables turn; and they discovered the way to make prophets of canaries, to give concerts without instruments, and to correspond by means of snails. The press, seriously offering these impostures to the public, increased its credulity'.[19] Flaubert's novel is about *bêtise*; stupidity and with-it gullibility. The first step in criticizing the fetishism of commodities and not exchanging people for things could and should

[19] Gustave Flaubert, *Bouvard and Pécuchet* (Goucester: Dodo Press, 2009), p. 204.

be the criticism of Human Follies (bêtise), which Flaubert saw advancing alongside science and technology. What is *bêtise*? Kundera refers to it as: the non-thought of conformism and clichés, which today is increasingly reinforced by the complicity of mass media and social networks. The first step in rethinking an alternative is by criticising bêtise, which unfortunately in almost all politics today tends to accept and to interpose in a frantic search for immediate consent because they are unable to overcome the condition of minority to which conformism and the clichés of neoliberalism condemn them. In 1985, with the uprise of Neoliberalism, Milan Kundera wrote: 'Flaubert's discovery is more important for the future of the world than the most startling ideas of Marx or Freud. For we could imagine the world without the class struggle or without psychoanalysis, but not without the irresistible flood of received ideas that - programmed into computers, propagated by the mass media - threaten soon to become a force that will crush all original and individual thought and thus will smother the very essence of the European culture of the Modern Era'.[20]

References

Baudrillard, Jean (1983), *Simulacra and Simulation*, Los Angeles: Semiotext[e].

Calvino, Italo (1999), *Mr. Palomar*, London: Vintage Random House.

Casetti, Francesco (2015), *The Lumière Galaxy: 7 Key Words for the Cinema to Come*, New York: Columbia University Press.

Debord, Guy (2013), *The Society of the Spectacle*, Detroit: Black & Red.

Deleuze, Gilles (1990), 'The Simulacrum and Ancient Philosophy', in: Gilles Deleuze (ed.), *The Logic of Sense*, London: The Athlone Press, pp. 253–79.

Derrida, Jacques (1994), *Spectres of Marx*, London: Routledge.

Flaubert, Gustave (2009), *Bouvard and Pécuchet*, Goucester: Dodo Press.

Harvey, David (2018), *Marx, Capital, and the Madness of Economic Reason*, Oxford: Oxford University Press.

Heidegger, Martin (2002), *Identity and Difference*, Chicago: University of Chicago Press.

Iacono, Alfonso Maurizio (2016), *History and Theory of Fetishism*, New York: Palgrave MacMillan.

Jameson, Fredric (1991), *Postmodernism, or, the Cultural Logic of Late Capitalism*, Durham: Duke University Press.

Kundera, Milan (1988), *The Art of the Novel*, New York: Grove Press.

Marx, Karl (1986), *Economic Manuscripts of 1857–61*, MECW, vol. 28.

[20] Milan Kundera, *The Art of the Novel* (New York: Grove Press, 1988), p. 77.

———. (1990), *Capital, Volume I*, London: Penguin Books.
———. (1996), *Capital, Volume I*, MECW, vol. 35.
Merleau-Ponty, Maurice (1964), *The Primacy of Perception: And Other Essays on Phenomenological Psychology, the Philosophy of Art, History and Politics*, Evanston: Northwestern University Press.
———. (1996), *Notes de cours 1959–61*, Paris: Gallimard.
Wollheim, Richard (1974), 'Walter Pater as a Critic of the Arts', in: Richard Wollheim (ed.), *On Art and the Mind*, Cambridge: Harvard University Press, pp. 155–76.

PART II

Environmental Crisis and the Struggle for Nature

CHAPTER 5

Primitive Accumulation as the Cause of Economic and Ecological Disaster

Kohei Saito

5.1 Introduction

Marx's theory of primitive accumulation is not a mere historical description of the origin of capitalism, but depicts its destructive character.[1] To comprehend this fully, the concept of primitive accumulation needs to be understood in relation to Marx's theory of metabolism. Doing so makes it possible to comprehend the historical process of primitive accumulation as the cause of both economic *and* ecological disaster. It also becomes clear how tightly both these crises are linked to each other precisely because capitalist development as a process of class formation radically transforms and reorganizes the entire metabolic exchange between humans and nature on an unprecedented scale.

[1] This study was supported by JSPS Kakenhi Grant Number JP20K13466 and by the Ministry of Education of the Republic of Korea and the National Research Foundation of Korea (NRF-2018S1A3A2075204).

K. Saito (✉)
Osaka City University, Osaka, Japan

M. Musto (ed.), *Rethinking Alternatives with Marx*, Marx, Engels, and Marxisms, https://doi.org/10.1007/978-3-030-81764-0_5

Famously enough, Fredric Jameson lamented that 'it is easier to imagine the end of the world than the end of capitalism'.[2] Only a solid understanding of the destructive impact immanent to capitalist development can make it possible to conceptualize an alternative postcapitalist society. The key to reviving a communist imaginary today is the concept of 'wealth' (*Reichtum*) in the opening passage of volume 1 of *Capital*. This concept reveals why capitalist development rather impoverishes the 'wealth' of society instead of augmenting it, because it constantly creates artificial scarcity (i.e. 'Lauderdale's paradox').

Later, in *Critique of the Gotha Programme*, Marx returned to this concept of wealth. In his famous description of the communist society, he seemed to fall back into the naïve Promethean idea of absolute domination over nature. However, this passage can be reinterpreted from an ecological perspective without falling into the productivist reading based on his ecosocialist critique of primitive accumulation, which he developed in volume 1 of *Capital*. This reinterpretation finally opens up a vision of an alternative postcapitalist society with 'radical abundance' of the common wealth that expands the 'realm of freedom' without increasing the productive forces.

5.2 Separation Between Humans and Nature as the Uniqueness of Capitalism

The historical process of 'primitive accumulation' is the precondition for capitalist development. As Marx argued in volume 1 of *Capital* by referring to the 'enclosure' in England, primitive accumulation of capital is a violent process of separation that is tantamount to forcefully 'divorcing the producer from the means of production'.[3] This definition often leads the reader to historical transformations through which social means of subsistence and production are turned into capital and the producers are turned into wage-labourers. Readers tend to concentrate on how the social condition for the increasing misery of workers was prepared by primitive accumulation and strengthened by the development of capitalism. In *New Imperialism* David Harvey succinctly summarizes the point that primitive accumulation 'entailed taking land, say, enclosing

[2] Fredric Jameson, 'Future City', *New Left Review*, vol. 21 (2003), n. 3: 76.

[3] Karl Marx, *Capital, Volume I* (London: Penguin, 1976), p. 875.

it, and expelling a resident population to create a landless proletariat, and then releasing the land into the privatized mainstream of capital accumulation'.[4]

Nevertheless, it is important to recall that Marx defined 'labor' in volume 1 of *Capital* as a process between humans and nature, a process 'by which man, through his own actions, mediates, regulates and controls the metabolism (*Stoffwechsel*) between himself and nature'.[5] This is why primitive accumulation as the separation of the original unity of the producers from their objective condition of production inevitably results in a great transformation both in the life of workers and in their relationship with nature. In fact, Marx, in the *Grundrisse*, highlighted this historically peculiar relationship between humans and nature as created by primitive accumulation, saying:

> It is not the *unity* of living and active humanity with the natural, inorganic conditions of their metabolic exchange (*Stoffwechsel*) with nature, and hence their appropriation of nature, which requires explanation or is the result of a historic process, but rather the separation between these inorganic conditions of human existence and this active existence, a *separation* which is completely posited only in the relation of wage labour and capital.[6]

In precapitalist societies, as Marx noted, humans and nature were not separated. Slaves and serfs were reduced to a part of the objective condition for production and reproduction next to cattle, but this treatment also secured the satisfaction of their basic needs. They became a part of inorganic nature like cattle, so that their metabolic exchange with nature was stabilized without disruption. This realized what Marx called 'original unity' between the producers and their objective condition of production.

In contrast, as a result of the coercive separation from nature, the immediate producers in capitalism became 'free' in a dual sense. Whereas they became free from the personal and political domination in precapitalist societies, they also became free of the objective means of realizing their labour. As a result of this historical alienation from nature, labour

[4] David Harvey, *The New Imperialism* (Oxford: Oxford University Press, 2005), p. 149.

[5] Marx, *Capital, Volume I*, p. 283.

[6] Karl Marx, *Grundrisse: Foundations of the Critique of Political Economy* (London: Penguin, 1973), p. 489.

as the mediation of human interactions with nature came to be exerted differently—now the entire production process is thoroughly reorganized in favour of capital valorization—, so that their metabolic exchanges with nature also began to take an utterly different form. As discussed below, this transformation came to exert a powerful influence on both economic and ecological spheres.

Marx consistently argued that it is necessary to re-establish the 'original unity' in the future society beyond this alienation from nature: 'The original unity can be reestablished only on the material foundation which capital creates and by means of the revolutions which, in the process of this creation, the working classand the whole society undergo'.[7] Indeed, Marx's famous remark on the 'negation of the negation' in volume 1 of *Capital* corresponds to this reestablishment of the 'original unity' as the process of overcoming the separation in the metabolic exchange between humans and nature. However, to comprehend what needs to be reestablished in communism, it is first necessary to grasp what is destroyed through the primitive accumulation in detail. According to Marx, wealth is negated under capitalism. It may sound dubious to argue that capitalism destroys wealth despite its magnificent power of production; but this constitutes the 'paradox of wealth'.[8]

5.3 Marx's Concept of 'Wealth'

Marx's discussion of primitive accumulation indicates that the beginning of *Capital*, although written in a logical manner, presupposes a historical process of enclosure that led to the universalization of the production of commodities. As a result, in the opening passage, there is a fundamental contradiction of capitalism created by a radical separation in the metabolic exchange between humans and nature. John Holloway presented a unique interpretation of this passage, where Marx wrote: 'The wealth of societies in which the capitalist mode of production prevails appears as an "immense collection of commodities;" the

[7] Karl Marx, *Economic Manuscript of 1861–1863*, MECW, vol. 33, p. 340.

[8] John Bellamy Foster and Brett Clark, *The Robbery of Nature: Capitalism and the Ecological Rift* (New York: Monthly Review Press, 2020), p. 152.

individual commodity appears as its elementary form. Our investigation therefore begins with the analysis of the commodity'.[9]

It is true that *Capital* starts with the 'analysis of the commodity'. However, as Holloway pointed out, the true beginning, which is the subject of the first sentence, is not commodity, but *wealth*.[10] Marx argued in this opening passage that the wealth of societies 'appears' as an 'immense collection of commodities' in capitalism. The verb 'appear' indicates that wealth and commodities 'are' not identical, and that the wealth of noncapitalist societiesdoes not necessarily appear as the commodity. Only under certain social relations, the wealth of societies 'appears' as the commodity.

It is important to recognize both the non-identity and the fundamental tensions between wealth and the commodity. Karl Polanyi once warned that land, labour, and money are 'fictitious commodities' that must not be completely commodified and subjected to the dictates of the market.[11] These three categories can be considered typical forms of the social 'wealth' that are incompatible with full commodification under the logic of capitalism.

Yet Marx's conception of wealth is even broader. His usage may be hard to grasp as the contemporary image of 'wealth' is often reduced to its 'bourgeois' form, so that being wealthy usually signifies having a lot of material wealth such as real estate and money. However, wealth does not have to be understood this way, as Holloway noted. The German term '*Reichtum*' can be translated to mean 'richness' because '*reich*' means 'rich'. Though 'richness' can signify the abundance of monetary wealth, it has a broader connotation such as richness in taste and smell, experience of life, and nature.[12]

Marx wrote in the *Grundrisse* about far-extended possibilities of noncapitalist wealth, saying:

[9] Marx, *Capital, Volume I*, p. 125.

[10] John Holloway, 'Read Capital: The First Sentence: Or Capital Starts with Wealth, Not with the Commodity', *Historical Materialism*, vol. 23 (2015), n. 3: 5.

[11] Karl Polanyi, 'The Self-Regulating Market and the Fictitious Commodities: Labor, Land, and Money', in: Karl Polanyi (ed.), *The Great Transformation: The Political and Economic Origins of Our Time* (Boston: Beacon Press, 2001), pp. 71–80.

[12] Holloway, 'Read Capital', p. 5.

> In fact, however, when the limited bourgeois form is stripped away, what is wealth other than the universality of individual needs, capacities, pleasures, productive forces etc., created through universal exchange? The full development of human mastery over the forces of nature, those of so-called nature as well as of humanity's own nature? The absolute working out of his creative potentialities, with no presupposition other than the previous historic development, which makes this totality of development, i.e. the development of all human powers as such the end in itself, not as measured on a predetermined yardstick? [...] In bourgeois economics—and in the epoch of production to which it corresponds—this complete working-out of the human content appears as a complete emptying-out, this universal objectification as total alienation, and the tearing-down of all limited, one-sided aims as sacrifice of the human end-in-itself to an entirely external end.[13]

The wealth or richness of societies is not about producing an ever-greater quantity of commodities, but rather about the full and constant development of total potentialities of human beings. Marx considered the richness of culture, skills, free time, and knowledge wealth, whose full realization requires the stripping away of the 'bourgeois form' of wealth because capitalist production *impoverishes* social wealthunder 'total alienation' by imposing 'an entirely external end' upon producers for the sake of endless capital accumulation.

Marx also used the expression 'natural wealth' (*natürlicherReichtum*) to designate the natural and material conditions of production and reproduction, as he wrote in volume 1 of *Capital*: 'External natural conditions can be divided from the economic point of view into two great classes, namely (1) natural wealthin the means of subsistence, i.e. a fruitful soil, waters teeming with fish, etc., and (2) natural wealthin the instruments of labour, such as waterfalls, navigable rivers, wood, metal, coal, etc.'[14] The richness of nature in the form of land, water, and forests is indispensable for humans as both means of subsistence and production, and they surely count as the fundamental 'wealth' of societies. Marx also wrote in volume 1 of *Capital* that 'labor is the father of material wealth, the earth is its mother'.[15] The abundance and sustainability of the natural wealth

[13] Marx, *Grundrisse*, p. 488.

[14] Marx, *Capital, Volume I*, p. 535.

[15] Ibid., p. 134.

provided by the earth constitutes the essential material foundation for the prosperity of society.

However, as Marx argued in the beginning of volume 1 of *Capital*, such social and natural richness all appear as an 'immense collection of commodities' in capitalism. There arises a tension here because commodities only focus one-sidedly on the value of the commodity and undervalue and marginalize what does not count as commodities. Commodity prioritizes exchange value, although the material characteristic of wealth remains the basis of use-value. As commodity without use-value loses its value, the material aspect of wealth functions as an essential 'bearer' (*Träger*) of value. However, use-value is subordinated to the logic of capital's valorization, which creates a tension because wealth is often something that capital did not itself create (capital neither creates knowledge and culture nor land and water), but simply utilizes and modifies it as a means for its valorization.

On the one hand, natural forces are thoroughly exploited by capital as free gifts: 'Natural elements which go into production as agents without costing anything, whatever role they might play in production, do not go in as components of capital, but rather as a free natural power of capital'.[16] Capital's treatment of nature as free gifts certainly strengthens the fundamental paradox of wealth because the destruction and squandering of the richness of nature in favour of capital's valorization undermines the natural conditions of production in the long run.

On the other hand, nature is also commodified because wild nature is worthless when left as it is. Its commodification, however, occurs by dissolving the abundance of social wealth and creating 'artificial scarcity'. Marx described this in his theory of primitive accumulation. Enclosure dissolved the commons, thus commodifying lands and expelling people living on them. Although primitive accumulation is often reduced to the separation of the producers from their means of production, its impact on the wealth of society was far-reaching. Quoting various reports, Marx highlighted the fact that nature is devastated after the expulsion of peasants from land in volume 1 of *Capital* (especially in the French edition). The most fertile lands in Scotland were totally laid waste because those who used to cultivate the lands were expelled, and were simply turned into a more profitable usage: 'Immense tracts of land, much of which is

[16] Marx, *Capital, Volume III* (London: Penguin, 1981), p. 879.

described in the statistical account of Scotland as having a pasturage in richness and extent of very superior description, are thus shut out from all cultivation and improvement, arid are solely devoted to the sport of a few persons for a very brief period of the year'.[17]

This transformation of land usage had an immense impact on the daily life of people in the countryside. The second enclosure is characterized by the general impoverishment of people's living conditions. Whereas the agricultural revolutionbased on the Norfolk four-course system significantly increased the production of wheat, peasants lost access to common lands and forests, where they used to raise pigs with acorns, collect mushrooms, wood, and fruits, and catch birds. Living in the countryside, they also had access to the river or the sea and caught fish. Now driven into the city, they lost access to such natural wealth. Even if they remained in the countryside, the previous activities in the commons were illegalized as acts of trespass and theft. Consequently, poor peasants came to suffer from the lack of availability of local food.

Enclosure concentrated lands in the hands of fewer capitalist farmers. As capitalist farmers hire peasants only during the busy farming seasons and fire them thereafter, the farming villages disappeared, and the small vegetable gardens maintained by the residents ceased to provide fresh vegetables for their own dinner tables. As it was no longer clear by whom and how the vegetables were grown and it was possible for them to be smeared with excreta of cattle and poultry, they became inedible raw, and fresh salads disappeared from the menu.

At the same time, all family members had to work in the factory to make a living. The loss of access to the commons significantly increased the financial burden on households. As they began working from when they were very young, children were not able to attend school and could not acquire basic cooking skills at home or during festivals and ceremonies where free luxurious meals were served for the village residents. Even if they acquired and maintained some cooking skills, working-class families in the city were no longer able to buy expensive meat but only cheap potatoes that were sold on the street. Consequently, the traditional English recipe based on ingredients available to the traditional rural village became useless to working-class families in the large cities.

[17] Marx, *Capital, Volume I*, p. 894.

Finally, English food culture was destroyed by adulteration. Marx documented this in volume 1 of *Capital*, that is, the falsification of bread adulterated with alum, soap, pearl-ash, and chalk, by referring to Arthur Hill Hassall's work *Adulterations Detected*. The worker 'had to eat daily in his bread a certain quantity of human perspiration mixed with the discharge of abscesses, cobwebs, dead cockroaches, and putrid German yeast, not to mention alum, sand, and other agreeable mineral ingredients'.[18] The problem was not limited to bread, as Hassall reported various adulterations in milk, butter, vegetables, and beer.[19] These foods were unhealthy and unsafe, but were also cheap, so the poor working class had to depend on them to fill their stomachs.

The consequences of dissolving the commons were disastrous for a great number of people. Skill and knowledge were impoverished, and natural wealthwas destroyed as a result of the total commodification of the world. From the perspective of capital, the same situation looks very different. Paradoxically, this is how capitalism took off, emancipating its full potentialities of productive forces, as workers became more and more dependent on commodities in the market.

This tension between wealth and the commodity is what underlies 'Lauderdale's paradox'.[20] According to James Maitland, the eighth Earl of Lauderdale, there is an inverse relationship between 'public wealth' and 'private riches', where if one increases, the other decreases. He defined 'public wealth' as consisting 'of all that man desires, as useful or delightful to him'. In contrast, 'private riches' has an additional character, in that it comprises 'all that man desires as useful or delightful to him; which exists in a degree of scarcity'.[21] Expressed in Marxian terms, public wealth has use-value, but not value because it exists abundantly. Public wealth turns into private riches when it becomes scarce. In other words, land, air, water, and food, must become scarce to attain value and function as a means to augment private riches (as well as the national riches that

[18] Ibid., p. 359.

[19] Arthur Hill Hassall, *Adulterations Detected, or Plain Instructions for the Discovery of Frauds in Food and Medicine* (London: Longman, Green, Longmans, and Roberts, 1861).

[20] Herman E. Daly, 'The Return of Lauderdale's Paradox', *Ecological Economics*, vol. 25 (1998), n. 1: 22.

[21] James Maitland Lauderdale, *An Inquiry Into the Nature and Origin of Public Wealth* (Edinburgh: Archibald Constable & Co., 1819), pp. 57–8.

comprise the sum total of individual riches). The obvious problem here is, as Lauderdale argued, that the increase in private riches is inevitably accompanied by the augmentation of scarcity and the decrease in the free and abundant common wealth. The common lands were gated and became inaccessible and thus scarce to peasants, which increased the misery of the masses.

This process of creating artificial scarcity augmented the individual private riches of the few. The scarcity of capitalism is 'artificial'—there is obviously 'natural' scarcity of arable lands and available water—because the richness of social and natural wealthin common must be destroyed and monopolized. Herein manifests the tension between wealth and the commodity, and this is the 'paradox of wealth' that marks the peculiarity of capitalism.

5.4 Paradox of Wealth Continued

Primitive accumulation brings about a fundamental shift in the metabolic exchange between humans and nature and produces disastrous consequences for natural wealth, as well. Marx was quite consistent in distinguishing between wealth and the commodity from the very beginning of *Capital*. He paid attention not only to 'free gifts of nature' to capital—this alone would be insufficient as it only treats the dimension of value—but also to its ecological-material impacts on nature as the common wealth of all human beings.

Marx especially focused on the problem of soil exhaustion, which caused great social anxiety at the time. With the development of capitalism, the aim of agricultural production came to be oriented towards short-term profit-making, and nutrients were extracted from the soil as far as possible without being replenished: 'the entire spirit of capitalist production, which is oriented towards the most immediate monetary profit—stands in contradiction to agriculture, which has to concern itself with the whole gamut of permanent conditions of life required by the chain of human generations'.[22] Another problem was excessive deforestation: 'The development of civilization and industry in general has always shown itself so active in the destruction of forests that everything

[22] Marx, *Capital, Volume III*, p. 754.

that has been done for their conservation and production is completely insignificant in comparison'.[23]

This environmental destruction under capitalism is what Marx repeatedly problematized in *Capital*:

> Capitalist production collects the population together in great centres, and causes the urban population to achieve an ever-growing preponderance. This has two results. On the one hand it concentrates the historical motive power of society; on the other hand, it disturbs the metabolic interaction between man and the earth, i.e. it prevents the return to the soil of its constituent elements consumed by man in the form of food and clothing; hence it hinders the operation of the eternal natural condition for the lasting fertility of the soil. Thus it destroys at the same time the physical health of the urban worker, and the intellectual life of the rural worker.[24]

Marx aimed to analyze how the metabolic interaction between humans and nature is thoroughly transformed and reorganized in the capitalist mode of production. The now celebrated passage in volume 3 of *Capital* also points to this tension between the commodity and wealth, which ultimately leads to the emergence of an 'irreparable rift' between social and natural metabolism:

> On the other hand, large landed property reduces the agricultural population to an ever decreasing minimum and confronts it with an ever growing industrial population crammed together in large towns; in this way it produces conditions that provoke an irreparable rift in the interdependent process between social metabolism and natural metabolism prescribed by the natural laws of the soil. The result of this is a squandering of the vitality of the soil, and trade carries this devastation far beyond the bounds of a single country.[25]

As Marx's theory of metabolism focuses on both sides of humans and nature, it is clear that the impacts of primitive accumulation cannot be limited to the formation of the working class alone. Different organizations of the metabolism between humans and nature in capitalism causes

[23] Marx, *Capital, Volume II* (London: Penguin, 1978), p. 322.

[24] Marx, *Capital, Volume III*, p. 637.

[25] Ibid., p. 949; translation modified following Karl Marx, *Das Kapital (Ökonomische Manuskript 1863–1865). Drittes Buch*, MEGA^2, vol. II/4.2, pp. 752–53.

significant damage to *all* wealth including the natural kind. Samir Amin, in *Modern Imperialism, Monopoly Finance Capital, and Marx's Law of Value,* grasped this point and noted: 'Marx concludes his radical critique in *Capital* with the affirmation that capitalist accumulation is founded on the destruction of the bases of all wealth: human beings and their natural environment'.[26] In this vein, Stefania Barca in her *Forces of Reproduction* rightly pointed to the interrelationship between the degradation of living conditions and that of the natural environment through primitive accumulation, and said: 'from a historical-materialist perspective, the working class, or proletariat, and metabolic rift originate from a unique, global process of violent separation of people from their means of subsistence, which also disrupts the biosphere. The ecological crisis is thus a direct consequence of class making'.[27] By clearly grasping the truly destructive impact of primitive accumulation upon both social and natural wealth, it becomes possible to envision an alternative society that truly repairs the metabolic rift and rehabilitates the 'abundance' of the common wealth. This is particularly relevant to Marx's famous assertion about the 'negation of the negation'.

5.5 The Negation of the Negation Revisited

Primitive accumulation of capital as the dissolution of the commons counts as the first negation, which dismantles individual property as founded on the labour of its proprietor. In contrast, communism aims at the 'negation of the negation'. In the famous passage that appeared in volume 1 of *Capital*, Marx wrote as follows:

> But capitalist production begets, with the inexorability of a natural process, its own negation. This is the negation of the negation. It does not re-establish private property, but it does indeed establish individual property on the basis of the achievements of the capitalist era: namely co-operation and the possession in common of the land and the means of production produced by labor itself.[28]

[26] Samir Amin, *Modern Imperialism, Monopoly Finance Capital, and Marx's Law of Value* (New York: Monthly Review Press, 2018), p. 85.

[27] Stefania Barca, *Forces of Reproduction: Notes for a Counter–Hegemonic Anthropocene* (Oxford: Oxford University Press, 2020), p. 42.

[28] Marx, *Capital, Volume I*, p. 929.

Communism, as Marx argued, aims at rehabilitating the commons at a higher scale for the sake of the full development of the richness of wealth for most working individuals. Against the logic of commodification by capital, communism seeks the commonification of wealth.

However, this statement must not be simply understood as the emancipation of human desire to enjoy the richness of the world. As is evident in the passages quoted in the previous section, Marx was already aware that the availability of natural wealthis limited and cannot be arbitrarily utilized for satisfying human desire. Communism as the negation of the negation transcends artificial scarcity, but not scarcity itself, as natural scarcity continues to remain.

The term 'land' used in the quote is '*Erde*' in German. It also means 'earth', which implies natural resources other than land. Marx argued that the earth must be controlled 'in common', meaning that its usage must be cautious enough to care about future generations. Marx also wrote in volume 3 of *Capital*, in which the term '*Erde*' is translated as 'earth', saying:

> From the standpoint of a higher socioeconomic formation, the private property of particular individuals in the earth will appear just as absurd as the private property of one man in other men. Even an entire society, a nation, or all simultaneously existing societies taken together, are not the owners of the earth. They are simply its possessors, its beneficiaries, and have to bequeath it in an improved state to succeeding generations, as *boni patres familias*.[29]

The earth is what the current generation succeeded from the previous one, and it is obligatory for them to pass it on to the next generation without destroying it. Sustainability is essential, but capitalism cannot guarantee it. System change is necessary. This is the basic insight of Marx's ecosocialism.

This ecosocialist insight needs to be contrasted with the popularized vision of socialist society where materialabundance is supposed to become almost infinite, so that the working class can enjoy the same luxurious life without natural limits. For example, in *Self-Ownership, Freedom, and Equality*, G. A. Cohen described the abundance in communism in this manner. According to Cohen, Marx's vision of an equal society in the

[29] Marx, *Capital, Volume III*, p. 911.

future is based on 'a conviction that industrial progress brings society to a condition of such fluent abundance that it is possible to supply what everyone needs for a richly fulfilling life'.[30] Infinite material abundance of wealth is the condition of material equality of all, which inescapably leads to the Promethean myth of absolute domination over nature by the limitless increase in productive forces. Such a productivist vision of the future society is incompatible with planetary boundaries that exist independently of human will. Thus, Cohen concluded that it is no longer possible to 'sustain Marx's extravagant, pre-green, materialist optimism' and it is necessary to 'abandon the vision of abundance'.[31]

Cohen is absolutely right in emphasizing the need to criticize the extravagant and productivist vision of social and economic equality in socialism. Yet it is not necessary to entirely abandon the 'vision of abundance' if one recalls the 'Lauderdale paradox' as the process of creating artificial scarcity. The transcendence of the artificial scarcity of private riches recreates the abundance of the common wealth, which is available without the mediation of monetary exchange. This rehabilitation of the common wealth does not have to negate the natural scarcitythat is imposed by natural limits. However, Cohen assumed that Marx envisioned the abundance of a postcapitalist society based on that of capitalist society, that is, the abundance of private riches for all. However, if this was so, Marx would have simply imposed the 'bourgeois form of wealth' upon the future society instead of 'stripping it out'.

Nevertheless, there is a certain ambivalence in the *Grundrisse*. As quoted above, Marx also explicitly stated that the 'full development of human mastery over the forces of nature, those of so-called nature as well as of humanity's own nature'.[32] Such a statement can be easily presented as strong proof of Marx's naïve endorsement of the capitalist development of productive forces, especially because he endorsed the idea of 'great civilizing influence of capital' in the *Grundrisse*.[33] Whereas John Bellamy Foster highlighted Marx's ecological critique of capitalism in the

[30] G. A. Cohen, *Self-Ownership, Freedom, and Equality* (Cambridge: Cambridge University Press, 1995), p. 10.

[31] There is another current that sticks to this technocratic optimism today, which can be categorized as 'eco-modernism'. See Aaron Bastani, *Fully Automated Luxury Communism: A Manifesto* (London: Verso, 2018).

[32] Marx, *Grundrisse*, p. 488.

[33] Ibid., p. 409.

Grundrisse,[34] it is not necessarily clear whether Marx was fully ecologically conscious.

However, the situation clearly changed in the 1860s. In 1864 and 1865, Marx carefully read the seventh edition of Liebig's *Agricultural Chemistry* (1862), to which this famous German chemist had added a long new introduction in order to criticize the irrationality of modern capitalist agriculture as 'robbery' (*Raubbau*), which takes as much nutrition as possible from the soil in the short-term without even replenishing it. Robbery agriculture is, as Liebig criticized, driven by the farmer's desire to maximize profits, but the material conditions of the soil under capitalism turns out to be incompatible with sustainable production. There is a grave gap between the favorable conditions for capital's valorization and nature's sustainable metabolism. Marx in volume 1 of *Capital* praised 'Liebig's immortal merits'[35] and immediately integrated his critique of modern capitalist agriculture.

Even after the publication of volume 1 of *Capital*, Marx continued to study various topics in natural sciences such as chemistry, geology, mineralogy, and botany in order to analyze the contradictory tendencies of capitalist development. Consequently, he became more nuanced in his future predictions and rejected the breakdown theory of capitalism, whereas Liebig fell into a rather Malthusian tone.[36] On the one hand, the development of new technologies allows capital to gain access to previously unavailable or unprofitable natural resources and to more elastically appropriate natural forces. On the other hand, such utilization of nature from the perspective of profit-making increasingly undermines material conditions for sustainable production, because capital can never repair the metabolic rift, but only 'shift' it elsewhere.[37] Capitalism does not simply collapse, but the ecological crisis deepens under capitalist development,

[34] John Bellamy Foster, 'Marx's *Grundrisse* and the Ecological Contradiction of Capitalism', in: Marcello Musto (ed.), *Karl Marx's Grundrisse: Foundations of the Critique of Political Economy 150 Years Later* (London: Routledge, 2008), p. 96.

[35] Marx, *Capital, Volume I*, p. 638. See also John Bellamy Foster, 'The Metabolism of Nature and Society', in: John Bellamy Foster (ed.), *Marx's Ecology: Materialism and Nature* (New York: Monthly Review Press, 2000), pp. 141–77.

[36] See Kohei Saito, 'Marx's Ecology After 1868', in: Kohei Saito (ed.), *Karl Marx's Ecosocialism: Capital, Nature, and the Unfinished Critique of Political Economy* (New York: Monthly Review Press, 2017), pp. 217–55.

[37] Richard York and Brett Clark, 'Rifts and Shifts: Getting to the Root of Environmental Crises', *Monthly Review*, vol. 60 (2008), n. 6: 14; and Kohei Saito, 'Marx's Theory

which can only be fixed through the rational regulation of the metabolic exchange between humans and nature by associated producers not just for the sake of satisfying their own needs, *but also* for the needs of future generations.

In the 1860s, Marx was far from being a productivist and even envisioned an ecosocialist future. Based on this understanding, it is worth revisiting Cohen's critique of Marx's vision of abundance. What Cohen criticized is the famous passage in Marx's *Critique of the Gotha Programme*, where he wrote about the future communist society:

> In a higher phase of communist society, after the enslaving subordination of the individual to the division of labour, and thereby also the antithesis between mental and physical labour, has vanished; after labour has become not only a means of life but life's prime want; after the productive forces have also increased with the all-round development of the individual, and all the springs of common wealth flow more abundantly—only then can the narrow horizon of bourgeois right be crossed in its entirety and society inscribe on its banners: From each according to his abilities, to each according to his needs![38]

Cohen is not alone here. Herman Daly in his *Steady–State Economics* similarly argued that for Marx, the 'materialistic determinist, economic growth is crucial in order to provide the overwhelming material abundance that is the objective condition for the emergence of the new socialist man. Environmental limits on growth would contradict "historical necessity"'.[39]

However, considering the ecosocialist background of Marx's *Capital* and his discussion of wealth, it is not necessary to read this passage as the celebration of productivist domination over nature to achieve the abundance of wealth. Otherwise, Marx would have become totally inconsistent. When he demanded that the metabolic exchange between humans and nature should be regulated more rationally in the postcapitalist society free from the pressure of capital accumulation, he did not mean that socialist society would entirely become free from natural limits. Marx

of Metabolism in the Age of Global Ecological Crisis', *Historical Materialism*, vol. 28 (2020), n. 2: 14.

[38] Karl Marx, *Critique of the Gotha Programme*, MECW, vol. 24, p. 87.

[39] Herman E. Daly, *Steady–State Economics* (London: Earthscan, 1992), p. 196.

was quite aware of the fact that metabolic exchange is an ecologically material process that cannot be socially transcended. In *Critique of Gotha Programme*, he emphasized that labour 'is not *the source* of all wealth. *Nature* is just as much the source of use values (and it is surely of such that material wealth consists!) as labor'.[40]

In this context, it is almost absurd to maintain that Marx demanded the saturation of all unlimited desire.[41] It is possible to imagine a different kind of abundance of common wealth here, because there is another kind of abundance, namely 'radical abundance'.[42] This form of abundance is *radically* different from the bourgeois form that is based on ever-increasing productivity and endless mass consumption. It is not equivalent to the unlimited access to abundant goods; otherwise communist society would simply repeat the capitalist form of private riches. As primitive accumulation created 'artificial scarcity', communism reverses the order of the Lauderdale paradox with the aim of recovering the 'radical abundance' of the common wealth, making it equally accessible to everyone at the cost of private riches.

This alternative ecosocialist reading of *Critique of Gotha Programme* makes the meaning of the 'negation of the negation' clearer: de-enclosing and expanding the commons for the sake of the many. The expansion of public commons through basic service would enable people to access the basic goods that they need to live well without constantly seeking after high levels of income. This way, it is possible to revisit Marx's famous discussion in volume 3 of *Capital* with regard to the distinction between the realms of 'freedom' and 'necessity':

> This realm of natural necessity expands with his development, because his needs do too; but the productive forces to satisfy these expand at the same time. Freedom, in this sphere, can consist only in this, that socialized man, the associated producers, govern the human metabolism with nature in a rational way, bringing it under their collective control instead of being dominated by it as a blind power; accomplishing it with the least expenditure of energy and in conditions most worthy and appropriate for their

[40] Marx, *Critique of the Gotha Programme*, p. 81.

[41] See Ernest Mandel, *Power and Money: A Marxist Theory of Bureaucracy* (London: Verso, 1992), p. 206.

[42] See Jason Hickel, 'Degrowth: A Theory of Radical Abundance', *Real–World Economics Review*, vol. 87 (2019): 54–68.

> human nature. But this always remains a realm of necessity. The true realm of freedom, the development of human powers as an end in itself, begins beyond it, though it can only flourish with this realm of necessity as its basis. The reduction of the working day is the basic prerequisite.[43]

This passage was also often celebrated as Marx's endorsement of the unlimited growth of productive forces and provocation for the absolute domination over nature so that the realm of freedom can expand by reducing the working day.

Such a reading would also be incompatible with the ecosocialist character of Marx's *Capital*. However, from the perspective of radical abundance, it is not necessary to solely depend on ever-increasing productive forces because once artificial scarcity is overcome, people, now free from the constant pressure to earn money thanks to the expanding commons, would attain an attractive choice to work less without worrying about the degradation of their quality of life. Consequently, such a society will produce less unnecessary stuff and thus reduce the burden on the natural environment.

In this vein, Jason Hickel argued: 'Liberated from the pressures of artificial scarcity, the compulsion for people to compete for ever-increasing productivity would wither away. We would not have to feed our time and energy into the juggernaut of ever-increasing production, consumption and ecological destruction'.[44] In other words, it is possible to reduce the realm of necessity not by increasing the productive forces, but by increasing the commons, which allows people to live more stably without pressure to conform to the wage-labour system. The fairer (re)distribution of income and resources would also shorten the working day. Without unnecessary production, it is possible to reduce consumption as well. Emancipated from the constant exposure to advertisement and ceaseless market competition, there emerges more room to autonomously self-limit production and consumption. This certainly contributes towards downscaling the current 'realm of necessity' especially because it is actually full of what is not necessary at all.

Humans can consciously limit their needs. This does not necessarily mean austerity and poverty because it would simultaneously enrich various non-commercial activities that are not necessarily reflected in the GDP.

[43] Marx, *Capital, Volume III*, p. 959.

[44] Hickel, 'Degrowth', p. 66.

This way, it is possible to significantly expand the realm of freedom by realizing radical abundance for everyone. This is the negation of endless economic growth, and also how the 'negation of the negation' in communism in the twenty-first century increases the chances for free and sustainable human development without repeating the failures of the socialism that prevailed in the twentieth century.

References

Amin, Samir (2018), *Modern Imperialism, Monopoly Finance Capital, and Marx's Law of Value*, New York: Monthly Review Press.

Barca, Stefania (2020), *Forces of Reproduction: Notes for a Counter–Hegemonic Anthropocene*, Oxford: Oxford University Press.

Bastani, Aaron (2018), *Fully Automated Luxury Communism: A Manifesto*, London: Verso.

Cohen, G. A. (1995), *Self-Ownership, Freedom, and Equality*, Cambridge: Cambridge University Press.

Daly, Herman E. (1992), *Steady–State Economics*, London: Earthscan.

———. (1998), 'The Return of Lauderdale's Paradox', *Ecological Economics*, vol. 25, n. 1: 21–3.

Foster, John Bellamy (2000), 'The Metabolism of Nature and Society', in: John Bellamy Foster (ed.), *Marx's Ecology: Materialism and Nature*, New York: Monthly Review Press, pp. 141–77.

———. (2008), 'Marx's *Grundrisse* and the Ecological Contradiction of Capitalism', in: Marcello Musto (ed.), *Karl Marx's Grundrisse: Foundations of the Critique of Political Economy 150 Years Later*, London: Routledge, pp. 93–106.

Foster, John Bellamy, and Clark, Brett (2020), *The Robbery of Nature: Capitalism and the Ecological Rift*, New York: Monthly Review Press.

Harvey, David (2005), *The New Imperialism*, Oxford: Oxford University Press.

Hassall, Arthur Hill (1861), *Adulterations Detected, or Plain Instructions for the Discovery of Frauds in Food and Medicine*, London: Longman, Green, Longmans, and Roberts.

Hickel, Jason (2019), 'Degrowth: A Theory of Radical Abundance', *Real–World Economics Review*, vol. 87: 54–68.

Holloway, John (2015), 'Read Capital: The First Sentence: Or Capital Starts with Wealth, Not with the Commodity', *Historical Materialism*, vol. 23, n. 3: 3–26.

Jameson, Fredric (2003), 'Future City', *New Left Review*, vol. 21, n. 3: 65–79.

Lauderdale, James Maitland (1819), *An Inquiry Into the Nature and Origin of Public Wealth*, Edinburgh: Archibald Constable & Co.

Mandel, Ernest (1992), *Power and Money: A Marxist Theory of Bureaucracy*, London: Verso.
Marx, Karl (1973), *Grundrisse: Foundations of the Critique of Political Economy*, London: Penguin.
———. (1976), *Capital, Volume I*, London: Penguin.
———. (1978), *Capital, Volume II*, London: Penguin.
———. (1981), *Capital, Volume III*, London: Penguin.
———. (1989), *Critique of the Gotha Programme*, MECW, vol. 24, pp. 75–99.
———. (1991), *Economic Manuscript of 1861–63*, MECW, vol. 33.
———. (1992), *Das Kapital (Ökonomische Manuskript 1863–1865). Drittes Buch*, MEGA^2, vol. II/4.2, Berlin: Dietz.
Polanyi, Karl (2001), 'The Self-Regulating Market and the Fictitious Commodities: Labor, Land, and Money', in: Karl Polanyi (ed.), *The Great Transformation: The Political and Economic Origins of Our Time*, Boston: Beacon Press, pp. 71–80.
Saito, Kohei (2017), 'Marx's Ecology After 1868', in: Kohei Saito (ed.), *Karl Marx's Ecosocialism: Capital, Nature, and the Unfinished Critique of Political Economy*, New York: Monthly Review Press, pp. 217–55.
———. (2020), 'Marx's Theory of Metabolism in the Age of Global Ecological Crisis', *Historical Materialism*, vol. 28, n. 2: 3–24.
York, Richard, and Clark, Brett (2008), 'Rifts and Shifts: Getting to the Root of Environmental Crises', *Monthly Review*, vol. 60, n. 6: 13–24.

CHAPTER 6

Marx and Environmental Catastrophe

Gregory Claeys

6.1 Introduction

Let me begin with a brief review of where we are today vis-à-vis the prospect of environmental catastrophe. As anyone who follows the woeful litany of environmental reports knows, the news has gotten much worse in the past two years or so. Humanity now faces a dire predicament in the coming decades, with the genuine prospect of the extinction of our species within this century, indeed possibly sooner. Here is why:

The dominant narrative of planetary warming from Rio (1992) to Paris (2016), with 1.5–2 °C increases regarded as 'tolerable', has been proven to be completely misleading. With current temperature rises averaging about 1 °C since the Industrial Revolutionwe are witnessing the melting of the polar icecaps (in the Arctic warming is at 2.2 °C) and the world's glaciers; the warming of the oceans, and consequent water shortages; extreme heat-waves and forest fires; desertification; the loss of many animal and insect species, and much else. Emissions are still rising. Far worse, we now face temperature increases of perhaps 4–5 °C as early as 2050. The Siberian tundra is melting, with billions of tons of methane soon to be released. The consequence of this is startling: this is one of

G. Claeys (✉)
University of London, London, UK

M. Musto (ed.), *Rethinking Alternatives with Marx*, Marx, Engels, and Marxisms, https://doi.org/10.1007/978-3-030-81764-0_6

the most feared potential tipping points. These developments imply not just humanity's possible, but its likely elimination. The planet will burn, and we will likely be exterminated fighting over the charred remnants.

The obvious conclusion is that the patterns of production, distribution and consumption which have emerged since the mid-eighteenth century have to be superseded, and rapidly too. Besides moving immediately away from fossil-fuel consumption, reforesting the world, reducing our population, and other practical measures to cope with the immediate effects of global warming, we need fundamentally to alter our relationship to commodities. Current patterns of consumption would require 1.7 planets to sustain: if we are all to have a middle class standard of living, five planets would be required. The argument for frugality is thus irrefutable. Ultra-clean renewable energy will not save us from certain destruction: we must reduce our consumption of many resources.

Rousseau or Gandhi might seem likely thinkers to consult in this emergency. The issue immediately before us here, however, is how Marx fits into the solution to these problems. Can Marx be legitimately construed as a proto-environmentalist thinker, and a theorist of post-consumer society, or do other aspects of his thought apply to these problems today? In my own view there is sufficient ambiguity in Marx's theory of needs to permit an environmentalist interpretation of his ideas, but it is clearly stretching the point. Here I will illustrate this ambiguity briefly; then illuminate some of its reception history, especially in the USSR; and then reconsider our situation today. We will see that other areas of Marx's thought also provide some insight into our present condition.

6.2 Marx

The ambiguity I have suggested that we find in Marx respecting environmental philosophy relates to his theory of needs. As is well known, Marx in the 'Paris Manuscripts' presents a theory of alienation which hints at a potential reunification of humanity with nature. He also offers in various writings of this period an account of the system of commerce as promoting alienation, where money leads man to regard 'his will, his activity and his relation to other men as a power independent of him and them'. In commerce people do not see each other as human, but as means of effecting self-enrichment. So 'things lose the significance of human, personal property'. Exchange, however, ought to be 'equivalent to *species-activity* and species-spirit, the real, conscious and true mode of existence which is *social* activity and social enjoyment'. And here too Marx asserted that 'Assume *man* to be *man* and his relationship to the world to be a human one: then you can exchange love only for love, trust for trust, etc.'[1] This idea, which is often linked to romanticism, implies that human relations can only be satisfactory where the mediation of money does not pervert them. It also implies that the satisfaction of basic needs must be balanced off with our desire for sociability, or 'species-activity', later more often construed in terms of 'solidarity'.[2] This sociability, together with a shift from private to public affluence, is to my mind one of the most important parts of any future programme and any radical Green New Deal.[3]

In his later writings, Marx assumes that while a basic range of material needs exists, most needs are shaped by circumstances, rather than being fixed. Such needs obviously proliferate under capitalism. In the *Communist Manifesto* (1848) Marx and Engels proposed that the new society would be built upon the highest stage of development of the old. Industry would have reached the capacity to meet the needs of the majority, provided a just distribution was introduced. Many earlier utopian ideals—and Marx was clearly a utopian in the common language meaning of the term—had been predicated upon restraining needs along Spartan and puritan lines. But Marx was no Spartan. He acknowledged that capitalism gave rise to 'new wants, requiring for their satisfaction the products of distant lands and climes'.[4] At various points, and particularly against Sergei Nechayev, he denounced *Kasernenkommunismus* or 'barracks-communism' as 'an absurd plan of practical organisation' of 'communal eating, communal sleeping, assessors and offices regulating

[1] Karl Marx, *Economic and Philosophic Manuscripts of 1844*, MECW, vol. 3, pp. 212–13, 216–17, 326.

[2] See Gregory Claeys, *Marx and Marxism* (London: Penguin Books, 2018), pp. 103–4.

[3] See Gregory Claeys, *After Consumerism: Utopianism for a Dying Planet* (Princeton: Princeton University Press, forthcoming).

[4] Karl Marx and Friedrich Engels, *Manifesto of the Communist Party*, MECW, vol. 6, p. 488. On anti-urbanism in the USSR in this period, see S. Frederick Starr, 'Visionary Town Planning During the Cultural Revolution', in: Sheila Fitzpatrick (ed.), *Cultural Revolution in Russia, 1928–1931* (Bloomington: Indiana University Press, 1978), pp. 207–40.

education, production, consumption, in a word, all social activity'.[5] Nor did Marx ever oppose any 'new needs' the proletariat might eventually embrace following the abolition of capitalism. The *Grundrisse* observed in passing that 'what earlier appeared as luxury is now necessary, and [...] so-called luxury needs appear e.g. as a necessity for the most natural industry rooted in the most basic natural need'.[6] There was no reason to presume this pattern would alter under socialism. The eventual goal of rewarding people on the principle, 'to each according to his needs' is thus only superficially simple, since needs are not fixed but mutable.

The ambiguity Marx leaves us with, then, is that his account of needs can be broadly described as a mixture of Stoic, republican, and romantic components, in which a slavish devotion to the consumption of commodities would clearly be impossible. But he also provides us with an account of expanding, potentially unlimited needs. Moreover, Marx does not rule out a post-revolutionary expansion of needs, such that the proletariat, having left penury behind and achieved a comfortable standard of living, would continue to pursue greater material comforts as well as higher and more refined cultural ends. The proletariat might become bourgeoisified, and moreover its needs too might become limitless. This ambiguity can be illustrated by briefly considering the history of consumerism in the most important Marxist experiment, the Soviet Union.

6.3 Consumption in the USSR

Both of these possibilities in fact developed in the USSR. Certainly at the outset of the revolution there were those who regarded the model proletarian as a 'paragon of virtue [...] a hero of virtue, who did not indulge in the imminent gratification of his needs'.[7] Many of the early revolutionaries adopted, in Hans Jonas's terms, 'a credo of public morality' which

[5] Karl Marx and Friedrich Engels, 'The Alliance of Socialist Democracy and the International Working Men's Association. Report and Documents Published by Decision of the Hague Congress of the International', MECW, vol. 23, p. 543. He associated such ideas with August Willich, a revolutionary rival amongst the German exiles, as well as Bakunin.

[6] Karl Marx, *Economic Manuscripts of 1857–61*, MECW, vol. 28, p. 451.

[7] Timo Vihavainen, 'Consumerism and the Soviet Project', in: Timo Vihavainen and Elena Bogdanova (eds.), *Communism and Consumerism: The Soviet Alternative to the Affluent Society* (Leiden: Brill, 2015), p. 29.

involved 'a spirit of frugality, alien to capitalist society', but commensurate with the aim of living 'for the whole' and thus involving asceticism and self-denial.[8] Yet the suspicion always existed that such asceticism was always temporary, required until the revolution had been won and plenty achieved, and then dispensable. At the very least its status was ambiguous. And the presence of a cult of technology within Bolshevism, with the promise of electrification and ever-expanding machinery, railways, tractors, tanks, and spaceships, belies any belief that growth would in principle be limited under socialism.

The trajectory of the development of a conflict between these two ideals can be easily traced. When the Bolsheviks seized power in 1917, luxury stood for the ostentatious extravagance of the bourgeoisie and aristocracy. Fashion was as such based on novelty, which bound it inexorably to waste and to conspicuous consumption. Luxury meant someone else had to labour harder. At least initially it was expected that the new Soviet Man and Woman would rise above such petty indulgences. Youth was regarded as extremely pliable, and an entirely new being was to be constructed, particularly among Party members. The Komsomol, or Communist Youth, formed in late 1918, was to be the breeding ground of the new type. Its new ideal was rooted in self-sacrifice, and a constant 'struggle' to make the Revolution succeed, often couched in military terms of a desire for 'strength, endurance, toughness and dexterity'. Austerity in personal dress and habits was necessary to attain such virtues. Many thought an 'undisciplined, slovenly appearance' (leather jackets, short hair for both sexes, patched shoes) exemplified the purity of their revolutionary morality. It was necessary to learn how to 'speak Bolshevik', and to look and act accordingly. But early on this also sometimes meant adopting pseudo-proletarian affections, such as speaking in street slang or wearing working class overalls (and even long hair and dark glasses), much as the student revolutionaries of the 1860s and 1870s had done (and those of the 1960s would do).[9]

In the communes where most Komsomols lived by the 1930s, daily life was strictly regimented, sometimes down to specifying the particular

[8] Hans Jonas, *The Imperative of Responsibility: In Search of an Ethics for the Technological Age* (Chicago: University of Chicago Press, 1984), p. 147.

[9] Anne E. Gorsuch, *Youth in Revolutionary Russia: Enthusiasts, Bohemians, Delinquents* (Bloomington: Indiana University Press, 2000), pp. 16, 89–90.

hours at which newspapers were to be read.[10] Here selfish interests were to give way to the common good, whether it meant sharing food, not drinking excessively, or having sex outside marriage. Frugality was the order of the day. Women were condemned for wearing make-up or gold jewellery, or anything which 'made you stand out from the larger working masses'. For amusement there were political and scientific lectures, and meetings—as many as fifty a month. We are not far off here, at points, from the revival of the Spartan model, now compounded with Bolshevik bureaucracy. Popular works portrayed them indeed as 'neither indulgent hedonists nor calculating utilitarians, but fiery soldiers of their cause' who 'very much looked like puritan moralists'.[11] Mere pleasure-seeking was 'bourgeois' (*burzhui*), and as such contemptible, especially for Party members and Young Communists. As late as 1960 indeed the official view was that 'Communism excludes those narrow-minded people for whom the highest goal is to acquire every possible luxurious object'.[12] Debates about consumption thus overlapped with a narrative which sought to abolish private life as such, or at least to merge it as closely as possible with public life, which is the ideal we associate with Stalin and the construction of communal flats for much of the urban population.[13]

The most substantial alteration in these ideals came about in the mid-1930s, when Stalin acknowledged that the surge in demand for consumer goods during the NEP period (1921–1928) remained powerful. Soon 'the public's interest in material goods was immense'.[14] After 1935 Stakhanovites, exceedingly productive 'shock workers', were offered luxuries like cars as inducements to labour—they were rarely available otherwise for anything other than official use, and were highly prized, despite

[10] Ibid., pp. 56, 89.

[11] Timo Vihavainen, 'The Spirit of Consumerism in Russia and the West', in: *Communism and Consumerism*, p. 15.

[12] Quoted in David Crowley and Susan E. Reid, 'Introduction: Pleasures in Socialism?', in: David Crowley and Susan E. Reid (eds.), *Pleasures in Socialism: Leisure and Luxury in the Eastern Bloc* (Chicago: Northwestern University Press, 2010), p. 23.

[13] Adele Marie Barker, 'The Culture Factory: Theorizing the Popular in the Old and New Russia', in: Adele Marie Barker (ed.), *Consuming Russia: Popular Culture, Sex, and Society Since Gorbachev* (Durham, NC: Duke University Press, 1999), pp. 32–3.

[14] Timo Vihavainen, 'The Spirit of Consumerism in Russia and the West', in: *Communism and Consumerism*, p. 4.

the great cost of maintaining them.[15] They were also given costly clothing at workers' congresses; one woman who earned nine times the average wage vowed to spend her surplus entirely on clothing, including ivory-coloured shoes and a crêpe de chine dress.[16] Variation in clothing in particular was widely desired, though the mass production of clothing also accompanied a desire to see ethnic groups like the Uzbeks dress like 'cultured' Muscovites, as A. I. Mikoian put it in 1936.[17] When Stalin proclaimed in 1936 that 'life has become more joyous', he meant that abundance had been achieved, and Soviet papers proclaimed: 'We endorse beauty, smart clothes, chic coiffures, manicures [...] Girls should be attractive. Perfume and make-up belong to the "must" of a good Comsomol girl [...] Clean shaving is mandatory for a Comsomol boy'. A magazine named *Fashion* opened, and dancing became all the rage. Then came a backlash against 'promiscuity', and arrests of young women for having an 'immoral appearance' for flaunting the new fashions.[18] The more puritanical and the more libertine aspects of the revolution, once again, danced together in a dialectic.

From this time onwards the USSR engaged in a contest with the United States to provide a potentially endless array of consumer goods. The retreat from asceticism was largely a post-war and Cold War phenomenon. By the 1950s socialistfashion began to emerge, though a taste for things American (especially cars, music and dance styles) also intensified. (Snack bars were called *amerikanki*, and ice-cream bars were also regarded as 'American').[19] This was notably evident during the 1957 Festival of Youth and Students, when some 30,000 foreigners descended on Moscow. Many must have gone home clothed only in roubles, for a roaring trade developed in their apparel, many of the buyers being Young

[15] Even as late as 1980, only 15% of Soviet citizens owned cars.

[16] Djurdja Bartlett, *FashionEast: The Spectre That Haunted Communism* (Boston: MIT Press, 2010), p. 68.

[17] Amy E. Randall, *The Soviet Dream World of Retail Trade and Consumption in the 1930s* (New York: Palgrave Macmillan), pp. 42–3.

[18] Nicholas S. Timasheff, *The Great Retreat: The Growth and Decline of Communism in Russia* (New York: E.P. Dutton & Co., 1946), pp. 317–20.

[19] Jukka Gronow, *Caviar with Champagne: Common Luxury and the Ideals of the Good Life in Stalin's Russia* (Oxford: Berg, 2003), p. 116.

Communists or *Komsomols*.[20] The resulting gap between promise and reality meant that 'the inability to fulfil the needs of consumers would become a major factor in destroying the Soviet regime, perhaps even the chief one'.[21] This implies that the Soviet paradigm mirrored that of the West in assuming that mass consumption was an inevitable by-product of industrial society, no less applicable to socialism than to capitalism. A similar process can be traced in the eastern European states incorporated into the Soviet bloc from 1945–1989. Whatever their possibility of maintaining an internal socialist ideal of restrained needs, the manifest desire to attain a constantly tantalising western standard of living, particularly as viewed through American commodities, made competition with the West in this area inevitable. The possibility of a systematic restraint of needs was therefore virtually ruled out from the outset.

6.4 The Problem Today

So where do we or ought we to stand today on this issue? How should we contemplate what appears for the later moderns to imply an unacceptably bleak and harsh transformation, to a regime of scarcity and regimented rationing akin to wartime? We cannot, some suppose, rise to any plea for Spartan civic virtue without falling into the pit of totalitarianism. We are ourselves—I speak here in terms of the western middle classes—so far and so deeply sculpted by the possession and consumption of commodities as to not be able to detach ourselves any longer from the process. We revere greed, we accept the normality of conspicuous consumption, and of planned obsolescence. We want more and newer, and better, and faster. The primitive holds no fascination for us: Sparta is dead for good. We cannot imagine a world in which instant gratification amidst a cornucopia of plenty will not take place. We argue instead about a fairer and just distribution of its delights, not the question of their further extension ad infinitum.

And yet we must contemplate the possibility of a finite world, in terms of both population and resources. To reduce our wants to something

[20] Larissa Zakharova, 'How and What to Consume: Patterns of Soviet Clothing Consumption in the 1950s and 1960s', in: Vihavainen and Bogdanova (eds.), *Communism and Consumerism*, pp. 104–5.

[21] Timo Vihavainen and Elena Bogdanova (eds.), 'About This Book', in: *Communism and Consumerism*, pp. xi, xviii.

approximating rational needs, we must conceive of a notion of self which is centred not on possession and having but on being and experiencing, and which places a priority on life lived in a manner which is qualitatively superior to the present. For there is no doubt that we cannot move sharply and rapidly away from consumerism unless we promise some compensatory advantage in the new society.

Let me now sketch just how we might conceive of this advantage. The first premise I will ask you to accept is that the consumerist mentality I have described, while 'normal' to us, is abnormal and even pathological in historical terms. Most societies have not embraced novelty, rapidity, and the definition of self based on commodity consumption. If our lifestyle is deviant, it also demonstrates many qualities akin to a serious illness. Societies which revere consumption routinely report greater degrees of anxiety and unhappiness than those which are more balanced in this respect (think of the index rankings of the United States and Britain compared to Scandinavia). Studies similarly indicate that societies which give greater stress to the value of shopping and consuming also experience higher levels of alienation, loneliness, and isolation than those which do not. Here we see the disadvantages of preferring having over being.

So how then can we compensate for the obviously reduced standard of living which we face in the future? Let us consider—in an extremely compressed manner—eight means of achieving this.

Firstly, while the private luxuries of the few will be suppressed, the public luxuries of the many can be maintained, in the form of free public transport, museums, theatres, concert venues, pleasure gardens, and the like. Yachts will disappear, along with private jets, corporate helicopters, and SUVs, even before petrol and diesel vehicles are banned. Private art collections will be housed in public galleries.

Secondly, we will soon be moving towards a dramatic reduction of work-time, firstly to a four-day week, then three. With the reduction of work-time will come the reduction of stress at work. A minimum sustainable wage will also be introduced within a few years.

Thirdly, our cities—where some 70% of humanity will live by 2100—will be remodelled in order to eliminate pollution and maximize user-friendly spaces. Subsidies for many more social spaces will encourage meeting and greeting on a scale hitherto impossible. Since social relationships are probably 'the single greatest cause' of our individual sense of well-being, we need to redesign our urban spaces in order to maximize their sociability potential.[22]

Fourthly, we will limit the consumption of commodities in a number of ways. Advertising will be drastically reduced if not eliminated. Planned obsolescence will be replaced by production for extended periods. A maximum will be placed on the ownership of property and some goods will be rationed and restricted. Waste and packaging will be reduced. Local sources for food in particular will be prioritized. Vegetarianism will be encouraged. Renting and borrowing will be given priority over buying.

Fifthly, when we reduce population growth we obviously reduce demand for commodities. A one-child policy would be most desirable, though its political feasibility is unlikely.

Sixthly, we will endeavour to reduce the tempo of life in other ways. The slow food movement indicates the way forward here. We need to reduce our expectations that speed of delivery and the volume of the product are the ultimate goals in consumption. This process, sometimes referred to as the McDonaldization of society,[23] places a premium on quantity over quality, and haste ('fast food') and instant gratification over sociability and delayed satisfaction.

Seventhly, we need to reduce the impact of the fashion movement on consumption, again perhaps by legislating against advertising as such, impossible though this sounds. This is bound up with cultivating a sense of luxophobia, or the definition of individuals by their possession and exhibition of luxury goods. A fine contempt for such excesses should do the trick. The passion for emulation and the obsessive display of social rank can be tempered, by ostracizing their extreme manifestations, as well as by sumptuary laws.

Eighthly, of course, we have to pay for this transition to sustainability, which will cost many trillions of dollars. This can be done in three ways: via a wealth tax, which sets a maximum on personal wealth (to a limit of perhaps $10 million); then a personal income tax which rises to 100% above a certain limit, say $200,000 per annum. Then finally we need to make the international financial system completely transparent, abolish

[22] Michael Argyle, *The Psychology of Happiness* (London: Routledge, 2001), p. 71. On this theme see, for example, Edward W. Soja, *Postmodern Geographies: The Reassertion of Space in Critical Social Theory* (London: Verso, 1989); and Edward W. Soja, *Thirdspace: Journeys to Los Angeles and Other Real-and-Imagined Spaces* (Oxford: Blackwell, 1996).

[23] George Ritzer, *The McDonaldization of Society* (London: Sage, 2019).

all 'off-shore' tax havens, equalize corporation tax across the globe, and increase it as well.

Marx's relevance to this potential programme is pretty obvious. Three areas in particular can be stressed.

Most obviously, firstly, much of the existing capitalist system will have to be replaced in the near future, not because it is exploitative, which is reason enough, but because it is destroying the planet, which is the most compelling argument of all. Marx remains our most important anti-capitalist writer. Much subsequent Marxist thinking on the command economy is relevant to the international mechanisms of control which a radical Green New Deal will necessarily require. The centralization of green redevelopment, and a supervisory international body to which sovereignty has been ceded by all nations, also have Marxian precedents. This is not to say that Marx should be the end-point of such discussions. But he is clearly the starting-point.

Secondly, the coming revolution will establish a much more egalitarian regime, since it will recognize that inequality is a leading cause of over-consumption (1% of the population produce as many carbon emissions as the poorest 50% of the world's population). The basic trend in Marx's thought was towards the support of an egalitarianism which was not mathematical, but eliminated extreme inequalities. Some differentiation of rank and inequality in wealth will inevitably take place in any society. But the present concentration of wealth is immensely harmful, as it was in the early stages of capitalism.

Thirdly, in seeking to supersede that commodification of life which results from capitalism, and produces a desire for superfluous consumption, Marx's theories of alienation and commodification remain extremely relevant. Obviously, these were sketchy, and often interwoven within critiques of other aspects of capitalism. There is some indication, however, that Marx continued broadly to adhere to his early critique of alienation in his later works. These can assist us in exonerating the humanist critique of a money—and commodity-centred society, and creating an alternative to it.

These measures, then, imply a shift in character not only towards sociability, but away from the all-encompassing ideal of consumption which has intoxicated us for the past two centuries and more. This means ending not only planned obsolescence of quality, but, as the great pioneer in this field, Vance Packard, stressed, eliminating obsolescence of desirability as well—the will to want the new.[24] We need to reduce our sense of self-identity as a reliance on having a choice of consumer goods. We must acknowledge that 'Material possessions serve as pacifiers for the self-induced helplessness we have created'.[25] This 'terminal materialism' has only developed in the last two centuries, and is not a result of 'the human condition' or our relationship with nature as such. Social solidaritycan only grow where an attachment to objects diminishes. As Georg Simmel indicated, and we can now prove clearly, there is less need for such an attachment to objects where warm, emotionally-satisfying personal relationships play a major part of our life.[26] There is no reason to presume that a substantial reduction in choice in consumer goods will make us proportionately less happy (and even if it did, we have to be willing to make this choice too).

There are precedents here for the transformation I am suggesting in a number of past rebellions against capitalism. Most recently the counterculture of the 1960s widely suggested that a rejection of a consumer-centred lifestyle was central to any qualitative movement forward for humanity, and effectively proposed the type of substitution of sociability for excess consumption which I am suggesting here. While the coming counterculture will necessarily vary from this model in many particulars, its central emphasis, anti-consumerism, and the prioritising of sociability over commodity-centred identity, is likely to be the same. The plea for a 'simple life' has been a recurrent theme in almost every second or third generation since the beginning of the Industrial Revolution, in the 1790s, in the 1840s, in the 1890s, in the 1930s, and again in the 1950s and 1960s. 'Back to the land' movements have often resulted from these reactions to modernity, as have nostalgic throwbacks to pre-modern, agricultural habits centring on 'authentic' patterns of consumption and social relations. Each generation recalls the efforts of its immediate predecessors, and then commences anew. With the decline of the small farm ideal, of republican simplicity, and of peasantries world-wide, such reversions now seem much less likely than ever. We no longer desire to flee the city, and small-scale community life holds little attraction to us. If we are to

[24] Vance Packard, *The Waste Makers* (London: Longmans, 1961), p. 69.

[25] Mihaly Csikszentmihalyi and Eugene Rochberg-Halton, *The Meaning of Things: Domestic Symbols and the Self* (Cambridge: Cambridge University Press, 1981), p. 230.

[26] Csikszentmihalyi and Rochberg-Halton, *The Meaning of Things*, p. 163.

simplify our lives in the twenty-first century, it will be largely in cities. The coming utopian simplicity will be urban, thus, paradoxical as this may seem.

No one can imagine, however, that the process of decommodifying our character will be easy. But if we do not adopt it voluntarily, we will have it forced upon us by extreme scarcity. The advantages of the former course of action are abundantly obvious. We have only a brief opportunity—perhaps ten years—to begin this revolution. The consequences of leaving things as they are, are too horrifying to contemplate as an alternative. It is clear, however, that relinquishing unsustainable consumption can only succeed if compensation is offered to the majority for the loss of pleasure which consumer society notionally offers. As Paul Wachtel contends, however, we can learn 'to think beyond material goods as the defining essence of life and to focus instead on the quality of our relations with others; on the clarity and intensity of our experiences; on intimacy, sensual and aesthetic experiences, and emotional freedom; and on the ethical, spiritual, and communal dimensions that give the entire enterprise meaning'.[27] This implies a new hedonism which will serve to compensate for the new asceticism. Once we recover from the fright of acknowledging what fate lies before us if we do not embrace this outlook, the possibility of hope is renewed.

6.5 Conclusion

Marx retains great power as a visionary and utopian who foresaw the possibility of relieving humanity of the oppressive exploitation and coercion which have made the everyday lives of so many a misery throughout human history. This vision retains great value today. Marx also anticipated that technology might provide a release from drudgery. He hinted at ways of making urban life in particular more pleasant, humane, and liveable which are worth recalling today. Some of his admirers, notably William Morris, moved even further in this direction.

From a socialist viewpoint, then, and specifically Marx's, the problem of dealing with the capitalist system of ownership and exploitation remains

[27] Paul L. Wachtel, 'Alternatives to the Consumer Society', in: David A. Crocker and Toby Linden (eds.), *Ethics of Consumption: The Good Life, Justice, and Global Stewardship* (Lanham: Rowman & Littlefield, 1998), p. 199.

much the same as it was in the nineteenth century. A transfer of ownership of public utilities back to public hands needs to be followed by greater workers' control over the means of production, including cooperative management and ownership, which Marx understood to be the most important bridge to the future. Wage differentials need to be reduced dramatically. Tax havens need to be abolished. The avoidance and evasion of taxation by the wealthy and by large corporations needs to be eliminated entirely, and replaced by a completely transparent financial model in which all forms of income are publicly known (as in Norway today). The model here is that of an egalitarian, social democratic economy and polity, with full public control over both, as Marx projected in his writings on the Paris Commune in particular. In politics as well as all financial transactions, a maximum transparency is desirable to minimize corruption. There is pressure now, too, to extend the voting age to perhaps 16; to eliminate private campaign spending, and to eliminate or sharply curtail the effects of lobbying. In terms of the eventual shape of government, many would today assert that Marx was insufficiently aware of the need to maintain a separation of executive, legislative, and judicial powers, and to maintain the independence of the judiciary and press in particular. The experience of Stalinism requires no reiteration here. Marx's understanding of the reliance of all forms of power, and especially political power, upon the system of property ownership and mode of production retains undiminished authority in our assessment of such relations today. Here, perhaps, more than anywhere else, we can use Marx's assessment of capitalism's propensity to crisis, to the concentration of wealth and power, to good effect.

References

Argyle, Michael (2001), *The Psychology of Happiness*, London: Routledge.

Barker, Adele Marie (1999), 'The Culture Factory: Theorizing the Popular in the Old and New Russia', in: Adele Marie Barker (ed.), *Consuming Russia: Popular Culture, Sex, and Society Since Gorbachev*, Durham, NC: Duke University Press, pp. 12–46.

Bartlett, Djurdja (2010), *FashionEast: The Spectre That Haunted Communism*, Boston: MIT Press.

Crowley, David, and Reid, Susan E. (2010), 'Introduction: Pleasures in Socialism?', in: David Crowley and Susan E. Reid (eds.), *Pleasures in Socialism: Leisure and Luxury in the Eastern Bloc*, Chicago: Northwestern University Press, pp. 3–51.

Csikszentmihalyi, Mihaly, and Rochberg-Halton, Eugene (1981), *The Meaning of Things: Domestic Symbols and the Self*, Cambridge: Cambridge University Press.

Claeys, Gregory (forthcoming), *After Consumerism: Utopianism for a Dying Planet*, Princeton: Princeton University Press.

———. (2018), *Marx and Marxism*, London: Penguin Books.

Gorsuch, Anne E. (2000), *Youth in Revolutionary Russia: Enthusiasts, Bohemians, Delinquents*, Bloomington: Indiana University Press.

Gronow, Jukka (2003), *Caviar with Champagne: Common Luxury and the Ideals of the Good Life in Stalin's Russia*, Oxford: Berg.

Jonas, Hans (1984), *The Imperative of Responsibility: In Search of an Ethics for the Technological Age*, Chicago: University of Chicago Press.

Marx, Karl (1975), *Economic and Philosophic Manuscripts of 1844*, MECW, vol. 3, pp. 229–346.

———. (1986), *Economic Manuscripts of 1857–61*, MECW, vol. 28.

Marx, Karl, and Friedrich, Engels (1976), *Manifesto of the Communist Party*, MECW, vol. 6, pp. 477–517.

———. (1988), 'The Alliance of Socialist Democracy and the International Working Men's Association. Report and Documents Published by Decision of the Hague Congress of the International', MECW, vol. 23, pp. 454–580.

Packard, Vance (1961), *The Waste Makers*, London: Longmans.

Randall, Amy E. (2008), *The Soviet Dream World of Retail Trade and Consumption in the 1930s*, New York: Palgrave Macmillan.

Ritzer, George (2019), *The McDonaldization of Society*, London: Sage.

Soja, Edward W. (1989), *Postmodern Geographies: The Reassertion of Space in Critical Social Theory*, London: Verso.

———. (1996), *Thirdspace: Journeys to Los Angeles and Other Real-and-Imagined Spaces*, Oxford: Blackwell.

Starr, S. Frederick (1978), 'Visionary Town Planning During the Cultural Revolution', in: Sheila Fitzpatrick (ed.), *Cultural Revolution in Russia, 1928–1931*, Bloomington: Indiana University Press, pp. 207–40.

Timasheff, Nicholas S. (1946), *The Great Retreat: The Growth and Decline of Communism in Russia*, New York: EP Dutton & Co.

Vihavainen, Timo (2015), 'Consumerism and the Soviet Project', in: Timo Vihavainen and Elena Bogdanova (eds.), *Communism and Consumerism: The Soviet Alternative to the Affluent Society*, Leiden: Brill, pp. 28–67.

———. (2015), 'The Spirit of Consumerism in Russia and the West', in: Timo Vihavainen and Elena Bogdanova (eds.), *Communism and Consumerism: The Soviet Alternative to the Affluent Society*, Leiden: Brill, pp. 1–27.

Vihavainen, Timo, and Bogdanova, Elena (2015), 'About This Book', in: Timo Vihavainen and Elena Bogdanova (eds.), *Communism and Consumerism: The Soviet Alternative to the Affluent Society*, Leiden: Brill, pp. x–xxiv.

Wachtel, Paul L. (1998), 'Alternatives to the Consumer Society', in: David A. Crocker and Toby Linden (eds.), *Ethics of Consumption: The Good Life, Justice, and Global Stewardship*, Lanham: Rowman & Littlefield, pp. 198–217.

Zakharova, Larissa (2015), 'How and What to Consume: Patterns of Soviet Clothing Consumption in the 1950s and 1960s', in: Timo Vihavainen and Elena Bogdanova (eds.), *Communism and Consumerism: The Soviet Alternative to the Affluent Society*, Leiden: Brill, pp. 85–112.

CHAPTER 7

Finding a Way Out of the Anthropocene: The Theory of 'Radical Needs' and the Ecological Transition

Razmig Keucheyan

7.1 Introduction: A New Type of Crisis

Throughout its history, capitalism has undergone many crises. Today, however, it is confronted with a new type of crisis: the environmental crisis. This crisis has at least four dimensions:[1] (1) climate change, meaning the modification of long-term weather patterns; (2) resource depletion, and especially the depletion of resources crucial for the functioning of modern societies, such as oil and water; (3) ever-new forms of pollution; and (4) the collapse of biodiversity, in what is sometimes called the 'sixth extinction'. These four dimensions are, of course, interconnected. But they nonetheless relate to separate natural processes. What is called the 'environmental crisis' results from their combination.

[1] John McNeill, *Something New Under the Sun: An Environmental History of the 20th Century* (London: Allen Lane, 2000).

R. Keucheyan (✉)
University of Bordeaux, Bordeaux, France

M. Musto (ed.), *Rethinking Alternatives with Marx*, Marx, Engels, and Marxisms, https://doi.org/10.1007/978-3-030-81764-0_7

All these patterns are caused by human activity: they are thus 'anthropic'. 'Anthropocene' is a concept often used in current debates about the environmental crisis, with reference to the age in which humanity itself became a geological force.[2] Even before the nineteenth century, indeed throughout human history, societies have often damaged their environments, for instance by depleting natural resources or damaging ecosystems. But these 'local' environment crises are fundamentally different from the current global one.

It is crucial to understand that it is not human activity per se that causes these processes. Rather, it is capitalism that does so, and especially capitalism in its industrial form.[3] The industrial revolutioncould not have taken place without fossil fuels: coal, gas, and oil.[4] Without the fossil energy system, there could not have been industrialization—in Great Britain and Europe, where this process began, or in any of the other places where it spread over the following two centuries. Fossil energies, and the logic of productivism and consumerism to which they give rise, are the main causes of the environmental crisis. Thus, in order to understand this crisis, we need to analyze the dynamic of industrial capitalism, and especially its globalization to new regions.

7.2 Ecological Marxism

What does this have to do with Marx and Marxism? It can be argued that new readings of Marx and the Marxist tradition tend to emerge when humanity is faced with new challenges.[5] This has been true since Marx's death, throughout the twentieth century, and it remains true today. Hence, since the 1980s the environmental crisis has led a group of Marxist thinkers, mostly based in the English-speaking world, but also

[2] Christophe Bonneuil and Jean-Baptiste Fressoz, *The Shock of the Anthropocene* (London: Verso, 2017).

[3] This is why certain authors have suggested replacing 'anthropocene' with 'capitalocene'. See Jason W. Moore (ed.), *Anthropocene or Capitalocene? Nature, History, and the Crisis of Capitalism* (Oakland: PM Press, 2016).

[4] Elmar Altvater, 'The Social and Natural Environment of Fossil Capitalism', *Socialist Register*, vol. 43 (2007): 37–59.

[5] For a version of this argument, see André Tosel, *Le marxisme du 20e siècle* (Paris: Syllepse, 2009).

in Latin America and Europe, to elaborate what they call an 'Ecological Marxism', or 'Eco-Marxism'.[6]

Ecological Marxismcan be defined as the use of Marx's and other Marxists' categories and insights to make sense of the environmental crisis. Marxism is a theory of capitalism, indeed one of the most sophisticated ones at our disposal. If, as we have said, the environmental crisis is the outcome of this system, then it is clear that Marxism has a lot to contribute to the understanding of its dynamic. Authors like James O'Connor (in 1988 founder of the leading journal *Capitalism Nature Socialism*), Ted Benton, Elmar Altvater, Paul Burkett, Michael Löwy, Jason Moore, Andreas Malm, among others, belong to this group. They form one of the most interesting currents of Marxism today.

The purpose of this article is to contribute to this collective effort to develop an Ecological Marxism.[7] However, it will do so by exploring a problem that Ecological Marxists have not yet tackled, namely the problem of the satisfaction of 'needs' during the ecological transition. First, we should outline what this problem is, in its most general form. In the context of the ecological transition that is going to take place in the years and decades to come, societies will not be able to satisfy all needs. The reason for this is that over the past two centuries, capitalism has driven a proliferation of needs, real or—mostly—artificial, especially through advertising[8] and the 'financialization of daily life'.[9] A significant part of these needs is unsustainable from an environmental standpoint, because their satisfaction puts too much pressure on the environment, in terms of resource extraction or various forms of pollution.

To quote a well-known observation: in 2019, the Global Footprint Network calculated if all the world's citizens had the same environmental footprint as the citizens of the United States, we would need 5 planet

[6] For an introduction, see Matthias Lievens, 'Towards an Eco-Marxism', *Radical Philosophy Review*, vol. 13 (2010), n. 1: 1–17.

[7] This article summarizes certain arguments developed in Razmig Keucheyan, *Les Besoins artificiels. Comment sortir du consumérisme* (Paris: La Découverte, 2019).

[8] Hannah Holleman, Inger L. Stole, John Bellamy Foster, and Robert W. McChesney, 'The Sales Effort and Monopoly Capitalism', *Monthly Review*, vol. 60 (2009), n. 11: 1–23.

[9] Randy Martin, *Financialization of Daily Life* (Philadelphia: Temple University Press, 2002).

Earths.[10] 3 would be required if everyone lived like Germans, 2.7 if they lived like the French, and 2.2 if they lived like the Chinese. Yet we only have one planet. Some kind of change, whether forced or deliberately chosen, is thus bound to take place. This change—some of us call it a revolution—will be either chaotic or planed. When this happens, every society will be faced with a simple question: which needs do we keep on satisfying, and which needs should we no longer satisfy, to alleviate the burden on ecosystems? Moreover, who decides? Who is sovereign when it comes to environment policy making? Is it the state, citizens themselves, cities, international organizations?

This article argues that we cannot answer these questions without a theory of needs: a theory of what human needsin their diversity and complexity are, and of how individual and collective needs come to be intertwined. Marx and Marxism are a good starting point to elaborate such a theory of needs. They don't answer all possible questions, of course, but they do offer a general framework to think about them. Again, new readings of Marx and the Marxist tradition take place when humanity is faced with new challenges. The problem of needs in the ecological transition is precisely such a problem.

Marx himself developed a concept of need, in several texts: the *1844 Manuscripts*, the *Critique of Hegel's Philosophy of Right*, the *German Ideology*, the *Grundrisse*, and in *Capital*. In fact, the concept of need is pervasive in Marx. To quote one famous definition of the commodity from the very beginning of *Capital*:

> A commodity is, in the first place, an object outside us, a thing that by its properties satisfies human wants of some sort or another. The nature of such wants, whether, for instance, they spring from the stomach or from fancy, makes no difference. Neither are we here concerned to know how the object satisfies these wants, whether directly as means of subsistence, or indirectly as means of production.[11]

[10] Global Footprint Network, 'Earth Overshoot Day is 29 July, the Earliest Ever', *Earth Overshoot Day*, 23 July 2019, https://www.overshootday.org/newsroom/press-release-july-2019-english/.

[11] Karl Marx, *Capital, Volume I*, MECW, vol. 35, p. 45. The German term Marx uses is 'Bedürfnis', translated into English (depending on the edition) as 'want' or 'need' ('besoin' in French).

In the Marxist tradition, Marx's insights were developed over the 1960s and 1970s by two authors in particular: André Gorz and Agnes Heller. Marx, Gorz and Heller form the backbone of what we will call *the Marxist theory of needs*. Obviously, each of them has their own specific approach to the issue of defining needs. But for the purposes of this article, we will combine them. We can learn a lot from these approaches, in order to begin answering our question: which needs should we satisfy during the ecological transition, and which needs should we give up?

The article will be organized around Gorz and Heller's theory of needs. It will also refer to certain crucial aspects of Marx's own theory. It will conclude with a few reflections on the actuality of the Marxist theory of needs for our present political conjuncture. The concept of need is not only an analytical tool, but a political one. It helps us understand how the critique of capitalism is rooted in the contradictions of capitalism itself.

7.3 André Gorz and Agnes Heller in Context

As mentioned above, André Gorz and Agnes Heller developed their theory of needs in the 1960s and 1970s. But they did so in two different types of societies. Gorz was French.[12] A long-time collaborator of Jean-Paul Sartre's journal *Les Temps modernes*, he was influenced by existentialism. Later in his life, he was also in sustained contact with certain members of the Italian *operaismo* current, especially Toni Negri, who was in exile in France in the 1980s. Gorz was one of the main representatives in France of an anti-authoritarian, anti-Stalinist, left, and he was also a pioneer of political ecology. Until his death in 2007 he tried to understand the transformations of capitalism, and their effects on society. He developed his theory of needs in several writings, among them *La Morale de l'histoire* (1959) and *Stratégie ouvrière et néocapitalisme* (1964).

The historical context in which he elaborated his theory of needs was the post-war economic boom in Western Europe and the United States (the 'Trente glorieuses', as they are called in France). With the rise of 'consumer society', capitalism constantly puts new commodities on the

[12] Willy Gianinazzi, *André Gorz, une vie* (Paris: la Découverte, 2016).

market, which have to be consumed.[13] In doing so, capitalism creates new needs, material and/or symbolic. The post-war economic boom saw capitalism at its most productivist and consumerist. This proliferation of commodities raised the question of the legitimacy of the underlying needs. Are the needs satisfied by these new commodities 'real' needs? Are they false needs, alienated needs? Thus, the starting point for Gorz's theory of needs is the rise of consumer society and its effects on individual and collective subjectivities.

Agnes Heller was Hungarian.[14] A disciple of György Lukács, she was, along with Ferenc Fehér and György Márkus, a member of the 'Budapest school'.[15] She wrote in the context of a communist country. In a planned economy, a bureaucracy decides what and how much to produce. In other words, it decides which needs to satisfy. This raises two questions. Firstly, how does this bureaucracy know which needs to satisfy? The answer is that it often doesn't, in other words planning is mostly top-down, and not bottom-up. Heller would come to qualify the USSR, like the other countries of the Eastern Bloc as a *dictatorship over needs*.[16] And a crucial problem that the planned economies couldn't resolve during the twentieth century was: how to gather and centralize information so as to satisfy the needs of the people, without waste or shortages?[17]

Hence the second question: what legitimacy does the bureaucracy have to decide which needs to satisfy? Why should bureaucrats decide which colour of shoes people should wear, or where they should go for their vacations? Again, the answer is: its legitimacy was traditionally weak. In sum, in planned economies, economic information is often imperfect, and legitimacy is fragile. The decision on whether to satisfy a need is not taken by the individual. Rather, it is taken by economic institutions, most of the time dysfunctional and authoritarian ones. Consequently, for

[13] For a history of this period through the prism of consumption, see Lizabeth Cohen, *A Consumer's Republic: The Politics of Mass Consumption in Postwar America* (New York: Vintage Books, 2003).

[14] Agnes Heller, *La valeur du hasard. Ma vie* (Paris: Rivages, 2020).

[15] André Tosel, 'The Late Lukács and the Budapest School', in: Jacques Bidet and Eustache Kouvélakis (eds.), *Critical Companion to Contemporary Marxism* (Leiden: Brill, 2008), pp. 163–73.

[16] Ferenc Feher, Agnes Heller, and György Markus, *Dictatorship over Needs* (London: Palgrave Macmillan, 1983).

[17] Michael Ellman, *Socialist Planning* (Cambridge: Cambridge University Press, 2014).

reasons different from Gorz's own, Heller was interested in the question of defining needs, and of determining what a legitimate need is, as opposed to an artificial one. In 1976, she published *The Theory of Need in Marx*, one of the greatest Marxist books written in that period.[18]

One aspect common to Gorz and Heller's work is their interest in the young Marx. During the 1960s and 1970s, many Marxist authors, both East and West, turned back to the concept of alienation.[19] Such was the case of Henri Lefebvre, Guy Debord, Jacques Ellul, and Jean Baudrillard, just to quote a few names from the French intellectual field. These thinkers were greatly influenced by Marx's *1844 Manuscripts*, and also by György Lukács's *History and Class Consciousness* (1923). Alienation became an important theoretical and political issue in the 1960s and 1970s, since post-war capitalism generated material well-being, at least in the North, with impressive growth rates, but without a corresponding rise in 'spiritual' well-being. Alienation designates the gap, increasingly experienced during the 1960s and 1970s, between material and spiritual well-being. The May '68 events can be interpreted as an attempt to fill this gap, and as an expression of the 'malaise' of the younger generations in particular.

Gorz and Heller were part of the group of Marxist thinkers who wrote about alienation. However, their originality lay in the fact that thinking about alienation gradually led them to the issue of needs. What link is there between alienation and needs? Alienation can be evaluated or measured in relation to 'authentic' needs. One is alienated from an initial, non-alienated, state. Fighting alienation means finding one's way back to that state, or finally reaching it for the first time. Capitalism's creation of ever-more artificial needs is precisely what alienation amounts to. Hence, the critique of alienation rests, explicitly or implicitly, on a concept of 'authentic' needs—that is, of non-alienated needs.

The concept of needs thus allows us to combine a critique of alienation with a critique of the capitalist destruction of nature. Underlying both phenomena, indeed, is the question of 'authentic' as opposed to 'artificial' needs. What makes needs such an interesting concept today not only from an analytical, but also from a political perspective, is that it encourages us

[18] Agnes Heller, *The Theory of Need in Marx* (London: Verso, 2018).

[19] Pierre Nora, 'Aliénation', in: Anne Simonin and Hélène Clastres (eds.), *Les Idées en France, 1945–1988* (Paris: Gallimard, 1989).

to think about previously separate issues in combination. This, in turn, can encourage the social and political movements fighting on these different fronts to converge.

7.4 The First Paradox of 'Radical Needs'

So, what does Gorz and Heller's theory of needs consist of? Their starting point is a specific kind of needs. These needs are not a condition for survival—they are not absolute or vital needs,[20] like eating, breathing, sleeping, or shelter from the cold. However, though they are not absolute needs, the needs Gorz and Heller refer to are 'essential' needs, in the sense that they contribute to the definition of what most people would call a good, meaningful, life. Examples of these meaningful needs are: loving and being loved, being autonomous, creative, and free, taking part in social and political life, having a relationship with the surrounding nature.

A human being could probably survive without satisfying most of these needs. But this, indeed, would be survival, and not life. Gorz calls these needs 'qualitative' needs. Heller calls them 'radical' needs. The notion of 'radical needs' is already present in Marx. In his *Contribution to the Critique of Hegel's Philosophy of Right* (1843–1844), Marx famously says: 'Only a revolution of radical needs can be a radical revolution'.[21] Marx clearly saw that needs in general, and radical needs in particular, are not only personal. They have a political, even revolutionary, dimension.

Qualitative or radical needs rest on two paradoxes. The first goes as follows. Capitalism is an exploitative system, which causes misery and pain. But it also generates some material well-being in the long run, for significant parts of the population. Inequalities are pervasive, but this doesn't mean that capitalism is unable to lift people out of extreme forms of poverty. As economist Branko Milanovic has shown with his famous 'elephant graph', since 1988, the income of the 2% poorest people on earth, who mainly live in the global south, underwent a 20% increase, and the income of the 30% poorest people underwent an increase of between 20 and 50% (there are, obviously, many differences also within each of

[20] Stephen McLeod, 'Absolute Biological Needs', *Bioethics*, vol. 29 (2014), n. 6: 293–301.

[21] Karl Marx, *Contribution to the Critique of Hegel's Philosophy of Law*, MECW, vol. 3, p. 183.

these groups).[22] Of course, this hasn't prevented the 1% richest people becoming 70% richer during the same period. Milanovic's data is in line with Marx's argument according to which capitalism, despite its exploitative and alienating dimensions, represents a form progress compared to precapitalist socioeconomic systems.

For qualitative needs to emerge, an economic surplus has to be generated, that enables people to think about satisfying other, non-material, needs. Capitalism liberates significant parts of the population from the obligation to fight on a daily basis for their survival. Consequently, qualitative needs become more and more important as history unfolds.

However—and herein lies the paradox—as these new qualitative needs emerge, capitalism prevents their full realization. It is unable to fulfil the promise of a truly better life, as embodied by qualitative needs. Why? The division of labour it rests on shuts people in more and more limited functions and skills, thus preventing them from developing the full spectrum of human capacities. Equally, consumerism substitutes artificial, unauthentic, needs instead of more authentic ones, hence damaging subjectivities.

These qualitative or radical needs are a constitutive part of our modern selves. They make up part of the definition of what most of us would consider a good life. But even if capitalist development is the condition for their development, it cannot satisfy them fully. In fact, it prevents them from being fulfilled. This is why qualitative or radical needs are the basis for many social and political movements. 'Needs contain the seeds of revolution' ('Le besoin est révolutionnaire en germe'), as Gorz says.[23] The quest for the satisfaction of these qualitative needs sooner or later leads people to criticize the capitalist system, which prevents their realization. The history of modern social and political movements can be seen as the history of the struggles that have aimed at satisfying unsatisfied, or only partially satisfied, needs.

In seeking to define her concept of 'radical need', Heller writes of 'The consciousness of alienation, in other words radical needs'.[24] Radical needs are the 'consciousness of alienation'. Her argument is the following.

[22] Branko Milanovic, *Global Inequality: A New Approach for the Age of Globalization* (Cambridge, MA: The Belknap Press, 2016).

[23] André Gorz, *La Morale de l'histoire* (Paris: Seuil, 1959), p. 235, our translation.

[24] Heller, *The Theory of Need in Marx*, p. 94.

When you are alienated, you don't know you are—this is precisely what being alienated is. You live in ignorance of the alienation you are the victim of. However, given certain circumstances, a person or a group of persons becomes conscious of its alienated condition, or fully realizes what it had perceived only confusedly.

This consciousness doesn't abolish alienation right away. Alienation is not only a question of 'consciousness', but essentially a question of alienating social structures. However, this consciousness leads to social and political struggles, which in the shorter or longer run will transform these structures, and consequently put an end to alienation. It will also lead to the broadening of the group of people conscious of their alienated condition, and who will take part in the struggle.

In sum, radical needs are the 'engine' underlying social and political struggles. Their development is made possible by capitalism, but they cannot be fulfilled within this system. The emergence of another, postcapitalist system, is necessary for them to become real.

7.5 Between Nature and History

According to the Marxist theory of needs, needs to stand at the intersection of nature and history. This is one of the most interesting aspects of this theory. Eating, breathing and sleeping are obviously rooted in some form of human natural necessity. However, these functions are also immediately connected to historical processes. Here is a famous quote by Marx from the *Grundrisse*: 'Hunger is hunger; but hunger that is satisfied by cooked meat eaten with knife and fork differs from hunger that devours raw meat with the help of hands, nails and teeth'.[25]

In this passage, Marx recognizes the existence of absolute biological needs—that is, needs whose fulfilment is a condition for survival. Hunger is hunger, whatever the historical period or region in question. But as well as being a biological fact, this need has evolved across history. In ancient societies, it was satisfied by raw meat eaten with the hands. According to Marx, this is not the same hunger, i.e. not the same need, as the one gratified by cooked meat eaten with a knife and fork later in human history. Marx may be exaggerating a bit to make his point. But the argument is rather simple: needs have a history, they are *simultaneously* both

[25] Karl Marx, *Economic Manuscripts of 1857–1858*, MECW, vol. 28, p. 29.

biological and historical. Traditional thought opposes nature and history, whereas Marx tries to combine them.[26] This leads him to elaborate his own, innovative, definitions of both nature and history.

But what does this history of human needsconsist of? The object being consumed at least partly alters the underlying need. According to Marx, needs themselves have a history—thus what changes historically is not only the ways in which they are satisfied. Hence the idea that hunger refers to two different kinds of needs, according to the way in which it is satisfied. This argument sets Marx apart from other social-science classics who have theorized needs, for instance Norbert Elias. In *The Civilizing Process*, Elias argues that throughout history civilizations have satisfied human needsin very variable ways.[27] This is illustrated through his famous analysis of the evolution of table manners, where he shows that the rise of the modern *habitus* implies that food is ever-more abstracted from the live animal it originates from. However, Elias doesn't argue that needs themselves evolve—only the ways in which they are satisfied. When it comes to needs, Elias is interested in history, Marx in the intertwining of history and nature.

Here lies the important point. Because the consumed object first has to be produced, in the last instance it is production—that is, capitalist production—which determines needs. The external object (the commodity) determines the need, production determines the object, and hence production determines the need. The quote from the *Grundrisse* above continues as follows:

> Production thus produces not only the object but also the manner of consumption, not only objectively but also subjectively. Production thus creates the consumer. Production not only supplies a material for the need, but it also supplies a need for the material.[28]

According to Marx, under capitalism, most of the time production is the decisive instance. If an evolution occurs in the productive sphere, for

[26] Alfred Schmidt, *The Concept of Nature in Marx* (London: Verso, 2013). Combining nature and history is in a sense also what modern biology has tried to do, but from a different perspective. See Pierre-Antoine Miquel, *Qu'est-ce que la vie?* (Paris: Vrin, 2006).

[27] Norbert Elias, *The Civilizing Process* (London: Wiley-Blackwell, 2000).

[28] Karl Marx, *Economic Manuscripts of 1857–1858*, p. 29.

instance following a technological innovation or a change in the relations of production, it is likely to lead to a new 'manner of consumption'. Sometimes, this new manner concerns a vital need, like eating, for example when humanity started cooking meat and eating it with a knife and fork, rather than eating it raw and with the hands.

But because production determines consumption, it often puts on the market goods that correspond to no prior need, vital or otherwise, and hence creates the need *artificially*. Artificial needs are a consequence of the productive process. Hence, as Marx says, 'Production creates the consumer'. It is abundantly clear that this is the basic logic of the world we live in. The environmental damage brought by this productivist logic, and the damage done to human subjectivity, are obvious.

7.6 The Second Paradox of 'Radical Needs'

Radical needs rest on a second paradox. At a collective level, needs evolve and become more sophisticated and diverse as history unfolds. But at the individual level, there takes place an impoverishment of needs and the ways in which they are satisfied. This is especially the case among the popular classes, but also the dominant ones. 'The wealth of the species and the poverty of the individual are reciprocally based and reproduce each other',[29] is the phrase Heller employs to sum up this second paradox of radical needs. This, in our opinion, is one of the most profound contributions that the Marxist theory of needs makes to our understanding of the ontology of needs in modern societies.

One way of defining progress is to say that more and more sophisticated needs are created over the course of history. A process takes place which broadens the spectrum of qualitative needs. According to Gorz, 'The richer a civilization is, the richer and more diverse the needs of men become'.[30]

This phrase echoes an important passage from the *Grundrisse*:

> the discovery, creation and satisfaction of new needs arising from society itself; cultivating all the qualities of social man and producing him in a

[29] Heller, *The Theory of Need in Marx*, p. 94.

[30] Gorz, *La Morale de l'histoire*, pp. 234–35, our translation.

> form *as rich as possible in needs* because rich in qualities and relations—producing man as the most total and universal social product possible (for in order to enjoy many different kinds of things he must be capable of enjoyment, that is he must be cultivated to a high degree)—all these are also conditions of production based on capital.[31]

In this quotation, Marx establishes a causal link between capitalism and the production of the 'social man' in a form 'as rich as possible in needs'. At the collective level, by 'socializing' the human being more and more, capitalism creates 'qualities' and capacities for 'enjoyment' unconceivable for earlier historical periods.

However—and herein lies the paradox—this progress at the collective level, the level of humanity as such, is accompanied by a deterioration or trivialization of individual needs. In other words, there is a growing gap between the 'social man' and each particular individual. This is precisely the 'poverty of the individual' argument made by Heller in the above quotation.

How are we to explain this second paradox? Three factors contribute to this outcome. Firstly, the degree of sophistication of needs depends on the time the person has to take care of his needs. The less time at your disposal, the more unsophisticated your needs will be and the more you will succumb to 'pre-formatted', standardized, needs. In capitalism, the individual—the subaltern individual especially—devotes most of his time and energy to labour. Today, for instance, in OECD countries, a worker dedicates 40% of his time to work.[32] The rest covers eating and sleeping, that is, the satisfaction of basic vital needs. Therefore, he has little time to spend on cultivating his qualitative needs.

This is the reason why in the Marxist theory of needs, the reduction of working time is a crucial, progressive, policy. Gorz was one of the first theoreticians of the reduction of working time, and also of the 'basic income'.[33] (The basic income is an income given unconditionally to every

[31] Karl Marx, *Economic Manuscripts of 1857–1858*, p. 336, emphasis added.

[32] See OECD Better Life Index, 'How's Life?', *OECD Better Life Index*, n.d., www.oecdbetterlifeindex.org/, accessed on 27 February 2021.

[33] Philippe Van Parijs, 'De la sphère autonome à l'allocation universelle', in: Christophe Fourel (ed.), *André Gorz, un penseur pour le XXIe siècle* (Paris: La Découverte, 2009). Gorz's position on this issue evolved over time, but we do not have the space to enter into the details here.

citizen, thus allowing him to decide to work or not, and how much to work.) The reduction of working time not only will allow the sharing of work, and thus lead to a decrease in unemployment levels. It will also liberate time, so that people will be able to take care of themselves and their needs.

The standardization of production is a second factor explaining the trivialization of individual needs under capitalism. The exact same commodities are produced in ever-greater quantities. Standardization is a long-term tendency of capitalist production.[34] It responds to the necessity of lowering production costs, and realizing economies of scale. It has been a central factor in the emergence of 'consumer society' since the nineteenth century, and even more so since the post-war economic boom. The invention of the shipping container in the 1950s, the 'containerization' that made globalization possible by reducing transportation costs, increased this tendency even further in the second half of the twentieth century.[35]

Standardization has a major influence on manners of consumption, and consequently on the definition of needs and the ways they are satisfied. The consumer consumes those commodities to which he has access, meaning, standardized commodities, which are the same for billions of people. Think about the smartphones we all carry in our pockets. Alternative, more sustainable, forms of consumption exist, especially among the middle classes with high 'cultural capital'.[36] But they remain marginal. Thus, standardized products tend to standardize individual needs.

A third factor that explains why the wealth of the species with regard to needs comes in tandem with an impoverishment of individual needs is the division of labour. The division of labour exists in diverse forms in every human society, and even in some animal groups. What is specific to the capitalist division of labour is that it is rooted in the division between manual and intellectual labour.[37] Capitalism confines certain individuals (a majority of humanity) to the side of manual labour, and other individuals (a minority) to the side of intellectual labour. Of course, labour

[34] Lawrence Busch, *Standards: Recipes for Reality* (Cambridge, MA: MIT Press, 2013).

[35] Marc Levinson, *The Box: How the Shipping Container Made the World Smaller and the World Economy Bigger* (Princeton: Princeton University Press, 2008).

[36] Geoffrey Pleyers (ed.), *La consommation critique* (Paris: Desclée de Brouwer, 2011).

[37] Ali Rattansi, *Marx and the Division of Labour* (London: Macmillan, 1982).

always has manual and intellectual aspects, but in very different degrees. The reason capitalism relies on this division is because it is supposed to increase productivity, and the constant rise in productivity is the fuel of capitalist accumulation.

The computerization of work, and the rise of so-called 'digital labor' over the past three decades, do not change this basic logic. They have led to a proliferation of repetitive tasks, like data capture and management, which in no way favour creativity. David Graeber famously named these forms of labour 'bullshit jobs'.[38]

Gorz and Heller are, after Marx himself, the great thinkers on the political effects of the division of labour. The division of labour confines a majority of individuals to a limited set of repetitive tasks across their entire professional career. Because of the centrality of labour in capitalist societies, this has an impact on every aspect of a person's existence. If your work is stultifying, if it gives you little time and energy to think about your true, authentic, needs, then this will also have its effects, for instance, on your love life, or your ability to enjoy art, or to be intellectually or manually creative. Hence, your life will be deprived of some of its important potentialities.

7.7 A Revolutionary Ecological Transition

Many other aspects of the Marxist theory of needs could be mentioned, here. Elaborating the different dimensions of this problem should become part of the collective work agenda of Ecological Marxists in the future.

To conclude, we shall go back to the question we started out from: during the ecological transition, which needs should we decide to satisfy, and which shouldn't we? Obviously, the Marxist theory of needs is not a detailed roadmap for this transition. To put together such a roadmap, we need to look at the ecological transition scenarios elaborated by contemporary (heterodox) ecological economists and social scientists, and also engineers working for instance on the energetic aspects of the environmental challenges ahead. But this theory provides a way to think about this problem, or at least some of its aspects.

During the ecological transition, satisfying the absolute biological needs of all people should, of course, be a primary aim. Today, according

[38] David Graeber, *Bullshit Jobs: The Rise of Pointless Work, and What We Can Do About It* (London: Penguin, 2019).

to the UN Food and Agriculture Organization (FAO), more than 800 million people still suffer from hunger.[39] This amounts to one out of every nine people across the planet. Capitalism not only generates an economic surplus allowing significant segments of the global population to devote themselves to qualitative needs. It also induces poverty and inequalities, which compel other segments to concentrate on their immediate, material needs, especially but not only in the Global South. Poverty and inequalities are not just remnants of the past which will fade away with the passage of time, as apologists of capitalism would have us believe. Capitalism reproduces these ills constantly; they are a consequence of its basic logic (which is not to say that nothing can be done about them within the context of capitalism—quite the contrary). Thus, a serious critique of capitalism is in order, so as to achieve this goal.

Radical needs will be a transformative force during the ecological transition. The reason for this is that they raise the question 'which needs should we satisfy?' *from below*. The definition and satisfaction of radical needs is more a matter of revolutionary social and political movements, than of state policies. More precisely, it is through the influence of such movements on the state that they will be satisfied.

The ecological transition should proceed by mobilizing people, their knowledges and know-how, in order to decide which needs to satisfy and which needs to renounce. This will require a deepening of democracy, through the creation of new 'deliberative' democratic institutions, in which a debate about 'real' as opposed to 'artificial' needs will take place. If the Marxist theory of needs teaches us one thing, it is that this distinction is essentially political. Except for a small number of vital needs such as eating, breathing, or sleeping, there is no such thing as a 'real' need defined in absolute terms. A 'real' need is one that a society considers as such at a given time in its history.

The form to be adopted by these new democratic institutions, in which the deliberation about needs will take place, remains an open question. Perhaps the workers' councils of the revolutions of the twentieth century can serve as a model. These councils, however, should be broadened

[39] See Food and Agriculture Organization of the United Nations, *The State of Food Security and Nutrition in the World 2020: Transforming Food Systems for Affordable Healthy Diets* (Rome: Food and Agriculture Organization of the United Nations, 2020).

to include all citizens, not only workers.[40] More precisely, the question 'which needs should we satisfy?' is as much a question for producers as it is for consumers. During the twentieth century, revolutionary movements mostly relied on workers' power, dismissing the consumer as politically less central. This strategy was rooted, among other things, in the Marxist labour theory of value: because workers were the ones producing value, they were also the ones considered able to transform society and lead us to communism.

Revolutionaries should stick to this argument. However, they should also try to imagine the multiple ways in which consumers could give a hand to workers, for instance by boycotting environmentally or socially damaging goods, and pursuing 'politically aware' forms of consumption. Focusing on alternative modes of consumption alone would be a political dead-end. Remember what Marx said: in capitalism, 'Production thus creates the consumer'. But this doesn't mean that the consumer has no role to play whatsoever in the struggle against productivism and consumerism, i.e., the accumulation of capital. He certainly has. In fact, alliances between workers' and consumers' organizations existed in the past, most importantly in the first half of the twentieth century, for instance in the US or France.[41] In the US, in the 1930s, the combination of workers' strikes and consumer boycotts was an effective way to attain substantial economic and political gains. This alliance should be reinvented, so as to help us find a way out of the anthropocene.

Radical needs are a false promise made by capitalism. But it is a false promise that people come to take seriously. This false promise allows social and political movements to emerge, and to fight for its fulfilment. In so doing, they necessarily question the legitimacy of capitalism, and of the capitalist state. Equally, the diversification of the spectrum of human needsover the course of history—i.e., progress—stands in sharp contrast with people's growing inability to find the time and energy to satisfy their

[40] See the proposals made by Patrick Devine, *Democracy and Economic Planning* (Cambridge: Polity, 2010).

[41] Hayagreeva Rao, 'Caveat Emptor: The Construction of Nonprofit Consumer Watchdog Organizations', *American Journal of Sociology*, vol. 103 (1998), n. 4: 912–61; and Marie-Emmanuelle Chessel, 'Aux origines de la consommation engagée. La Ligue sociale d'acheteurs (1902–1914)', *Vingtième siècle*, vol. 77 (2003), n. 1: 95–108.

needs. This also leads to the questioning of the legitimacy of the system. What revolutionary movements need to do, in sum, is take capitalism at its word, and demand that our vital and qualitative needs be at last fulfilled. As for the concrete form of the organizations and institutions who will carry forward these demands in the twenty-first century, that remains for us to invent.

References

Altvater, Elmar (2007), 'The Social and Natural Environment of Fossil Capitalism', *Socialist Register*, vol. 43: 37–59.

Bonneuil, Christophe, and Fressoz, Jean-Baptiste (2017), *The Shock of the Anthropocene*, London: Verso.

Busch, Lawrence (2013), *Standards: Recipes for Reality*, Cambridge, MA: MIT Press.

Chessel, Marie-Emmanuelle (2003), 'Aux origines de la consommation engagée. La Ligue sociale d'acheteurs (1902–1914)', *Vingtième siècle*, vol. 77, n. 1: 95–108.

Cohen, Lizabeth (2003), *A Consumer's Republic: The Politics of Mass Consumption in Postwar America*, New York: Vintage Books.

Devine, Patrick (2010), *Democracy and Economic Planning*, Cambridge: Polity.

Elias, Norbert (2000), *The Civilizing Process*, London: Wiley-Blackwell.

Ellman, Michael (2014), *Socialist Planning*, Cambridge: Cambridge University Press.

Féher, Ferenc, Heller, Agnes, and Márkus, György (1983), *Dictatorship over Needs*, London: Palgrave Macmillan.

Food and Agriculture Organization of the United Nations (2020), *The State of Food Security and Nutrition in the World 2020: Transforming Food Systems for Affordable Healthy Diets*, Rome: Food and Agriculture Organization of the United Nations.

Gianinazzi, Willy (2016), *André Gorz, une vie*, Paris: la Découverte.

Global Footprint Network (2019), 'Earth Overshoot Day is 29 July, the Earliest Ever', *Earth Overshoot Day*, 23 July 2019, https://www.overshootday.org/newsroom/press-release-july-2019-english/.

Gorz, André (1959), *La Morale de l'histoire*, Paris: Seuil.

———. (1964), *Stratégie ouvrière et néocapitalisme*, Paris: Seuil.

Graeber, David (2019), *Bullshit Jobs: The Rise of Pointless Work, and What We Can Do About It*, London: Penguin.

Heller, Agnes (2018), *The Theory of Need in Marx*, London: Verso.

———. (2020), *La valeur du hasard. Ma vie*, Paris: Rivages.

Holleman, Hannah, Stole, Inger L., Bellamy Foster, John, and McChesnay, Robert W. (2009), 'The Sales Effort and Monopoly Capitalism', *Monthly Review*, vol. 60, n. 11: 1–23.

Keucheyan, Razmig (2019), *Les Besoins artificiels. Comment sortir du consumérisme*, Paris: La Découverte.

Levinson, Marc (2008), *The Box: How the Shipping Container Made the World Smaller and the World Economy Bigger*, Princeton: Princeton University Press.

Lievens, Matthias (2010), 'Towards an Eco-Marxism', *Radical Philosophy Review*, vol. 13, n. 1: 1–17.

Martin, Randy (2002), *Financialization of Daily Life*, Philadelphia: Temple University Press.

Marx, Karl (1975), *Contribution to the Critique of Hegel's Philosophy of Right*, MECW, vol. 3, 3–129.

———. (1986), *Economic Manuscripts of 1857–1858*, MECW, vol. 28.

———. (1996), *Capital, Volume I*, MECW, vol. 35.

McLeod, Stephen (2014), 'Absolute Biological Needs', *Bioethics*, vol. 29, n. 6: 293–301.

McNeill, John (2000), *Something New Under the Sun: An Environmental History of the 20th Century*, London: Allen Lane.

Milanovic, Branko (2016), *Global Inequality: A New Approach for the Age of Globalization*, Cambridge, MA: The Belknap Press.

Miquel, Pierre-Antoine (2006), *Qu'est-ce que la vie?* Paris: Vrin.

Moore, Jason W. (ed.) (2000), *Anthropocene or Capitalocene? Nature, History, and the Crisis of Capitalism*, Oakland: PM Press.

Nora, Pierre (1989), 'Aliénation', in: Anne Simonin and Hélène Clastres (eds.), *Les Idées en France, 1945–1988*, Paris: Gallimard.

OECD Better Life Index (n.d.), 'How's Life?', *OECD Better Life Index*, www.oecdbetterlifeindex.org/. Accessed on 27 February 2021.

Pleyers, Geoffrey (ed.) (2011), *La consommation critique*, Paris: Desclée de Brouwer.

Rao, Hayagreeva (1998), 'Caveat Emptor: The Construction of Nonprofit Consumer Watchdog Organizations', *American Journal of Sociology*, vol. 103, n. 4: 912–61.

Rattansi, Ali (1982), *Marx and the Division of Labour*, London: Macmillan.

Schmidt, Alfred (2013), *The Concept of Nature in Marx*, London: Verso.

Tosel, André (2008), 'The Late Lukács and the Budapest School', in: Jacques Bidet and Eustache Kouvélakis (eds.), *Critical Companion to Contemporary Marxism*, Leiden: Brill, pp. 163–73.

———. (2009), *Le marxisme du 20e siècle*, Paris: Syllepse.

Van Parijs, Philippe (2009), 'De la sphère autonome à l'allocation universelle', in: Christophe Fourel (ed.), *André Gorz, un penseur pour le XXIe siècle*, Paris: La Découverte.

PART III

Migration, Labour and Globalization

CHAPTER 8

Accumulation and Its Discontents: Migration and Nativism in Marx's *Capital* and Late Manuscripts

David Norman Smith

8.1 Introduction

Migration is not the first word that comes to mind when people discuss Karl Marx.[1] But in fact migration—and in particular, *forced* migration—is one of the cornerstones of Marxian theory, which revolves around

[1] I am grateful to many people for their help with Marx's late manuscripts. I am particularly indebted to Dr. Gerald Hubmann of the Berlin-Brandenburgische Akademie der Wissenschaften, who, in his capacity as secretary of the Internationale Marx-Engels-Stiftung and MEGA^2 project leader, granted me permission to cite from MEGA^2 manuscripts and transcripts. At the International Institute for Social History in Amsterdam, I benefited from the knowledge and support of Mieke Ijzerman and Götz Langkau. I also owe a great deal to the outstanding scholars with whom I have been associated in connection with Karl Marx, *Exzerpte und Notizen, 1879 bis 1881*, MEGA^2, vol. IV/27, above all, Jürgen Rojahn, Kevin Anderson, Norair Ter-Akopian, and Georgi Bagaturia. I also express my warmest thanks to the National Endowment for the Humanities (NEH), which funded a research grant proposal, co-authored by Kevin Anderson, that financed a series of transcriptions of Marx's late texts.

D. N. Smith (✉)
University of Kansas, Lawrence, KS, USA

M. Musto (ed.), *Rethinking Alternatives with Marx*, Marx, Engels, and Marxisms, https://doi.org/10.1007/978-3-030-81764-0_8

two basic realities: the expropriation of farmers and the exploitation of workers.

Exploited workers are the crux of Marx's worldview. They are both the engine of capitalism and the potential engine of socialism. But they occupy this double role thanks not to what they have, but to what they *lack,* above all, means to produce and subsist independently. Workers lack what their forebears lost—land. That land was expropriated, turning farmers into *former farmers* who could survive only by working for wages.

When Marx began his career in early 1840, only a small fraction of the world's farmers had yet been expropriated. That was still true four decades later when he wrote his final reading notes. But that reality was eroding, and Marx's account of that erosion was central to *Capital.* In the final chapters of Volume 1, Marx showed that, in order for capitalists to have labour to employ and exploit, farmers had to be swept off the land: 'The thinning (*Verdünnung*) of the self-sufficient, independent rural populace', Marx wrote, is essential 'to the thickening (*Verdichtung*) of the industrial proletariat'.[2]

In other words, the accumulation of capital requires the attenuation of the peasantry. This is the corollary of Marx's familiar claim that the accumulation of capital is 'at the same time increase of the proletariat'.[3] Peasants, forced from the land, become a reserve army of what is, initially, artisanal, pre-industrial labour. When—if—they obtain paid employment, they are thereby 'proletarianized'.[4]

For the expropriated, 'if' is the operative word here, since neither former farmers nor their descendants are guaranteed employment. Until recently, when scholars began to attend more carefully to the plight of the 'precariat',[5] it was not uncommon to treat the interval between expropriation and exploitation as a kind of hiatus, like the moment of silence between lightning and thunder. But in fact proletarianization is

[2] Karl Marx, *Das Kapital* (Hamburg: Meissner, 1867), p. 728; cf. Karl Marx, *Capital, Volume I*, MECW, vol. 35, p. 734. Below, I cite the original German and French editions of *Capital* when they contain subtleties that are unavailable elsewhere.

[3] Marx, *Das Kapital* (1867), p. 600; and Karl Marx, *Le Capital* (Paris: Lachâtre, 1875), p. 272. Cf. Marx, *Capital, Volume I*, MECW, p. 609.

[4] Marx stresses that 'proletarianization' can occur pre-industrially as well as industrially. The idea is just that a new class relationship arises when people enter into wage labour.

[5] See especially Mike Davis, *Planet of Slums* (London: Verso, 2006); and Saskia Sassen, *Expulsions: Brutality and Complexity in the Global Economy* (Cambridge: Harvard University Press, 2014).

not inevitable. Only one outcome is certain when farmers are expelled from the land: migration and precarity.

8.2 Accumulation by Forced Migration

Many aspects of Marx's worldview are hidden in plain sight in *Capital*. Others lie buried in his manuscripts and reading notes, many of which remain unpublished. In what follows, with expropriation as the cause and migration as the effect, I attempt to connect the analysis of peasant expropriation in *Capital* to phenomena that Marx probes in a pair of hitherto unpublished late manuscripts which will appear in future volumes of the *Marx-Engels Gesamtausgabe* (MEGA^2).[6] Despite the unfamiliarity of these texts, what I report below may sound familiar, since the trends and events that Marx reports anticipate many features of what we now call 'globalization'.

Writing about Egyptian finances, Marx maps a tangled story of predatory lending by Anglo-French financiers which ensnared Egypt in unsustainable debt. The beleaguered Egyptian regime responded by hyper-exploiting the peasantry and withholding pay from soldiers, with predictable consequences: flight from the land, followed by a military revolt, followed by a British invasion. Marx's reading notes on this crisis, written in late 1882, are among his very last texts.

Writing about social conflict in San Francisco, Marx documented a classic instance of what would now be called right-wing populism: a violent campaign against Chinese migrants by the nativist 'Workingmen's Party'. Many latter-day themes which scholars rarely associate with Marx's name appear in his notes on this subject: xenophobia, antisemitism, electoral corruption, and working-class authoritarianism. Here, as in his Egypt notes and in his so-called 'ethnological notebooks', Marx goes well beyond the bounds of what is ordinarily construed as Marxian discourse.[7] This fact has wide implications for our understanding of the role of

[6] See my acknowledgements, below, for a full list of the MEGA^2 collaborators and others to whom I am indebted for access to Marx's unpublished manuscripts and transcripts.

[7] See my English edition of Marx's ethnological notes, *Marx's World: Global Society and Capital Accumulation in Marx's Late Manuscripts* (New Haven: Yale University Press, 2022, forthcoming), which also includes Marx's closely related letter drafts to Vera Zasulich.

dispossession and displacement—so-called 'primitive accumulation'—in Marx's critique of political economy.[8] Accumulation requires the attenuation of the peasantry, which, in turn, requires the dispossession of peasants. Those peasants, displaced, become a floating population, with uncertain prospects.[9]

For Marx, dispossession is a technical term, the conceptual core of a cluster of categories which appear and reappear throughout his writings. Old modes of possession and production are 'destroyed', 'dissolved', 'decomposed', 'splintered' (*zerstört, aufgelöst, zersetzt, zerschnitten*). Vulnerable social formations and class relations fall victim to destruction (*Zerstörung*), dissolution (*Auflösung*), decomposition (*Zersetzung*), and fragmentation (*Zerschneidung*). These terms are not simply rough synonyms. A classic example of Marx's use of this vocabulary appears in his excerpt notes of 1851, when, with reference to John Francis Bray's tract *Labour's Wrongs and Labour's Remedy*, he notes the destructive, dissolving power of money. Bray, as paraphrased by Marx, had written that money is a 'means to splinter (*zerschneiden*)' things 'into countless fragments, piece by piece, through exchange'. Marx generalized this point: 'Destructive, dissolving effect of money. *Sans* money, a mass of inexchangeable, hence inalienable objects'.[10]

The language and the intent of this remark had been anticipated in Marx's Paris Manuscripts of 1844. There he cites the soliloquy that opens Shakespeare's *Timon of Athens*: 'Gold? yellow, glittering, precious gold? [...] This yellow slave / Will knit and break religions, bless the accurst; / Make the hoar leprosy adored, place thieves / And give them title, knee and approbation'.[11] Marx quoted these lines, however, not directly from Shakespeare but from August Schlegel's famous translation: 'Yes, this ruddy slave dissolves and binds (*löst und bindet*) / sacred bonds;

[8] For Marx, primitive accumulation was 'so-called', since his topic was not capital accumulation per se but the separation of labour-power from means of production. In an address in 1865 to the General Council of the International Workingmen's Association, Marx said that this separation is what 'the economists call: "The Previous or Original Accumulation, but which ought to be called the Original Expropriation"', Karl Marx, 'Value, Price and Profit', MEGA^2, vol. II/4.1, p. 412.

[9] Marx explores the dialectic of active and reserve armies of labour in *Capital, Volume I*, Chapter 25, 'The General Law of Capital Accumulation', MECW, vol. 35, pp. 607–703. See below for further details.

[10] Karl Marx, 'Bullion', MEGA^2, vol. IV/8, p. 9: 'Zerstörende, auflösende Wirkung'.

[11] *Timon of Athens*, Act 4, Scene 2.

blesses the accursed; / Makes leprosy alluring, honors the thief'.[12] Corresponding language appears in Marx's meditation on this point: 'If *money* is the bond that ties me to *human* life, [to] society, nature and people, is it not the bond of all bonds? Can it not dissolve and bind all ties? Is it not, therefore, also the universal *agent of separation*?'.[13]

The significance of this passage lies not simply in the direct repetition of this language of binding and dissolving but in the characterization of money as an 'agent of separation' (*Scheidungsmittel*). In the chemistry of Marx's day, this term simply meant *solvent*. In other words, Marx, who would later call money the 'universal equivalent' commodity, was now calling it a universal solvent. This might appear to be a metaphor, but as Marcel van der Linden and Gerald Hübmann have recently observed, when we take Marx's 'chemical, geological, and physiological excerpts into consideration, it becomes evident that [we are dealing with] more than just metaphors, [that such usages function, rather, as] scientific analogies'.[14] Marx, in the next sentence, shows the plausibility of this claim. Money, he writes, 'is the true *Scheidemünze*, the true binding agent, the *(galvano)chemical* power of society'.[15]

This line returns us to Bray, since *Scheidemünze* were coins minted to mediate small-scale exchanges.[16] But Marx is now also directly formulating a scientific analogy. Money is the social equivalent of electrochemical force. It has both solvent and binding properties. It dissolves in its role as universal solvent; it binds, it reconnects, in its role as universal equivalent. It is in this dual sense that money acts as 'the alienated (*entäusserte*) ability of mankind'—that is, as subjective agency dissolved

[12] Karl Marx, 'Ökonomische–philosophische Manuskripte', MEGA^2, vol. I/2, p. 319. Cf. *Shakspeare's dramatische Werke*, Bd. 7 (Berlin: Reimer, 1832). Schlegel's unrevised translation (Vienna: Pichler, 1811, pp. 81–2) is closer to the original, rendering 'yellow' as *gelbes* rather than *Rothe*, 'ruddy'. The version of this passage which appears in the MECW, vol. 3, p. 323, cites Shakespeare in the original English.

[13] Karl Marx, 'The Power of Money', MECW, vol. 3, p. 324.

[14] Marcel van der Linden and Gerald Hubmann, 'Introduction', in: Marcel van der Linden and Gerald Hubmann (eds.), *Marx's Capital: An Unfinishable Project?* (Leiden: Brill, 2018), pp. 1–30.

[15] Marx, 'Ökonomische–philosophische Manuskripte', p. 320.

[16] Marx read Bray in 1845 and again in 1851. See Lucia Pradella, *Globalisation and the Critique of Political Economy* (New York: Routledge, 2015), pp. 80ff.

and replaced. Money is quite literally the fatal electricity, the alienated energy, of an inhuman, inverted world.[17]

8.3 Force and Fetishism

Dispossession, however, results from other forces as well, not least from sheer destructive force. As early as 1842, Marx had pointed out that money itself, in the form of silver and gold, was often acquired by wholly destructive means. Castigating the dispossession of Moselle peasants, Marx found a parallel, and a parable, in the experience of the Taíno of Cuba and Hispaniola, who, knowing that Columbus and a Spanish fleet were approaching and 'that gold was [their] fetish', placed all their gold in a basket, 'held a feast in its honor [...] and hurled it into the sea', hoping by this means to evade plunder and exploitation.[18] They failed, tragically. Forced into servitude and exposed to ghastly diseases, the Taíno fought back, but in vain. By the end of the sixteenth century, they were extinct.[19]

Capital, however, needs workers, not corpses. The accumulation of the proletariat is not advanced by the annihilation of noncapitalist peoples. Force benefits capital only when it 'frees' labour-power and land for capital investment. That was the consequence, however unintended, in Tudor England shortly after the Spanish conquest of Cuba, when warlords violently 'cleared' the land to raise sheep for the Flemish wool market. The uprooted farmers who streamed into the cities were initially an outcast precariat, starving or surviving as vagabonds. But before long they were driven from the streets, too. Measures stunningly harsh

[17] Marx, 'The Power of Money', p. 324.

[18] Marx, 'Exzerpte aus Charles De Brosses', MEGA^2, vol. IV/1, p. 322. The original source of this anecdote is Bartolemé de las Casas, *A Short Account of the Destruction of the Indies* (London: Penguin, 2004), first published in 1542.

[19] Karl Marx, 'Verhandlungen des 6. Rheinischen Landtags. Dritter Artikel', MEGA^2, vol. I/1, p. 236. On the Moselle, see Peter Linebaugh, 'Karl Marx, the Theft of Wood, and Working-Class Composition', *Social Justice*, vol. 40 (2014), n. 1/2: 137–61; and Daniel Bensaïd, *Les dépossédés* (Paris: La fabrique, 2007). On Marx and the Taíno, see Roland Boer, *In the Vale of Tears* (Leiden: Brill, 2013), pp. 295–6. Hatuey, the Taíno *cacique* who led the ritual to exalt and remove the gold, also led the ensuing resistance. He was burned at the stake in 1513.

forced them into the rough-hewn factories of the dawning age of manufacture, which they were the first to populate.[20] 'Thus', Marx wrote, 'were the country people forcibly expropriated, chased from their homes into vagabondage, and—by grotesquely terroristic laws, by the whip and branding iron, by torture and enslavement—broken to the discipline needed by the wage labor system'.[21]

This tragic episode, which Marx regarded as the most primitive moment of primitive accumulation, was the blood-soaked ground on which the edifice of English capitalism was erected. It was the destroying, dissolving moment when labour-power became available for exploitation. But money had to be present too—and in many instances, money sufficed to unravel the fabric of old social ties. Money, in the modern age, is as much the 'midwife' of history as force itself.

Marx revisited and developed the theme of money's solvent effects in every installment of his voluminous, unfinished critique of political economy.

In the fragment *Bastiat and Carey*, which he drafted in June 1857, on the eve of writing the *Grundrisse*, he wrote that the unity of manufacture and agriculture, which money had dissolved (*aufgelöst*) in England, was now being destroyed (*zerstört*) by English capital 'everywhere'.[22] In the *Grundrisse* itself, under the rubric '*Auflösende Wirkung des Geldes*', Marx reproduced his earlier remark on Bray,[23] and in his final paragraph, he gave this observation historical content, saying that shared property, which had been the 'starting point' for cultural development, was also the starting point for cultural dissolution, which took place serially, in waves. The first wave dissolved shared property, setting the stage for private commodity production.[24] Ensuing waves then dissolved

[20] Marx, *Capital, Volume I*, Part VIII, Chapters 26–28, MECW, vol. 35, pp. 704–31. Cf. Karl Marx, *Das Kapital* (Hamburg: Meissner, 1872), Chapter 24, pp. 742ff.

[21] The MECW version of this line dilutes this point. Marx speaks of '*grotesk-terroristische Gesetze*' in *Das Kapital* (1867), p. 718, italics in original, and '*lois d'un terrorisme grotesque*' in *Le Capital*, but the MECW translation (vol. 35, p. 726) refers simply to 'laws grotesquely terrible'. My version of the full passage, above, blends the original French and German versions.

[22] Karl Marx, 'Bastiat und Carey', MEW, vol. 42, p. 6.

[23] Karl Marx, *Grundrisse*, MEW, vol. 42, pp. 757–8.

[24] Ibid.: 'The production system based on private exchange is before all else the historical dissolution (*Auflösung*) of [...] naturally grown communism', ibid., p. 768. Cf. Karl Marx, *Economic Manuscripts of 1857–61*, MECW, vol. 29, p. 253.

the 'whole series of economic systems which have, as their foundation, dissolved common property'. Some of these post-communal systems made commodity exchange an ancillary feature of their activities—selling, e.g., their unneeded surpluses—but it was not until the rise of modern capitalism that production came to be 'dominated in its whole depth and breadth by exchange value'.[25]

Many of these same points reappear, in bullet-point form, in the index to the *Grundrisse*, which Marx wrote in June 1858 as a projected table of contents for *A Contribution to the Critique of Political Economy* (1859).[26] And Marx concludes this text with the remark that coined money, which had mediated local exchanges, had now been displaced by 'completed' world money, bullion assessed by weight alone. Even coins which had served as quasi-universal equivalents, mediating regional exchanges (Mexican dollars, Russian imperials, and English sovereigns) had been 'stripped' (*abstreift*) of their mediating roles.[27] Every parochial, concrete form of money was now reduced to the common denominator of abstract equivalence. Money and commodity relations which, until this point, had retained hints of geographic and cultural particularity were now rendered entirely uniform.

Marx returned to these themes in the fall of 1858, when he wrote the so-called *Urtext 'Zur Kritik'*, the first draft of *A Contribution to the Critique of Political Economy*.[28] Once again reproducing his Bray note verbatim, Marx now appended a line of explanation: If there were no money, only 'inexchangeable, inalienable objects' would exist because only money gives them 'an existence [...] independent of the nature of their use value'.[29] Marx quickly adds that money gives producers, too, a social existence detached from the immediacy of their useful labours, since they relate to each other through the social relations between their

[25] Ibid., p. 768. Cf. Marx, *Economic Manuscripts of 1857–61*, p. 253. This concluding line is followed by just two words—*ohne daß*—and then breaks off in mid-sentence, bringing the *Grundrisse* to an abrupt conclusion.

[26] Karl Marx, 'Index zu den 7 Heften', MEGA^2, vol. II/2, pp. 22–8.

[27] Ibid., p. 14. Cf. Marx, *Economic Manuscripts of 1857–61*, pp. 428–9.

[28] Karl Marx, 'Fragmente des Urtextes von 'Zur Kritik der politischen Oekonomie', in: Karl Marx, *Grundrisse der kritik der politischen Ökonomie (Rohentwurf), 1857–1858* (Berlin: Dietz, 1953), pp. 871–947.

[29] Marx, *Economic Manuscripts of 1857–61*, p. 445.

commodities, which money mediates. These 'relations of individuals to each other', Marx says, 'appear as *social relations* of things'.

This, plainly, is an early statement of Marx's canonical definition of commodity fetishism,[30] and Marx now proceeds to make a novel point, which he had previously only implied—namely, that fetishism itself is a dissolving power. Merchant-raiders, bewitched by bullion, were driven to scour the globe for gold by an extraordinary, limitless avarice, the *auri sacra fames*, Virgil's accursed greed for gold.[31] This was the wish, not only to enrich themselves in the usual way, but to amass and hoard gold in particular, to entomb the object of fetishistic desire in a vault. The precious metals were also enchanted. Invulnerable to oxidization and insoluble in acids, gold, and silver seemed more astral than material, like 'crystallized light raised from the underworld'.[32] The historian Sempéré, in a passage cited by Marx, noted that in 1593 Spain's *Cortes* had asked emperor Philip II to restrict the exchange of gold for foreign goods—'*as if Spaniards were Indians*'—on the ground that gold alone is truly valuable.[33]

This, of course, was a perverse misreading of gold, but capitalism, Marx says, is perverse from top to bottom, turning money 'from means into end' and degrading all it touches.[34] He cites Creon, from Sophocles' *Antigone:* 'Money – you demolish cities, root men from their homes'.[35]

[30] Marx, 'Fragmente des Urtextes von 'Zur Kritik der politischen Oekonomie', p. 889.

[31] Virgil, *Virgil's Aeneid* (New York: D. Appleton, 1860), Book 3, Line 57. See also Karl Marx, 'The Greed for Surplus Labor: Manufacturer and Boyar', in: Marx, *Capital, Volume I*, pp. 243ff.

[32] Karl Marx, *Zur Kritik der politischen Ökonomie* (Berlin: Duncker, 1859), pp. 133–4. In English this book is known as *A Contribution to the Critique of Political Economy* (New York: International, 1970). Cf. Marx, *Economic Manuscripts of 1857–61*, pp. 257–417.

[33] Karl Marx, 'The Original Text of the Second and the Beginning of the Third Chapter of *A Contribution to the Critique of Political Economy*', in: Marx, *Economic Manuscripts of 1857–61*, p. 446, citing Juan Sempéré, *Considérations sur les causes de la grandeur et de la décadence de la monarchie espagnole*, Tome 1 (Paris: Renouard, 1826), pp. 275–6, italics in original.

[34] Marx, *Economic Manuscripts of 1857–61*, p. 447.

[35] Sophocles, *Antigone*, in: Sophocles, *The Three Theban Plays* (London: Penguin, 1984), Lines 297–8, cited above from the translation by Robert Fagels which the MECW reproduces (Marx, *Economic Manuscripts of 1857–61*, p. 451). This appears in the original Greek in the *Grundrisse* (1953), p. 894: *Κακών νόμισμ' έβλαστε, ταυτο και πόλεις/Πορθεî, τόδ' άνδρας εξανίστησιν δόμων.*

And he revisits *Timon of Athens* to repeat that gold does in fact 'knit and break religions'. The 'yellow slave' knits money fetishism and tears apart its rivals.[36] The Taíno were early victims of this process, which, spreading outward from Europe, exerted its solvent effects in continent after continent.

Money too soon lost its lingering immediacy. Gold and silver, denuded of their 'natural-ethnic' identity as coins, now seemed to embody value by virtue of their unstamped substance alone. That inspired an idealization of bullion and a reckless disregard for any kind of wealth that did not take money form.

8.4 Accumulation Mania

World money, the binding and separating agent of the world market, connected and divided people in new ways. Cultures were not only connected to a previously unimagined extent—the whole world now felt like a single city, Montanari said, hosting a perpetual fair, with all the world's goods on display[37]—but in newly alienated, detached ways. People who had been strangers to each other were now entwined, yet their social relations were reified and estranged. Their concrete personal labour, buried in their products, remained anonymous. Individuality melted, as if in an acid bath.

Marx elaborated these themes in *A Contribution to the Critique of Political Economy*. Writing, again, that world money is stripped (*abstreift*) 'of its shape and stamp', he now says that it returns, full circle, to the unworked formlessness of *aes rude*, the rough ingots of early Roman trade.[38] Local, regional, and national forms of money which had been

[36] Marx, *Economic Manuscripts of 1857–61*, pp. 451–2, citing Shakespeare's English. Neither citation, from Sophocles or Shakespeare, appears in *Zur Kritik der politischen Ökonomie*, hereafter cited as *Zur Kritik*.

[37] Geminiano Montanari, 'Della moneta, trattato mercantile', in: Pietro Custodi (ed.), *Scrittori Classici Italiani di Economia Politica: Parte Antica*, Tomo III (Milan: G. G. Destefanis, 1804), cited in Marx, *Zur Kritik*, p. 134. Money, Montanari added, that 'marvelous invention', brings commodities from every corner of the world right into our homes.

[38] Marx, *Zur Kritik*, p. 129: '*aes rude*', in ancient Italy, referred to unstamped, uncoined bronze ingots.

quasi-universal equivalents now gave way to a global equivalent.[39] World money mediated exchanges everywhere—and the world market, by its extension, increasingly assured that products would assume commodity form everywhere.[40]

Marx credits this expansion, in no small part, to fetishism itself. The world market arose as the unplanned consequence of globe-girdling commerce pursued by merchants whose greed for gold was inflamed by the conviction that gold has miraculous properties—'just as chemistry grew up behind the backs of alchemists, who wanted only to make gold'.[41] Max Weber, much later, would cite the greed of a legendary Dutch sea-captain, who swore that he would sail through hell, though it scorched his sails, in pursuit of profit.[42] Marx said that avarice of this kind, which he dubbed 'enrichment mania' (*Bereicherungssucht*), was a defining force in the age of world money. 'Money is not only an object of enrichment mania, it is *the* object of that mania. It is essentially *auri sacra fames*'.[43] Previously, greed had fastened on use-values—'clothes, jewelry, flocks, etc.' But money permitted an addiction to abstract wealth, which can be amassed without limit, and is hence 'both the object and the wellspring of enrichment mania'.[44]

In the mercantilist stage of the world market, the *auri sacra fames* was in tension with circulation, since what the money fetishist wanted

[39] 'When national coins like Russian imperials, Mexican thalers, and English sovereigns circulate abroad, their denominations become irrelevant and only their substance counts', ibid., p. 129.

[40] Ibid., pp. 131–2.

[41] Ibid., p. 132.

[42] Melville's Ahab, though his grail was a whale, not gold, was a similar figure. On the Dutch sea-captain, see Max Weber, 'Die protestantische Ethik und der 'Geist' des Kapitalismus', *Archiv für Sozialwissenschaft und Sozialpolitik*, vol. 20 (1904): 20.

[43] Marx, *Grundrisse*, MEW, vol. 42, p. 96; cf. pp. 149–50, 244. This term is translated in the MECW as 'craving' and 'quest' for enrichment, see Karl Marx, *Economic Manuscripts of 1857–58*, MECW, vol. 28, pp. 100, 155. Paresh Chattopadhyay, *Marx's Associated Mode of Production* (London: Palgrave, 2016), discusses this theme deftly, under the rubric of 'enrichment mania', p. 41.

[44] Marx, *Zur Kritik*, p. 112, cites Plinius, *Historia Naturalis* (I, XXXIII): 'Money created the first basis for avarice [...] Soon avarice in its ferocity burned hot and became a hunger for gold (*sed auri fames*)', pp. 3, 48, translation amended. See Jacob Isager, *Pliny on Art and Society: The Elder Pliny's Chapters on the History of Art* (London: Routledge, 2013), p. 63.

was not simply means of circulation, but gold's immortal 'money soul'. Hoarding gold, viewed as treasure, was thus a constant temptation, but that temptation faded as money owners came to a better understanding of capital accumulation.[45] When money *as capital* became the object of enrichment mania, that passion evolved, becoming what Marx—coining a term—called 'accumulation mania' (*Akkumulationssucht*).[46] That mania consisted of an abstract social *auri sacra fames*, oriented wholly to the accumulation of value in the form of capital.[47]

Fetishism, which is often regarded as essentially cognitive, is ultimately a matter of praxis, affective as well as cognitive. The wish to sell products rather than sharing them, to pursue enrichment or accumulation ad infinitum, is above all a *wish*.[48] Just as the profit motive is a motive, fetishism is a fever. That fever orbits around the mystic imputation of value to commodities and money—but that mysticism is active, not contemplative. Value mystics travel the world like missionaries, converting concrete labour into abstract labouron every continent. Old social relations dissolve and displaced peasants, now 'free as birds', are either proletarianized or left in limbo.[49]

In short, money achieves its real-world effects in part because fetishists hunger for its miracle-working powers.[50] Gold is materially powerful because people believe it has magical powers. Enrichment, pursued in

[45] Marx, *Zur Kritik*, pp. 111–2. In many places this passage reproduces the discussion of this theme in the *Grundrisse* (1953), pp. 133–4, almost verbatim.

[46] Marx, *Grundrisse* (1953), p. 180. *Bereicherungssucht* was a common term, found, for example, in Karl Dietrich Hüllmann, *Geschichte des Ursprungs der Stände in Deutschland* (Berlin: Eichhoff & Krafft, 1830), p. 497. But *Akkumulationsssucht* was new. Until 1935, when part of the *Grundrisse* appeared in the Institut Marksa-Engel'sa-Lenina, *Arkhiv Marksa i Engel'sa*, vol. 4 (Moscow: Partizdat, 1934), see p. 100, only one writer besides Marx had used the term—the economist Mentor Bouniatian, *Wirtschaftskrisen und Ueberkapitalisation* (Munich: Ernst Reinhardt, 1908), pp. 147–52, and not with reference to Marx. It appeared also in Karl Marx, *Zur Kritik der politischen Ökonomie (Manuskript 1861–1863)*, MEGA^2, vol. II/3, p. 1711.

[47] Marx, *Grundrisse* (1953), p. 180.

[48] On this see David Norman Smith, 'Sharing, Not Selling: Marx Against Value', *Continental Thought & Theory*, vol. 1 (2017), n. 4: 653–95.

[49] Marx often calls expropriated peasants '*vogelfrei*', 'free as the birds', which colloquially meant *outcast*. Birds, free of property, roamed unprotected by law. See, for example, Marx, *Das Kapital* (1867), p. 701, n. 189, where Marx discusses the 'outcast proletarian' (*vogelfreien Proletarier*) of early Italian capitalism.

[50] Marx, *Zur Kritik*, p. 132: '*Zauberwirkung*'.

enchanted form, has world-changing consequences. Nor, Marx adds, has faith in money's magic ceased to work its magic. On the contrary, the fascinated awe that greeted the discovery of gold in California and Australia just a decade earlier had sprung directly from fetishism, which made people 'cosmopolitans', citizens of what Marx now called 'the commodity world' (*die Waarenwelt*).[51] 'Commodities rise above religious, political, national, and linguistic barriers by their very nature. Their universal language is price and their shared essence is money'.[52]

Objects worshipped for other reasons had to be disenchanted if exchange-value was to be recognized as their essence. All things holy *had* to be profaned, if they were to sell at their value. Sensing this, value fetishists pitted the austerities of 'practical reason' against any 'prejudices' that stood in the way of circulation.[53] The poet Burns had written, at the height of the French and Haitian revolutions, that 'rank is but the guinea's stamp,/The man's the *gowd* [gold] for a' that'.[54] Marx now said that commodity owners *en masse* were coming to that conclusion: 'That nationality "is but the guinea's stamp" is proven to commodity owners by the fact that the same gold which, in England, becomes sovereigns after landing in the form of American eagles, circulates three days later in Paris as napoleons and just weeks later in Venice as ducats, all the while

[51] This rare term was not coined by Marx, but he embraced it. Appearing once in the *Grundrisse* (1953), p. 139, it appeared a dozen times each in *Zur Kritik* and *Das Kapital* (1867) and then 21 times in *Das Kapital* (1872).

[52] Marx, *Zur Kritik*, p. 132.

[53] Ibid., p. 132.

[54] Robert Burns, 'A Man's a Man for a' That', in: [No Author], *A Musical Banquet of Choice Songs* (Glasgow: A. MacGoun, 1790), p. 38. Burns had recently read the comedy of William Wycherly, *The Plain-Dealer: A Comedy* (London: Magnes & Bentley, 1677), which contains these lines: 'I weigh the man, not his Title; 'tis not the king's stamp can make the metal better or heavier', p. 4. In 1788, Burns' friend Helen Maria Williams had written an abolitionist poem: 'Chained on the beach the Captive stands/Where Man, dire merchandise! Is sold/And bartered life is paid for gold', Helen Maria Williams, *A Poem on the Bill Lately Passed for Regulating the Slave Trade* (London: T. Cadell, 1788), p. 16. And in 1796, a Scottish mercenary wrote that slaves in 'the Guinea trade' were 'branded [...] with the initial letters of the new master's name', J. G. Stedman, *Narrative of a Five Year's Expedition Against the Revolted Negroes of Surinam*, vol. 1 (London: J. Johnson, 1796), p. 106. For commentary, see Nigel Leask, 'Burns and the Poetics of Abolition', in: Gerard Carruthers (ed.), *The Edinburgh Companion to Robert Burns* (Edinburgh: Edinburgh University Press, 2009), pp. 56–7.

retaining its unchanged value. The sublime idea to which the whole world is reduced is that of a market – *the world market*'.[55]

The *auri sacra fames* returns to centre stage in *Capital*, in familiar form. 'Greed for gold (*Goldgier*) awakens', Marx writes, when it becomes possible to catch and hold 'fleet-footed, absolutely social wealth' in the form of a precious metal.[56] 'Gold', Columbus wrote from Jamaica in 1503, 'is a wonderful thing! Whoever possesses it is the lord of all he desires. With gold one can even get souls into Paradise!'[57] Socially, money has every negative power: 'Everything becomes salable and buyable. Circulation becomes the great social retort into which everything that flies in re-emerges as a money crystal. Not even saints' bones can resist this alchemy'.[58]

What money reconstructs, it first dissolves. 'All qualitative differences between commodities are dissolved'; money 'as a radical leveller dissolves all differences'.[59] Societies of antiquity, perturbed by this leveling, denounced all money as dissolving, destroying *Scheidemünze*.[60] Later societies, including our own, have been no less perturbed by this radical levelling. Marx quotes the *Manifesto of the Communist Party* to underline that the bourgeois epoch has been marked to a unique degree by 'constant upheaval in production, ceaseless disturbance of all social conditions, perpetual insecurity and movement'. 'All fixed, timeworn relations with

[55] Marx, *Zur Kritik,* pp. 132–3. Marx, *Economic Manuscripts of 1857–61*, p. 384, omits Marx's reference to value.

[56] Marx, *Das Kapital* (1867), p. 92. 'Precious', from the Latin for 'price', denotes non-material values which can nevertheless be embodied in objects.

[57] Ibid., pp. 92–3. Marx appears to have found these unattributed lines in Wilhelm Kiesselbach, *Der Gang des Welthandels und die Entwicklung des europäischen Völkerlebens im Mittelalter* (Stuttgart: J. G. Cotta, 1860), p. 317. Marx criticizes Kiesselbach elsewhere for his residual mercantilism.

[58] Ibid., p. 93. France's Henry III, Marx notes, sold relics stolen from cloisters.

[59] Ibid. These references to dissolution (*ausgelöscht, löscht* [...] *aus*) appear as 'extinguished' and 'does away with' in Marx, *Capital, Volume I*, MECW, p. 142.

[60] He cites *Antigone* and *Timon of Athens* (pp. 93, 94). Goethe expressed a similar chagrin about the distorting effects of '*Scheidemunze oder Papiergeld*' on modern society in Arnold Zweig, *Berliner Ausgabe*, Bd. 3 (Berlin and Weimar: Aufbau-Verlags, 1965), p. 231. Aristotle, meanwhile, named chrematistics per se as the problem, see Marx, *Das Kapital* (1867), pp. 113–4, 127, citing Aristotle, *Aristotelis Opera, vol. 8: De re publica* (Berlin: Georg Reimer, 1855); and cf. Aristotle, *The Politics of Aristotle*, vol. 1 (Oxford: Clarendon Press, 1885).

their train of venerable old ideas and opinions dissolve, all newly formed ones become obsolete before they can ossify'.[61]

Capital's solvent effects reached an early apogee with the rise of the modern colonial system, which, Marx wrote, 'proclaimed the making of surplus-value the ultimate and sole purpose of humanity, throwing all the old idols into a heap with a shove and a bang!'.[62] This was a tacit allusion to Hegel's contention that the skeptical rationalism of the Enlightenment had 'insinuated' itself like an 'invisible and unperceived spirit' into the unguarded fortress of faith, until, 'one fine morning', it toppled the old idols 'with a shove and a bang!'.[63]

Hegel, in turn, was alluding to a passage in *Rameau's Nephew* by the arch-enlightener Diderot in which the nephew, lamenting vulgar trends, insisted that his own trinity—the father, *truth*, the son, *goodness*, and the holy spirit, *beauty*—could not be denied for long.[64] His new god would 'place himself on the altar beside the nation's idol; step by step, he would gather strength until, one fine day, he would take his companion by the neck and *presto!* we would see the idol at our feet'.[65] Marx, in effect, was now saying that the role Diderot had assigned to enlightenment was actually played by the idols of the marketplace—thereby old

[61] Marx, *Das Kapital* (1867), p. 479, citing Karl Marx and Friedrich Engels, *Manifest der Kommunistischen Partei* (London: J.E. Burghard, 1848), p. 5 (hereafter cited as *Manifesto*; cf. Karl Marx, *Manifesto of the Communist Party*, MECW, vol. 6, pp. 477–519). In all, the *Manifesto* is cited just twice in *Capital, Volume I*. Marx, *Capital, Volume I*, MECW, p. 489, renders *aufgelöst* in this passage as 'swept away'.

[62] Marx, *Das Kapital* (1867), p. 737; Marx, *Das Kapital* (1872), p. 785: '*schub und bautz*'.

[63] G. W. F. Hegel, *The Phenomenology of Mind, Vols. 1 & 2* (London: Sonnenschein, 1910), pp. 564–5.

[64] Ibid., p. 493. Hegel was citing Goethe's translation, which was then the only extant version, since Goethe had translated the dialogue from a posthumous manuscript. See Johann Wolfgang von Goethe, 'Rameau's Neffe: ein Dialog', in: Johann Wolfgang von Goethe, *Goethe's Werke: XX Band* (Stuttgart: J.G. Cotta, 1820; Vienna: Carl Armbruster, 1820), p. 119. For details, see James Schmidt, 'The Fool's Truth: Diderot, Goethe, and Hegel', *Journal of the History of Ideas*, vol. 57 (1996), n. 4: 625–44.

[65] Ibid., citing Denis Diderot, *Rameau's Nephew and Other Works* (Indianapolis, IN: Hackett, 2001), p. 119. This, the nephew explained, is 'how the Jesuits are said to have planted Christianity in China and India'—'without uproar, bloodshed, or martyrs', Denis Diderot, *Le neveu de Rameau* (Paris: Gallimard, 1972), p. 105.

fetishes were displaced by new ones, embodying not reason *sans phrase* but the 'practical reason' of circulation, elevating quantity over quality.[66]

Hegel had despised Diderot's iconoclasm, his '*dieu étranger*' of doubt, which he called a 'serpent of wisdom', enticing the faithful. Marx felt similarly about the counting-house rationality of surplus-value. The world, reduced to a market, becomes featureless, stripped of its pre-existing cultural distinctiveness. Much of that distinctiveness had been inhumane, but it had now been replaced by social relations that are either radically dehumanizing or, quite literally, depopulating.

8.5 Nomads of the Proletariat

Clearing the land, the defining moment of expropriation, was the concrete process which cleared the way for the triumph of abstraction. The hegemony of money was thus made possible by material means, by means of coercion. Marx's account of that process in the closing chapters of *Capital* is too well known to require elaboration here. But I want to note, *en passant*, that under the skin of Marx's narrative we see continuing evidence of his dialectic of dissolution and reconstitution. Capitalism requires 'the separation (*Scheidung*) of workers from the ownership of means of production', which it both 'sustains [and] reproduces on an ever-widening scale. [This] *Scheidungsprozess* [...] converts the social means of life and production into *capital* [and] the direct producers into *wage laborers*. [Indeed,] capital's prehistory, [...] so-called original accumulation, [...] is nothing other than the historical *Scheidungsprozess* between producers and means of production'.[67]

This process, this prehistory, is far from over, Marx says. It began in Tudor England but it has since extended concentrically to the world as a whole, and it has followed many paths. 'One sees at a glance that this *Scheidungsprozess* includes a whole series of historical processes' which unfold along two defining, parallel lines: the dissolution (*Auflösung*) of pre-existing class relations (feudal, slave) and the dissolution (*Auflösung*)

[66] Marx intimated his debt to Diderot less obliquely in *Le Capital* (1875), p. 337, where he substituted Diderot's original French ('*le dieu étranger*', etc.) for Goethe's translation.

[67] Marx, *Das Kapital* (1867), p. 700, italics in original.

of any surviving communal relations. In England the penumbra of dependents around the great lords was dispersed, while free farmers were chased from the land by 'fitful, forcible expropriation'.[68]

The newly dispossessed, if they were to be proletarianized—to be 'transformed into wage laborers'—had to make their way to the 'seaports or flatlands' which, because they were outside 'the old urban system and its guild charter', became the earliest manufacturing centres. This prompted 'bitter struggle' between the cities and the 'new industrial nurseries',[69] a struggle which ultimately led to the dissolution of the guilds. Viewed *in toto*, Marx concludes, 'this *Scheidungsprozess* is thus coterminous with the whole developmental history of modern bourgeois society'.[70]

Once expelled, labour enters a liminal state of precarity which cannot be overcome, even by employment. Wage earners are always potentially outcast. They are always vulnerable to a second expropriation, from employment itself. They are always actually or potentially migratory, oscillating in and out of the labour force, moving from one job or continent to another. Marx addressed this theme in his discussion of the 'Lazarus layers' of the proletariat, which divides, he said, into three principal groups: active and reserve armies of labour and the truly outcast, those who would now be called structurally unemployed. Many workers float between employment and joblessness, remaining 'latent' wage earners even when they vegetate in enforced idleness for extended periods. When they eventually do return to work, they regain a modicum of stability.[71] But there are some workers whose migratory status is effectively permanent. Marx calls one such category *das Wandervolk*. These workers, he says, are the '*nomades du proletariat*'—'a stratum of the populace', displaced from the land, 'whose employment is mainly industrial. This is the light infantry of capital, which (thrown here, now there, as capital

[68] Ibid., p. 719.

[69] Ibid., p. 734.

[70] Ibid., pp. 700–1. Here as elsewhere in my rendering of Marx's German, if I use the word 'dissolution', I am always translating some variation of the word *Auflösung*.

[71] See Marx, 'The General Law of Capital Accumulation'. The phrase 'Lazarus layers'—'*Lazarusschichte*' (Marx, *Das Kapital* (1867), p. 631), is another of Marx's neologisms and refers to a miracle in the Gospel of John in which Jesus resurrects Lazarus from entombment. When Lazarus walks into the light, he is swathed in strips of cloth, as if he had been mummified.

requires) "camps" when not on the march'. These transient workers build roads and railroads, make bricks and mortar for construction projects, and work episodically in fields and mining encampments.[72] They are, for all intents and purposes, homeless. 'In capital-intensive enterprises like railway building', Marx says, the employers build temporary housing for the workers—huts, 'without any health precautions'—thus exploiting them twice, both 'as industrial soldiers and as tenants'.[73]

Similar principles apply in mining camps. In 1865, just 12 health inspectors monitored no fewer than 3217 coal mines in Great Britain,[74] and though wages were often fairly high, the miners led profoundly unsettled lives. Mine operators recruited armies of miners 'and the craftsmen, shopkeepers, etc.', who cluster around them. 'Here, as always when people are crowded together, rents are high'. As renters themselves, leasing the mines from land owners, the mine operators 'treat the whole colony as if it were only camping, not residing'. With only one overriding concern—'abstinence' from 'all spending that is not absolutely unavoidable'—they 'throw up' as much makeshift housing as they can fit in 'the narrowest possible building space at the mouth of the mines'.[75]

The miners were thus very much at the mercy of their employers. They returned in rent much of what they earned in the mines,[76] and in the spirit of the reigning 'truck system' they returned still more for groceries and water.[77] New to the locale, without local roots, they accepted what

[72] Marx, *Das Kapital* (1872), p. 692. The phrase '*nomades du prolétariat*' appears in *Le Capital*, p. 293. That matches the 1867 German edition, where Marx called this group '*einer Wandervölkerung*', p. 652. How rarely this theme has been discussed is shown by the fact that the phrases 'Karl Marx' and '*Wandervölkerung*' appear together only in Marx, *Das Kapital* (1867). 'Karl Marx' and '*nomades du prolétariat*' appear together only in *Capital* and in three other sources.

[73] Marx, *Das Kapital* (1872), p. 692. One rough equivalent of this kind of migratory labour in corporate agriculture is what Marx, *Le Capital*, calls '*le systeme de bands ambulantes (Gangsystem)*', p. 305.

[74] Marx, *Das Kapital* (1872), p. 526, n. 321.

[75] Ibid., p. 695.

[76] Ibid. Marx cites an inspector, who said that the miners' homes 'are perhaps on the whole the worst and the dearest of which any large specimens can be found in England' at this level, citing Dr. Henry Julian Hunter, 'Inquiry on the State of the Dwellings of Rural Labourers', in: Public Health, *Seventh Report of the Medical Officer of the Privy Council* (London: H.M. Stationery Office, 1864), p. 180.

[77] Ibid. 'It appears to me that no part of the "truck system" can be worse than what obtains in these densely-populated districts', wrote another inspector. The worker relies

amounted to indentured servitude. All miners in Durham, an inspector reported, 'are bound [to the] owner for twelve months'. 'Bound', Marx paused to explain, is 'a term which, like *bondage*, dates from the days of serfdom'. And yet the miners, unlike serfs, remained insecure. 'If the workers complain, or in any way annoy the overseer, a mark of memorandum is placed by their names in the oversight book and, at the yearly 'binding', such men are turned away'.[78]

Even virtual bondage, it seems, was no protection from precarity in the age of capital. This precarity, in turn, was contagious, figuratively and literally, since the unsanitary conditions in mining areas made them nests of contagion, while the nomad proletariat per se was 'a flying column of pestilence, importing outbreaks of smallpox, typhus, cholera, scarlet fever, and so forth, everywhere it camps'.[79]

Was this kind of squalor and insecurity predestined for the world beyond Europe? Marx, in the drafts of his 1881 letter to Vera Zasulich, expressly rejected the claim of early 'Marxists' that capitalism in England should be regarded as the ineluctable fate of peoples outside western Europe.[80] But that claim is still often credited to Marx himself, a fact

on the owner even for water, in 'pestilential' conditions. 'Good or bad [...] he has to pay for [it], or rather he suffers a deduction for [it], from his wages', ibid., p. 695, citing Dr. William Stevens, 'Sanitary State of Colliery Settlements at Gilesgate Moor', in: Public Health, *Seventh Report*, p. 517.

[78] Ibid., pp. 695–6, where Marx cites Dr. Stevens again: 'he is to all intents and purposes a serf', p. 517. This report led the Privy Council's Medical Officer Dr. John Simon to conclude that, so weak is the miners' position, they can be counted upon to submit to even the 'obscenest' and 'foulest' conditions without striking, in: Public Health, *Seventh Report*, p. 16, cited by Marx, ibid., p. 697.

[79] Ibid., p. 692. Among the very few discussions of Marx's views on this subject is a shallow account by Paul Leroy-Beaulieu, who simply denies that 'modern industry [and its] system of temporary migrations [...] deprives workers of all stability'. In fact, he assures us, industry has provided 'all the security human destiny permits [...] for hundreds of thousands of those called proletarians, even millions; we can cite the railroad companies, the insurance companies', etc. See Paul Leroy-Beaulieu, *Le collectivisme* (Paris: Guillaumin, 1903), p. 314. Among contemporary scholars, Ranabir Samaddar stands out for his call to study how nomad proletarians ('dispersed, informal and unorganized [...] moving from one site to another') are managed in the age of postcolonial capitalism. See Ranabir Samaddar, *Karl Marx and the Postcolonial Age* (London: Palgrave Macmillan, 2018), p. 88.

[80] See the new translations of these drafts which are forthcoming in Smith, *Marx's World*.

which would seem to attest, in part, to the force and clarity of his insistence on the dissolving effects of commerce, money, and capital. It has been assumed that the universal 'dissolution of private property based on one's own labor' should be an article of faith for Marxists.[81] Marx, however, rejected that assumption, most tellingly in his letters to Zasulich, Danielson, and others with respect to the Russian peasant commune.[82] The ground for that stance can be found in a theme which threads its way, inconspicuously, through many of Marx's writings.

In the *Grundrisse*, Marx caps his discussion of money's solvent power with this reflection: 'Trade naturally reacts back (*zurückwirken*) [...] on the communities [which it connects]. It increasingly subjects production to exchange-value [and] drives use-value into the shadows by making [producers] more dependent on the product's sale than on its immediate use. It dissolves the old relations [...] But its dissolving effect (*auflösende Wirkung*) depends very much on the nature of the producing communities between which it operates. [Trade] e.g. has barely shaken the ancient Indian communities and Asian conditions in general'.[83]

This exact language appears again in Marx's *Economic Manuscript of 1861–63*.[84] His point, clearly, is that different social formations offer trade and capital different prospects. The question that arises is plain: What features of producing communities render them more or less soluble

[81] Marx, *Das Kapital* (1867), p. 742.

[82] Nikolai Sieber, departing sharply from Marx, took this inevitabilist stance to an extreme, defending even expropriations: 'We shall get nowhere', he reportedly said, 'until the peasant is boiled down in the factory cauldron' and becomes a proletarian. See, on this, the sources cited in David Norman Smith, 'The Spectral Reality of Value', *Research in Political Economy*, vol. 19 (2001): 52. Nikolai Danielson, who was close to Marx on this subject, reported this aperçu in a letter to Engels, see James D. White, *Karl Marx and the Intellectual Origins of Dialectical Materialism* (New York: St. Martins, 1996), p. 294.

[83] Marx, *Grundrisse*, MEW, vol. 42, p. 747.

[84] Karl Marx, 'Mercantile Capital. Money-Dealing Capital', in: Karl Marx, *Economic Manuscript of 1861–63*, MECW, vol. 33, p. 20. This is a lightly edited extract from the *Grundrisse* which Marx included a few years later in a manuscript that Karl Kautsky published, in part, under the title *Theorien über den Mehrwert*, see Karl Marx, *Theorien über den Mehrwert: aus dem nachgelassenen manuskript 'Zur kritik der politischen ökonomie', Bd. 2, David Ricardo* (Stuttgart: J. H. W. Dietz, 1905); and Karl Marx, *Theorien über den Mehrwert, Bd. 3, Von Ricardo zur vulgärökonomie* (Stuttgart: J. H. W. Dietz, 1910). This manuscript, known in English as *Theories of Surplus Value*, appears with other related texts in MECW, vols. 30–34.

under the impact of money? The answer to that question is provided, broadly speaking, in Marx's 1864–1865 manuscript, which was the source from which Engelsdistilled *Capital, Volume III*, three decades later.[85]

Once again, Marx repeats the key passage from the *Grundrisse* verbatim.[86] But now he amplifies this point: 'Trade always has, to a greater or lesser degree, a solvent effect on the pre-existing organizations of production, which in all their various forms are principally oriented to use-value. But how far it leads to the dissolution of the old mode of production depends first and foremost on the solidity (*Festigkeit*) and inner articulation (*innern Gliederung*) of this mode of production itself [...] And what *results from* this process of dissolution, that is, what *new mode of production* arises in place of the old, does not depend on trade, but rather on the character of the old mode of production itself'.[87]

Marx is now sounding a new theme. His interest in pre-capitalist social forms dates back to his earliest excerpt notes, and he had often cited the impact of capitalist on pre-capitalist societies. Now, though, he looks through both ends of the telescope, stressing that link between capitalist and pre-capitalist societies is dialectical. To grasp their *external* articulation, we need to grasp their inner articulation as well. Marx is driven to this point by his concern with capital accumulation. Trade can be either 'a system of plunder' *á la* Columbus or a gateway to capitalism. It can be either opportunist or accumulationist.

'With respect to less developed modes of production', he writes, 'mercantile capital, when hegemonic, [...] is always a system of plunder, [of] piracy, slave stealing and (in colonies) subjugation'.[88] But plunder yields only wealth, not capitalism. In modern times, in contrast, mercantile capital gives rise to precisely 'the *capitalist mode of production*'.

[85] Surmising that Marx wrote *Capital, Volume III* (London: Penguin, 1991) after he wrote *Capital, Volume II* (London: Penguin, 1991) would be reasonable. But in fact, the manuscript that Engels published in 1894 as the third volume of *Das Kapital* had actually been written before he even wrote the first volume. See the unedited manuscript in Karl Marx, *Ökonomische Manuskripte 1863–1867*, Teil 2, MEGA^2, vol. II/4.2, which is available in English as Karl Marx, *Marx's Economic Manuscript of 1864–1865* (Leiden: Brill, 2016).

[86] Marx, *Marx's Economic Manuscript of 1864–1865*, p. 435. Citations from this superb translation, below, appear with just a few minor modifications, e.g., lines or words from Marx's original texts.

[87] Ibid., p. 438.

[88] Ibid., p. 435.

This difference in outcomes—the generation of a system of profit, not booty—stems, Marx says, from factors other than the inner nature of mercantile capital. Merchants *qua* buccaneers can destroy old social forms, but they cannot build new ones. They can scavenge, but they are unable to produce a new mode of production. Only trade which has exchange-value as its premise and purpose has the capacity to reconstitute societies which, formerly, produced for use. 'The world market itself forms the basis for [the capitalist] mode of production. Yet at the same time, the need inherent [within] this mode of production] to produce on an ever-greater scale drives it to the constant expansion of the world market'.[89] That expansion, driven by capital's need to valorize itself on an ever-expanding scale, is the geographic correlate of what Marx calls 'the extended reproduction of capital'.[90] Capital accumulation, infinite in principle, requires ever new fields for investment in ever new domains—hence, physical as well as fiscal expansion. But that expansion is not a foregone conclusion, or frictionless. Social as well as material borders must be permeable, if capital is to successfully reproduce itself on an extended scale.[91]

Capital often suffers what Marx calls 'realization crises'. When products fail to realize their values in exchange, they are doubly stillborn, since they will remain unused as well as unsold. Failures to extend the world market are crises in a similar sense, since the exchange-values that capitalists conjure and display go unrecognized. 'Bring paper money into a country where this use of paper is unknown, and everyone will laugh at your

[89] Ibid., p. 438, translation amended.

[90] This is the principal subject of 'Manuscript VIII' in *Capital, Volume II*, about which, see below.

[91] A major recent literature has emerged around the theme of 'accumulation by dispossession'. This concept, introduced by David Harvey in 2004 in 'The 'New' Imperialism: Accumulation by Dispossession', *Socialist Register*, vol. 40 (2004): 63–87, has already been discussed by thousands of authors. But Harvey himself remains almost the only author in this field who has consistently invoked Marx on the solvent powers of money and trade. See David Harvey, 'The Geography of Capitalist Accumulation: A Reconstruction of the Marxian Theory', *Antipode*, vol. 7 (1975), n. 2: 9–21; and David Harvey, *A Companion to Marx's Capital, Volume 2* (London: Verso, 2013). On dispossession per se, see now Robert Nichols, *Theft Is Property!* (Durham: Duke University Press, 2019).

subjective fancy', Marx wrote in 1841.[92] Products are only commodities if they are regarded and treated as commodities, and that recognition can be withheld, in practice as well as in theory. Cultures which are committed to use-value can resist exchange-value. Whether they resist successfully depends on the internal character of their social structure. 'The obstacles that the inner solidity and articulation (*innere Festigkeit und Gliederung*) of earlier national modes of production oppose to the dissolving effect of trade are strikingly apparent in England's commercial intercourse with India and China', Marx writes. 'There the broad basis of the mode of production is formed by the union between small-scale agriculture and household industry, which, [...] in the Indian case, [takes] the form of self-sustaining communities'.[93] 'In India that unity was disrupted by England's [...] experiments', which left the community 'torn to pieces'. But even in India, Marx emphasized, the 'work of dissolution (*Auflösungswerk*) is succeeding only very gradually. These effects are felt still less in China', where England is not politically dominant and where 'the great economy and time saving that results from the *direct* union (*Verbindung*) of agriculture and manufacture presents a very stubborn resistance to [English] products, whose prices include the overhead expenses of circulation'.[94]

To illustrate this point, Marx cited a report showing that China's cloth production was so cheap and efficient, so solid and deeply rooted in integrated farming and handicrafts, that Chinese textile production remained

[92] 'Real dollars exist in the way that imagined gods exist. Has a real dollar any existence other than in the [...] common imagination of humanity? Come with your gods into a country where other gods are worshipped, and you will be shown to suffer from fantasies and abstractions. And justly so. Anyone who would have brought a Wendish god to the ancient Greeks would have found proof of this god's non-existence. Indeed, for the Greeks he did not exist'. This is from Marx's 1841 dissertation, Karl Marx, *Difference Between the Democritean and Epicurean Philosophy of Nature*, MECW, vol. 1, p. 104.

[93] Marx, *Marx's Economic Manuscript of 1864–1865*, p. 438. Engels substituted 'pre-capitalist' for 'earlier' in this passage, see Karl Marx, *Das Kapital, Bd. 3* (Hamburg: Otto Meissner, 1894), p. 317. He also omitted a note: 'It can be seen from Abel, etc., that in China too this was the original form, derived from a spontaneously arising communism'. This is a reference to I. I. Sacharoff, 'Ueber das Grundeigenthum in China', in: Carl Abel and F. A. Mecklenburg (eds.), *Arbeiten der Kaiserlich russischen gesandtschaft zu Peking über China* (Berlin: Heinecke, 1858), pp. 3–43. Sacharoff, in turn, relied principally upon Mă Duānlín, *Wen xian tong kao jing ji kao* [Textual Examination of Confucian Classics] (Shanghai: East China Normal University Press, 1985).

[94] Marx, *Marx's Economic Manuscript of 1864–1865*, pp. 439–40, n. 31.

undisturbed, despite concerted English efforts to compete. This was the conclusion reached by the expatriate businessman 'Mr. Mitchell', who, in a letter to the British embassy in 1852, attested to 'the beautiful and simple economy' of the Chinese system, 'an economy which renders the system literally impregnable against all the assaults of foreign competition'. This impregnability sprang, Mitchell saw, from the fact that, in Fujian and elsewhere in China, 'the farmer is [...] not merely a farmer, but an agriculturist and a manufacturer in one!'.[95]

8.6 Powers of Resistance

Shortly after publishing *Capital, Volume I* in 1867, Marx turned to the second volume, penning an early fragment which, thanks to Engels, we now know as Manuscript II. One of the themes of that manuscript is the kind of realization crisis which affects people who produce use-values—the failure to realize the usefulness of what they make. Floods, droughts, and other natural disasters occupy central places in the pantheon of such crises. But social disasters are central, too, in a world which has been knitted into a predatory unity by the extension of the world market.

Marx points out that when products are converted into commodities, stockpiles of back-up products—which shield us from need in times of crisis—assume commodity form as well. Adam Smith had thought that stockpiling is unique to the *Waarenwelt.* But stockpiled reserves of use-values have always been a vital necessity, which capitalism now undermines and disfigures. The 'change of form' which stored use-values experience when they become stored exchange-values 'causes the most violent and dangerous crises', Marx says, in the sphere of consumption. 'In India, e.g. the age-old practice of storing surplus grain [...] has been sustained until very recently'. But 'the sudden vast increase in demand for cotton', triggered by the blockade of the South during the American civil war, 'caused great restrictions on rice cultivation, increases in the price of rice, and the sale of rice stocks [in 1864–1866] to Australia, Madagascar, etc.' In Mysore, peasants who needed cash to buy supplies and repay money

[95] Ibid., p. 440, n. 32. Engels omitted this note from *Das Kapital, Bd. 3* (1894). Mitchell's letter, which drew upon his experience in Fujian and elsewhere, is well known to historians, see for example, Shinkichi Eto, 'Mitcheru hokokusho ni tsuite' ['A Study on the Mitchell Report'], in: Shinkichi Eto, *Kindai chugoku seijishi kenkyu* [Studies of Modern Chinese Politics] (Tokyo: University of Tokyo Press, 1968), pp. 215–33.

lenders took advantage of the 'extravagant' prices to export grain they had stored for years, and as a result, 'in many places, there was an absolute shortage of even seed-grain'. An artificial shortage ensued, with the grimmest of consequences. This explains, Marx says, 'the acute character of the 1866 famine, which in the Orissa district alone killed a million people'.[96]

This tragedy was far from unique. 'The same thing happened [...] in Algeria. There is no doubt that the reconstitution of the old Arab system of grain storage, which was caused by the export of grain to France, aggravated the recent famine terribly'—a famine which a historian calls 'an unthinkable humanitarian and demographic disaster. Most scholars estimate that [about] eight hundred thousand Algerians died, [that is], between a quarter and a third of the total indigenous population'.[97]

Entanglement in the world market thus heightens risks of destitution for peasants. They can remain self-sufficient only to the extent that they have active and reserve stores of means of subsistence and production—and they need both. Even if they still own land, if they are forced or tempted to sell their reserves of means of production (e.g., seed grain) or means of subsistence (e.g., rice), they are left unprotected against the vagaries of the seasons. They may not yet be expropriated, but they are already feeling money's dissolving effects.[98]

This is a bleak picture, but there is, Marx says, another side to the coin. Peasants who remain independent, with direct personal or collective access to land or use-values, still have what he calls *Widerstandskraft*—resistance power. 'English official reports', Marx writes, were not wrong

[96] Karl Marx, *Manuskripte zum zweiten Buch des 'Kapitals' 1868 bis 1881*, MEGA^2, vol. II/11, pp. 61, 62. Marx drew these points from official sources: House of Commons, *Return, East India, Bengal, and Orissa Famine*, Part I (Parliament: House of Commons, 1867, pp. 230, 231; and Henry Waterfield, 'Statement Exhibiting the Moral and Material Progress and Condition of India, During the Year 1865–66', in: House of Lords, *Accounts and Papers*, vol. XIII (Great Britain: House of Lords, 1867), p. 41.

[97] Marx, *Manuskripte zum zweiten Buch des 'Kapitals' 1868 bis 1881*, p. 62; and Yan Slobodkin, *Empire of Hunger: Famine and the French Colonial State, 1867–1945* (PhD, Stanford University, 2018), p. 29. The French governor-general of Algeria opened an 1867 report to Napoleon III on an upbeat note: 'there is reason to hope that when the sun will have acted efficiently on the corpses of poorly-buried people, the oasis will return to its normal state', ibid., p. 29.

[98] Market vicissitudes, in other words, weaken peasants with respect to natural vicissitudes. Money famine often leads to actual famine.

to blame the 1866 famine in part on the fact that 'people who have been converted into wage laborers have to buy their food'; but the scale of famine could have been even worse if so many of India's peasants had not remained self-sufficient. Despite the tragic scale and horror of the famine, the peasantry was still shielded from unmitigated reliance on the market. In Western Europe, in contrast, the share of the populace which relied entirely on wages was greater than in India. This made it 'impossible for the English and French working classes', Marx wrote, 'to withstand [rising food] prices [with as much] resistance power (*Widerstandskraft*) as the Indian masses'. Even peasants who had begun to feel the deadly effects of the market, in other words, were not yet wholly captured by commerce.[99] This was especially true for Indian village communities. The net consequence was that the 'resistance power' of European workerswas 'far below [...] the Asian level'.[100]

The arrow of Marx's thinking was subtly changing direction. Not long before, in *Capital* he had stressed the morbid effects of the 'destruction process' (*Zerstörungsprozess*) which brought farming under the heel of capital. The result, he said, was 'the martyrology of the producers', the conversion of life-sustaining means of production into 'means of subjugation, exploitation, and immiseration'. Labour was intensified, labour-power was deskilled, the land was depleted, and 'socially combined labor processes' were splintered, making separation, not cooperation, the dominant mode of sociality.[101]

[99] The concept of the 'captured peasantry' has loomed large in agrarian studies since Göran Hydén coined the term in 1980, in his *Beyond Ujamaa in Tanzania* (Berkeley: University of California Press). But as I argue in 'Capital and the Thrill of Domination', in: Alan Sica (ed.), *The Routledge Handbook of Max Weber Studies* (London: Routledge, 2021, forthcoming), it is equally applicable to the working class in periods when its powers of self-organization are compromised.

[100] Marx, *Manuskripte zum zweiten Buch des 'Kapitals' 1868 bis 1881*, pp. 1009, 1010. These citations are drawn from variant versions of lines that appear in MEGA^2, vol. II/11, where Marx concludes as follows: 'Compared with earlier social conditions, capitalist society thus shows a *decrease* in the *consumption reserve in its immediate form*, i.e., as a consumption reserve in the hands of consumers themselves, and [a] corresponding *increase* in the consumption [stock that exists] as a *commodity reserve* [in the hands of capitalists]', pp. 61–2.

[101] Marx, *Das Kapital* (1867), p. 494.

The breakdown of collectivity was especially debilitating, since self-defense required collective strength. 'Just as the offensive power (*Angriff-skraft*) of a cavalry squadron or the resistance power (*Widerstandskraft*) of an infantry regiment is essentially different from [and greater than] the sum of individual offensive and resistance powers', so the sum of isolated individual powers falls below the 'power potential that emerges when many hands join together in the same undivided operation'.[102] In cooperation there is strength; in separation, weakness.[103]

What this implied for peasants was dispiriting. Factory workers had recovered from the 'martyrdom' of their original expropriation and atomization. As industry grew, they were enlisted into new relations of cooperation. Soaring industrial growth went 'hand in hand', Marx said, 'with the physical and moral rebirth of the factory workers' whose new relations of cooperation enabled them to wrest a shorter working day from capital. When, after 'a half-century of civil war, [...] the factory magnates bowed to the inevitable, [...] the *Widerstandskraft* of capital weakened and the offensive power (*Angriffskraft*) of the working class increased'.[104] This inflection point, which came after 1853, resulted from the urbanization of factory workers, which enhanced their mass strength. But the same could not be said for agrarian workers, who faced ongoing separation: 'The dispersal (*Zerstreuung*) of rural workers over larger areas breaks their resistance, while concentration increases that of urban workers'.[105]

Marx had been even more pessimistic about the prospect of rural resistance in 1853, in an article that prefigured *Capital*. 'The rural population', which had always been 'the most stationary and conservative element' of society, was being forced to migrate and 'disappear' under the pressure of expropriation and mechanization, while city workers gathered 'in mighty centers', which, once the scene of their 'martyrology', had

[102] Ibid., p. 306.

[103] This point is central to 'Cooperation', in: Marx, *Capital, Volume I*, MECW, pp. 326–41.

[104] Marx, *Das Kapital* (1867), p. 273. Mario Tronti is among the few who have highlighted this passage. Hoping that workers, reduced to personified labour-power, will leap the synapse from life *an sich* to *für sich*, Tronti concludes with a flourish: '*Arbeitskraft* can and must become *Angriffskraft*'. See Mario Tronti, 'Selections from *Workers and Capital*', *Genre*, vol. 43 (2010), n. 3–4: 339.

[105] Marx, *Das Kapital* (1867), pp. 494–5.

become citadels of proletarian strength. Where will capital find 'the power of resisting them? Nowhere!'.[106]

The overconfidence of this estimate of city workers' *Angriffskraft* was matched by Marx's underestimate of country workers' *Widerstandskraft*. Farm proletarians, he wrote, starving and forced into emigration—'not the emigration caused by the gold mania, but [...] compulsory emigration' under the pressure of landlordism—were powerless in the face of history's remorseless advance. 'Society is undergoing a silent revolution, which must be submitted to, and which takes no more notice of the human existences it breaks down than an earthquake regards the houses it subverts'.[107]

This early inevitabilism was not destined to last. Marx, too, changed after 1853. By the time he wrote *Capital*, his thinking had become far less mechanical and complacent. He devoted many pages of *Capital* to the agrarian proletariat, without predicting its imminent demise. Still, at this point Marx had not yet carefully considered the possibility of rural or indigenous resistance to capital's extended reproduction. His remarks about the impregnability of the Chinese economy and about Indian peasant *Widerstandskraft*—remarks which appeared, in both instances, in unpublished manuscripts—reflected a shift in emphasis, but that shift, at this stage, remained only a hint of things to come.

Scholars who discuss Marx's so-called ethnological notes—his excerpts from books by Phear, Maine, Morgan, and Lubbock in the final years of his life, from 1878 to 1882—generally assume that his interests had migrated away from *Capital*. I see things differently. It is not an accident, in my opinion, that Marx excerpted these books at the very moment when he was writing the section of *Capital, Volume II* on the global extension

[106] Marx concludes this article with a version of his later prediction that the expropriators, too, will ultimately be expropriated: Karl Marx, 'Forced Emigration', MEGA^2, vol. I/12, 1984, p. 59. Cf. Karl Marx, 'Forced Migration', MECW, vol. 11, pp. 528–34. Ralph Waldo Emerson found this passage inspiring, see Robert Richardson, *Emerson: The Mind on Fire* (Berkeley: University of California Press, 2015), p. 508. See also the excellent discussion by Nicolas Eyguesier, 'Marx, Primitive Accumulation, and the Impact of Sismondi', *The European Journal of the History of Economic Thought*, vol. 25 (2018), n. 50: 846ff.

[107] Marx, 'Forced Emigration', MEGA^2, p. 59.

of capital.[108] The text which resulted from that attempt, which Engels called 'Manuscript VIII' and published as the final third of *Capital, Volume II*,[109] was Marx's most ambitious attempt to explain the world market in the age of ***industrial*** capital. Commercial capital had proven its solvent powers, but capitalism per se could not be created by commerce alone. Capitalism could only realize surplus-value on an expanding scale by growing beyond the Euro-Atlantic sphere. Its systemic needs were dual: not only to separate labour-power from means of production but to reunite them. That, hence, was capital's global mission. But Marx no longer believed that rural peoples were defenseless before capital's incursions, or that capital alone had the creative power to industrialize society and reproduce use-value on an extended scale.

From October 1877 to July 1878, on the eve of writing Manuscript VIII, Marx wrote a short text in which he discussed the plight of 'Russian landowners, who [...] now conduct their rural operations with wage-laborers instead of enserfed forced laborers'. They complain, he wrote, that the labour-power they need to buy 'is not available in sufficient quantity and at the right time. This', Marx explains, 'is because the Russian rural worker is not yet fully separated (*getrennt*) from his means of production[110] and is thus still not a "free wage-laborer" in the full sense of the word. But the availability of the latter on a society-wide scale is the *sine qua non* without which' capitalist commodity production is impossible.[111]

Will that 'fully separated' labour become fully available to Russian employers? Not necessarily. In November 1877, with that question in mind, Marx wrote a letter to the Russian journal *Otechestvenniye Zapiski* (*Notes from the Fatherland*) in which he asked, 'must Russia begin, as

[108] In *Capital, Volume I*, Marx analyzes the production process. In *Capital, Volume II*, to which he devoted the remainder of his life, Marx analyzes the dialectical unity of capitalist production and circulation.

[109] This volume too can be consulted in its raw, original, pre-Engels form: Marx, *Manuskripte zum zweiten Buch des 'Kapitals' 1868 bis 1881*. In this, see especially Karl Marx, 'Manuskript VIII', pp. 698–828, which is Marx's most sustained discussion of capital accumulation.

[110] Engels inserted a clarifying phrase at this point: 'owing to the common ownership of the soil by the village community'. See Karl Marx, *Das Kapital, Bd. 2* (Hamburg: Otto Meissner, 1885), p. 117; and cf. Karl Marx, *Das Kapital, Bd. 2*, MEGA^2, vol. II/12, pp. 17ff.

[111] Marx, *Manuskripte zum zweiten Buch des 'Kapitals' 1868 bis 1881*, p. 695.

the liberal economists allege, by destroying the rural commune in order to pass over into the capitalist regime, or can she appropriate its fruits [...] without suffering [its] tortures?'. Since 1870 he had studied Russian conditions intensively, and 'I arrived at this result: If Russia remains on the path to capitalism, as it has since 1861, it will lose the finest chance that history has ever offered a people, only to suffer all the fatal vicissitudes of the capitalist regime'.[112]

The triumph of capitalism over communalism, in other words, was not inevitable. Resistance and noncapitalist industrialization could not be ruled out. Only in the British isles, in fact, had the transition to wage labour been effectively completed.[113] Elsewhere, even in Western Europe, the commodification of labour-power remained a work in progress. That was all the more true in more remote regions. In the final paragraph of his 1877–1878 manuscript, which Engels made the opening of *Capital, Volume II*, Marx restated his founding premise, namely, that everything conducive to capitalist commodity production has 'a destructive and dissolving effect (*wirkt sie zersetzend u. auflösend*) on all those forms of production which [...] convert only excess products into commodities'. Trade is the spearhead of the assault. 'It makes selling the product the main interest, without at first appearing to attack the mode of production itself'; this was, e.g., 'the first effect of capitalist world trade on such peoples as the Chinese, Indians, Arabs, etc.' But ultimately, if producers are tempted or forced to sell their products abroad on a more than incidental basis, their traditional mode of production is undermined. Where capitalist commodity exchange 'takes root', Marx writes, 'it destroys all forms of commodity production which are based either in the producers' own labor or simply in the sale of excess products as commodities'.[114]

[112] Karl Marx, 'Letter to *Otechestvenniye Zapiski*', in: Nicolai-On, *Die Volkswirtschaft in Russland nach der Bauern-Emancipation* (Munich: Lukaschik, 1899), pp. 528–30, in Marx's original French. Cf. Karl Marx, 'Letter to Otechestvenniye Zapiski', MECW, vol. 24, pp. 196–201; and Karl Marx, 'L'article "Karl Marx devant le tribunal de M. Joukowski"', MEGA^2, vol. I/25, pp. 112–6. Marx quotes often here from *Le Capital* about the *séparation radicale* of the peasants from the means of production. Hal Draper, *Marx–Engels Chronicle* (New York: Schocken, 1985), pp. 153, 203, is the source for the dates cited above.

[113] Marx, 'Letter to *Otechestvenniye Zapiski*'.

[114] Ibid.

This raises fundamental questions. To what extent is exchange of this kind contingent and resistible? Under what circumstances does it take root? Under what circumstances, in contrast, may it falter or fail?

In the period when Marx wrote to the editors of *Отечественные записки* and wrote Manuscripts VII and VIII of *Capital, Volume II*, he was in regular dialogue with Nikolai Frantsevich Danielson, who was among his principal interlocutors. It was to Danielson, who would ultimately translate all three volumes of *Capital*, that he sent the handwritten manuscript of the *Отечественные записки* letter.[115] Not long afterwards, Marx and Danielson exchanged a series of letters of great importance to understand what Marx intended for *Capital, Volume II*. Danielson, like Marx, was trying to grasp the effects of world trade on Russia, which he was studying by statistical and archival means. In early 1879, he wrote to Marx to report his findings. Russia's agrarian economy, he said, was caught in a bind. Railways and banks had penetrated deep into Russian society, converting subsistence goods into export commodities on a grand scale. This not only harnessed peasants to the exigencies of global circulation but exposed them to the risk of famine.[116] Railways above all were central to this process, attracting a majority of all Russian corporate investments while leaving the government, as the railways' main financier, deeply in debt—a debt redressed, but only in part, by taxing and exploiting the peasantry.[117]

Marx replied to Danielson's letter at length, in English. 'The railways sprang up first as the *couronnement de l'oeuvre* in those countries where *modern industry was most developed*, England, United States, Belgium, France, etc. I call them the '*couronnement de l'oeuvre*' not only in the sense that they were at last (together with steamships for oceanic

[115] This letter, which initially went unpublished, first appeared when a brief thaw in Russian despotism after the 1905 revolution enabled Danielson to publish his correspondence, see Karl Marx and Friedrich Engels, *Pis'ma Karla Marksa i Fridrikha Engel'sa k Nikolaiyu-onu [N. F. Daniel'sonu]* [Letters from Karl Marx and Friedrich Engels to Nikolai-on (N. F. Danielson)] (St.-Petersburg: Tip A. Benke, 1908).

[116] The tragic accuracy of this forecast was shown by Russia's epic famine a dozen years later.

[117] On Danielson, see Esther Kingston-Mann, 'Marxism and Russian Rural Development', *The American Historical Review*, vol. 86 (1981), n. 4: 731–52; and now James D. White, 'The Development of Capitalism in Russia in the Works of Marx, Danielson, Vorontzov, and Lenin', in: Paul Zarembka (ed.), *Class History and Class Practices in the Periphery of Capitalism* (Bingley, UK: Emerald, 2019).

intercourse and the telegraphs) the *means of communication* adequate to the modern means of production, but also in so far as they were the basis of immense joint stock companies [....] they gave [...] an impetus never before suspected to the *concentration of capital*, and also to the accelerated and immensely *enlarged cosmopolitan activity of loanable capital*, thus embracing the whole world in a network of financial swindling and mutual indebtedness, the capitalist form of "international" brotherhood'.[118]

For societies, however, at the periphery of modern industry, as Danielson had seen, the consequences of this 'crowning achievement' were less than happy: 'the appearance of the railway system [...] allowed, and even forced, states where capitalism was confined to a few summits of society, to suddenly [...] enlarge their capitalistic superstructure [to the detriment] of production in the traditional modes. There is [...] not the least doubt that in those states the railway creation has accelerated the social and political disintegration'. Nearly everywhere, 'governments enriched and fostered the railway companies at the expense of the Public Exchequer', which led them to raise taxes, often steeply, to pay their debts. The masses also suffered when, 'from the moment every local product could be converted into cosmopolitan gold, many articles *formerly* [...] invendible [...] became *dear* and were withdrawn from the consumption of the people, while [...] *production itself* [...] was changed according to its [...] *suitableness for exportation*', with predictable consequences. Marx cites, as an example, a case in which land 'was converted into pasture, because the export of cattle was more profitable', with the result that 'the agricultural population was driven away'.[119]

This web of themes was central to Marx's work on *Capital, Volume II*, which Danielson said he hoped would be ready for translation soon. Marx said that, given the darkening political climate in Germany—Bismarck's anti-socialist law had just been enacted—his publisher, Meissner, had told him publication would have to be delayed. 'This news', Marx told Danielson, 'I must confess, was far from annoying me', for a few reasons—most notably, his wish to study the mass of materials he had gathered about Russia and the United States, and his wish to monitor the unfolding global crisis, which had started in 1873. In the meantime, Marx encouraged Danielson to publish his findings, which resulted, a year

[118] Karl Marx to Nikolai Danielson, 10 April 1879, MECW, vol. 45, p. 356.

[119] Ibid., p. 357.

later, in a lengthy article in the journal *Slovo*.[120] Marx carefully annotated this article, urged the author to expand it into a book, and paraphrased Danielson's core argument in his correspondence with Vera Zasulich in 1881.[121]

In the years that followed Marx pursued these themes further, with respect to developments in many places, including Russia and the United States. His very final set of reading notes, on Egypt's exploitation by European capital, shed light on the ongoing progress and direction of that research.

8.7 Egypt Dispossessed

Marx excerpted Michael George Mulhall's article 'Egyptian Finance' in the fall of 1882, after returning to London from sojourns in Algeria and France, where he had travelled in the hope of restoring his failing health. Momentarily reinvigorated, Marx purchased an armful of factory reports and volumes of agricultural statistics.[122] He was, plainly, still hoping to return to *Capital*. Though that wish was not to be granted, his unpublished excerpts from Mulhall's article reflect the same wish.

Egypt was already, as it remains, one of the principal economies on the outer edge of Euro-Atlantic capitalism. As the granary of the Ottoman empire in the seventeenth and eighteenth centuries, Egypt's Nile breadbasket supplied the Sultan with wheat, rice, and lentils while Egypt also served as the transit hub for the inter-regional trade in spices and coffee. Hence Egypt had been entangled in trade for centuries, with appreciable but, overall, minor dissolving effects, when Napoleon invaded in 1798.

[120] This article appeared under the pseudonym Nikolai-on, Nikolai Danielson, 'Otcherki Nashego Poreformenogo Obschestvenogo Hoziatsva' ['Essays on Our Post-Reform Social Economy'], *Slovo*, no. 10 (1880): 77–142. Marx, respectful of Danielson's need for anonymity, signed his letters 'A. Williams'.

[121] Marx's notes on Danielson's article, introduced by Raisa Pavlovna Koniushaia, appear in Russian translation in Institut Marksa-Engel'sa-Lenina, *Arkhiv Marksa i Engel'sa*, vol. 12 (Moscow: Gospolitizdat, 1952), pp. 118–20. For details, see White, 'The Development of Capitalism in Russia in the Works of Marx, Danielson, Vorontzov and Lenin'.

[122] Karl Marx to Philip King, 9 November 1882, MECW, vol. 46, pp. 367–8. Marx also asked Eduard Bernstein to send him an article which discussed the founding concepts in *Capital, Volume I*, ibid., p. 364.

Fighting between the local warlords, aggravated by epidemics and competition from French Caribbean coffee growers, had shaken Egypt, and the warlords had increased taxes to finance their conflicts, driving a stream of peasants from the land. But Egypt was not infirm when Napoleon invaded, and an Ottoman army led by the Albanian *condottiere* Mehmed ‘Ali soon repelled the French invaders and restored the *status quo ante*.[123]

In 1805, when Mehmed ‘Ali officially became the ruler of the semi-autonomous Ottoman province of Egypt, the peasantry was still oriented to subsistence.[124] Rural life had been disturbed by incipient monetization and the depredations of the warlords, 300 of whom had claimed title to nearly two thirds of all farmland. But trade was still mainly regional (only 15% of Egypt's exports went to Europe), village communalism remained intact, and Mehmed ‘Ali soon expropriated and, in 1811, massacred the warlords.

Restoring the old order was not, however, Mehmed ‘Ali's aim, and though he ultimately drew Egypt far more deeply into the world market, his original aim had been to rival European capitalism, not serve it. No sooner had he freed the peasants from the burden of warlord taxes than he subjected them to intensive state control. In 1812 he seized the grain crop and his Albanian cavalry slaughtered anyone who resisted. Soon after, he mandated export production at below-market rates, with all profits accruing to the regime. In 1823, he began to export Egypt's main cash crop, cotton, and in 1829 he imposed a law regulating every aspect of production.

Timothy Mitchell, noting that Mehmed ‘Ali was advised by Jeremy Bentham's protégé John Bowring, has called his regime ‘panoptical’.[125]

[123] Details here and below, unless otherwise noted, are from the following: Raouf Abbas and Assem el-Dessouky, *The Large Landowning Class and the Peasantry in Egypt, 1837–1952* (Syracuse: Syracuse University Press, 2011); Alan R. Richards, ‘Primitive Accumulation in Egypt, 1798–1882’, *Review*, vol. 1 (1977), n. 2: 3–49; Juan R. I. Cole, *Colonialism and Revolution in the Middle East* (Princeton: Princeton University Press, 1993); Zachary Lockman, ‘“Worker” and “Working Class in Pre-1914 Egypt’, in: Zachary Lockman (ed.), *Workers and Working Class in the Middle East: Struggles, Histories, Historiographies* (Albany: SUNY Press, 1994), pp. 71–110; and Joel Beinin, *Workers and Peasants in the Modern Middle East* (Cambridge: Cambridge University Press, 2001).

[124] Many other variations on Mehmed ‘Ali's first name are current in the literature: Mehemed, Mehmet, Mohamed, Muhammad, etc.

[125] Timothy Mitchell, *Colonising Egypt* (Berkeley: University of California Press, 1991), pp. 24, 35, 185.

It was, indeed, all-encompassing in its ambitions. Not content with forced commodity production in agriculture, Mehmed 'Ali set up arms and textile factories which ultimately employed as many as 30,000–40,000 workers.[126] He built shipyards and a small armada, with the aim, it seems, of building a kind of state capitalism. But his industrial regime was as much Elizabethan as it was modern, resting on the labour of displaced peasants who had been forced into the factories, where they were tattooed with the names of their factories, so that they could be captured if they fled.

This regime provoked resistance, first from the peasants. Between 1820 and 1827 there were five peasant revolts, including three in Qina in upper Egypt. In 1821, 40,000 peasants rose in revolt, and in 1823 an even larger uprising broke out. But, at this stage, the *Angriffskraft* of Mehmed 'Ali's cavalry prevailed over the *Widerstandskraft* of the peasantry. Demoralized, many peasants simply fled, abandoning up to a quarter of the cultivable land in Upper Egypt by 1831. The regime chased after them, returning 6000 from Alexandria in a single round-up.[127]

European resistance proved more effective. Unwilling to countenance Mehmed 'Ali's swelling imperial and industrial ambitions, England and Austria sent a flotilla to Egypt's shores, forcing him to shutter his factories and clear the path to European commerce while sharply reducing the scale and reach of his military.

At this point, Egypt's traditional mode of production had been shaken, but its basis, the village community, had been neither dissolved nor destroyed. Village land was still held in common, it was still periodically redistributed and villagers remained collectively responsible for taxes and corvée labour.[128] It was only after Mehmed 'Ali's reign ended in 1848, that deeper, more solvent effects began to be felt. Those effects were the prime focus of Marx's notes.

The floodgates to European influence were opened from 1854 to 1863 by Sa'id Pasha, who privatized the most common form of land tenure,

[126] This was a non-negligible but small step towards the creation of an industrial labour force, since Egypt's population in this period hovered around 3–4 million.

[127] Gabriel Baer, 'Submissiveness and Revolt of the Fellah', in: Gabriel Baer, *Studies in the Social History of Modern Egypt* (Chicago: University of Chicago Press, 1969), p. 98.

[128] Gabriel Baer, 'The Dissolution of the Egyptian Village Community', *Die Welt des Islams*, vol. 6 (1959), n. 1: 56, 59.

abolished land redistribution, individualized taxes and granted vast fiefdoms to his family and vassals, thereby laying the ground for a new landed nobility with close ties to European trade and finance.[129] When southern cotton exports were blocked during the US Civil War, this new nobility moved quickly to expand cotton production and profits, and the regime borrowed £3,300,000 from a European lender to finance the needed infrastructure—railways, canals, and telegraphs. (Construction of the Suez Canal had recently begun.) That was the situation when Isma'il Pasha became viceroy in 1863.

The extent to which Isma'il came to depend on European finance was stunning. Marx noted that, by the end of his 16 year reign, Isma'il had swollen the debt *over 30-fold*. In each of the four years after he became viceroy, he took out large new loans, raising the grand total in this phase to £17,471,000. When cotton profits fell after the Civil War, as Isma'il found it ever harder to pay his debts, he borrowed at a frantic pace, taking out new loans totaling £51,033,000 over the next five years. The effects were ruinous, above all for the peasants.

Hounded by his European creditors, Isma'il turned to the peasantry. The 'basis' of his system, Marx wrote, 'was the *landtax*'. That tax was harrowingly steep, ultimately amounting to one eighth of the total value of Egyptian crops. Ordinary peasants, *fallāḥīn*, who held their land by *kharajī* tenure, owned 64.3% of the land but paid 79.7% of total taxes.[130] And there were extraordinary land taxes as well, of which the *Muqabala* (a forced payment of future taxes, which Isma'il introduced in 1871 and stiffened in 1874) was the most notable. 'The landholders', Marx observed, '*paid under the Muqabala 17 Million £*'—nearly triple the ordinary annual tax revenue.[131]

Isma'il's default method of forcing delinquent tax payments was an ancient torture known as *bastinado*—caning victims on the soles of their feet. Marx noted that, hounded by his European creditors, Isma'il now ensured that the *fallāḥīn* were '*bastinadoed*' even more regularly and

[129] Ibid., pp. 64, 66, 69.

[130] In contrast, *zawats* ('rich proprietors', holding land by *'ushurī* tenure) and those favoured with special *ab'adiya* grants owned over a third of the land yet paid just one fifth of the taxes.

[131] Marx reproduced Mulhall's archaic spelling, which I have replaced with today's equivalents.

energetically than usual.[132] Each year their plight worsened, and the consequence was unsustainable misery. Marx quoted Britain's Consul General, 'Mr. Vivian'—Hussey Crespigny Vivian, 3rd Baron Vivian—who expressed chagrin in 1877 that Isma'il was being forced by European pressure '*to collect nine months taxes in advance. I fear this will cause the utter ruin of the peasantry, an that the bondholders will find out perhaps too late, that they have destroyed the working-bees that made the honey*'.[133]

That fear was entirely realistic. As Rosa Luxemburg would later write, the peasants grew so desperate that, across Upper Egypt, they fled their villages and destroyed their homes, their cattle, and their date palms. Many starved, and many others came to the brink.[134]

What did Isma'il buy with his ill-gotten revenue? Above all, railways, canals, bridges, and harbours, in a pattern reminiscent of Russian spending in the same years. Of the £46,264,000 that the regime spent on public works from 1863 to 1879, Marx found that railway costs (£13,361,000) were the largest single item, amounting to 28.9% of the total. The Suez Canal, which was completed in 1869, had cost £6,770,000 and, *in toto*, spending for means of transport accounted for 83.3% of public expenditures.[135] Of the remainder, the majority paid for sugar mills, which were intended to yield export revenue when cotton sales declined.

The value of exports tripled in this period, and revenue nearly doubled. But those gains, which were largely achieved by forcing or tempting peasants to grow cotton, paled next to Isma'il's towering debt. The outcome was calamitous and, for Marx, entirely predictable. The regime, destitute

[132] As Cole, *Colonialism and Revolution in the Middle East*, wrote later: 'The buffalo-hide whip, or *kurbaj*, expressed in its rasping whisper the state's extractive determination', p. 74.

[133] These italics represent Marx's underlining.

[134] Rosa Luxemburg, *The Accumulation of Capital: A Contribution to the Economic Theory of Imperialism*, in: Peter Hudis and Paul Le Blanc (eds.), *The Complete Works of Rosa Luxemburg, Volume II: Economic Writings 2* (London: Verso, 2015), p. 317. Cole, *Colonialism and Revolution in the Middle East*, cites a British official who said that 'not less than ten thousand [...] had died of starvation' in 1878–1879, all from 'poverty arising from over-taxation', p. 74.

[135] As early as 1868, over 70% of all state employees worked for the railways as drivers, signalers, vehicle loaders, labourers, etc. See Mohammed Saleh, *The Reluctant Transformation* (Toulouse: Toulouse School of Economics and the Institute for Advanced Study in Toulouse, 2014).

and desperate, vainly attempted to shift the costs of its debt to the peasantry, which not only plunged the *fallāḥīn* into misery but, structurally, further corroded the 'inner articulation' of traditional Egyptian production relations, at long last. The residue of village communalism which had survived Mehmed 'Ali's autarky and Sa'id Pasha's privatizations now came almost entirely undone. The last straw, Marx wrote, came when Isma'il was confronted with the '*demands of Sir George Elliott and Messrs. Greenfield*, in connection with the harbour-works of Alexandria'.

The regime had been 'virtually bankrupt' since 1873, due to what had been delicately called 'the unwise haste of the bondholders to get back their money'.[136] But now the regime was utterly penniless. Under the pressure of '*2,500 bondholders*' and the 'crocodiles' who represented them, an attempt was made 'to remodel Egyptian finance on a different basis'. Isma'il was forced to cede financial control to an Anglo-European commission, the *Caisse de la Dette Publique*, and soon, European money lenders were plying their trade in rural areas, authorized, for the first time, to evict peasants who defaulted on their debts. The regime, as Juan Cole has said, was now not a panopticon, but a panklepticon.[137]

Isma'il himself was far from innocent in this drama. In return for recognizing his descendants as his vice-regal heirs, Ismail paid the Ottoman Sultan 8% of Egypt's annual gross revenue. And by maneuvers one of Marx's sources called 'adroit and unscrupulous', he expanded his private landholdings *33-fold* during his reign—thus personally depriving the peasants of 20% of all of the country's arable land. To work his estates, he pressed peasants into forced labour. 'The result', Marx remarked, was that he became 'a slavedriver on the largest scale'.[138]

[136] Marx called this phrase an 'alias' for greed.

[137] Cole, *Colonialism and Revolution in the Middle East*, p. 85.

[138] Marx drew some of his information about the 'great peasant evictions' in Isma'il's Egypt from Edward Dicey, see his *England and Egypt* (London: Chapman & Hall, 1881), pp. 110ff.

8.8 Resistance, Empire, Terror

The *fallāḥīn* grew increasingly rebellious as Isma'il's tenure drew to a close. Not only were they coerced, exploited, and expropriated—Roger Owen said that one-third of the peasantry was landless in the 1870s[139]—but they also suffered as pawns of the world market. Railways and canals expedited exports, which raised prices.[140] Peasants who were tempted to substitute cotton for food risked hunger if their harvest failed or their cattle became ill. Misfortunes of that kind were common, in part because the land tax was so steep that, for all intents and purposes, 'having to pay the tax meant that the peasant would have to grow cotton'.[141] So often did peasants abandon all or some of their land to evade this burden that a special category was formally recognized: the *mutasahib*, or *fallāḥ* who parted with his land.[142]

Other peasants, however, resisted. In 1879, tax collectors in part of Upper Egypt were met with armed force, and revolts against forced labour broke out the next year in rice-growing regions. The military itself grew restive in the same period. In early 1879, when their pay was delayed, a riot erupted in Cairo 'by 2,500 unpaid officers; [this] would have resulted', Marx said, 'in [the] murder of Isma'il Pasha and the massacre of all Europeans', had the 'cunning' Isma'il not ousted the '2 blacklegs' of the Debt Commission, Sir Rivers Wilson, and the Marquis de Blignières. Barely months later, under intense European pressure, the Sultan deposed Isma'il in favour of his eldest son, 'the dastard Tewfik'.

Unrest continued to brew and a colonel with village roots, Ahmed 'Urabi, became the leader of a popular movement for military and constitutional reform. Protests by junior officers in 1881 won wide support among merchants, craft, and labour guilds, and at least some peasants. Later that year 'Urabi, as the leader of the new National Party, joined a reform cabinet. In April 1882, coal heavers in Port Said went on strike against their British employers, with 'Urabi's support. Tenants at one

[139] Roger Owen, cited by Cole, *Colonialism and Revolution in the Middle East*, p. 30.

[140] Between 1800 and 1880, food costs for Egyptian peasants quadrupled. The overall cost of the full panoply of peasant expenses rose 320% in that period.

[141] Abbas and El-Dessouky, *The Large Landowning Class and the Peasantry in Egypt*, p. 35.

[142] Abandoned land, after 1865, was formally known as *al-matruka*.

of Tewfik's estates also struck. On May 25th, a Franco-British memorandum ordered the cabinet to dissolve and told 'Urabi to take a leave from the army. This provoked riots in Alexandria, which, on July 11th, were answered by deadly force. With bitter irony, Marx wrote that Ismail's lavish spending for harbours had finally proven its 'value'—to *the British*, who could now dock their ironclads with ease, which enabled 'old saintly Gladstone to bombard Alexandria' with impunity.

Marx concluded his notes at this point, but the resistance to England's assault continued for two months after the bombing began. Anti-English riots swept Tanta and other towns in northern Egypt, and 'Urabi assumed the formal leadership of the government. On July 29, he convened a National Congress to rally support for the struggle, which was nearing its zenith. On that same day a 'Grand Public Meeting' was held in Paris under the auspices of Marx's followers in France, whose aim was to show solidarity with the Urabist resistance.[143] With 3000 people in attendance, Marx's son-in-law Paul Lafargue joined Jules Guesde and others, including Louise Michel, to propose and pass these resolutions: 'We rally to support the protests of English and Italian workers against the bombing of Alexandria', 'a cowardly atrocity' which serves only 'the systematic bleeding of Egypt by Western money merchants'. We reject 'acts of piracy' against small states. 'The repudiation of the usurious foreign debt, the National Party's first act in power, is a matter of simple justice. We thus voice our admiration for ['Urabi's] Party [...] and our hope for its impending triumph'.

The final resolution was a stirring statement of solidarity: We hear, the speakers reported, that veterans of the Paris Commune have entered 'the service of the Egyptian national cause' and we salute them for 'doing, for the *fallāḥīn* of the Nile, what Frankel, Wrobleswki, Cipriani and other valiant "internationals" did in 1871 for the proletarians of the Seine'.[144]

Marx, who had been in Argenteuil since early June, came to Paris on August 1st to have lunch with Guesde, Paul, and Laura Lafargue, and

[143] The details below are drawn from the newspaper published by Marx's supporters in Paris, *Le Citoyen* (28 July–3 August 1882). Eduard Bernstein, who edited *Der Sozialdemokrat* for the German Social Democrats, echoed *Le Citoyen's* account of the Paris meeting (3 August). That led Engels to warn him on 9 August that support for the peasants did not require support for 'Urabi, who was likely to betray them. See Friedrich Engels to Eduard Bernstein, 9 August 1882, MECW, vol. 46, p. 301.

[144] Leo Frankel, Walery Wróblewski, and Amilcare Cipriani are cited here as 'combatants of March 18th'—that is, they fought to defend the Paris Commune in its decisive final

others.[145] The visit—which did not go unnoticed by the police[146]—went well, and Marx reported to Engels that 'the *Citoyen* people seem to be succeeding with their public MEETINGS on the Egyptian, etc., affaires'.[147]

Egypt officially became a British colony when 'Urabi's forces were defeated in battle on September 13, 1882. Engels, one day earlier, had written to Karl Kautsky to say that a revolution was likely in India and that 'the same thing could also happen elsewhere, say in Algeria or Egypt, and that would certainly suit us best'.[148] Marx, writing to Danielson in 1881, had predicted that 'serious complications, if not a general outbreak, [are] in store for the British in India [...] What [they] take from them annually in the form of rent, dividends for railways useless to the Hindus, [and so on...] amounts to more than the total [...] income of the 60 millions of agricultural and industrial laborers of India. This is a bleeding process, with a vengeance!'.[149]

How any given people will respond to that kind of bleeding process remains an open question. Marx hoped, to the last, that colonies like India and Egypt would retain enough *Widerstandskraft* to reverse their subjugation. He also remained cautiously hopeful that Russia's village communes could forge a path to modern industry without being swept into capital's event horizon. But he was well aware that other, less happy outcomes were possible. One such possibility was a movement of nativist or chauvinist reaction, in response to the forced migrations of the dispossessed.

battle. Frankel and Wróblewski served with Marx on the General Council of the International Workingman's Association and Cipriani, following his repatriation from penal exile in New Caledonia, worked for a time on *Le Citoyen*.

145 'Papa came to Paris' to dine with his *Le Citoyen* friends, Laura Lafarge reported to Engels the next day, see Frederick Engels, Paul Lafargue, and Laura Lafargue, *Correspondence, Volume I: 1868–1886* (Moscow: Foreign Languages Publishing House, 1956), p. 90.

146 The Paris police, when they learned of Marx's arrival, feared he had come 'to reorganize the International' and 'provoke trouble', Leslie Derfler, *Paul Lafargue and the Founding of French Marxism, 1842–1882* (Cambridge: Harvard University Press, 1991), p. 206.

147 Karl Marx to Friedrich Engels, 3 August 1882, MECW, vol. 46, p. 298.

148 Friedrich Engels to Karl Kautsky, 12 September 1882, MECW, vol. 46, p. 322.

149 Karl Marx to Nikolai Danielson, 19 February 1881, MECW, vol. 46, p. 63.

8.9 Chinese and Nativist Workers in California

Shortly after finishing his Egypt notes, Marx wrote to his daughter Eleanor from the Isle of Wight. He was still preoccupied with Egypt, which would be the subject of his very final letter to Eleanor in January, 1883: 'there could be no more blatant example of Christian hypocrisy than the "conquest" of Egypt – conquest in the midst of peace!'.[150] But in November, he wanted Eleanor to search his home for a 'report on the glorification by official economists in Paris of cheap Chinese labour in Europe'. That report, he said, could be found either in a copy of *L'Égalité* 'on the table by my bed' or in a copy of Benoît Malon's *Revue socialiste*, which is 'behind the sofa on a shelf in my book case'.[151]

Both of those journals reported on a session of the *Société d'économie politique* which, on May 5, 1880, considered 'The question of the Chinese in California'.[152] Three sharply opposed perspectives appeared in these reports. George Walker, Consul General of the United States, defended the anti-Chinese spirit which had swept California. 'The Chinese are always Chinese'—clannish, immoral, and 'refractory to assimilation', even in San Francisco, 'a Chinese city'. 'It is impossible to deny that all this furnishes a basis for popular prejudice'. Walker was echoed by a right-wing socialist, Charles-Mathieu Limousin, who warned that white workers would understandably claim the barbaric 'right to eliminate the Chinese by force' if the Chinese were granted the right to 'starve the white worker' by working for inhumanly low wages. Malon, applauding Walker and Limousin, went further, saying that the menacing approach of '100 million Chinese' portended 'the substitution of the yellow race

[150] Karl Marx to Eleanor Marx, 9 January 1883, MECW, vol. 46, p. 423. Marx was appalled that even the old Chartist Joseph Cowen, 'the best' of English parliamentarians, blinded by 'THE DAZZLE OF OUR MILITARY PARADE', saw the invasion as a 'heroic exploit', pp. 423–4. On this, and on Marx's final years in general, see Marcello Musto, *The Last Years of Karl Marx: An Intellectual Biography* (Stanford: Stanford University Press, 2020).

[151] Karl Marx an seine Tochter Eleanor, 10 November 1882, MEW, vol. 35, p. 398.

[152] See the full transcript of this session, reporting on 5 May 1880, meeting of the Société d'économie politique, in Société d'économie politique, 'La question des Chinois en California. – Celle des juifs en Roumanie, etc.', *Journal des économistes*, vol. 29 (1880): 298–312.

for the white race, the destruction of European civilization'.[153] The economists took a diametrically opposed stance. 'To attack the Chinese because they consume little is to attack the freedom of consumers; a crime well worthy of protectionist America'. The hardest of hard workers, they contribute mightily to the 'marvelous' advance of civilization, as they showed by their central role in building the Pacific half of the transcontinental railway 'from Sacramento to Missouri'. Furthermore, since the 'wage of a Chinese worker is [roughly] a fourth that of his European peer', Paul Leroy-Beaulieu looked forward to the day when competition from Chinese labour would reduce European wages 'to a normal level'. If, by their frugal habits, the Chinese teach European workers'to be less turbulent', another economist said, 'to leave the workshop less often for the cabaret, to drink less and save more, they will render them an immense service. *Vive le Chinois!*'.[154]

That cry, Guesde and Lafarge said in *L'Égalité*, came from the heart. For bourgeois economists, competition between workers is an unmitigated good—a stance Guesde and Lafargue scorned. But it was not until 1882, in their updating of the programme of the *Parti ouvrier*, that they fully drew out their own distinctive approach to immigration. That programme, which was ratified at a party congress on October 1, 1882, took an unequivocal stance: 'Workers' France must remain open to workers from everywhere'. The remedy for wage competition between foreign and native workers is not exclusion, but a minimum wage, prohibiting employers from paying immigrant workerssub-standard wages. Guesde and Lafargue knew that increasing wage competition was inevitable: 'the day will come', they wrote, when the employers begin to actively recruit Chinese labour: 'the bourgeois economists are already thinking about it'. Guesde and Lafargue noted that the US Consul

[153] Malon added that the Chinese 'sacrifice everything'—'dignity, personality'—'to low greed', while remaining 'contented with the grossest satisfaction of animal life', practicing 'infamous customs in filthy kennels'.

[154] These citations are drawn from several sources: the transcript in the *Journal des économistes*, cited above; Arthur Mangin, 'Les discussions de la *Société d'économie politique*', *L'économiste français*, vol. 1 (1880), n. 20 (15 May): 597–600; and the two sources cited by Marx: Jules Guesde and Paul Lafargue, 'Le patriotisme de la bourgeoisie et les Chinois', *L'Égalité*, vol. 21 (1880), n. 2 (9 June): 3–4; and Benoît Malon, 'La question chinoise devant les économistes', *La Revue Socialiste*, vol. 1880, n. 9 (5 July): 408–13. The economists cited—besides Leroy-Beaulieu, who hoped for falling wages—are Joseph Garnier, Louis Simonin, Charles Lavollée, and Louis Marchal de Robinot.

General had objected to Chinese immigration at the 1880 meeting. But the French economists had 'replied sternly' to his objection: 'In California, where a white man demands 10 francs per day, a yellow [man] is satisfied with 2.5 francs'. 'Let these good Chinese come, and too bad for the French workers if that bothers them'.[155]

Guesde and Lafargue warned that the bourgeoisie will often attempt to stir hatred of immigrants. They condemned Malon for inciting *la lutte des races*, stressing that French socialists advocate the unity of all workers, 'irrespective of sex or race'. They noted that, when France invaded Tunisia in 1881, financiers who wanted to dissuade Italy from intervening had 'sparked bloody brawls' between French and Italian workers in Marseille.[156] In short, they were well aware of the colonial and racial implications of anti-immigrant nativism. But they did not make nativism per se an object of inquiry and criticism.

In 1880, Guesde and Lafargue had written that 'the white and black working class' in America, threatened by the importation of Chinese workers, demanded 'an end to this trade in yellow flesh', a demand which, in California, 'took a revolutionary turn'.[157]

That casual, passing mention of the anti-Chinese campaign in California—a campaign of often violent and reactionary bent—was left undeveloped. Marx dug deeper.

Marx's budding interest in Chinese labour in the 1880s sprang from his long-standing concern with the cultural constitution of the value of labour-power. He had argued, in *Capital*, that unlike other commodities, labour-power is valued in proportion to the sum of average labour

[155] Jules Guesde and Paul Lafargue, *Le programme du Parti ouvrier: son histoire, ses considérants, ses articles* (Paris: Henri Oriol, 1883), p. 4. They cite Walker, et al. from the reports cited above. On this programme, cf. Gilles Candar, 'Socialistes et Migrations (1880–1914)', *Fondation Jean-Jaurès*, 5 October 2016, https://jean-jaures.org/nos-productions/jaures-et-les-migrations.

[156] The remark about Tunisia appeared in the party programme, op cit. The rebuke of Malon appeared in Jules Guesde and Paul Lafargue, 'Sixième Congrès National du Parti Ouvrier, tenu à Roanne du mardi 20 septembre au dimanche 1er octobre', *L'Égalité*, vol. 44 (1882), n. 3 (8 October): 1–3 (unsigned, but almost certainly by Guesde and Lafargue). The phrase 'irrespective of sex or race' appeared in *L'Égalité* often in this period. A general criticism by J. M., 'La Théorie des Races', *L'Égalité*, vol. 23 (1882), n. 3 (14 May): 2 (grotesque, reactionary, propagated by despots and chauvinists to divide workers and incite attacks on Jews).

[157] Guesde and Lafargue, 'Le patriotisme de la bourgeoisie et les Chinois', p. 3.

which goes into the goods and services that are regarded as acceptable for the maintenance of a suitable standard of life. Living standards vary, and they revolve around what Marx calls 'historical and moral' judgements.[158] Workers in different cultures who work in nearly identical ways to make nearly identical products are often paid strikingly different wages—and yet, Marx says, that disparity does not necessarily mean that any of them are paid above or below the value of their labour-power, since what matters for the determination of that value is the level at which pay is regarded as *fair*.

Indian cotton spinners, for example, can accept wages far below what English spinners receive without selling themselves short if those wages enable them to achieve a standard of living which lives up to their cultural expectations. What workers regard as a fair wage differs radically from place to place and time to time—and those discrepancies ignite conflict when different concepts of wage fairness collide in the labour market. If Indian cotton spinners had emigrated to England, their English peers would have found their established wages undermined.

In the first two editions of *Capital*, to illustrate a basic point about the cross-national valuation of commodities, Marx drew a contrast between Indian and English cotton spinners. In 1875, in *Le Capital*, Marx changed that passage to contrast English and Chinese spinners.[159] Elsewhere in *Le Capital*, Marx showed his growing interest in Chinese labour in two new passages. He quoted a speech by a British parliamentarian which anticipated the views expressed by the *Société des politiques économiques* in 1880. If China were to industrialize on a large scale, Mr. Stapleton warned, 'I don't see how the European working-class population can endure the struggle without falling to the level of their competitors'. That outcome, Marx said, reflects the capitalists' desire to substitute Chinese wages for European wages—a desire which US employers also manifest when they replace 'a Yankee worker with three Chinese'.[160]

[158] Marx, *Das Kapital* (1867), pp. 134–5.

[159] This passage appears in Marx, *Das Kapital* (1867), p. 592; Marx, *Das Kapital* (1872), p. 629; Marx, *Le Capital* (1875), p. 265; and Marx, *Das Kapital* (1883), p. 621.

[160] Engels omitted the latter passage, which appears in Marx, *Le Capital*, p. 281, from the third German edition of 1883. He moved Marx's earlier point (*Le Capital*, p. 263, vis-à-vis Stapleton) from the text into a note (*Das Kapital* (1883), p. 615, n. 53), which readers often credit to Engels.

This emerging interest in inter-ethnic labour conflict had several roots. On the one hand, Chinese emigration itself was a recent development. Until the eve of the Opium Wars of the 1840s, Chinese westward migration had been minimal, restrained by ancestor cults, which required home-based rituals, and by imperial bans which remained in effect until 1859, when Guangzhou province relaxed the ban, recognizing that migration over the past twenty years had become a reality which could no longer be stemmed. The first reference to overseas employment had come in 1839 from Guangzhou's imperial commissioner, who observed that 'every year at winter time, when foreign ships return to their homelands, there are some unemployed paupers who [...] accept employment abroad'.[161] A decade later, a few contract labourers were brought to California to work in gold mining; they were followed by others, and by 1852 a grand total of 20,000 had arrived.[162] But that wave slowed, some of the workers returned home, and it was not until 1865, when major construction began on the Central Pacific Railroad, that truly major migrations occurred. The motive for their recruitment was clearly stated by the railway owners in their private correspondence: 'Without them it would be impossible to go on with the work'. They do almost all the digging and 'they [are] equally as good as white men, and less inclined to quarrels and strikes'.[163]

'Each white man costs us in board and wages $2.50 each 8 hours, but Chinamen cost us $1.19 each 8 hours'.[164] In June 1867, the Chinese miners did in fact strike. But they were defeated, and by mid-1869, when the Central Pacific completed its half of the transcontinental railroad, 20,000 Chinese workers had worked for the company, forming the backbone of their labour force. This was, Gordon Chang writes, and remained until the late nineteenth century, 'likely the single largest workforce in

[161] June Mei, 'Socioeconomic Origins of Emigration', *Modern China*, vol. 5 (1979), n. 4: 472, 477.

[162] Ping Chiu, *Chinese Labor in California, 1850–1880* (PhD, University of Wisconsin, 1967), pp. 12–3, cited by Mae M. Ngai, 'Chinese Gold Miners and the 'Chinese Question' in Nineteenth-Century California and Victoria', *The Journal of American History*, vol. 101 (2015), n. 4: 1086.

[163] 'Mark Hopkins to Collis Huntington, 31 May 1865', *Huntington Papers*, cited by Manu Karuka, *Empire's Tracks: Indigenous Nations, Chinese Workers, and the Transcontinental Railroad* (Oakland, CA: University of California, 2019), p. 87.

[164] 'E. B. Crocker to Collis Huntington, 14 January 1867', *Huntington Papers*, cited by Karuka, *Empire's Tracks*, p. 89.

a private enterprise in the United States'.[165] Collis Huntington, one of the Central Pacific's owners, said in 1868 that California needed a half million more Chinese workers.[166] That total was never reached, but by 1876 there were 148,000 Chinese workers in California, representing a significant percentage of the total population of the state.[167]

Marx first alluded to Chinese immigrants in a letter in 1869.[168] This was at a time when the International Workingmen's Association was growing rapidly in the United States, not least in San Francisco, where a German section had formed in 1868, followed by a French section in 1870 and an English-speaking section in late 1871.[169] Reports on the founding meeting of the English section testified to the contradictory character of socialist thinking about Chinese immigration at this early stage. The convenor of the meeting gave a recital of IWA principles, concluding with 'the reading of a poetical tribute to the Communists of Paris'. But he also paired support for 'entire' equality before the law with resistance to 'the importation of [any] cheap labor', 'Chinese or other', which would degrade native labour, not elevate it.[170]

In 1881, when Marx studied Henry George's account of anti-Chinese nativism in California, the agitation which would result in the passage of the Chinese Exclusion Act in 1882 was simmering, after several years of explosive violence. In effect, what had occurred was the collision of two sets of displaced, *Vogelfrei* nomads: Irish and other 'white' workers

165 Gordon H. Chang, 'Chinese Railroad Workers and the US Transcontinental Railroad in Global Perspective', in: Gordon H. Chang and Shelley Fisher Fishkin (eds.), *The Chinese and the Iron Road* (Stanford: Stanford University Press, 2019), p. 33.

166 Ibid., p. 31.

167 Mei, 'Socioeconomic Origins of Emigration', p. 485, citing a US Senate report. In all, since about 200,000 Chinese workers had migrated to California, Mei deduces that by 1876 about 25% had either died or returned to China.

168 Karl Marx to Friedrich Engels, 10 August 1869, MECW, vol. 43, pp. 343–4.

169 General Council of the First International, *Minutes*, vol. 3 (Moscow: Progress Publishers, 1966), p. 50; and General Council of the First International, *Minutes*, vol. 4 (Moscow: Progress Publishers, 1967), pp. 92, 167–8.

170 William West, 'Formation of an English-Speaking Section of the International Workingmen's Association at San Francisco, CA', *Woodhull & Claflin's Weekly*, 16 December 1871, p. 8. Marx regularly read this weekly, which was published by an eccentric dissenting faction in the I.W.A., so he may have seen this report. He himself reported positively on the founding of the section. See General Council of the First International, *Minutes*, vol. 5 (Moscow: Progress Publishers, 1968), p. 61.

from the east, who could now migrate west in growing numbers thanks to the transcontinental railroad; and a parallel set of nomads from southeastern China who could migrate to California thanks to the Pacific Mail Steamship Company, which had been founded in 1848. As Danielson had shown, the ongoing revolution in the means of transportation was enabling job-seekers to travel. The dissolving effects of that revolution were now coming home to roost, not only in noncapitalist countries like China but in advanced capitalist countries. California was an early site of that revolution, and collision. White workers, without land or secure employment, found themselves facing Chinese migratory workers who also lacked land and steady work.

Southeastern China had long since been entangled in dissolving trade, radiating from Hong Kong and Guangzhou (which Europeans called Canton) to Macao, and elsewhere in the region. Cotton spinners, silver miners, and foundry workers had worked for pay on a modest but growing scale since the middle of the Ming Dynasty (1368–1644), and money exchange was increasingly common. All of this was accentuated in the decades leading up to the opium wars in the 1840s, as English force and commerce drew China ever further into the world market.[171] Southeastern China, shaken sociopolitically as well as economically, was rocked not only by the opium wars but, in 1854, by a provincial war which resulted in 70,000 executions in Guangzhou alone. Two years later, the Taiping rebellion, which had begun three years earlier, spilled over catastrophically into the Pearl River Delta. The effects of that rebellion were felt particularly acutely in Xinning, in the hinterland of the province. That single district—one of four which were collectively known as Sze-yap—was the point of origin for at least half of the ultimate Chinese migration to California.[172]

Xinning, a land-poor coastal district, had for centuries been a destination for migrants from elsewhere in China. In 1856, the district was divided between two mutually exclusive groups: the *pun-ti*, or 'natives', and the Hakka-speaking *k'echia*, or 'guest people', who had arrived in the region a few centuries earlier. Large-scale fighting between these groups erupted when the *pun-ti* joined the Taiping rebels and the Hakkas were

[171] Mei, 'Socioeconomic Origins of Emigration', pp. 468ff.

[172] For a full overview of the migration, see Kil Young Zo, *Chinese Emigration into the United States* (PhD, Columbia University, 1971). On the local wars, see the sources cited by Mei, 'Socioeconomic Origins of Emigration'.

enlisted to suppress them. That ruinous conflict, in which the Hakkas gained the upper hand, left Xinning in disarray. Much of the ensuing emigration was an attempt by Xinning 'natives' to find safety and opportunities elsewhere—in overseas realms where they, in turn, were regarded as a guest people.[173]

Anti-Chinese violence began on a small scale soon after the first miners arrived in 1849, but sustained agitation began only in the 1870s, when Chinese labourers who had worked for the Central Pacific joined other Chinese migrants *en masse* in fruit orchards, quartz and lumber mills, and road construction sites. Rancho Chico, in Butte County, became the single largest employer of Chinese workers, and similar employment trends elsewhere in California became a sore point for many white workers, especially after the economy fell into depression in 1873. In 1876, a secret group calling itself the 'Supreme Order of Caucasians' began a campaign of anti-Chinese arson and murder in the town of Chico and nearby Oroville. That same year, a former California attorney general, speaking as a member of the 'Anti-Coolie Union', told a Congressional committee 'that he longed to stand on Telegraph Hill and watch Chinese hang from the yardarms of burning immigrant ships entering San Francisco Bay'.[174] This was the context in which the 'Caesarist' anti-Chinese movement discussed by Henry George burst on the scene in San Francisco in 1877.

8.10 Nativism and Caesarism

Marx, writing to Danielson about the United States in late 1878, had said that the best way to map the 'baneful influence of the great *compagnies* swaying industry, commerce, property in land, railroads [and] finance' is to 'look, not to the older States of the Atlantic, but to the newer ones [...]

[173] Zo, *Chinese Emigration into the United States*, pp. 73ff., 123ff.; cf. Mei, 'Socioeconomic Origins of Emigration', pp. 473–4. Zo shows that, of the 150,000 Chinese immigrants whose presence in California was documented by Chinese organizations, over half were Xinning emigrants.

[174] Jean Pfaelzer, *Driven Out* (Berkeley: University of California Press, 2008), pp. 89–90, 104–5. The Chinese in California were not, in fact, 'coolies' (that is, indentured labourers). The so-called coolie trade sent emigrants to Cuba and Peru, but not to California.

and the newest (*California* f.i.)'.[175] Marx followed his own advice, paying fine-grained attention not only to the great companies per se—of which few were greater than Leland Stanford's Central Pacific Railroad—but to their disruptive influence. His excerpts from Henry George's *Popular Science* article 'The Kearney Agitation in California' beam a bright light on that subject.[176]

George's subject is nativist hostility to immigrants, which he traces to influences both general and particular. The most general influence is the impulse to scapegoat: 'If there is not one Jonah, another will be found'. Again and again, 'popular discontent has been fixed upon the Jews, and [now many people] make the "ignorant foreigner" the same sort of a scapegoat'. Why that was true in San Francisco was due largely to the '*greater mobility* of society (IN CALIFORNIA)', springing, in large measure, from '*the increase of facilities of movement*'—that is, railroads and steamships.[177] China, which had formerly been divided from the industrial reserve army in the United States by the Pacific ocean, was now a source of labour competition. This fact has seemed to many workers to offer 'a sufficient explanation of the fall of wages and difficulty of finding employment'. The real causes lie elsewhere, in the 'concentration of the whole railway system' in California 'in the hands of one close corporation' and in the 'grand culture' of mechanized agriculture, which employs 'large gangs of men at certain seasons, setting them adrift when the crop is gathered'.

'Socialists and communists are more tolerant of the Chinese than any [others who] are threatened by their competition'. That was true of 'thoughtful' and organized workers in general. 'The impulse [for] these California agitations came from Pittsburgh and the great railway strikes of 1877. In California, where a similar strike was [imminent — the railroad company had given notice of a like reduction of wages – [the Pittsburg strike] excited an interest that became intense when the telegraph [reported] burning and fighting [...] The railroad magnates, alarmed, rescinded their notice, but [...] a meeting to express sympathy with the

175 Karl Marx to Nikolai Danielson, 15 November 1878, MECW, vol. 45, p. 344.

176 George's article appeared in August 1880. Marx's notes were written in the autumn of 1880 or the spring of 1881. My thanks to the International Institute of Social History (IISH) in Amsterdam and the senior MEGA editors for sharing the transcript.

177 Phrases cited below generally reproduce Marx's mixed German and English in English, and I omit much of his italicization.

Eastern strikers had been called [...] Though among the promoters and speakers [there was] no lawless talk or allusion to the Chinese [...] there arose the cry: "To Chinatown!" [and] some Chinese washhouses were raided by gangs'.

Historians have learned that these raids, on July 23, 1877, were the work of Anti-Coolie Club members, who 'pushed their way to the front of the rally and demanded that it denounce the Chinese. When the crowd refused, the infuriated anti-coolie men [set] buildings ablaze' in Chinatown.[178] Days later, a mob tried to burn the Pacific Mail Steamship docks. 'Es war nicht *Kearney*, but *a Republican*, rich, [...] influential [...] who *first proposed that the Pacific Mail steamers should be burned at their docks if they did not cease to bring Chinese*'. In Oakland, armed guards were dispatched to defend the Central Pacific, which had refused to fire its Chinese employees. In the ensuing days, Dennis Kearney became the face of the 'Pick Handle' campaign to oust the Chinese.

Marx paid close attention to Kearney's class background: 'On this *"pick-handle brigade"— Dennis Kearney*, a *drayman* [...] accumulated [...] a comfortable little property'. In 1876, as a Hayes Invincible—a partisan of President Rutherford B. Hayes, who opened the door to Jim Crow by ending Reconstruction that same year[179]—'Kearney joined a Republican club, [where he stood out for] the *venom with which he abused the working classes* and his partisanship (*Parteiergreifen*) *for the capitalistic side at every opportunity*; [he] declared the wages of the labouring class *far too high* and defended Chinese immigration'. His subsequent turn to anti-Chinese labour politics was, Marx noted, 'hastened by some recent losses in stock'.[180]

'The knot of men who had called the meeting of sympathy with the [Pittsburgh] strikers had afterwards organized a workman's party [...] *Kearney* [called them] fools, he would start a *party of "bread or blood"*'. Railing about 'the *Chinese Question* [...] he [described] the burning of

[178] Pfaelzer, *Driven Out*, p. 105.

[179] See Edlie L. Wong, *Racial Reconstruction: Black Inclusion, Chinese Exclusion, and the Fictions of Citizenship* (New York: NYU Press, 2015).

[180] Marx extensively excerpted passages saying that this plebeian violence was prefigured and influenced by a long history of business vigilantism in San Francisco which was still very much part of the scene and reflected '*the disposition towards sharp repressive measures which is aroused among the wealthy classes by symptoms of dissatisfaction and aggression by the poor*'.

Moscow as a suggestion of what might be in store for San Francisco'. He 'appropriated' the name '*Workingman's Party*' for his new association and called a meeting 'for *the top of California Street*', which is 'crowned by the palaces of the railroad nabobs. In Kearney's meetings, [now] largely composed of the unemployed men who after the harvest begin to collect in San Francisco', he made ominous threats. In a famous speech, as reproduced by a modern historian, he was unrestrained: 'When the Chinese question is settled, we can discuss whether it would be better to hang, shoot, or cut the capitalists to pieces. In six months we will have 50,000 men ready to go out [...] and if "John" don't leave here,[181] we will drive him and his aborts into the sea [...] We are ready to do it [...] If the ballot fails, we are ready to use the bullet'. Kearney warned the owners of the railroad and the steamship company that if they didn't fire their Chinese workers, they should 'remember Judge Lynch'.[182]

Some of his followers were arrested when they went too far in their rhetoric, but Kearney played it safe: '*Wise guy (Schlaumeier) Kearney* [...] always kept [...] his wild declamations' just short of '*direct incitement to violence* [...] by an *"if"* (like O'Connell)'.

Marx devoted many pages to Kearney's machinations, which quickly went from the street to the ballot box and soon resulted in a predictable betrayal. All 'denunciations of the railroad magnates' ceased and 'all the officials elected by the workingmen [are] either employees or friends of the railroad'. But his attention was riveted above all by Kearney's petty Bonapartism. Kearney knew, by demagogic intuition, that 'feeling on the Chinese question had been so strong for so long' in San Francisco that the best way to win a following was to wage an anti-Chinese crusade. When the authorities arrested his followers and took a 'mass of illegal steps' against them, Kearney was buoyed by indignation over the 'drunken spirit of arbitrary repression'—repression which seemed to confirm his standing as a populist rebel.

Kearney 'understood the *connexion between Caesar and the proletariat*; [he] appeared on all occasions in rough working-dress; announced [that] as soon as he had led the people to victory, he would retire from the fray, and must in the meantime be supported by collections'. By winning

[181] 'John' was short for 'John Chinaman', which was then a common slang term in nativist circles.

[182] Pfaelzer, *Driven Out*, p. 107.

'the *floating element* which [does] the most shouting he commanded his party' and 'BECAME FOR THE MASSES THE INCARNATION OF THE MOVEMENT'. Kearney's support came, above all, 'from people so utterly disgusted with the workings and corruptions of old parties as to welcome "anything for a change"'. He expertly 'EXPLOITED the *feeling against politicians*' and ensured his 'SUPREMATIE' in his own party by castigating rivals as politicians. In the end, 'by a *coup d'état* he swept out *the whole Central Committee*'.

One of the few figures in the movement who was able to establish an independent following was 'the *Reverend Dr. Kalloch, a leading Baptist clergyman, great stump-speaker*. This *lumpacius* had at the start of [the anti-Chinese] events the largest Chinese Sunday school in the city, preached against mobs the virtues of *loading [guns] with grape and firing low* (UPON THEM): but as soon as the movement assumed political force, *he shut up his Chinese Sunday-school*, preached so [well] that he "completely captured the Workmen," was finally—*nicht by Kearney's wish!*—nominated by them for *Mayor*', an office he soon won.

When Kearney went to the east in 1880, a new movement of the jobless began, 'demanding of large employers the discharge of the Chinese'. But 'the advance of the season and the consequent demand for laborers in the interior' depleted the movement before long. That, and 'bitter disappointment' among workers when Kearneyite enactments and officials proved to be 'JUST AS AWFUL AS THEIR PREDECESSORS', spelled the beginning of the end of the movement. But the damage had been done. Chinese exclusion legislation, which would remain in effect for six decades, passed in 1882, and further outbreaks of Kearney-like Caesarism remained a danger.

What happened in California 'betokens the social unrest and discontent from which destructive forces are generated'. 'The man *(Kearney)* who now talks about wading through blood and hanging people to lamp-posts is *but the vendor of a nostrum*'. He is not a *fanatical reformer*, but a politician, a herald of '*the coming Caesar*'. His followers 'demanded *only quack remedies*', but his success showed 'how easily our political struggles may pass into all the bitterness [...] of excited class-feeling without [bringing] improvement or reform'.

Society, George concluded, now pivots around wealth—'*capital is becoming organized in greater and greater masses* and the railroad companies dwarf the State'. Marx echoed him. And he appears to have shared George's concern that capital and nativist reactions are fundamentally destabilizing forces which 'demoralize and corrupt', rewarding only venal Caesarists who seek to 'ride to power' by 'exciting class jealousies'.

8.11 Outrage and Right-Wing Rebellion

How Marx would have developed this argument, if he had lived to pursue it further, can only be a matter of conjecture. But he had been a critic of Bonapartism for thirty years, and he had used the platform of the International Workingmen's Association to highlight the danger of national and ethnic antagonisms a decade earlier.[183] How far this removed him from the innocent triumphalism of his erstwhile comrades is shown by the reporting on Kearney and Kalloch which appeared in *Der Sozialdemokrat*, which, after the passage of the anti-socialist laws, Eduard Bernstein edited in Zurich. On October 5, 1879, *Der Sozialdemokrat* rejoiced that 'the successes of the labor party in America are steadily increasing. The admittedly not *purely* socialist Workingmen's Party of California won the San Francisco mayoral election'. That election brought the Reverend Isaac Kalloch into office. On December 28, *Der Sozialdemokrat* ran an enthusiastic account of Kearney's 'ballots or bullets' harangue. 'Of course', the author ironized, 'the bourgeois press of all lands and tongues will make a great fuss over the peace-breaking, thieving, murderous California workers. But our comrades will know what to think of that chatter'.

We do know what Marx thought of those events, and those demagogues. He could tell the difference between nativist Bonapartism, which preyed on the precarity and prejudice of migratory workers, and workers' solidarity. August Bebel, who saw matters similarly, would later call antisemitism the socialism of fools.[184] Like Marx, he wanted a socialism without borders, or blinders. But few of Marx's other avowed heirs have squarely or creatively confronted the issue of nativism or Bonapartism. Marx himself left an ambiguous legacy in this respect. His occasional,

[183] On Bonapartism, which Marx first dissected in his *The Eighteenth Brumaire of Louis Bonaparte*, MECW, vol. 11, pp. 99–209, see Hal Draper, *Karl Marx's Theory of Revolution, Volume 1: State and Bureaucracy* (New York: Monthly Review Press, 1977); and Maximilien Rubel, *Karl Marx devant le Bonapartisme* (The Hague: Mouton, 1960). On ethnic divisions among workers, see Marx's 1 January 1871 statement in General Council of the First International, *Minutes*, vol. 3, pp. 359ff.

[184] Benoît Malon, in the 1890s, was one of the 'socialist' antisemites who aroused Bebel's ire. See Stephen Wilson, *Ideology and Experience* (Madison, NJ: Fairleigh Dickinson University Press, 1982), pp. 69, 332–4, et seq.

well-known denunciations of anti-Black and anti-Irish bigotry—and now, his clear-eyed appraisal of anti-Chinese demagoguery—testify to his overall humanism. But the dissolving and disturbing effects of capitalism and the world market are felt, not only at the frontiers of self-expanding value, but within the working class itself; and those effects are psychological as well as political.

Marx hinted at this point in more than one place, but he left those hints undeveloped. The ambiguity that results is apparent, *sub rosa*, in his best known prophecy of working-class victory—that 'the expropriators will be expropriated'. Marx roots this prediction in the *Empörung* of the workers, which, he says, grows as the mass of degradation, subjection, and misery accumulates with capital. In other words, the more the solvent effects of expropriation and exploitation are felt, the more, Marx says, the immiserated will resist. But *Empörung* is a deeply ambiguous term. Rendered, in most editions of *Capital*, as 'revolt' or resistance, *Empörung* literally means indignation or outrage—as Marx made clear when he translated the term into English himself.[185] That indignation can attach itself to other workers, not just against capital, and the migratory precariat, in particular, is a natural target—a Jonah. When migrant and native notions of wage fairness collide, both are called into question. Solidarity across borders dissolves when the *Empörung* of native workers is directed against diasporas of the *Vogelfrei*.

Sustained critical thinking on the contradictions of class indignation awaited the appearance, in the 1920s and 1930s, of the psychological concept of authoritarianism, which was pioneered by the critical Marxists of the Frankfurt School, most notably Erich Fromm and Hilde

[185] *Empörung* appears in Marx, *Le Capital* (1875), p. 342, as 'résistance'. But in the Russian edition, Karl Marx, *Kapital: Kritika politicheskoi ekonomii, Tom 1. Protsess proizvodstva kapitala* [Capital: A Critique of Political Economy, Volume I. The Production Process of Capital] (Saint-Petersburg: N. P. Polyakova, 1872; St.-Petersburg: Tipografiya A. Benke, 1878), p. 673, it appears as 'возмущение' (indignation), and in the 1872 German edition, translating a letter by Dr. Charles Parsons to the Children's Employment Commission Parsons (Charles Parsons, 'Letter to F. D. Longe', in: House of Commons, *Children's Employment: Factories. Reports from Commissioners, vol. 18. Appendix: Reports and Evidence of Assistant Commissioners* (Parliament: House of Commons, 1863)), p. 22, Marx himself rendered 'indignation' as *Empörung*, Marx, *Das Kapital* (1872), p. 247.

Weiss.[186] Research in that tradition—which, in effect, analyzes 'the Bonapartist personality'—has proven powerful, not least with respect to key twenty-first century instances of demagogic authority.[187]

Marx's late notes offer us many further insights into the extended reproduction of capital and its ramifying solvent effects. His notes on India, Australia, Indonesia, the Americas, Africa, and Algeria—where the *Parti ouvrier* had a section—shed light on many subjects he addressed with respect to Egypt and California. Marx pays minute attention to what Engels would later call, on the basis of Marx's reading of Lewis Henry Morgan's *Ancient Society*, 'the world historic defeat of the female sex'. Often, Marx directly discusses 'manworship', which, when clan relations in ancient Ireland were beginning to be disrupted, took the form of a kind of proto-Bonapartism, in which chiefs enhanced their power by recruiting warriors from broken tribes to their personal service. In other instances, 'man-worship' dressed itself in the raiment of personalized fetishism, which was one of the subjects of Marx's very last set of ethnological notes, on *The Origin of Civilisation* by John Lubbock.[188] These final notes, which he completed in tandem with his excerpts from Mulhall's article on Egypt, bring his readings full circle—since, in every essential respect, they extend and deepen the study of fetishism he had begun forty years earlier, in his notes on Charles de Brosses.

The issues raised in these notes remain, alas, as timely as ever, since migrations, in the age of trade globalization and climate chaos, are large and growing, and demagogues, inciting nativist reaction and fetishistic man-worship, are still very much with us.

[186] See David Norman Smith, 'Anti-Authoritarian Marxism', in: Kieran Durkin and Joane Braune (eds.), *Erich Fromm's Critical Theory* (London: Bloomsbury, 2020), pp. 131–65.

[187] See David Norman Smith, 'Authoritarianism Reimagined', *The Sociological Quarterly*, vol. 60 (2019), n. 2: 210–23; as well as David Norman Smith and Eric Hanley, 'The Anger Games: Who Voted for Donald Trump in the 2016 Election, and Why?', *Critical Sociology*, vol. 44 (2018), n. 2: 195–212.

[188] See David Norman Smith, 'Capital Fetishism and the Authoritarian Personality', in: Jeremiah Morelock (ed.), *How to Critique Authoritarian Populism: Methodologies of the Frankfurt School* (Leiden: Brill, 2021), which briefly links Marx's ethnological discussion of authority and fetishism to his long-standing concern about capital fetishism.

References

Abbas, Raouf, and el-Dessouky, Assem (2011), *The Large Landowning Class and the Peasantry in Egypt, 1837–1952*, Syracuse: Syracuse University Press.

Aristotle (1855), *Aristotelis Opera, vol. 8: De re publica*, Berlin: Georg Reimer.

———. (1885), *The Politics of Aristotle*, vol. 1, Oxford: Clarendon Press.

Baer, Gabriel (1959), 'The Dissolution of the Egyptian Village Community', *Die Welt des Islams*, vol. 6, n. 1: 56–70.

———. (1969), 'Submissiveness and Revolt of the Fellah', in: Gabriel Baer, *Studies in the Social History of Modern Egypt*, Chicago: University of Chicago Press, pp. 93–108.

Beinin, Joel (2011), *Workers and Peasants in the Modern Middle East*, Cambridge: Cambridge University Press.

Bensaïd, Daniel (2007), *Les dépossédés: Karl Marx, les voleurs de bois et le droit des pauvres*, Paris: La fabrique.

Boer, Roland (2013), *In the Vale of Tears*, Leiden: Brill.

Bouniatian, Mentor (1908), *Wirtschaftskrisen und Ueberkapitalisation*, Munich: Ernst Reinhardt.

Burns, Robert (1790), 'A Man's a Man for a' That', in: [No Author], *A Musical Banquet of Choice Songs*, Glasgow: A. MacGoun.

Candar, Gilles (2016), 'Socialistes et Migrations (1880–1914)', *Fondation Jean-Jaurès*, 5 October, https://jean-jaures.org/nos-productions/jaures-et-les-migrations.

Casas, Bartolomé de las (2004), *A Short Account of the Destruction of the Indies*, London: Penguin.

Chang, Gordon H. (2019), 'Chinese Railroad Workers and the US Transcontinental Railroad in Global Perspective', in: Gordon H. Chang and Shelley Fisher Fishkin (eds.), *The Chinese and the Iron Road: Building the Transcontinental Railroad*, Stanford: Stanford University Press, pp. 27–41.

Chattopadhyay, Paresh (2016), *Marx's Associated Mode of Production*, London: Palgrave Macmillan.

Chiu, Ping (1967), *Chinese Labor in California, 1850–1880*, Ph.D., University of Wisconsin.

Cole, Juan R. I. (1993), *Colonialism and Revolution in the Middle East*, Princeton: Princeton University Press.

Danielson, Nikolai (1880), 'Otcherki Nashego Poreformenogo Obschestvenogo Hoziatsva' ['Essays on Our Post-Reform Social Economy'], *Slovo*, no. 10: 77–142.

Davis, Mike (2006), *Planet of Slums*, London: Verso.

Derfler, Leslie (1991), *Paul Lafargue and the Founding of French Marxism, 1842–1882*, Cambridge: Harvard University Press.

Dicey, Edward (1881), *England and Egypt*, London: Chapman & Hall.

Diderot, Denis (1972), *Le neveu de Rameau*, Paris: Gallimard.

———. (2001), *Rameau's Nephew and Other Works*, Indianapolis, IN: Hackett.
Draper, Hal (1977), *Karl Marx's Theory of Revolution, Volume 1: State and Bureaucracy*, New York: Monthly Review Press.
———. (1985), *Marx–Engels Chronicle*, New York: Schocken.
Engels, Frederick, Lafargue, Paul, and Lafargue, Laura (1959), *Correspondence, Volume 1: 1868–1886*, Moscow: Foreign Languages Publishing House.
Eto, Shinkichi (1968), 'Mitcheru hokokusho ni tsuite' ['A Study on the Mitchell Report'], in: Shinkichi Eto, *Kindai chugoku seijishi kenkyu* [Studies of Modern Chinese Politics], Tokyo: University of Tokyo Press, pp. 215–33.
Eyguesier, Nicolas (2018), 'Marx, Primitive Accumulation, and the Impact of Sismondi', *The European Journal of the History of Economic Thought*, vol. 25, n. 5: 833–58.
General Council of the First International (1966), *Minutes*, vol. 3, Moscow: Progress Publishers.
———. (1967), *Minutes*, vol. 4, Moscow: Progress Publishers.
———. (1968), *Minutes*, vol. 5, Moscow: Progress Publishers.
George, Henry (1880), 'The Kearney Agitation in California', *Popular Science Monthly*, vol. XVII: 433–53.
Goethe, Johann Wolfgang von (1820), *Rameau's Neffe: ein Dialog*, in: Johann Wolfgang von Goethe, *Goethe's Werke*, Bd. 20, Stuttgart: J.G. Cotta; Vienna: Carl Armbruster, pp. 3–222.
———. (1965), *Berliner Ausgabe, Bd. 3: Poetische Werke. Gedichte und Singspiele III*, Berlin & Weimar: Aufbau-Verlags.
Guesde, Jules, and Lafargue, Paul (1880), 'Le patriotisme de la bourgeoisie et les Chinois', *L'Égalité*, vol. 21, n. 2 (9 June): 3–4.
———. (1882), 'Sixième Congrès National du Parti Ouvrier, tenu à Roanne du mardi 20 septembre au dimanche 1er octobre', *L'Égalité*, vol. 44, n. 3 (8 October): 1–3.
———. (1883), *Le programme du Parti ouvrier: son histoire, ses considérants, ses articles*, Paris: Henri Oriol.
Harvey, David (1975), 'The Geography of Capitalist Accumulation: A Reconstruction of the Marxian Theory', *Antipode*, vol. 7, n. 2: 9–21.
———. (2004), 'The "New" Imperialism: Accumulation by Dispossession', *Socialist Register*, vol. 40: 63–87.
———. (2013), *A Companion to Marx's Capital, Volume 2*, London: Verso.
Hegel, G. W. F. (1910), *The Phenomenology of Mind, Vols. 1 & 2*, London: Swan Sonnenschein.
House of Commons (1867), *Return, East India, Bengal, and Orissa Famine*, Part I, May 31, Parliament: House of Commons.
Hüllmann, Karl Dietrich (1830), *Geschichte des Ursprungs der Stände in Deutschland*, Berlin: Eichhoff & Krafft.

Hunter, Dr. Henry Julian (1864), 'Inquiry on the State of the Dwellings of Rural Labourers', in: Public Health, *Seventh Report of the Medical Officer of the Privy Council*, London: H.M. Stationery Office, pp. 126–302.

Hydén, Göran (1980), *Beyond Ujamaa in Tanzania: Underdevelopment and an Uncaptured Peasantry*, Berkeley: University of California Press.

Institut Marksa-Engel'sa-Lenina (1934), *Arkhiv Marksa i Engel'sa*, vol. 4, Moscow: Partizdat.

———. (1952), *Arkhiv Marksa i Engel'sa*, vol. 12, Moscow: Gospolitizdat.

Isager, Jacob (2013), *Pliny on Art and Society: The Elder Pliny's Chapters on the History of Art*, London: Routledge.

J. M. (1882), 'La Théorie des Races', *L'Égalité*, vol. 23, n. 3 (14 May): 2.

Karuka, Manu (2019), *Empire's Tracks: Indigenous Nations, Chinese Workers, and the Transcontinental Railroad*, Oakland, CA: University of California.

Kiesselbach, Wilhelm (1860), *Der Gang des Welthandels und die Entwicklung des europäischen Völkerlebens im Mittelalter*, Stuttgart: J.G. Cotta.

Leask, Nigel (2009), 'Burns and the Poetics of Abolition', in: Gerard Carruthers (ed.), *The Edinburgh Companion to Robert Burns*, Edinburgh: Edinburgh University Press, pp. 47–60.

Leroy-Beaulieu, Paul (1903), *Le collectivisme*, Paris: Guillaumin.

Linden, Marcel van der, and Hubmann, Gerald (2018), 'Introduction', in: Marcel van der Linden and Gerald Hubmann (eds.), *Marx's Capital: An Unfinishable Project?*, Leiden: Brill, pp. 1–30.

Linebaugh, Peter (2014), 'Karl Marx, the Theft of Wood, and Working-Class Composition', *Social Justice*, vol. 40, no. 1/2: 137–61.

Lockman, Zachary (1994), 'Worker' and 'Working Class' in Pre-1914 Egypt', in: Zachary Lockman (ed.), *Workers and Working Classes in the Middle East: Struggles, Histories, Historiographies*, Albany: SUNY Press, pp. 71–109.

Luxemburg, Rosa (2015), *The Accumulation of Capital: A Contribution to the Economic Theory of Imperialism*, in: Peter Hudis and Paul Le Blanc (eds.), *The Complete Works of Rosa Luxemburg, Volume II: Economic Writings 2*, London: Verso, pp. 3–344.

Mă Duānlín (1985), *Wen xian tong kao jing ji kao* [Textual Examination of Confucian Classics], Shanghai: East China Normal University Press.

Malon, Benoît (1880), 'La Question chinoise devant les économistes', *La Revue Socialiste*, vol. 9, (5 July): 408–13.

Mangin, Arthur (1880), 'Les discussions de la *Société d'économie politique*', *L'économiste français*, vol. 1, n. 20 (15 May): 597–600.

Marx, Karl (1859), *Zur Kritik der politischen Ökonomie*, Berlin: Duncker.

———. (1867), *Das Kapital: Kritik der politischen Oekonomie, Bd. 1: Der Produktionsprocess des Kapitals*, Hamburg: Otto Meissner.

———. (1872a), *Das Kapital: Kritik der politischen Oekonomie, Bd. 1: Der Produktionsprocess des Kapitals, Zweite verbesserte Auflage*, Hamburg: Otto Meissner.

———. (1872b), *Kapital: Kritika politicheskoi ekonomii, Tom 1. Protsess proizvodstva kapitala* [Capital: A Critique of Political Economy, Volume I. The Production Process of Capital], Saint-Petersburg: N. P. Polyakova.

———. (1875), *Le Capital*, Paris: Éditeurs, Maurice Lachâtre et Cie.

———. (1877), 'Letter to *Otechestvenniye Zapiski*', in: Nicolai-On, *Die Volkswirtschaft in Russland nach der Bauern-Emancipation*, Munich: Hermann, pp. 528–30.

———. (1880–81), 'H. George, The Kearney Agitation in California', in: *Karl Marx/Friedrich Engels Papers, Exzerpte von Karl Marx*, B_161, Heft CXLV, Amsterdam: Internationaal Instituut voor Sociale Geschiedenis, pp. 8–14.

———. (1883), *Das Kapital: Kritik der politischen Oekonomie, Bd. 1: Der Produktionsprocess des Kapitals, Dritte vermehrte Auflage*, Hamburg: Otto Meissner.

———. (1885), *Das Kapital: Kritik der politischen Oekonomie, Bd. 2: Der Cirkulationsprocess des Kapitals*, Hamburg: Otto Meissner.

———. (1894), *Das Kapital: Kritik der politischen Oekonomie, Bd. 3: Der Gesammtprocess der kapitalistischen produktion*, Hamburg: Otto Meissner.

———. (1898), *Kapital: Kritika politicheskoi ekonomii, Tom 1. Protsess proizvodstva kapitala* [Capital: A Critique of Political Economy, Volume I. The Production Process of Capital], St. Petersburg: Tipografiya A. Benke.

———. (1905), *Theorien über den Mehrwert: aus dem nachgelassenen manuskript "Zur kritik der politischen ökonomie", Bd. 2, David Ricardo*, Stuttgart: J. H. W. Dietz.

———. (1910), *Theorien über den Mehrwert, Bd. 3, Von Ricardo zur vulgärökonomie*, Stuttgart: J. H. W. Dietz.

———. (1952), 'Notes on Danielson's Article, 1880', in: Institut Marksa-Engel'sa-Lenina, *Arkhiv Marksa i Engel'sa*, vol. 12, Moscow: Gospolitizdat, pp. 118–20.

———. (1953a), *Grundrisse der kritik der politischen Ökonomie (Rohentwurf), 1857–1858*, Berlin: Dietz.

———. (1953b), 'Fragmente des Urtextes von 'Zur Kritik der politischen Oekonomie', in: Karl Marx, *Grundrisse der kritik der politischen Ökonomie (Rohentwurf), 1857–1858*, Berlin: Dietz, pp. 871–947.

———. (1962a), 'Entwürfe einer Antwort auf den Brief von V. I. Sassulitsch', MEW, vol. 19, pp. 384–406.

———. (1962b), 'Briefe an V. I. Sassulitsch', MEW, vol. 19, pp. 242–3.

———. (1966), 'Le Conseil générale au conseil fédéral de la Suisse romande', in: General Council of the First International, *Minutes*, vol. 3, Moscow: Progress Publishers, pp. 354–63.

———. (1967), *Briefe Januar 1881-März 1883*, MEW, vol. 35.
———. (1970), *A Contribution to the Critique of Political Economy*, New York: International.
———. (1972), 'Verhandlungen des 6. Rheinischen Landtags. Dritter Artikel', MEGA^2, vol. I/1, pp. 266–304.
———. (1975a), *Difference Between the Democritean and Epicurean Philosophy of Nature*, MECW, vol. 1, pp. 25–105.
———. (1975b), 'Debates on the Law on the Theft of Wood: Third Article', MECW, vol. 1, pp. 224–63.
———. (1975c), 'Index zu den 7 Heften', MEGA^2, vol. II/2, pp. 22–8.
———. (1976a), 'Exzerpte aus Charles De Brosses', MEGA^2, vol. IV/1, pp. 320–8.
———. (1976b), 'The Power of Money', in: Karl Marx, *Economic and Philosophic Manuscripts of 1844*, MECW, vol. 3, pp. 322–5.
———. (1979a), *The Eighteenth Brumaire of Louis Bonaparte*, MECW, vol. 11, pp. 99–209.
———. (1979b), 'Forced Migration', MECW, vol. 11, pp. 528–34.
———. (1982), 'Ökonomische–philosophische Manuskripte: Heft III [IX]', MEGA^2, vol. I/2, pp. 318–20.
———. (1983a), 'Bastiat und Carey', MEW, vol. 42, pp. 3–13.
———. (1983b), *Grundrisse der kritik der politischen Ökonomie*, MEW, vol. 42, pp. 15–770.
———. (1985), 'L'article «Karl Marx devant le tribunal de M. Joukowski»', MEGA^2, vol. I/25, pp. 112–6.
———. (1986a), 'Bullion: Das vollendete Geldsystem', MEGA^2, vol. IV/8, pp. 3–74.
———. (1986b), *Economic Manuscripts of 1857–58*, MECW, vol. 28.
———. (1987a), *Economic Manuscripts of 1857–61*, MECW, vol. 29.
———. (1987b), 'The Original Text of the Second and the Beginning of the Third Chapter of *A Contribution to the Critique of Political Economy*', in: Karl Marx, *Economic Manuscripts of 1857–61*, MECW, vol. 29, pp. 430–532.
———. (1987c), 'The Original Text of the Second and the Beginning of the Third Chapter of *A Contribution to the Critique of Political Economy*', MECW, vol. 29, pp. 430–507.
———. (1989), 'Letter to *Otechestvenniye Zapiski*', MECW, vol. 24, pp. 196–201.
———. (1990), '*Das Kapital*' *und vorarbeiten*, MEGA^2, vol. II/9.
———. (1991a), *Capital, Volume II*, London: Penguin.
———. (1991b), *Capital, Volume III*, London: Penguin.
———. (1991c), *Economic Manuscript of 1861–63*, MECW, vol. 33.
———. (1991d), 'Mercantile Capital. Money-Dealing Capital', in: Karl Marx, *Economic Manuscript of 1861–63*, MECW, vol. 33, pp. 9–68.

———. (1996a), *Capital, Volume I*, MECW, vol. 35.
———. (1996b), 'Cooperation', in: Karl Marx, *Capital, Volume I*, MECW, vol. 35, pp. 326–41.
———. (1996c), 'The Greed for Surplus Labor. Manufacturer and Boyar', in: Karl Marx, *Capital, Volume I*, MECW, vol. 35, pp. 243–51.
———. (1996d), 'The General Law of Capital Accumulation', in: Karl Marx, *Capital, Volume I*, MECW, vol. 35, pp. 607–703.
———. (2006), *Ökonomische Manuskripte 1857/58. (Grundrisse der Kritik der politischen Ökonomie)*, MEGA^2, vol. II/1.1–II/1.2.
———. (2008a), *Manuskripte zum zweiten Buch des 'Kapitals' 1868 bis 1881*, MEGA^2, vol. II/11.
———. (2008b), 'Vorrathbildung', in: Karl Marx, *Manuskripte zum zweiten Buch des 'Kapitals' 1868 bis 1881*, MEGA^2, vol. II/11, pp. 61–2.
———. (2008c), 'Manuskript VIII', in: Karl Marx, *Manuskripte zum zweiten Buch des 'Kapitals' 1868 bis 1881*, MEGA^2, vol. II/11, pp. 698–828.
———. (2008d), 'Vorrathbildung', in: Karl Marx, *Manuskripte zum zweiten Buch des 'Kapitals' 1868 bis 1881*, MEGA^2, vol. II/11, pp. 1009–10.
———. (2011), 'Value, Price and Profit', MEGA^2, vol. II/4.1, pp. 383–432.
———. (2012), *Ökonomische Manuskripte 1863–1867*, Teil 2, MEGA^2, vol. II/4.2.
———. (2013), *Zur Kritik der politischen Ökonomie (Manuskript 1861–1863)*, MEGA^2, vol. II/3.
———. (2016), *Marx's Economic Manuscript of 1864–1865*, Leiden: Brill.
———. (2017), *Das Kapital. Kritik der politischen Ökonomie. Zweites Buch: Der Zirkulationsprozeß des Kapitals. Redaktionsmanuskript von Friedrich Engels 1884/1885*, MEGA^2, vol. II/12.
Marx, Karl, and Engels, Friedrich (1848), *Manifest der Kommunistischen Partei: veröffentlicht im Februar 1848*, London: J. E. Burghard.
———. (1908), *Pis'ma Karla Marksa i Fridrikha Engel'sa k Nikolaiyu-onu [N. F. Daniel'sonu]* [Letters from Karl Marx and Friedrich Engels to Nikolai-on (N. F. Danielson)], St-Petersburg: Tip A. Benke.
———. (1976), *Manifesto of the Communist Party*, MECW, vol. 6, pp. 477–519.
———. (1988), *Letters 1868–70*, MECW, vol. 43.
———. (1991), *Letters 1874–79*, MECW, vol. 45.
———. (1992), *Letters 1880–83*, MECW, vol. 46.
Mei, June (1979), 'Socioeconomic Origins of Emigration', *Modern China*, vol. 5, n. 4: 463–501.
Mitchell, Timothy (1991), *Colonising Egypt*, Berkeley: University of California Press.
Montanari, Geminiano (1804), 'Della moneta, trattato mercantile', in: Pietro Custodi (ed.), *Scrittori Classici Italiani di Economia Politica: Parte Antica*, Tomo III, Milan: G. G. Destefanis, pp. 9–285.

Musto, Marcello (2020), *The Last Years of Karl Marx: An Intellectual Biography*, Stanford: Stanford University Press.

Ngai, Mae M. (2015), 'Chinese Gold Miners and the 'Chinese Question' in Nineteenth-Century California and Victoria', *The Journal of American History*, vol. 101, n. 4: 1082–105.

Nichols, Robert (2019), *Theft Is Property! Dispossession and Critical Theory*, Durham: Duke University Press.

Parsons, Charles (1863), 'Letter to F. D. Longe', in: House of Commons, *Children's Employment: Factories. Reports from Commissioners, vol. 18. Appendix: Reports and Evidence of Assistant Commissioners*, Parliament: House of Commons.

Pfaelzer, Jean (2008), *Driven Out: The Forgotten War Against Chinese Americans*, Berkeley: University of California Press.

Pliny the Elder (2004), *Natural History*, London: Penguin.

Pradella, Lucia (2015), *Globalisation and the Critique of Political Economy*, New York: Routledge.

Richards, Alan R. (1977), 'Primitive Accumulation in Egypt, 1798–1882', *Review*, vol. 1, n. 2: 3–49.

Richardson, Robert D. (2015), *Emerson: The Mind on Fire*, Berkeley: University of California Press.

Rubel, Maximilien (1960), *Karl Marx devant le Bonapartisme*, The Hague: Mouton.

Sacharoff, I. I. (1858), 'Ueber das Grundeigenthum in China', in: Carl Abel and F. A. Mecklenburg (eds.), *Arbeiten der Kaiserlich russischen gesandtschaft zu Peking über China*, Berlin: Heinecke, pp. 3–43.

Saleh, Mohammed (2014), *The Reluctant Transformation*, Toulouse: Toulouse School of Economics and the Institute for Advanced Study in Toulouse, http://publications.ut-capitole.fr/15736/.

Samaddar, Ranabir (2018), *Karl Marx and the Postcolonial Age*, London: Palgrave Macmillan.

Sassen, Saskia (2014), *Expulsions: Brutality and Complexity in the Global Economy*, Cambridge: Harvard University Press.

Schmidt, James (1996), 'The Fool's Truth: Diderot, Goethe, and Hegel', *Journal of the History of Ideas*, vol. 57, n. 4: 625–44.

Sempéré, Juan (1826), *Considérations sur les causes de la grandeur et de la décadence de la monarchie espagnole*, Tome 1, Paris: Renouard.

Shakespeare, William (1811), 'Timon von Athen', in: William Shakespeare, *Shakspeare's dramatische Werke*, Bd. 17, Vienna: Anton Pichler.

———. (1832), 'Timon von Athen', in: William Shakespeare, *Shakspeare's dramatische Werke*, Bd. 7, Berlin: G. Reimer.

Slobodkin, Yan (2018), *Empire of Hunger: Famine and the French Colonial State, 1867–1945*, PhD, Stanford University.

Smith, David Norman (2001), 'The Spectral Reality of Value: Sieber, Marx, and Commodity Fetishism', *Research in Political Economy*, vol. 19: 47–66.

———. (2017), 'Sharing, Not Selling: Marx Against Value', *Continental Thought & Theory*, vol. 1, n. 4: 653–95.

———. (2019), 'Authoritarianism Reimagined: The Riddle of Trump's Base', *The Sociological Quarterly*, vol. 60, n. 2: 210–23.

———. (2020), 'Anti-Authoritarian Marxism', in: Kieran Durkin and Joane Braune (eds.), *Erich Fromm's Critical Theory*, London: Bloomsbury, pp. 131–65.

———. (2021a, forthcoming), 'Capital and the Thrill of Domination', in: Alan Sica (ed.), *The Routledge Handbook of Max Weber Studies*, London: Routledge.

———. (2021b), 'Capital Fetishism and the Authoritarian Personality', in: Jeremiah Morelock (ed.), *How to Critique Authoritarian Populism*, Leiden: Brill.

———. (2022, forthcoming), *Marx's World: Global Society and Capital Accumulation in Marx's Late Manuscripts*, New Haven: Yale University Press.

Smith, David Norman, and Hanley, Eric (2018), 'The Anger Games: Who Voted for Donald Trump in the 2016 Election, and Why?', *Critical Sociology*, vol. 44, n. 2: 195–212.

Société d'économie politique (1880), 'La question des Chinois en California. – Celle des juifs en Roumanie, etc., réunion du 5 mai 1880', *Journal des économistes*, vol. 29: 298–312.

Sophocles (1984), *Antigone*, in: Sophocles, *The Three Theban Plays*, London: Penguin.

Stedman, J. G. (1796), *Narrative of a Five Year's Expedition Against the Revolted Negroes of Surinam*, vol. 1, London: J. Johnson.

Stevens, Dr. William (1864), 'Sanitary State of Colliery Settlements at Gilesgate Moor', in: Public Health, *Seventh Report of the Medical Officer of the Privy Council*, London: H.M. Stationery Office.

Tronti, Mario (2010), 'Selections from *Workers and Capital*', *Genre*, vol. 43, n. 3-4: 337–52.

Virgil (1860), *Virgil's Aeneid*, New York: D. Appleton.

Waterfield, Henry (1867), 'Statement Exhibiting the Moral and Material Progress and Condition of India, During the Year 1865–66', in: House of Lords, *Accounts and Papers*, vol. XIII, Great Britain: House of Lords, pp. 3–52.

Weber, Max (1904), 'Die protestantische Ethik und der 'Geist' des Kapitalismus, I. Das Problem', *Archiv für Sozialwissenschaft und Sozialpolitik*, vol. 20: 1–54.

West, William (1871), 'Formation of an English-Speaking Section of the International Workingmen's Association at San Francisco, CA', *Woodhull & Claflin's Weekly*, 16 December, p. 8.

White, James D. (1996), *Karl Marx and the Intellectual Origins of Dialectical Materialism*, New York: St. Martins.

———. (2019), 'The Development of Capitalism in Russia in the Works of Marx, Danielson, Vorontzov, and Lenin', in: Paul Zarembka (ed.), *Class History and Class Practices in the Periphery of Capitalism*, Bingley, UK: Emerald.

Williams, Helen Maria (1788), *A Poem on the Bill Lately Passed for Regulating the Slave Trade*, London: T. Cadell.

Wilson, Stephen (1982), *Ideology and Experience: Antisemitism in France at the Time of the Dreyfus Affair*, Madison, NJ: Fairleigh Dickinson University Press.

Wong, Edlie L. (2015), *Racial Reconstruction: Black Inclusion, Chinese Exclusion, and the Fictions of Citizenship*, New York: New York University Press.

Wycherley, William (1677), *The Plain-Dealer: A Comedy*, London: Magnes & Bentley.

Zo, Kil Young (1971), *Chinese Emigration into the United States*, PhD, Columbia University.

Zweig, Arnold (1965), *Berliner Ausgabe*, Bd. 3, Berlin: Aufbau-Verlags.

CHAPTER 9

Marx on Migration and the Industrial Reserve Army: Not to Be Misused!

Pietro Basso

9.1 A Key Contradiction That Is Insoluble

Amid the new attention to Marx's ideas, his authority has sometimes been invoked on the left and even the right, especially in Italy and Germany, to legitimize the anti-immigrant 'border closure' policies that are running wild in Europe and beyond. This misuse of his thought cites his analysis of the function of migration and the industrial reserve army under capitalism, while (partly) distorting it and (completely) severing it from his political conclusions. Here I shall consider such shameless misuse, addressing the logic behind certain cases of falsification. First, however, we need to look very briefly at what Marx really said on the matter.

In Marx's critique of political economy and the capitalist mode of production, the category of 'industrial reserve army' occupies a particularly important place. Already in the *Grundrisse*, Marx presents a *key*

Translated by Patrick Camiller.

P. Basso (✉)
Ca' Foscari University, Venice, Italy

M. Musto (ed.), *Rethinking Alternatives with Marx*, Marx, Engels, and Marxisms, https://doi.org/10.1007/978-3-030-81764-0_9

contradiction insoluble in the mode of expansion of capital. Capital, he argues, has one end in view: unlimited self-valorization. For this purpose, it needs to constantly increase surplus labour time, the uncompensated portion of the time provided by workers, as well as to increase the number of working days, and therefore the mass of wage labourers. Capital has two ways of increasing the surplus labour time of this mass of workers: it can lengthen the working day and it can increase the productivity of labour through the employment of technology. But a higher productivity of labour produces a (relative) decline in the number of hired workers. In short, as Marx put it: 'It is the tendency [of capital] to increase the labouring population [as a prerequisite for an increase in surplus value], as well as constantly to posit a part of it as surplus population – population which is useless until such time as capital can utilize it'.[1] This contradiction presents itself in different forms and degrees according to the location and historical conjuncture, but it is insoluble in and by capitalism. Today it is clearer than ever, when we see before us a simply huge and growing mass of unemployed and underemployed workers.[2]

The tight nexus between accumulation and overpopulation is analysed at even greater length in *Capital*,[3] where it is explicitly related to the *composition of capital* as well as to labour productivity. With the progress of capital accumulation, Marx shows, even if the composition of capital (the ratio of capital-machinery to living labour-power) remains unchanged, the demand for labour-power increases. But as a normal rule, with the progress of capital accumulation and the concentration of capital, constant capital (means of production) grows more than proportionately in relation to variable capital (labour-power). In other words, with the increase in total capital, the demand for labour *declines in relative terms*, while it grows in absolute terms. Hence, *a growing surplus population is created as the capitalist mode of production advances world-wide and supplants precapitalist social relations*. One part of this surplus population functions as the industrial reserve army—a phenomenon generated

[1] Karl Marx, *Grundrisse: Foundations of the Critique of Political Economy* (London: Penguin, 1993), p. 399.

[2] The latest International Labour Organization report, *World Employment and Social Outlook: Trends 2020* (Geneva: International Labour Office, 2020) gives the following estimates: unemployed and underemployed workers make up 470 million out of a global labour forceof 3.3 billion, and 1.4 billion of the latter are informal workers who 'live in vulnerable conditions and earn much less than salaried workers', p. 3. Of these, a significant number may be considered as part of the proletarian reserve army.

[3] Karl Marx, *Capital, Volume I* (London: Penguin, 1976), pp. 781–98.

by capitalist commodity production and unknown in earlier modes of production.

Variable in extent, the industrial reserve army is also non-homogeneous, internally differentiated. Marx identifies four layers for his own time, each with its distinctive living conditions and functions for capital: (a) a shifting top stratum, composed of industrial and skilled workers, who periodically become unemployed but sooner or later resume work in their own or other branches of industry; (b) a second layer, which Marx calls 'latent', comprising the mass of workers from the countryside who flow into the cities and make themselves available in all branches of industry; (c) a stagnant layer which, on the margins of the active army of workers but with irregular employment, consists of people constantly looking for any kind of work; and (d) the poorest bottom layer, itself subdivided into those who are capable of work but can only find back-breaking jobs off and on, those who have become incapable of work, and those who have fallen into the subproletariat. Marx's main field of investigation is Great Britain, although at the end of Chapter 25 this shifts to Ireland, where Marx's study founds 'similar phenomena' to those facing the English rural proletariat. In fact, the formation of a relative surplus population and an industrial reserve army depends on the *general laws of motion* of the capitalist mode of production—a mode which, for the first time in history, has made existential insecurity of the working masses and chronic poverty of broad layers among them a 'normal phenomenon of society'.[4] This process occurred in both England and Ireland, which Marx analysed first separately and then in their colonial relationship, and we subsequently find the process again in *every* other country taken over by capitalism. This is evidently the case in the global South today, where the all-out development of capitalist relations of production, under the aegis of agribusiness multinationals, is leading to massive emigration from the countryside (30–40 million people a year) at an unprecedented pace.

The industrial reserve army is a product of capitalist development but also its precondition, in the sense that it is always available at any moment to satisfy 'just in time' the changing needs of capital accumulation. This is essential in periods of stagnation or crisis as well as periods of productive paroxysm, since in both cases it puts pressure on the active army of labour

[4] Rosa Luxemburg, *Introduction to Political Economy*, in: Peter Hudis (ed.), *The Complete Works of Rosa Luxemburg, Volume I: Economic Writings 1* (London: Verso, 2013), p. 281.

by curbing its demands and containing or lowering the average value of labour-power (through no choice of the workers, of course!). Marx's analysis here rounds off his definition of the 'absolute general law of capitalist accumulation', valid for all countries and all stages of this mode of production and reproduction of the life of society: 'The greater the social wealth, the functioning capital, the extent and energy of its growth ..., the greater is the industrial reserve army'. This nexus connecting capital accumulation, active army of labour and industrial reserve army has a profound effect on the terrain of class struggle: it 'rivets the worker to capital more firmly than the wedges of Hephaestus held Prometheus to the rock'.[5]

The orderly functioning of this mechanism, which permanently *divides* the class living from wage labour and fuels competition between the employed and the unemployed or underemployed, is of fundamental importance for capital. For centuries now, it has supplied it with policies and imagery that have tended to entrench the dividing lines between the two armies of labour. This is why Marx, a sworn enemy of the modern chains for the exploitation of human labour, unconditionally promotes 'planned co-operation between the employed and the unemployed in order to obviate or weaken the ruinous effects of this natural law of capitalist accumulation on their class'. For 'every combination between employed and unemployed disturbs the "pure" action of this law'.[6] For Marx, therefore: (1) the production of an industrial reserve army is a *law*, not a passing accident or dysfunction of capitalism linked to this or that social policy or—to keep with our main theme—this or that policy on migration; (2) the only force that can challenge it is the *combined struggle* of the employed and the unemployed. To omit this twofold political and historical-theoretical conclusion is brazenly to falsify Marx's and Marxist theory on the question.

[5] Marx, *Capital, Volume I*, pp. 798–9.

[6] Ibid., pp. 793–4.

9.2 Migrant Workers and Industrial Reserve Army Are Not the Same Thing

In Marx there is a parallel and an intertwining between migration and industrial reserve army—but the two are not superimposed.[7] Let us begin with the parallelism. In a manner as 'automatic' and necessary to its development as the production of a surplus population and an industrial reserve army, capitalism has never ceased to generate migratory movements, both within individual countries and on an international level. In fact, mass migrations are integral to the capitalist mode of production and its expanded reproduction on a world scale; they bring about the formation of a global labour market. Another key point for Marx is that mass migration in the capitalist epoch is *essentially forced*: nothing is further from his thought than the frivolous liberal image of the 'free migrant', rich in romantic left variants that reduce the phenomenon to a chaotic, random collection of individual life-stories and choices, glossing over its causes and its brutal social and collective character.

The European dimension of this secular process was the theme of many of Marx's journalistic pieces, particularly memorable ones being those on the Duchess of Sutherland, which exposed the terroristic methods she used to clear the farmers from her land and force them to emigrate. Marx clearly shows that the capitalist agricultural revolutionbrought ruthless violence to bear on farm workers and tenant-farmers in the Scottish Highlands, and that countless rural producers were later driven from the countryside all over the Continent and forced to seek shelter in small towns and cities.

Outside Europe, the *colonial* aspect of this global spread of capitalist relations of production, including through the large-scale forced emigration of workers, featured a series of even more abominable chapters: the rise of the African slave trade industry, the violent ejection of more than 100 million slaves from their lands and homes, and the transplanting and superexploitation of those who survived the journey to the Americas, where they were used to repopulate areas after the holocaust of indigenous peoples in the Centre and South, and later the North. There followed the exploitation of Chinese coolies, Indians, Indonesians, and Japanese, all forced into temporary migration as half-slaves/half-wage

[7] Pietro Basso, 'Migration', in: Marcello Musto (ed.), *The Marx Revival: Key Concepts and New Interpretations* (Cambridge: Cambridge University Press), pp. 232–46.

labourers. Not by chance did Marx stress several times that capital feeds on 'dual slavery': indirect wage slavery in Europe and direct slavery 'pure and simple' of coloured peoples in the colonies.

Advances of the agricultural and industrial revolution, worldwide expansion of capitalist social relations: such was the basis for the parallel between the creation of an industrial reserve army and the spread of national and international migration. Let us now consider the intertwining of the two phenomena, confining ourselves to Europe, where the process first developed. As the growth of capitalist market relations generated an ever-greater surplus population in Europe, the new industries proved unable to absorb all the dispossessed masses, and large-scale migratory flows headed towards the Americas and Australasia. Only in the British case was this mainly a case of non-labourers; elsewhere in Europe workers made up by far the largest component. For some groups, even among working-class emigrants, North America and large parts of South America were veritable promised lands, where many had an immediate opportunity to become small, or not so small, landowners. By 1867, Marx already declared that this 'golden age' of emigration had come to an end. He did so, as he often did, far in advance of the real situation. But the fact remains that over the past 150 years, as he foresaw, no mass emigration on a world scale has replicated the characteristics of the outflow from Britain in the eighteenth century and the first half of the nineteenth. There would be no more promised lands like North America, Australasia, or even South America, cleared through the extermination of indigenous peoples by the colonial powers. An overwhelming majority of the UN's estimated 270 million emigrants in today's world consist of proletarians, wage earners, or others destined to become such in the countries where they resettle.[8] For these masses of people, no land of plenty awaits them with free spaces to take over or gold deposits to plunder. On the contrary, the horn of plenty overflows only for countries that can employ labouring capacity (brain, muscles, heart) without having spent anything to produce it, at a *differential* rate of exploitation fuelled by discriminatory racist laws and practices that strike immigrant workers everywhere at the hands of national states—except when struggles counteract them, of course! Only with the passing of generations and the sinking of social and cultural roots does a minority (or small minority) of the immigrant population manage

[8] One of the novelties in today's world is the high presence of women and their leading role in opening up migration 'chains' or networks.

to climb out of the proletariat and join the middle classes, particularly in the activities involving small-scale capital accumulation that have been on the decline for decades, or, unusually, in more privileged strata up to the top of the social ladder.

But in contrast to what so-called left 'sovereigntists' like to claim, the great mass of Europe's immigrant wage earners in recent decades cannot be considered *en bloc* as a new industrial reserve army. Indeed, many are quite stably inserted in various sectors of the economy. In Italy, for example, while redundancies among immigrant workers have increased since the great crisis of 2008, the rate of unemployment of the immigrant labour force in 2017 was 14.3%, barely 3.5% higher than that of Italians. Conversely, in the early twenty-first century, the proportion of Italian born workers made redundant (certainly not by choice or through any fault of the immigrant workers, nor as a result of their 'disloyal competition') was so high that over a period of thirteen years (2006–2019) more than two million people left Italy for good.[9] In the European Union, the gap between the unemployment rate of non-EU immigrants and that of EU citizens is a little wider, but the official statistics indicate that four out of five immigrant workers have a more than temporary work relationship.[10] Much as one wishes to remove imprecision and the well-known tendency of official data to mask job insecurity, it remains the case that the great majority of immigrant workers in the EU *are within the active army of labour*, not the industrial reserve army.

The fact is that the independent variable regulating the scale of unemployment and underemployment is not the openness or closure of borders and migration policy, but the course of capital accumulation. And if migration policies are to be seriously challenged for what they really are, we would have to say that for decades in Italy and Europe they have been discriminatory, repressive, and selective—the opposite of the 'no borders' approach that left and right 'sovereigntists' jabber on about. That is the type of policy that often drives millions of working men and women into

[9] See Fondazione Migrantes, *Rapporto Italiani nel mondo 2019* (Todi: Editrice Tau, 2019); and Iside Gjergji (ed.), *La nuova emigrazione italiana. Cause, mete e figure sociali* (Venice: Edizioni Ca' Foscari, 2015).

[10] Eurostat, *Migrant Integration Statistics, 2018 Edition* (Luxembourg: Eurostat, 2018).

conditions of forced irregularity, and almost always of economic, juridical, political, and symbolic inferiority.[11]

9.3 Emigrants as the Vanguard of the Working Class

Marx, therefore, denounces the essentially forced character of the internal and international migration generated by the advance of capital, as well as the capitalistic use made of it against the working class as a whole. But it is impossible to find in the writings of that perennial political refugee a portrait of migrants as supine victims of capital. The dialectical power of his analysis, which mirrors the contradictions and antagonisms of the international spread of capitalist social relations, is all there in the dazzling finale to Chapter 25.

> Like all good things in the world, this profitable mode of proceeding [the depopulation of Ireland driven by rent-bloated landowners] has its drawbacks. The accumulation of the Irish in America keeps pace with the accumulation of rents in Ireland. The Irishman, banished by the sheep and the ox, reappears on the other side of the ocean as a Fenian. And there a young but gigantic republic rises, more and more threateningly, to face the old queen of the waves.[12]

Beyond its brief and eventful span of activity, the Fenian Brotherhood—founded in Chicago in 1858 by the emigrants John O'Mahony and Michael Doheny, and present in Ireland, Canada, Australia, and Latin America—gave the decisive impetus for the birth of the Irish freedom struggle against British rule. And what of the vanguard role of émigré proletarians in the battles of the international workers' movement, a long and glorious history? Were not German immigrants in the United States—August Spies, Albert Parsons, Adolph Fischer, George Engel—the magnificent heralds of the international workers' struggle for the eight-hour day, hanged on 11 November 1887 in a prison courtyard in Chicago? And was it not Bohemian, Polish, German, Russian, and Irish emigrants who gave mass and strength to that struggle?

[11] See Pietro Basso (ed.), *Razzismo di stato. Stati Uniti, Europa, Italia* (Milan: Angeli, 2015).

[12] Marx, *Capital, Volume I*, p. 870.

In *The German Ideology*, Marx and Engels already noted that in North America the speed of historical developments was faster precisely because 'the most advanced individuals of the old countries' (the emigrants) brought with them the 'correspondingly most advanced form of intercourse'.[13] And in the *Manifesto of the Communist Party*, they hailed the reverse side of the brutal violence with which the peasantry was driven from the countryside: namely, that it 'rescued a considerable part of the population from the idiocy of rural life'.[14] Later, following his two revolutionary predecessors, Lenin saw in the large metropolitan areas, with their concentrations of nationalities, the great mills grinding down the ethnic differences and hatreds that had long ravaged human existence, the melting pot that would permit the birth of the empirically universal individuals envisaged in *The German Ideology*.

Economists, including the towering classical figures, have not been capable of seeing workers, proletarians, as anything other than work-machines or Aristotle's animated instruments of labour, a merely subordinate factor of production. The young Marx, however, chancing upon meetings of the French socialist *ouvriers*, already saw with his own eyes how capable they were of something very different, how eager to engage with theoretical questions, how expressive of a new fundamental need for true fraternity and genuine cooperation—and how in practice this involved a radical negation of the alienation of labour and of the capitalist's absolute sway over his wage-slaves.

9.4 Italian 'Social Nationalist' Demagogy

Let us now turn to those who have claimed to be drawing on Marx's analysis of the industrial reserve army and its place in forced migration, but who have distorted it and severed it from his political conclusions, using false pictures of reality and specious justifications to join the ranks of 'social' nationalism.

In Italy, the most skilled in juggling with words and coining new formulas is the 'philosopher' Diego Fusaro, who is often asked via video to come up with slogans that can be marketed as radical but

[13] Karl Marx and Friedrich Engels, *The German Ideology* (London: Lawrence & Wishart, 1965), p. 91.

[14] Karl Marx and Friedrich Engels, *Manifesto of the Communist Party*, MECW, vol. 6, p. 488.

are really reactionary in the true sense of the term. In his latest book, *Glebalizzazione*, he repeatedly endeavours to cover himself with Marx's shadow:

> In opposition to all who celebrate today's immigration as an inherently positive model, at once integrative and emancipatory, we should forcefully underline, from a staunchly Marxist viewpoint, that it is always such only for capital and the globalist Master, who can unreservedly employ migrants in various branches of production, at rock-bottom prices and without a proper recognition of their rights. [...] In the practices of mass immigration and the capitalist uprooting associated with it, the winners are neither migrants nor workers, who both form the emerging pole of the new precarious Slave.[15] Migrants lose out because they figure as slaves subject to blackmail, and as human material deprived of rights and dignity. [...] Native-born workers also are losers, because they find themselves competing with migrant workerswho promote a race to the bottom. The big winner is the globalist liberal-libertarian elite ... the neofeudal Master and Capital, with its insatiable thirst for hands and brain cells available to do the same for a lower price.[16]

So, Fusaro begins by setting up a straw man: where can we ever find his phantom-subject, who celebrates migration in such a naïve, infantile manner and is here quackishly described as if he were the Almighty? Then our 'philosopher' stages a jeremiad, with not a whit in it that is 'staunchly Marxist'. First of all, it is no monopoly of Marx's thought to note the competition among wage earners in the capitalist mode of production, nor the competition between native-born and immigrant workers. And the apparent (never clear) broaching of this theme has no other purpose than the anti-Marxist one of depicting both immigrants and native-born proletarians as new serfs: the former as mere things, weak, wretched, desperate, vulnerable to blackmail; the latter as beings reified and nullified by the unfortunate arrival of new migrants. All this therefore serves to

[15] The whole book suggests that, with the globalization of capital and capitalist social relations, workers are being transformed into new serfs (*servi della gleba*)—hence the wordplay in the title *La glebalizzatione*. There is no need to highlight that Fusaro completely ignores the long history of serf rebellions, and that only this disregard allows him to present serfs as the ideal figure of 'slaves born to be slaves'.

[16] Diego Fusaro, *Glebalizzazione. La lotta di classe al tempo del populismo* (Milan: Rizzoli, 2019), e-book.

reverse the perspective that Marx already set out in his *Speech on the Question of Free Trade*, where, having exposed the spurious demand for free trade as nothing other than a call for the freedom of capital to pulverize the workers and to establish a monopoly in the world market that will oppress more backward countries, he concludes by arguing *in favour* of free trade because of its indubitably *revolutionary impact*. Although it is true that the free trade system has a destructive effect, it has this in relation to the 'old nationalities'. And for Marx this is a merit, in so far as it 'carries the antagonism of bourgeoisie and proletariat to the uttermost point', by globalizing it and thereby 'hastening the Social Revolution'.[17] That was in Brussels, on 9 January 1848, the dawn of the first year in European social history which, particularly because of the June Days in Paris, would be marked in golden letters on the calendar of the proletarian revolution.

Fusaro's account moves in the *diametrically opposite* direction, bringing onto the stage the avenging angel of the immigrant and indigenous serf-workers: His Majesty the National State(bourgeois, of course) supposedly becomes sovereign again against 'globalism', thanks to the restoration of the order associated with the Peace of Westphalia. In his view, the present context of class struggle has completely changed:

> The class struggle in the age of globalism presents itself [...] as a conflict between the financial openness of the dominant cosmopolitan layer and the national autonomy of the dominated national-popular pole (the national self-sufficiency that was Keynes's focus). The former aims for a fundamental opening of reality and the imaginary, so that the commodity form can circulate in every direction free from barriers and frontiers, walls and enclosures. The latter has every interest in reinstating boundaries and limit, so that the deregulated, unbounded space of the commodity is normatized by politics and the *wildes Tier* (wild beast) of the market, as Hegel called it, and disciplined by society as a function of its actual needs. [Moreover], Marx himself was fully aware – he said so explicitly, above all in Volume One of *Capital* – that the conquests of the workers' movement always occur in the framework of national states, through limits on the working day and norms defending the proletarian condition and protecting labour.[18]

[17] Karl Marx, 'Speech on the Question of Free Trade', MECW, vol. 6, p. 465.

[18] Fusaro, *Glebalizzazione*.

What a cocktail of little truths and barefaced lies! The true admission is that Fusaro and his cohorts dream of an Italian *capitalist* state capable of regulating the anarchy of capital and the market, and powerful enough to be 'sovereign' in relation to the 'globalist power-elite'.[19] It is an empty idealism, which ignores the barriers introduced in the past—and still more today—against this retrograde shopkeeper's fantasy. Much more important are the quasi-leftist falsehoods. It escapes the 'philosopher' and his Red-Brown cronies that we are witnessing an acute class polarization (between capitalists and the class that lives on its own labour) in Western societies, and a more radical subsumption than ever of politics under economics, not only on a global scale but *also within individual nations*. Those who speak of the need to reinstate frontiers, walls, and boundaries fail to see one little aspect of them: the instruments of torture against migrants that have been up and running in Europe, at least since the Schengen agreement in 1985.[20] Not only have these multiplied in the form of physical, electronic, legal, and symbolic walls, at the level of the EU, national statesand private gangs, on land, sea, and air; for the migrants, women, men, and children, there is an *embarras de choix* as to how and where they should risk their lives (and often die) in the attempt to cross over.[21] But the height of falsification is reached when, 'in the name of the class struggle harking back to Marx', our author invokes 'political control over the flows of capital and people', and when he claims

[19] This theme of sovereignty—repeatedly described as national, popular, or democratic—is sometimes developed with more arguments, but is always turned inward in a (social) nationalism of the heart. This is also true of other exponents of 'left sovereigntism' in Italy, such as Alessandro Somma, *Sovranismi. Stato, popolo e conflitto sociale* (Rome: Derive Approdi, 2018); Carlo Formenti, *Utopie letali: contro l'ideologia post–moderna* (Milan: Jaca Book, 2013); Carlo Formenti, *La variante populista. Lotta di classe nel neo–liberismo* (Rome: Derive Approdi, 2016); and Vladimiro Giacché, *Costituzione italiana contro Trattati europei. Un conflitto inevitabile* (Reggio Emilia: Imprimatur, 2015). Another of Fusaro's inspirers is, of course, Régis Debray, *Éloge des frontières* (Paris: Gallimard, 2010).

[20] These *structurally* include torture in the strict sense of the word, as we can see from the outstanding research compilation: Fabio Perocco (ed.), *Tortura e migrazioni/Torture and Migration* (Venice: Edizioni Ca' Foscari, 2019).

[21] See Tim Marshall, *Divided: Why We're Living in an Age of Walls* (London: Elliott & Thompson, 2018); and Ainhoa Ruiz Benedicto, Mark Akkerman, and Pere Brunet, *A Walled World Towards a Global Apartheid* (Barcelona: Centre Delàs d'Estudis per la Pau, 2020).

that Marx himself glorified the national stateas the protector of workers' rights—two complete untruths. From the earliest documents of the First International, on which the Moor worked with great dedication, he established its very foundation as fraternal solidarity between the working classes of various countries and the struggle against national prejudices. And he considered that, at a time (1867) when the bosses were importing 'foreign workers' and 'transferring manufacture to countries where there is a cheap labour force', the only possibility of successful resistance was that 'the national organizations must become international'.[22] Anything but 'political control of cross-border flows' and the closing of frontiers!

Equally unsustainable is the idea that Marx saw the national stateas friendly to the workers' aims, in setting limits to the working day in the mid-nineteenth century. Having forced the reader to sample some of the most toxic atmosphere to be found in the Po valley, it is time for some breaths of healthy mountain air:

> In the United States of America, every independent workers' movement was paralysed as long as slavery disfigured a part of the republic. *Labour in a white skin cannot emancipate itself where it is branded in a black skin.* However, a new life immediately arose from the death of slavery [which owed so much to the tireless struggle of the slaves descended from forced migrants from Africa]. The first fruit of the American Civil War was the eight hours' agitation, which ran from the Atlantic to the Pacific, from New England to California, with the seven-league boots of the locomotive. The General Congress of Labour held at Baltimore in August 1866 declared: 'The first and great necessity of the present, to free the labour of this country from capitalistic slavery, is the passing of a law by which eight hours shall be the normal working day in all the States of the American Union. We are resolved to put forth all our strength until this glorious result is attained'. At the same time (the beginning of September 1866), the Congress of the International Working Men's Association, held at Geneva, passed the following resolution, proposed by the London General Council: 'We declare that the *limitation of the working day* is a preliminary condition without which all further attempts at improvement and emancipation must prove abortive [...] the Congress proposes eight hours as the legal limit of the working day'.[23]

[22] Karl Marx, 'The General Council of the International Working Men's Association on the Lausanne Congress', MECW, vol. 20, p. 422.

[23] Marx, *Capital, Volume I*, pp. 414–5, emphases added.

That is a far cry from the national stateas the workers' friend and protector! Instead, we read of an international and internationalist struggle of self-emancipation, in which 'the workers have to put their heads together and, as a class, compel the passing of a law, an all-powerful social [not state or institutional] barrier by which they can be prevented from selling themselves and their families into slavery and death by voluntary contract with capital'.[24] The national stateis neither friend nor protector: the workers must use the power of their own general organization to force action that protects them as a class from the craving of capital for profit—and also from any temptation to sell themselves as isolated individuals. *Dixit* Marx.

9.5 Germany: The Case of *Aufstehen*

Now let us turn to Germany, where we come across two high-profile exponents of the *Aufstehen* movement: Sahra Wagenknecht and Wolfgang Streeck. The first, a glittering, photogenic writer, who comes from the Communist Platform in the PDS and is now a leading spokesperson of Die Linke, has been outrageously compared to Rosa Luxemburg by the German international broadcaster Deutsche Welle. The second, a celebrated sociologist, is one of the reference intellectuals of the movement.[25]

[24] Ibid., p. 416.

[25] See Sahra Wagenknecht, *Reichtum ohne Gier: Wie wir uns vor dem Kapitalismus retten* (Frankfurt: Campus Verlag, 2018), and a semi-autobiography Sahra Wagenknecht, *Couragiert gegen den Strom. Uber Goëthe, die Macht and die Zukunft* (Munich: Piper Verlag, 2017); Wolfgang Streeck, *How Will Capitalism End? Essays on a Failing System* (London: Verso, 2016), a work on the primacy of the nation; and Wolfgang Streeck, 'Between Charity and Justice: Remarks on the Social Construction of Immigration Policy in Rich Democracies', *Culture, Practice & Europeanization*, vol. 3 (2018), n. 2: 3–22. The positions of *Aufstehen* on immigration have met with a number of responses, ranging from gentle to caustic. See Colin Crouch, 'Sahra Wagenknecht: Brauchen wir eine Sammlungsbewegung?', *Die Zeit*, 17 August 2018; Thomas Sablowsky and Hans-Günter Thien, 'Die AfD, die ArbeiterInnenklasse und die Linke – kein Problem?', *PROKLA*, vol. 48 (2018), n. 1: 55–71; and Silke van Dyk and Stefanie Graefe, 'The Reality of Exclusive Solidarity: A Response to Wolfgang Streeck's "Between Charity and Justice"', *Culture, Practice & Europeanization*, vol. 4 (2019), n. 1: 149–54. A clear early emphasis on the 'need to control and regulate' immigration is contained in Oskar Lafontaine, *Politik für Alle. Streitschrift für eine Gerechte Gesellschaft* (Berlin: Ullstein, 2006), pp. 232–5.

In this case, unlike that of the word-jugglers, the falsification of Marx's thought relies on classical Teutonic 'rational' and 'realistic' argument; nor is it quite so 'upfront'. Still, there is no shortage of appeals to a counterfeit Marx and Marxism. And the posture of both our heroes is of people who stand firmly on the side of the weakest, of the 'lower classes', the working class, against the strong powers of global capital that inordinately swell the industrial army with immigrants. The only difference between Wagenknecht and Streeck is that she bows compassionately towards poor refugees struck by adversities, whereas he, using isolated cases, manages to construct the refugee as a threatening figure, seemingly a victim but in reality a lucid schemer and lawbreaker. But they are always ready to get back into step with each other, in the imperious wish to help refugees 'return home', or as near as possible to 'home'—anyway, as far as possible from German soil.

On the question of immigration, their 'rationality' and 'realism' rests upon the following arguments: (1) immigrant workers exert downward competitive pressure on native-born workers in the labour market; (2) there are not enough resources to ensure decent welfare benefits for both poor Germans and immigrants (resource scarcity being a theme that Streeck is forever beating out); and (3) a sort of 'cultural war' is underway against the German subaltern classes, because the arrival en masse of (especially Muslim) immigrants is shaking their traditional habitat of ideas and customs, and because immigrants have a tendency to create culturally homogeneous and impermeable ghettoes. And since the material and spiritual suffering of the native proletarians carries little or no weight for the wild-eyed 'no borders' Left, 'the old working class is *forced* into a coalition with the protectionist wing of the capitalist class and the remnants of the anti-liberal, nationalist Right'.[26] Their argument naturalizes every single aspect of the question: the competition between immigrant and native-born, the scarcity of resources, austerity policies, the self-ghettoization of immigrant populations, the impermeability of cultures, xenophobia, racism. Without becoming the new serfs of Fusaro's imaginings, both German proletarians and new immigrant proletarians or asylum-seekers are presented as pawns in the historical game staged by evil liberal policies of 'open borders', and as *naturally* inimical to each other.

[26] Streeck, 'Between Charity and Justice', p. 20, emphasis added.

Once more, the twin targets of their polemic are the 'globalism' of capitalist elites and international working-class solidarity. Indeed, the latter is downgraded to mere dangerous rhetoric, so dangerous that Streeck picks it up and attacks it even when it wears the institutional trappings of Mrs Merkel's 'Christian charity',[27] which he regards as a perilously 'anarchic' (non-law-abiding) surrogate for the old decomposing internationalism. Here, too, the approach is a *repêchage* of the national 'social state', which has the supposed merit of being able to tame the economy and 'make capitalism less capitalist' (Wagenknecht), making the lives of 'ordinary people', the most vulnerable workers, secure from the terrifying dangers of immigration and multiculturalism, through the closing of borders and a 'responsible nationalism'. The 'social question'—that is, class antagonisms—thus transmute into the 'national question', into conflicts between global powers and national states. And the operation rounds off 'sovereigntism' with a social content, which it actually claims to be internationalist in so far as it aims (ideally) to help immigrants to go back 'home'.

The bitter truth contained in all this swill is that such a position is not alien to the (worst) traditions of the German workers' movement, and not only the German. The leaders of *Aufstehen* do not lie when they proclaim that they 'courageously' recovering the traditional positions of the Social Democratic Left, its 'historical pro-regulation agenda', and its customary 'politics of law and (national) order'. The big lie, however, is their 'harnessing of Marx-esque phraseology' to present a 'politics at odds with Marxism' as is if it were pro-working class.[28] And the big lie is their obscuring the fact that for decades immigrants in Germany (and elsewhere in Europe) are subject to endless regulations and additional discriminatory controls, to hair-raising special laws that can force people into illegality[29]; and that at least since 11 September 2001 a veritable European war on emigrants and immigrants has been piling up the

[27] Streeck's polemic is directed at Angela Merkel's decision in 2015 to admit hundreds of thousands of Syrian refugees.

[28] Angela Mitropoulos, 'Wolfgang Streeck's Neo–Romantic Sociology', *S0metim3s*, 27 March 2019, https://s0metim3s.com/2019/03/27/streeck-sociology/. This misuse of 'Marx-esque' phrases, notes Mitropoulos, serves Streeck as 'a hallmark of both Polanyian conservatism and Sorelian fascism', a 'craft' dating back more than a century in which the economic sociologist is the latest newcomer.

[29] See Peter Kammerer, 'Germania: un secolo di politica migratoria', in: Pietro Basso and Fabio Perocco (eds.), *Gli immigrati in Europa. Disuguaglianze, razzismo, lotte* (Milan:

dead bodies between the Sahara and the Mediterranean. As Sablowski has shown, it is another lie to claim that the whole of the 'old' German working class holds an anti-immigrant position; or to pass over the fact that immigrant workers waged struggles alongside German workers in the post-war period, not in competition with them but in many cases at their head. Have our authors never heard of one of the most memorable cycles of working-class history in West Germany, in the spring/summer of 1973? Or of the strikes at John Deere in Mannheim, at Hella in Lippstadt and Paderborn, at Ford's of Cologne, at AEG in Gelsenkirchen, Opel in Bochum, and others in Aachen, Bielefeld, Duisburg, Hagen, and so on? Or of the role that Turkish, Yugoslav, and Italian[30] proletarians played in all this—yes, the very 'wretched of the earth' provoking a race to the bottom in the toxic narratives of Wagenknecht and Streeck? Do they know, when they speak of a cultural war underway against the German 'lower classes' and their traditions, that at least 25% of today's population in Germany, and more of the working class, has a *Migrationshintergrund*, an immigrant background, and that the figure will soon reach 33%? What traditions do they have in mind if Germany is now a structurally multinational, multiracial, multicultural country? And breaking out of the perimeter of the nation-prison, were immigrant proletarians not at the head of the great cycle of working-class struggles between 1968 and 1973, which shook the factories and the entire life of society in France, Belgium, and Northern Italy (where the immigrant workers were Italians, from the South)? What collective strength was capable of launching the first great *international* strike in the whole of US history, on 1 May 2006, if not that of immigrants from Mexico, South America, and Asia furious at the criminalization of people without documented status? At the other pole of contemporary capitalist development, in a rising China, who if not the *mingong* (the young and very young internal migrants) filled the stage with myriad strikes that became so widespread and embarrassing that official statistics were forced to suspend the recording of social conflicts? And in today's benumbed Italy, who keeps the strike weapon alive, who renews the great traditions of class solidarity ('Touch one of us, you touch us all!'), if not the logistics workers and deliverers of dozens of nationalities,

Angeli, 2003), pp. 163–88; and the articles by Dirk Vogelskamp and Tobias Pieper in Basso (ed.), *Razzismo di stato*, pp. 215–50.

[30] See Karl Heinz Roth, *Die "andere" Arbeiterbewegung und die Entwicklung der kapitalistischen Repression von 1880 bis zur Gegenwart* (Munich: Trikont Verlag, 1974).

often led by the North African 'Islamics' who so repel left 'sovereigntists' throughout Europe?[31]

As to the German workers' movement, it may have been a minority, but there has always been another, internationalist tradition, which Karl Liebknecht expressed in his report to the Essen Conference in 1907:

> I have had many opportunities to observe the wretched conditions of immigrants in Germany, especially their dependence on the police. I know the difficulties they have to confront. Their legal status as "proscribed" [illegals] should impel us German Social Democrats in particular to concern ourselves energetically with the laws regarding the rights of foreigners, and to work hard to eliminate the disgrace of deportation. The congress resolution therefore calls for the complete equality of foreigners with nationals also with regard to the right to stay in the country. Away with the Damocles sword of deportation! That is the first prerequisite for foreigners to cease to be the pre-eminent reducers of wages and strike-breakers.[32]

That is the solution *à la Marx* of the contradictions described (and instrumentalized) by Wagenknecht and Streeck! Liebknecht well knew, as we do too, that bosses and rulers strengthened by the spontaneous dynamics of the market operate methodically and skillfully to set native-born and immigrant workers at each other's throats, the more easily to exploit and oppress them both. That is why he called for them to have complete, effective equality of working conditions and rights—still today a fundamental demand. And that should be addressed by fighting for the *unconditional regularization of all immigrant workers present in the European Union, with permission to remain in the EU for an unlimited time.* To Streeck—who blows up implausible single cases to paint a picture of the refugee (and transitively, the immigrant) as an individual inclined to law-breaking, almost naturally attracted to illegality—I would say that the German language provides us with the right word to characterize the situation into which so many immigrants are forced, against their will and their interests: *illegalisierten*. In other words: illegalized, driven into irregularity. *That* is the rule—not the cunning, well-off Afghan refugee.

[31] SI COBAS, *Carne da macello. Le lotte degli operai della logistica* (Rome: Red Star Press, 2017).

[32] Karl Liebknecht, *Gesammelte Reden und Schriften*, Bd. 2 (Berlin: Dietz, 1960), pp. 71–3, author's translation.

As for borders, it would be naïve to think that their removal would solve everything—that is true. But we can be sure that none of the workers' problems would be solved through the closing of borders, with all the associated rhetoric and racist practices. The real social borders pass between the exploited and the exploiters of all nationalities, the more so in a world like today's that is so united (in inequality).

Fears, prejudices, an instinctive aversion among impoverished social layers shaken by insecurity and deprivation (in cultural terms, too): these must be fought against in a perspective of joint social struggle by native-born and immigrant workers—a struggle based on common conditions, needs and prospects. Are the genuine needs of those born in and outside a country really so different? Is it not pathetic nonsense to speak of a 'lack of resources' to satisfy these needs, at the very apex of the historical development of the productive forces by capital, which is also the apex of unnecessary and harmful production that must be sharply reduced?

9.6 Marx Saw Very Far Ahead

So, we have every reason in the world to remonstrate with those who, lining up with the European Right, think they can attack immigrants 'from the left' and do so by playing on people's ignorance to manipulate Marx's writings on migration and the industrial reserve army. Hands off Marx!

Whereas they delude themselves that the social plagues of unemployment and structural insecurity can be cured, and that the mechanisms of the system at the origin of international migration can be kept at bay through 'social nationalism' and the creation of new barriers, it seems to me all too obvious that such processes can only become sharper, whatever the policies of individual states. For their causal determinants lie deep down in the *impersonal*, '*automatic*' laws of capitalism, not in the neoliberal globalization that is but a product of those laws. The proletarian reserve army will grow, in the West, mainly through the relentless slowing of the rate of accumulation (the independent variable that all our authors forget), and in the East, mainly through the furious capitalist penetration of agriculture. Alongside this, external debt, ecological disasters, and the endless chain of wars will produce huge new contingents of migrants from the South and East to the North and West of the world, but, as Italy shows, there will also be significant migratory movements within the global North and South. A further impetus in this direction, in both the West and East, will come from the capitalist obsession with higher labour productivity, the 'fourth industrial revolution' and the 'Great Reset' after the pandemic, which has already been announced by the World Economic Forum and the IMF.[33] The quest for 'completely different ways of creating value', that is, *surplus-value*, which is the sacred mission of Schwab and other architects of a horrendous 'trans-human' hypercapitalist future, points in the same direction. And the current pushing of the 'general, absolute law of capitalist accumulation' to the extreme, with an ontological inequality reminiscent of Dr. Strangelove between an elite of 'winners' and a discountable mass of 'losers', gives the measure of the depth of the crisis of capitalist civilization. Its false promises of liberty, equality, and fraternity are being pulverized before our eyes.

With just a minimum of objectivity, anyone would have to recognize that Marx saw far ahead in the matters that concern us here. Very far ahead. That means to the world we now live in. There is a way to *abolish* today's huge industrial reserve army and the ever more gruelling extra burden of work that is its reverse side, to abolish forced migrationwith its torments and struggles and its accompanying national and racist discrimination. But that possibility entirely depends on an epochal class confrontation to affirm an alternative social system, at once anticapitalist, anti-colonial and fully human, which Marx sketched for us in its broad outlines.

References

Basso, Pietro (ed.) (2015), *Razzismo di stato. Stati Uniti Europa Italia*, Milan: Angeli.

———. (2020), 'Migration', in: Marcello Musto (ed.), *The Marx Revival: Key Concepts and New Interpretations*, Cambridge: Cambridge University Press, pp. 232–46.

Crouch, Colin (2018), 'Sahra Wagenknecht: Brauchen wir eine Sammlungsbewegung?', *Die Zeit*, 17 August 2018.

Debray, Regis (2010), *Éloge des frontières*, Paris: Gallimard.

[33] Klaus Schwab and Nicolas Davis, *Shaping the Future of the Fourth Industrial Revolution: A Guide to Building a Better World* (Geneva: World Economic Forum, 2018); Klaus Schwab and Thierry Malleret, *Covid-19: The Great Reset* (Geneva: World Economic Forum, 2020); and Massimo Gaddi, *Industria 4.0. Più liberi o più sfruttati?* (Milan: Edizioni Punto Rosso, 2019).

Eurostat (2018), *Migrant Integration Statistics, 2018 Edition*, Luxembourg: Eurostat.

Fondazione Migrantes (2019), *Rapporto Italiani nel mondo 2019*, Todi: Editrice Tau.

Formenti, Carlo (2013), *Utopie letali: contro l'ideologia post–moderna*, Milan: Jaca Book.

———. (2016), *La variante populista. Lotta di classe nel neo–liberismo*, Rome: Derive Approdi.

Fusaro, Diego (2019), *Glebalizzazione. La lotta di classe al tempo del populismo*, Milan: Rizzoli, e-book.

Gaddi, Massimo (2019), *Industria 4.0. Più liberi o più sfruttati?*, Milan: Edizioni Punto Rosso.

Giacché, Vladimiro (2015), *Costituzione italiana contro Trattati europei. Un conflitto inevitabile*, Reggio Emilia: Imprimatur.

Gjergji, Iside (ed.) (2015), *La nuova emigrazione italiana. Cause, mete e figure sociali*, Venice: Edizioni Ca' Foscari.

International Labour Organization (2020), *World Employment and Social Outlook: Trends 2020*, Geneva: International Labour Office.

Kammerer, Peter (2003), 'Germania: un secolo di politica migratoria', in: Pietro Basso and Fabio Perocco (eds.), *Gli immigrati in Europa. Disuguaglianze, razzismo, lotte*, Milan: Angeli, pp. 163–88.

Lafontaine, Oskar (2006), *Politik für Alle. Streitschrift für eine Gerechte Gesellschaft*, Berlin: Ullstein.

Liebknecht, Karl (1960), *Gesammelte Reden und Schriften*, Bd. 2, Berlin: Dietz, pp. 71–3.

Luxemburg, Rosa (2013), *Introduction to Political Economy*, in: Peter Hudis (ed.), *The Complete Works of Rosa Luxemburg, Volume I: Economic Writings 1*, London: Verso, pp. 89–300.

Marshall, Tim (2018), *Divided: Why We're Living in an Age of Walls*, London: Elliott & Thompson.

Marx, Karl (1975), 'Speech on the Question of Free Trade', MECW, vol. 6, pp. 451–65.

———. (1976), *Capital, Volume I*, London: Penguin.

———. (1985), 'The General Council of the International Working Men's Association on the Lausanne Congress', MECW, vol. 20, pp. 421–3.

———. (1993), *Grundrisse: Foundations of the Critique of Political Economy*, London: Penguin.

Marx, Karl, and Engels, Friedrich (1965), *The German Ideology*, London: Lawrence & Wishart.

———. (1975), *Manifesto of the Communist Party*, MECW, vol. 6, pp. 477–517.

Mitropoulos, Angela (2019), 'Wolfgang Streeck's Neo–Romantic Sociology', *S0metim3s*, 27 March, https://s0metim3s.com/2019/03/27/streeck-sociology/.

Perocco, Fabio (ed.) (2019), *Tortura e migrazioni. Torture and Migration*, Venice: Edizioni Ca' Foscari.

Pieper, Tobias (2015), 'Germania: I campi come strumenti variabili di controllo delle Migrazioni', in: Pietro Basso (ed.), *Razzismo di stato. Stati Uniti Europa Italia*, Milan: Angeli, pp. 239–50.

Roth, Karl Heinz (1974), *Die 'andere' Arbeiterbewegung und die Entwicklung der kapitalistischen Repression von 1880 bis zur Gegenwart*, Munich: Trikont Verlag.

Ruiz Benedicto, Ainhoa, Akkerman, Mark, and Brunet, Pere (2020), *A Walled World Towards a Global Apartheid*, Barcelona: Centre Delàs d'Estudis per la Pau.

Sablowsky, Thomas, and Thien, Hans-Günter (2018), 'Die AfD, die ArbeiterInnenklasse und die Linke – kein Problem?', *PROKLA*, vol. 48, n. 1: 55–71.

Schwab, Klaus, and Davis, Nicolas (2018), *Shaping the Future of the Fourth Industrial Revolution: A Guide to Building a Better World*, Geneva: World Economic Forum.

Schwab, Klaus, and Malleret, Thierry (2020), *Covid-19: The Great Reset*, Geneva: World Economic Forum.

SI COBAS (2017), *Carne da macello. Le lotte degli operai della logistica*, Rome: Red Star Press.

Somma, Alessandro (2018), *Sovranismi. Stato, popolo e conflitto sociale*, Rome: Derive Approdi.

Streeck, Wolfgang (2016), *How Will Capitalism End? Essays on a Failing System*, London: Verso.

———. (2018), 'Between Charity and Justice: Remarks on the Social Construction of Immigration Policy in Rich Democracies', *Culture, Practice & Europeanization*, vol. 3, n. 2: 3–22.

van Dyk, Silke, and Graefe, Stefanie (2019), 'The Reality of Exclusive Solidarity: A Response to Wolfgang Streeck's "Between Charity and Justice"', *Culture, Practice & Europeanization*, vol. 4, n. 1: 149–54.

Volgelskamp, Dirk (2015a), 'La gestione dell'immigrazione in Germania: monitoraggio, controllo ed esclusione repressiva', in: Pietro Basso (ed.), *Razzismo di stato. Stati Uniti Europa Italia*, Milan: Angeli, pp. 215–25.

———. (2015b), 'La produzione sociale di razzismo e violenza contro immigrati e richiedenti asilo nella Repubblica federale tedesca', in: Pietro Basso (ed.), *Razzismo di stato. Stati Uniti Europa Italia*, Milan: Angeli, pp. 227–37.

Wagenknecht, Sahra (2017), *Couragiert gegen den Strom. Uber Goëthe, die Macht and die Zukunft*, Munich: Piper Verlag.

———. (2018), *Reichtum ohne Gier: Wie wir uns vor dem Kapitalismus retten*, Frankfurt: Campus Verlag.

CHAPTER 10

Globalization, Migrant Labour, and Capitalism: Past and Present

Ranabir Samaddar

10.1 Introduction: Migration as a Crucial Factor in the Global History of Capitalism

Migrant labour has been a feature of global capitalism since the latter's beginning. Capitalism needed labour from colonies, semi-colonies, and other parts of the world. Thus, while Atlantic slavery was supplying labour across the ocean, there was an increase in the mobility of labour in post-manumission age, when capital became global and global trade became a defining feature of global capitalism. While discussing primitive accumulation Marx wrote that labour was like an army in encampment waiting to move on to wherever ordered. He also said that much of the capital had no birth-ticket attached to it.[1]

The second half of the nineteenth century was the great age of plantations and massive construction of railway lines and telegraph poles across

[1] Karl Marx, *Capital, Volume I* (Moscow: Progress Publishers, 1978). Marx wrote, 'A great deal of capital, which appears today in the United States without any certificate of birth, was yesterday, in England, the capitalized blood of children', p. 536.

R. Samaddar (✉)
Calcutta Research Group, Kolkata, India

M. Musto (ed.), *Rethinking Alternatives with Marx*, Marx, Engels, and Marxisms, https://doi.org/10.1007/978-3-030-81764-0_10

the globe. While we know this age as the age of nationalism, this was also a distinct age of labour mobility required for these plantations, railway lines, telegraph, and mining, and thus the consequent development of the modes of managing and controlling migration. It was the age of imperial infrastructure-making, requiring labour deployment in a particular mode.[2] Yet, for long, in writings on general labour history including Marxist writings in labour history, migrant labour did not appear analytically as a key factor. However, the new crop of historical studies on various aspects of the welfare state and schemes suggest a different way of understanding migrant labour, where a study of the nation as a stable territorial-political form is not at the centre of our political understanding. In its place we have the still largely unwritten history of governing a mobile, unruly world of population flows occupying a much more critical place of significance. Studies of hunger in the nineteenth century, of itinerant movements, transportations of coolies, spread of famines, shipping of children, adult girls, trafficking in sex, labour, and human organs, and welfare legislations to cope with this great infamy, tell us how actually we have arrived at our own time. This is certainly different from the tradition of nation-centred histories, which exercised an overwhelming influence over Marxist historical writings on labour too. As this short article will try to explain, one of the main reasons of this shortcoming in Marxist writings was the failure to consider colonialism as a principal gradient of the history of modern capitalism, and by inference the history of the modern working class.[3] At the same time, analysis of the composition of the population that made the working class—a dynamic process in which migration

[2] On this see Ned Rossiter, 'Imperial Infrastructures', in: Ned Rossiter, *Software, Infrastructure, Labour: A Media Theory of Logistical Nightmares* (London: Routledge, 2017), pp. 138–83; and Michael Adas (ed.), *Essays on Twentieth Century History* (Philadelphia: Temple University Press, 2010). Adas has commented, 'If the period from the 1870s is included in a long twentieth century (and perhaps even if it is not), migration served as a mode of escape from oppression and poverty and, in many instances, as an avenue towards advancement for an unprecedented number of people that soared well into the hundreds of millions by century's end. But for a clear majority of these migrants, movement was coerced by flight from war and oppression or was enticed by labour recruiters who preyed on the desperately poor. The prospects for the great majority were almost invariably lives of drudge labour in urban sweatshops, on tropical plantations, or on the wharves of an expansive, global export economy', p. 2.

[3] This is partly surprising given Marx's unequivocal reference to colonialism as a foundational element of capitalism in his discussions on primitive accumulation. For instance, he wrote in *Capital, Volume I*, 'The colonial system ripened, like a hot-house, trade

had been an absolutely important element—was lacking. Not only had we failed to draw the full significance of Marx-Malthus debate on the question of population, we also neglected the factor of mobility in the making of the working class and working masses. One can say roughly that only with the publication of Stephen Castles' co-authored work, *Immigrant Workers and Class Structure in Western Europe* (1973), migration began to be considered as a serious factor in the making of the working class.[4] Now of course with *Border as Method: Or, the Multiplication of Labour* (2013), Marxist analytical method has come to accept transit labour as a critical component of labour formation.[5] However a review of this historiography calls for a separate occasion. Here we must come back to the question of colonialism in the global history of the formation of working class.

Indentured labour from countries such as India formed an important segment of nineteenth-century labour migration. Nearly a million workers left India to labour under indenture in plantations in various parts of the colonial world.[6] In many cases they were sought as replacements of the newly freed African slave labour and the emphasis was on direct labour

and navigation. The "societies Monopolia" of Luther were powerful levers for concentration of capital. The colonies secured a market for the budding manufactures, and, through the monopoly of the market, an increased accumulation. The treasures captured outside Europe by undisguised looting, enslavement, and murder, floated back to the mother-country and were there turned into capital', p. 535.

[4] Stephen Castles and Godula Kosack, *Immigrant Workers and Class Structure in Western Europe* (Oxford: Oxford University Press, 1973).

[5] Sandro Mezzadra and Brett Neilson, *Border as Method: Or, the Multiplication of Labour* (Durham: Duke University Press, 2013).

[6] The literature on indentured labour is substantial, see for instance the site Sundari Anitha and Ruth Pearson, 'A History of Migration', *Striking Women*, www.striking-women.org/module/migration/history-migration, accessed on 1 January 2021; Galutra Bahadur, *Coolie Woman: The Odyssey of Indenture* (Chicago: University of Chicago Press, 2014); John Wareing, *Indentured Migration and the Servant Trade from London to America, 1618–1718: 'There Is Great Want of Servants'* (Oxford: Oxford University Press, 2017); Khal Torabully and Marina Carter, *Coolitude: An Anthology of the Indian Labour Diaspora* (London: Anthem Press, 2002); and Hugh Tinker, *A New System of Slavery: The Export of Indian Labour Overseas, 1830–1920* (Oxford: Oxford University Press, 1974). Among these works on indentured labour, classic is of course by Jan Breman, *Taming the Coolie Beast: Plantation Society and the Colonial Order in Southeast Asia* (New Delhi: Oxford University Press, 1989); and also Rana P. Behel and Marcel van der Linden (eds.), *Coolies, Capital, and Colonialism: Studies in Indian Labour History* (Cambridge: Cambridge University Press, 2007).

input. The preference for imported over locally settled labour was shaped besides other important factors by gender. Gender was of central concern in recruitment operations as well as labour deployment in the indentured system. South Africa refused to allow male emigrants to bring in more than one wife and demanded proof of marriage and birth from women and children wishing to join their husbands and fathers in the colony. Gender, far from being marginal, occupied a central place in the making of migrant labour. Labour had to be identified with a family system, and labour made governments aware of the need to manage populations. The 'slavery' into which Indian labourers emigrated was a strong issue in anti-indenture thinking. Soon, women's recruitment for indentured emigration became a part of anti-colonial thought. After the expiry of the indenture of exported labour post First World War, the return of large sections of indentured labour back to native country in the early decades of the twentieth century—also owing to improved transportation and communication facilities—made circular migration of labour possible.

10.2 Variegated Forms of Migrant Labour

There were various other forms of exporting labour under coercive conditions. Take the case of transportation of children—again as an important component of the development of capitalism.[7] We know something of

[7] In the 'Preface' to the first German Edition of *Capital, Volume I*, Marx had commented, 'We should be appalled at the state of things at home, if, as in England, our governments and parliaments appointed periodically commissions of inquiry into economic conditions; if these commissions were armed with the same plenary powers to get at the truth; if it was possible to find for this purpose men as competent, as free from partisanship and respect of persons as are the English factory-inspectors, her medical reporters on public health, her commissioners of inquiry into the exploitation of women and children, into housing and food. Perseus wore a magic cap down over his eyes and ears as a make-believe that there are no monsters', p. 7; and then towards the end of the book he came back to the role of child labour in the development of capitalism with these words, 'Colonial system, public debts, heavy taxes, protection, commercial wars, &c., these children of the true manufacturing period, increase gigantically during the infancy of Modem Industry. The birth of the latter is heralded by a great slaughter of the innocents. Like the royal navy, the factories were recruited by means of the press-gang. Blasé as Sir F. M. Eden is as to the horrors of the expropriation of the agricultural population from the soil, from the last third of the fifteenth century to his own time; with all the self-satisfaction with which he rejoices in this process, "essential" for establishing capitalistic agriculture and "the due proportion between arable and pasture land"—he does not show, however, the same economic insight in respect to the necessity of child-stealing and child-slavery

the transportation of the coolie labour, but we know very little of the ways in which children were sent across seas and deserts as labour force. In a volume titled *Uprooted: The Shipment of Poor Children to Canada, 1867 to 1917* (2008) the historian of the transportation of child labour Roy Parker gives us detailed account of exportation of hundreds of boys and girls from England to Canada in the second half of the nineteenth century and the first few decades of the twentieth century—to work in Canada, to be beaten, sexually abused, slave laboured—all to build up Canada and to rid England of its poor destitute children.[8] This was also roughly the time, immediately after the American Civil War when Chinese labour was imported to the United States to build the Central Pacific Railway Line. Chinese peasants from the Canton Province began arriving on California's shores in 1850. Initially, they took five-year stints in the mines, after which they prospected or accepted jobs as labourers, domestic workers, and fishermen. They faced intense prejudice and increasingly restrictive laws limiting work opportunity. In early 1865 the Central Pacific Railway Company started recruiting Chinese labour because of acute labour shortage. The early workers were mostly Irish immigrants. Railroad work was hard, and management was chaotic, leading to a high attrition rate. The Chinese labour replaced the Irish labour.[9] Similarly during the mass importation of labour for mining in Australia, girls, boys, and single women were transported in the decades of the last half of the nineteenth century and specially in the first half of the twentieth century to the stark Edwardian homes in Australia, where (for instance in Adelaide, today the building being known as the Migration Museum) it would be written on the wall by the charity institutions and city councils, 'You who have no place else on earth enter this home—never to look back to the outside world, but to take this as home'. There is this astonishing collection of documents and writings, done by Mary Geyer, and

for the transformation of manufacturing exploitation into factory exploitation, and the establishment of the "true relation" between capital and labour power', p. 537.

[8] Roy Parker, *Uprooted: The Shipment of Poor Children to Canada, 1867–1917* (Bristol: The Policy Press, 2008). See also Robert Coles, *Uprooted Children: The Early Life of Migrant Farm Workers* (Pittsburgh: University of Pittsburgh Press, 1970).

[9] For details of the construction of the Railway Line and the nature of labour employed, see for instance: David Haward Bain, *Empire Express: Building the First Transcontinental Railroad* (New York: Penguin Books, 2000); and Stephen E. Ambrose, *Nothing Like It in the World: The Men Who Built the Transcontinental Railroad 1863–1869* (New York: Simon & Schuster, 2001).

published by the Migration Museum on the occasion of the Women's Suffrage Centenary in South Australia (1894–1994), titled, *Behind the Wall: The Women of the Destitute Asylum, Adelaide, 1852–1918*, which tell us the destitute migrants' lives behind the walls.[10]

In capitalist economies like the United Kingdom, hunger marches began in the second half of the nineteenth century and continued in the twentieth century—in fact in both new and old worlds, colonial and colonized countries—in search for food and job.[11] It is important to see the exportation of coolie labour as part of this broader history of dispossession and displacement much of which is still concealed. This broader history will also help us understand better the dialectical relation between *labour form* and the *nation form*, and if we like *nation as history* and *labour as history*. Crucial in shaping this relation was the development of the basic technologies of governing population flows towards achieving in each case the right composition of the population, *the right mix*, as it is termed now, leading to partitions and new boundary making exercises. All these, as said earlier, happened after the manumission of slavery. The post-manumission period was one of several changing modes of labour process—the slave, indentured, the contract, and the free. These modes historically never appeared as pure types, because much of the availability of labour depended on labour's mobility—making the labour mobile. Indeed the truth is that largely on the condition of making labour mobile that globalization proceeded. This would always be the underside of the official story of globalization—the subaltern or the primitive aspect. Transit labour then as now occupies a crucial place in capitalist production.

Clifford Rosenberg, the historian of *Policing Paris—The Origins of Modern Immigration Control Between the Wars* (2006) have shown how colonial authorities gave shape to their immigration policies, precisely when part of the colonial political class was voicing humanitarian concerns in order to institute some protection measures for the immigrants. Drawing extensively on the police files in Paris of that time Rosenberg presents for us a critical moment in the history of migration control and political surveillance. He shows how in the years after the First World

[10] Mary Geyer, *Behind the Wall: The Women of the Destitute Asylum, Adelaide, 1852–1918* (Adelaide: Migration Museum, 1994).

[11] James Vernon, *Hunger: A Modern History* (Cambridge: Harvard University Press, 2007).

War the French police, terrified by the Bolshevik Revolution and the spectre of immigrant criminality, became the first major force anywhere to systematically enforce distinctions of citizenship and national origins. As the French capital emerged as a haven for refugees, dissidents, and workers from throughout Europe and across the Mediterranean in the 1920s, police officers raided immigrant neighbour hoods to scare illegal aliens into registering with authorities and arrested those whose papers were not in order. Transformed by their enforcement, legal categories that had existed for hundreds of years began to matter as never before. These categories determined whether or not families could remain together and whether people could keep their jobs or were forced to flee. During World War II, identity controls marked out entire populations for physical destruction.[12] It was again then that the basic control systems were put in place, such as the introduction of the passport and the visa system, recording the foreigner, developing labour market management tools in order to use immigrant labour for a capitalist market and for control of domestic labour, and finally developing a detailed surveillance system.[13] The feature of modern democracies practising various social exclusions developed during that time. This is how the societies of the settled with their pre-ordained divisions of labour wanted to return to equilibrium.[14]

[12] Clifford Rosenberg, *Policing Paris: The Origins of Modern Immigration Control Between the Wars* (Ithaca: Cornell University Press, 2006); and also Mary Dewhurst Lewis, *The Boundaries of the Republic: Migrant Rights and the Limits of Universalism in France, 1918–1940* (Stanford, CA: Stanford University Press, 2007).

[13] John Torpey, *The Invention of Passport: Surveillance, Citizenship, and the State* (Cambridge: Cambridge University Press, 1999). For a broader history, see Martin Lloyd, *The Passport: The History of Man's Most Travelled Document* (Gloucestershire: Sutton Publishing, 2003). Significant is the study by Mahmoud Keshavarz, *The Design Politics of the Passport: Materiality, Immobility, and Dissent* (London: Bloomsbury Visual Arts, 2019). Keshavarz speaks of 'passport situations', which are 'those situations when and where a passport is important, thus rendering it as an operative as well as illuminative agent of making relationships', p. 13. Passport produces the immigrant situation, and the passport situations 'are experienced, confronted, contested, or negotiated'.

[14] Saskia Sassen, 'Europe's Migrations: The Numbers and the Passions Are Not New', *Third Text*, vol. 20 (2006), n. 6: 635–45. Sassen has written, 'Part of the difficulty for old Europe is, ironically, the lack of a historical perspective. Europe has a barely recognized history of several centuries of internal labour migrations. This is a history that hovers in the penumbra of official European History dominated by the image of Europe as a continent of emigration, never of immigration. In the 1700s, when Amsterdam built its polders and cleared its bogs, it brought in northern German workers; when the French built up their vineyards they brought in Spaniards; when Milan and Turin developed they

The history of immigrant labour as a sub-citizen population group is thus long. Along with that the fiction of a juridical figure of the worker as a citizen accessing rights also has a long lineage. The history alluded to here has relation with the question of the visibility of the immigrant worker—a question to which we shall return soon.

10.3 Labour Migration and Forced Migration

Migration history is thus the 'the shadowy cone' over the history of capitalism—that symbolizes the unreported histories of masses of errant, deported, and eradicated individuals who live in foreign lands, in countries that do not recognize their 'belonging', and join the labouring classes there in hundreds and thousands. These migratory movements have fractured the national, ethnic, and linguistic features of polities and political societies. Today, in a global postcolonial setting, labour flows from 'New Europe' to 'Old Europe' (or, from Mexico or Puerto Rico to the United States) threaten the imperial-civilisational core of the Euro-Atlantic continent. The border/confine in this way is continually under pressure, and the stress reproduces itself in continuous remaking of migrant labour management techniques. Governing strategies have to ensure that labour flows must not be directionless; they must conform to the rules the regime of division of labour lays down. The reserve army or the army of surplus labour must conform to the institutional rules of the global labour market. The logic of these institutional rules forming labour immigration quota system, skill absorption, wage remittance procedures, and supervisory procedures was formed in the period we have referred to previously in this article.

The fact remains that globalization means among others globalization of the recruitment of migrant labour. The situation obtaining today reminds us of the time we have been speaking of till now, the late nineteenth and early twentieth century: for instance the exploitation inherent in global supply chains (we can today think of the Burmese migrant

brought in workers from the Alps. In the 1800s, when Haussmann redid Paris, he brought in Germans and Belgians; when London built its infrastructure for water and sewage, it brought in the Irish; when Sweden decided to become a monarchy and needed handsome palaces, it brought in Italian stoneworkers; when Switzerland built the Gotthard Tunnel, it brought in Italians; and when Germany built its railroads and steel mills it brought in Italians and Poles', p. 644.

workers in Thailand), creation of new economic space virtually out of nothing (for instance Macao), Filipino nightclub hostesses and girls in Hong Kong or the Nepali labour there, women migrant workers in Taiwan, and the massive cities marked by migrant workers and trafficked labour (including sex workers) for instance of Georgian or Armenian care giving women in Athens is not much different in procedure to that of the earlier time. The globalization of sex work now proceeds apace with the Internet playing a critical role. A study by *The Economist* (9 August 2014) discusses the entry of sex workers of different ethnic origins in an equally differentially constituted global flesh market.[15] Sex workers from Eastern Europe to older Europe and the United States, from Africa and Central Asia to different parts of the globe following the expansion of the European Union and the global financial clash now feature prominently in sex trade.[16]

In many senses today's care industry and the logistical industry represent what the plantation and railway construction industries signified in the period referred to in this article. Thousands upon thousands of migrant workers serving worldwide from the United States to the Middle East to South East Asia to the Far East as masons, plumbers, coolies, nurses, ayahs, sex workers, workers in entertainment and construction industry, temporary work hands in container shipping, loaders and unloaders including crane drivers, cable-layers, truck, and motor cycle drivers and others employed in the gig economy and delivery services remind us again of the recruitment practices of the colonial era that marked the late nineteenth and early twentieth century. Nursing schools are booming in the developing countries to produce the necessary labour.[17] Yet in these

[15] The Economist, 'Briefing Prostitution and the Internet: More Bang for Your Buck', *The Economist*, 9 August 2014, pp. 15–8.

[16] Report by TAMPEP (European Network for HIV/STI Prevention and Health Promotion Among Migrant Sex Workers), *Sex Work in Europe: A Mapping of the Prostitution Scene in 25 European Countries* (Amsterdam: TAMPEP International Foundation, 2009).

[17] For a picture of the booming nursing industry in the postcolonial world in the last decade (before the Corona crisis), see United Nations Population Fund, *The State of the World's Midwifery, 2011: Delivering Health, Saving Lives* (New York: United Nations Population Fund, 2011); and Department for Professional Employees, *The Stem Workforce: An Occupational Overview* (Washington: DPE Research Department, 2012). On US figures, see Department for Professional Employees, *Nursing: A Profile of the Profession* (Washington: DPE Research Department, 2014). On Asian figures, see World Health

discussions we forget that these new areas of production of labour power had to be secured in this round of globalization with coercive means much like the situation in the nineteenth century when colonial population had to be sent as part of the armed forces in sea voyages to the areas where plantation industry was to come up not much later. The coincidence of securing areas for occupation and production is and was not god ordained. Accounts of colonial military expeditions throw light on an early phase of this process.[18] The echoes of such expeditions in the hinterlands of India or the Amazons or the forests of Indonesia or the deserts of the Middle East can be heard today. Then too, as now, globalization was accompanied by de-peasantisation on wide scale. Then too as now the process was preceded by massive application of force.

Migration, economy, and force were invariably the blood brothers of an earlier age, as they are now.

10.4 Refugee and Immigrant Economy in Global Capitalism: Some Theoretical Reflections

We shall close this paper with a brief discussion on the scholarly studies on the refugee and immigrant economy in global capitalism today. Most writings on refugee economy or the immigrant economy discuss in the main changes in the immigrant labour absorption policies of the Western governments. They refer to the economic activities of the refugees and other victims of forced migration, and reflect on latter's economic activities. Refugees are seen as economic actors in the market. The idea is that refugees and other victims of forced migration want to be economically viable; they are economically relevant, but are unfortunately discriminated against. These writings showcase refugees' attempts to survive meaningfully in the camps, cities, and other settlements, in ethnically homogenous or mixed settings, and the ways they prove useful to market, big business, and organized trade. While these writings recognize that most refugees and illegal immigrants are denizens of informal economies, the guiding

Organization, *South–East Asia Nursing and Midwifery Educational Institutions Network: Report of the Second Meeting, Yangon, Myanmar, 28–30 April 2009* (New Delhi: World Health Organization, 2020).

[18] See for instance the accounts of military expeditions from India to Southeast Asia by Premansu Kumar Bandopadhyay, *Sepoys in the British Overseas Expeditions, Volume 1 (1762–1826)* (Kolkata: K.P. Bagchi, 2011).

thread once more is that these economies and their actors can be of relevance to market.[19] In such thinking, the refugee or the illegal immigrant as the labouring subject is absent. Yet camps are transforming. From being places of protection, they are becoming like holding territories of mobile labour, since they hold at one place an enormous quantity of reserve labour. Camps are becoming towns, and other types of big, quasi informal quasi formal settlements.

Governments have learnt to treat the arrival of refugees and other forced migrants as opportunities, triggering growth of their economies. They realize that the situation calls for labour market integration, which would help absorb migrant labour force, given the specific skill profile of the migrants say those from Syria in Europe. Informal economies would produce greater profit. Refugees and other immigrant labour market actors, such as climate migrants, illegal immigrants, economic migrants, etc., carry the signatures of footloose labour, and the refugee economies are in turn subsumed in the dynamics of informal economy. Recall Michael J. Piore's classic study, *Birds of Passage* (1979), which argued that the conventional push and pull theory is simply wrong, and industrial development in one place always creates informal, low paid economy, and calls for the import of informal, low wage labour for jobs that otherwise would not be performed.[20] Indeed, informality and segmentation go hand in hand; between stereotyped and regularized skills and jobs, there is a range of work arrangements creating transitory forms of labour, which

[19] For instance, Alex Betts, Louise Bloom, Josiah Kaplan, and Naohiko Omata, *Refugee Economies: Forced Displacement and Development* (Oxford: Oxford University Press, 2017); Naohito Omata, 'Refugees' Engagement with Host Economies in Uganda', *Forced Migration Review*, vol. 58 (2018): 19–21. The theme of the issue is 'Economies: Rights and Access to Work'. Also see report by Martin Ledstrup and Marie Larsen, 'From Refugee to Employee: Work Integration in Rural Denmark', *Forced Migration Review*, vol. 58 (2018): 14–6; and an analytic report by Paul Collier, 'Refugee Economics', *Milken Institute Review*, 2 May 2016, www.milkenreview.org/articles/refugee-economics. For a picture of job-segments in refugee or immigrant economy, see for instance J. Edward Taylor, Mateusz J. Filipski, Mohamed Alloush, Anubhab Gupta, Ruben Irvin Rojas Valdes, and Ernesto Gonzalez-Estrada, 'Economic Impact of Refugees', *PNAS* (Proceedings of the National Academy of Sciences of the United States of America), vol. 113 (2016), n. 27: 7449–53.

[20] Michael J. Piore, *Birds of Passage: Migrant Labour and Industrial Societies* (Cambridge: Cambridge University Press, 1979). Piore argued that such low paid, informal labour from outside never comes to settle permanently in the place they migrate to, and in this connection, he analysed the migration of Afro-American labour to the north of the United States.

navigate several institutional spaces of the market. The global now houses the informal within the formal.

Yet strangely, the absorption of the refugees and the migrants in the informal labour market and the informal mode of production also produce the labouring subject's duality. For long, it was a case of political visibility of the migrant appearing as refugee, but economic closure. Now it is the case of economic opening (entry in the informal labour market), but political closure. Yet the migrant as the footloose labouring subject copes with this upside down world of politics/economics with his/her autonomy to move. As I have argued elsewhere, it was the fact of *moving*, the phenomenon of *mobility* or *motion*, which enabled the footloose labouring subject to emerge in the political sphere as a subject during the Covid-19 lockdown in India—literally crashing through the invisibility of labour in bourgeois political order.[21]

Indeed reflecting on the two times we have been constantly referring to here—the colonial era of migration and our postcolonial age of migration, the one always playing on the other clamouring for our attention—we are also revisiting the history of Marxian thought on the question of migrant labour, colonialism, and incessant wars associated with the bourgeois age. To put it bluntly, there is a strange reticence in Marxist discussions on the issue of migration and forced migration, and therefore borders and border management. We do not have scope here to go to the bottom of the discomfort of Marxist scholars (excepting some) to come to terms with the phenomenon of migrant labour occupying a crucial place in the evolution of capitalist economy, particular in the neoliberal age, and the bourgeois political order today. But we can at least note the following:

First, Marxist scholars did not give adequate attention to the question of population management of which a crucial part is the management of the migrants and refugees. Wars had caused repeated rounds of dispossession and renewed rounds of accumulation—often through primitive modes. The phenomenon of war as a factor in economy got prominent attention with Lenin and other thinkers of the early twentieth century, only to slip behind again in discussions on accumulation by most Western Marxists in the last seventy years. Yet given the history of Marx-Malthus controversy the neglect of population question as crucial part of studying

[21] Ranabir Samaddar, 'Introduction', in: Ranabir Samaddar (ed.), *Borders of an Epidemic: Covid-19 and Migrant Workers* (Kolkata: Calcutta Research Group, 2020), pp. 1–23.

a labouring society this neglect has cost Marxism dearly in responding to the class question in the neoliberal age. Recall Marx who had argued that there was no permanent law of population or a permanent theory of overpopulation or unproductive population. There could be only relative surplus and a reserve army of labour. Yet it is also true that the Malthusian ghost has to be re-engaged in the neoliberal time, when global capitalism once again is busy in reframing the population question, and thus the two Malthusian issues of 'surplus' population and the 'productive' population. Punitive measures, confinement, new spatial strategies, informalisation of labour, global commodity supply chain, logistics, and the expansion of global market in order to make the last accessible person in society a 'market-enabled actor'—these redefine the population strategy of global capitalism of our time. This of course speaks of the interface of neoliberal economy and postcolonial capitalism. Immigrant labour stands on the meeting ground of the two. It epitomizes postcolonial capitalism in the neoliberal age. Without the postcolonial gradient in the determination of the population question in this neoliberal age we cannot make sense of Marx's insights regarding the population question under capitalism. Nor can we place properly the migration question in the political agenda of the Left today.

Second, Marx's *Capital* (Volume I), as everyone knows, is about capital: capital as relation, capital as commodity, capital as the progenitor of wage labour, capital as the crystallization of labour, and capital as realization of surplus labour. But capital is also the crystallization of several borders that capital in its own present history must cross in the forms of several exchanges to remain functional as capital, always suggesting thereby the borders labour had had to cross in order to become capital. *Capital* is thus a double story—of labour and capital—in which we find the story of the transition to a capitalist mode of production and of how labour in order to be socially relevant has to become wage labour (including the continuing story of capitalism's ever newer ways of accumulation by crossing new borders and boundaries). In this long account of a series of transitions we have a hidden history of borders, migrations, and constant flux of territories and markets. To get a sense of this hidden history one can read the famous section on primitive accumulation in *Capital* first when re-reading *Capital.* As if in an allegory couched in historical description this section is telling us of an eternal account of how capital turns the society again and again into a society of working population subjected to laws of capital. Continuing through to Volume III of *Capital* Marx noted how the ever-changing but always present, boundaries of commodity production, money, circulation, and again commodity production, ordain the dynamics of the reproduction of capital, and the necessary reproduction of labour—a process enacted today on a global scale. Yet it was through this analysis that Marx brought out from the obscurity of biologism the question of population and pointed towards the need to study the way capitalism created laws of population in different epochs. From the preparatory manuscripts of the *Grundrisse*, one of his main targets of critique was Malthus' claim to have formulated a general law of population and overpopulation for mankind based on a simple relation between natural reproduction of men and women and social reproduction of means of subsistence. For Marx as we know the natural reproduction of men and women was always a social reproduction of a population predicated by the historical process of a particular social formation. The two central concepts crucial for him in this task were *production* and *surplus*. On the basis of these two concepts Marx read Malthus and built his own arguments of peasant dispossession and primitive accumulation, relative surplus population, industrial reserve army, and the wandering army of labour, whom Marx called the foot soldiers migrating from site to site. If this is the way in which the society would become a society of working population, today this is also the process of appearance and reappearance of destitution and the emergence of ecologically marginal population groups (ravaged by wars, famines, and floods). Policies of managing and stabilizing destitute population groups such as setting up the Africa Fund (1966–2001) in the previous century[22] or the UN Millennium Goals (2015–2030) this century[23] emerged in this context. Since the writings of Marx, in all the discussions on pauperised

[22] The purpose is to encourage investment in Africa, the second largest continent with several languages spoken by its 1.1 billion population strength. Commonwealth Funds has developed the Africa Fund, designed to benefit from the emerging African economies and growing consumer strength. The Fund aims to access companies involved in enterprises in financial products, healthcare initiatives, transportation, tourism, and power generation facilities. Towards this aim it studies inter-government networks and other private networks, particular marketplaces where the financial instruments of the companies are traded, legal frameworks and governance modes and procedures, and financial systems for providing information for the investors.

[23] On this see United Nations (n.d.), 'News on Millennium Development Goals', *Millennium Development Goals and Beyond 2015*, www.un.org/millenniumgoals/, accessed on 1 October 2017.

labour we have the repeated emergence of the population question at the core of which is the issue of migrant labour—labour that is transiting from one work form to another, one place to another, one work process to another. This is broadly the context in which we need to situate the issue of migration and forced migration. Not surprisingly, the two Global Compacts on the protection of refugees and migrants draw from the UN Millennium Goals.[24]

To repeat: The context is one of the relations between capitalism and population. Capitalism is once again producing a new law of population spread on a global scale, creating once more the 'human masses' that capital will exploit for its reproduction, the 'relative surplus' population on a global scale with clearly discernible but fluctuating boundaries between the *necessary* working population and the *relative* surplus population.

Third, as an initial step towards understanding the relation between migration and the making of a global surplus population ready to be drawn into various kinds of enterprises, we may reflect on the way a new type of power that emerged in the wake of what Marx termed as primitive accumulation, the condition of dispossession, the condition of bare life, to which labour is reduced, and which provides the ground for capital to begin accumulation. We cannot but appreciate the absolute relevance of Marx's formulations on conditions of life when it has been reduced to the minimum, when the labourer has been stripped of all assets save his/her own labour power so that s/he can produce capital, in order to show, let us say, the original conditions of the emergence of a distinct type of power over life. We must note, in vast areas of the postcolonial world primitive and the most advanced forms of accumulation have combined in installing and deepening the capitalist mode of production. The needs of accumulation have made management of populations an imperative of our age. Social governance emerged in this context of population management in a society that would have to reproduce labouring life as value producing power. In the postcolonial condition we have besides the factory form and other forms of assembly other forms—dispersed, informal, and unorganized—with labouring subjects moving from one site to another. We need to study as to how this dispersed labouring population is managed under postcolonial capitalism and the specific form of power that managing such

[24] On the two global compacts, Ranabir Samaddar, 'The Global Gaze of Care, Protection, and Power', *Refuge*, vol. 36 (2000), n. 1: 75–86.

a state of affairs produces. And in this, we have still to learn from Marx to make sense of this transitory state of labour, and the combination of a dispersed state of power and centralized state power, in other words, a new form of bio-power. In Sections 3-5 of Chapter 25 in *Capital* (Volume I) Marx discussed the phenomenon of relative surplus population and its different forms. He discussed the nomad population, whom he described as a class of people whose origin is agricultural, but whose occupation is in great part industrial. They are the light infantry of capital, thrown by it, according to its needs, now to this point, now to that. When they are not on the march, they camp. These sections suggest the ways in which the formulation of bio-power and bio-politics can profitably proceed, namely by identifying its foundational elements—primitive accumulation, laws of population, violence, migration, and government of market economy.

A dialectical understanding will allow us to understand the interplay of the migration and insecurity of labour with the way security has functioned as the major rationale of liberal rule and the subjection of population groups to liberal governmental order. Insecure labour (that is insecurity of labour) will be made not only secure for reproduction of capital (that is security of capital), but to borrow a phrase from Julian Reid and others, bio-politically 'resilient' amidst conditions of insecurity to face those conditions of insecurity.[25]

Fourth, as hereditary and accumulated wealth becomes crucial for the expansion of capital (in fact there is never a pure aristocrat!) in form of rent, interest, and social capital, capital's expansionary logic tries to avoid the albatross of a population hanging around its neck. Idle bourgeoisie, idle towns, idle assets, and idle countries may become a big feature of global capitalism.[26] Coupled with the re-emergence of a bourgeoisie wallowing in interest and rent produced wealth, there is a rise in penal populations everywhere sought to be confined to islands, penal

[25] Brad Evans and Julian Reid, *Resilient Life: The Art of Living Dangerously* (London: Polity Press, 2014); and also David Chandler and Julian Reid, *The Neoliberal Subject: Resilience, Adaptation, and Vulnerability* (London: Rowman and Littlefield, 2016).

[26] This is the context in which one has to read Marx's analysis in Section 3 of Chapter 24 of Marx, *Capital, Volume I*, titled, 'Separation of Surplus-Value into Capital and Revenue: The Abstinence Theory', pp. 417–20.

colonies, and at times entire countries marked as penal lands such as parts of Africa, Central America, and the Middle East. Again they remind us of a nineteenth-century history of penal colonies such as Penang, Malacca, or the Andaman Islands. These penal lands are also lands whose millions of people have been punished through war (Libya, Iraq, Syria, Guatemala, El Salvador, or Afghanistan). In fact, as already mentioned, war reappearing as the other side of wealth periodically rearranges population groups for global labour market—a fact underplayed by demographers and economists.[27] The consequent re-ordering of space in its relation to population results in distinct spaces of war, deluge, exclusion, and flight, and on the other hand the spaces of production, consumption, and wealth.

The global reserve army of labour today has among its ranks refugees, internally displaced, dispossessed peasants, convicts, child labour, workers under new forms of servitude, ecologically marginal groups, and all those who are at the receiving end of what Michel Foucault would have perhaps called 'just measure of punishment'—punishment according to the requirements of the bourgeois society. And yet, and by the same token, it is not only the punitive policy under capitalism that contributes to the growth of penal populations, it is machines and technologies also that work to an increasing extent as the 'measure of men'. Liberal society has now dissolved into a punitive society. But the characteristic of this punitive society is that the migrant population must not be seen as 'unfairly punished'. The migrant population will be publicly punished only exceptionally. From visible punishment the order shifts the punitive task from the domain of visible perception to abstract consciousness, from visible intensity to inevitability of a production order.

There is thus a fetishism of the 'regular', the 'settled', the 'just', and hides the reality of mobility, motion, and direction. Yet these realities of mobility, motion, and direction effect large-scale social, geographic, and durational nature of labour formation. Remember Marx used the word 'secret' in the title of Chapter 1 (Section 4, 'The Fetishism of Commodities and the Secret Thereof') and Chapter 26 ('The Secret of Primitive Accumulation'—perhaps only twice in the chapter titles in book, *Capital*,

[27] The question of war in this context is brought out by among others, see for instance Partha Chatterjee, 'Land and the Political Management of Primitive Accumulation', in: Anthony P. D'Costa and Achin Chakraborty (eds.), *The Land Question in India: State, Dispossession, and Capitalist Transition* (Oxford: Oxford University Press, 2017), pp. 1–15.

and thus remarkably linked fetishism with the production of the secret as part of a production process. Colonial order hid the way value was being created much as primitive accumulation appeared as a story of past. It all became a matter of history, ancient past that nobody remembers. Production of value was like as Marx recalled Robinson Crusoe's diligence in an innocent island untouched by man's industry. The condition of the 'appearance' of migrant labour as a given part of an island where today's Robinsons create wealth is the naturalization of what we call labour. Yet is the anarchy that migration introduces in the process of labour—the motion that will always disturb the order of economy. Therefore the challenge to this order is: how to flexibilise itself when migration cannot be made orderly?

In this article we have spoken of 'direction'—the direction that the element of migrant labour lends to capitalism. In this invocation of the 'direction' we are only following the footsteps of Marx's famous formulations of 'tendency'. 'Tendency' is never absolute, never completes itself. It will be always becoming, never fully realized. Migrant economies and societies indicate 'directions'—the malleable reality of the neoliberal age, which is contrary to fixed, machinic compositions of industrial capitalism. Migration brings in the reality of 'direction' or if you will, 'tendency', and thus will give you no structure or any voluntary transfer of will. We may say, only a monastic order of direction to sit out and to come in when directed to work.

Migration, economy, and force were invariably the blood brothers of an earlier age, as are now.

References

Adas, Michael (ed.) (2010), *Essays on Twentieth Century History*, Philadelphia: Temple University Press.

Ambrose, Stephen E. (2001), *Nothing Like It in the World: The Men Who Built the Transcontinental Railroad 1863–1869*, New York: Simon & Schuster.

Anitha, Sundari, and Pearson, Ruth (2013), 'A History of Migration', *Striking Women*, www.striking-women.org/module/migration/history-migration. Accessed on 1 January 2021.

Bahadur, Galutra (2014), *Coolie Woman: The Odyssey of Indenture*, Chicago: University of Chicago Press.

Bain, David Haward (2002), *Empire Express: Building the First Transcontinental Railroad*, New York: Penguin Books.

Bandopadhyay, Premansu Kumar (2011), *Sepoys in the British Overseas Expeditions, Volume 1 (1762–1826)*, Kolkata: K.P. Bagchi.

Behel, Rana P., and van der Linden, Marcel (eds.) (2007), *Coolies, Capital, and Colonialism: Studies in Indian Labour History*, Cambridge: Cambridge University Press.

Betts, Alex, Bloom, Louise, Kaplan, Josiah, and Omata, Naohiko (2017), *Refugee Economies: Forced Displacement and Development*, Oxford: Oxford University Press.

Breman, Jan (1989), *Taming the Coolie Beast: Plantation Society and the Colonial Order in Southeast Asia*, New Delhi: Oxford University Press.

Castles, Stephen, and Kosack, Godula (1973), *Immigrant Workers and Class Structure in Western Europe*, Oxford: Oxford University Press.

Chandler, David, and Reid, Julian (2016), *The Neoliberal Subject: Resilience, Adaptation, and Vulnerability*, London: Rowman and Littlefield.

Chatterjee, Partha (2017), 'Land and the Political Management of Primitive Accumulation', in: Anthony P. D'Costa and Achin Chakraborty (eds.), *The Land Question in India: State, Dispossession, and Capitalist Transition*, Oxford: Oxford University Press, pp. 1–15.

Coles, Robert (1970), *Uprooted Children: The Early Life of Migrant Farm Workers*, Pittsburgh: University of Pittsburgh Press.

Collier, Paul (2016), 'Refugee Economics', *Milken Institute Review*, 2 May, www.milkenreview.org/articles/refugee-economics.

Department for Professional Employees (2012), *The Stem Workforce: An Occupational Overview*, Washington: DPE Research Department, http://uwua.net/wp-content/uploads/2017/01/protech-The-STEM-workforce-2012.pdf.

Department for Professional Employees (2014), *Nursing: A Profile of the Profession*, Washington: DPE Research Department, https://docplayer.net/9346993-Nursing-a-profile-of-the-profession.html.

The Economist (2014), 'Briefing Prostitution and the Internet: More Bang for Your Buck', *The Economist*, 9 August. https://www.economist.com/briefing/2014/08/07/more-bang-for-your-buck.

Evans, Brad, and Reid, Julian (2014), *Resilient Life: The Art of Living Dangerously*, London: Polity Press.

Geyer, Mary (1994), *Behind the Wall: The Women of the Destitute Asylum, Adelaide, 1852–1918*, Adelaide: Migration Museum.

Keshavarz, Mahmoud (2019), *The Design Politics of the Passport: Materiality, Immobility, and Dissent*, London: Bloomsbury Visual Arts.

Ledstrup, Martin, and Larsen, Marie (2018), 'From Refugee to Employee: Work Integration in Rural Denmark', *Forced Migration Review*, vol. 58: 14–6.

Lewis, Mary Dewhurst (2007), *The Boundaries of the Republic: Migrant Rights and the Limits of Universalism in France, 1918–1940*, Stanford, CA: Stanford University Press.

Lloyd, Martin (2003), *The Passport: The History of Man's Most Travelled Document*, Gloucestershire: Sutton Publishing.

Marx, Karl (1978), *Capital, Volume I*, Moscow: Progress Publishers.

Mezzadra, Sandro, and Neilson, Brett (2013), *Border as Method: Or, the Multiplication of Labour*, Durham: Duke University Press.

Omata, Naohito (2018), 'Refugees' Engagement with Host Economies in Uganda', *Forced Migration Review*, vol. 58: 19–21.

Parker, Roy (2008), *Uprooted: The Shipment of Poor Children to Canada, 1867–1917*, Bristol: The Policy Press, 2008.

Piore, Michael J. (1979), *Birds of Passage: Migrant Labour and Industrial Societies*, Cambridge: Cambridge University Press.

Rosenberg, Clifford (2006), *Policing Paris: The Origins of Modern Immigration Control Between the Wars*, Ithaca: Cornell University Press.

Rossiter, Ned (2017), 'Imperial Infrastructures', in: Ned Rossiter, *Software, Infrastructure, Labour: A Media Theory of Logistical Nightmares*, London: Routledge, pp. 138–83.

Samaddar, Ranabir (2020), 'The Global Gaze of Care, Protection, and Power', *Refuge*, vol. 36, n. 1: 75–86.

———. (2020), 'Introduction', in: Ranabir Samaddar (ed.), *Borders of an Epidemic: Covid-19 and Migrant Workers*, Kolkata: Calcutta Research Group, pp. 1–23.

Sassen, Saskia (2006), 'Europe's Migrations: The Numbers and the Passions Are Not New', *Third Text*, vol. 20, n. 6: 635–45.

TAMPEP (2009), *Sex Work in Europe: A Mapping of the Prostitution Scene in 25 European Countries*, Amsterdam: TAMPEP International Foundation.

Taylor, J. Edward, Filipski, Mateusz J., Alloush, Mohamed, Gupta, Anubhab, Valdes, Ruben Irvin Rojas, and Gonzalez-Estrada, Ernesto (2016), 'Economic Impact of Refugees', *PNAS*, vol. 113, n. 27: 7449–53.

Torabully, Khal, and Carter, Marina (2002), *Coolitude: An Anthology of the Indian Labour Diaspora*, London: Anthem Press.

Torpey, John (1999), *The Invention of Passport: Surveillance, Citizenship, and the State*, Cambridge: Cambridge University Press.

Tinker, Hugh (1974), *A New System of Slavery: The Export of Indian Labour Overseas, 1830–1920*, Oxford: Oxford University Press.

United Nations (n.d.), 'News on Millennium Development Goals', Millennium Development Goals and Beyond 2015, www.un.org/millenniumgoals/. Accessed on 1 October 2017.

United Nations Population Fund (2011), *The State of the World's Midwifery, 2011: Delivering Health, Saving Lives*, New York: United Nations Population Fund.

Vernon, James (2007), *Hunger: A Modern History*, Cambridge: Harvard University Press.

Wareing, John (2017), *Indentured Migration and the Servant Trade from London to America, 1618–1718: 'There Is Great Want of Servants'*, Oxford: Oxford University Press.

World Health Organization (2020), *South-East Asia Nursing and Midwifery Educational Institutions Network: Report of the Second Meeting, Yangon, Myanmar, 28–30 April 2009*, New Delhi: World Health Organization.

PART IV

Communism as a Free Association

CHAPTER 11

The Experience of the Paris Commune and Marx's Reflections on Communism

Marcello Musto

11.1 The Transformation of Political Power

The bourgeois of France had always come away with everything.[1] Since the revolution of 1789, they had been the only ones to grow rich in periods of prosperity, while the working class had regularly borne the brunt of crises. But the proclamation of the Third Republic would open new horizons and offer an opportunity for a change of course. Napoleon III, having been defeated in battle at Sedan, was taken prisoner by the Prussians on 4 September 1870. In the following January, after a four-month siege of Paris, Otto von Bismarck obtained a French surrender and was able to impose harsh terms in the ensuing armistice. National elections were held and Adolphe Thiers installed at the head of the executive power, with the support of a large Legitimist and Orleanist majority. In the capital, however, where the popular discontent was greater than elsewhere, radical republican and socialist forces swept the board. The

[1] This work was supported by the Social Science and Humanities Research Council of Canada (SSHRC), Insight Development Grant (Project n. 430-2020-00985).

M. Musto (✉)
York University, Toronto, ON, Canada

M. Musto (ed.), *Rethinking Alternatives with Marx*, Marx, Engels, and Marxisms, https://doi.org/10.1007/978-3-030-81764-0_11

prospect of a right wing government that would leave social injustices intact, heaping the burden of the war on the least well-off and seeking to disarm the city, triggered a new revolution on 18 March. Thiers and his army had little choice but to decamp to Versailles.[2]

To secure democratic legitimacy, the insurgents decided to hold free elections at once. On 26 March, an overwhelming majority of Parisians (190,000 votes against 40,000) approved the motivation for the revolt, and 70 of the 85 elected representatives declared their support for the revolution. The 15 moderate representatives of the *parti des maires*, a group comprising the former heads of certain *arrondissements*, immediately resigned and did not participate in the council of the Commune; they were joined shortly afterwards by four Radicals. The remaining 66 members—not always easy to distinguish because of dual political affiliations—represented a wide range of positions. Among them were twenty or so neo-Jacobin republicans (including the renowned Charles Delescluze and Félix Pyat), a dozen followers of Auguste Blanqui, 17 members of the International Working Men's Association (both mutualist partisans of Pierre-Joseph Proudhon and collectivists linked to Karl Marx, often at odds with each other), and a couple of independents.[3] Most leaders of the Commune were workers or recognized representatives of the working class, 14 originating in the National Guard. In fact, it was the central committee of the latter that invested power in the hands of the Commune—the prelude, as it turned out, to a long series of disagreements and conflicts between the two bodies.

On 28 March a large number of citizens gathered in the vicinity of the Hôtel de Ville for festivities celebrating the new assembly, which now officially took the name of the Paris Commune. Although it would survive for no more than 72 days, it was the most important political event in the history of the nineteenth-century workers' movement, rekindling

[2] On the main events leading up to the revolution, see Maurice Choury, *Les origenes de la Commune* (Paris: Éditions sociales, 1960); Alain Dalotel, Alain Faure, and Jean-Claude Freiermuth, *Aux origines de la Commune. Le movement des reunions publiques à Paris, 1868–1870* (Paris: Maspero, 1980); and Pierre Milza, *L'année terrible. I: La guerre franco–prussienne (septembre 1870–mars 1871)* (Paris: Perrin, 2009).

[3] See Jacques Rougerie, *Paris libre 1871* (Paris: Seuil, 1971), p. 146; Pierre Milza, *L'année terrible. II: La Commune* (Paris: Perrin, 2009), pp. 236–44; and also the more recent Claude Latta, 'Minorité et majorité au sein de la Commune (avril-mai 1871)', in: Michel Cordillot (ed.), *La Commune de Paris 1871. Les acteurs, l'événement, les lieux* (Ivry-sur-Seine: Les Éditions de l'Atelier/Éditions Ouvrières, 2021).

hope among a population exhausted by months of hardship. Committees and groups sprang up in the popular quarters to lend support to the Commune, and every corner of the metropolis hosted initiatives to express solidarity and to plan the construction of a new world. One of the most widespread sentiments was a desire to share with others. Militants like Louise Michel exemplified the spirit of self-abnegation—Victor Hugo wrote of her that she 'did what the great mad souls do […] glorified those who are crushed and downtrodden'.[4] But it was not the impetus of a leader or a handful of charismatic figures that gave life to the Commune; its hallmark was its clearly collective dimension. Women and men came together voluntarily to pursue a common project of liberation. Self-government was not seen as a utopia. Self-emancipation was thought of as an essential task.

Two of the first emergency decrees to stem the rampant poverty were a freeze on rent payments and on the selling of items valued below 20 francs in pawn shops. Nine collegial commissions were also supposed to replace the ministries for war, finance, general security, education, subsistence, labour and trade, foreign relations and public service.[5] A little later, a delegate was appointed to head each of these departments.

On 19 April, three days after further elections to fill 31 seats that became almost immediately vacant, the Commune adopted a *Declaration to the French People* that contained an 'absolute guarantee of individual liberty, of liberty of conscience, and liberty of labour' as well as 'the permanent intervention of citizens in communal affairs'. The conflict between Paris and Versailles, it affirmed, 'cannot be ended by illusory compromises'; the people had a right and 'duty to struggle and to conquer!'.[6] Even more significant than this text—a somewhat ambiguous synthesis to avoid tensions among the various political tendencies—were the concrete actions through which the Communards fought for a total transformation of political power. A set of reforms addressed not only the modalities but the very nature of political administration. The Commune provided for the recall of elected representatives and for control over their

[4] Victor Hugo, 'Viro Major', in: Nic Maclellan (ed.), *Louise Michel* (New York: Ocean Press, 2004), p. 24.

[5] Jacques Rougerie, *La Commune de 1871* (Paris: Presses Universitaires de France, 1988), pp. 62–3.

[6] The Commune of Paris, 'Declaration to the French People', in: Robert Tombs, *The Paris Commune 1871* (London: Longman, 1999), pp. 218–9.

actions by means of binding mandates (though this was by no means enough to settle the complex issue of political representation). Magistracies and other public offices, also subject to permanent control and possible recall, were not to be arbitrarily assigned, as in the past, but to be decided following an open contest or elections. The clear aim was to prevent the public sphere from becoming the domain of professional politicians. Policy decisions were not left up to small groups of functionaries and technicians, but had to be taken by the people. Armies and police forces would no longer be institutions set apart from the body of society. The separation between state and church was also a *sine qua non*.

But the vision of political change was not confined to such measures: it went more deeply to the roots. The transfer of power into the hands of the people was needed to drastically reduce bureaucracy. The social sphere should take precedence over the political—as Henri de Saint-Simon had already maintained—so that politics would no longer be a specialized function but become progressively integrated into the activity of civil society. The social body would thus take back functions that had been transferred to the state. To overthrow the existing system of class rule was not sufficient; there had to be an end to class rule as such. All this would have fulfilled the Commune's vision of the republic as a union of free, truly democratic associations promoting the emancipation of all its components. It would have added up to self-government of the producers.

11.2 The Commune as Synonym of Revolution and Social Reforms

The Commune held that social reforms were even more crucial than political change. They were the reason for its existence, the barometer of its loyalty to its founding principles, and the key element differentiating it from the previous revolutions in 1789 and 1848. The Commune passed more than one measure with clear class connotations. Deadlines for debt repayments were postponed by three years, without additional interest charges. Evictions for non-payment of rent were suspended, and a decree allowed vacant accommodation to be requisitioned for people without a roof over their heads. There were plans to shorten the working day (from the initial 10 hours to the eight hours envisaged for the future), the widespread practice of imposing specious fines on workers simply as a wage-cutting measure was outlawed on pain of sanctions, and minimum wages were set at a respectable level. As much as possible was done to increase food supplies and to lower prices. Night-work at bakeries was banned, and a number of municipal meat stores were opened. Social assistance of various kinds was extended to weaker sections of the population—for example, food banks for abandoned women and children—and discussions were held on how to end the discrimination between legitimate and illegitimate children.[7]

All the Communards sincerely believed that education was an essential factor for individual emancipation and any serious social and political change. School attendance was to become free and compulsory for girls and boys alike, with religiously inspired instruction giving way to secular teaching along rational, scientific lines. Specially appointed commissions and the pages of the press featured many compelling arguments for investment in female education. To become a genuine 'public service', education had to offer equal opportunities to 'children of both sexes'. Moreover, 'distinctions on grounds of race, nationality, religion or social position' should be prohibited.[8] Early practical initiatives accompanied such advances in theory, and in more than one *arrondissement* thousands of working-class children entered school buildings for the first time and received classroom material free of charge.

The Commune also adopted measures of a socialist character. It decreed that workshops abandoned by employers who had fled the city, with guarantees of compensation on their return, should be handed over to cooperative associations of workers. Theatres and museums—open for all without charge—were collectivized and placed under the management of the Federation of Parisian Artists, which was presided over by the painter and tireless militant Gustave Courbet. Some three hundred sculptors, architects, lithographers and painters (among them Édouard Manet) participated in this body—an example taken up in the founding of an Artists' Federation bringing together actors and people from the operatic world.[9]

[7] See Rougerie, *Paris libre 1871*, p. 100.

[8] Cited in Hugues Lenoir, 'La Commune de Paris et l'éducation', in: Cordillot (ed.), *La Commune de Paris 1871*, pp. 495–8.

[9] See Gonzalo J. Sanchez, *Organizing Independence: The Artists Federation of the Paris Commune and Its Legacy, 1871–1889* (Lincoln: University of Nebraska Press, 1997);

All these actions and provisions were introduced in the amazing space of just 54 days, in a Paris still reeling from the effects of the Franco-Prussian War. The Commune was able to do its work only between 29 March and 21 May, in the midst of heroic resistance to attacks by the Versailles that also required a great expenditure of human energy and financial resources. Since the Commune had no means of coercion at its disposal, many of its decrees were not applied uniformly in the vast area of the city. Yet they displayed a remarkable drive to reshape society and pointed the way to possible change.

The Commune was much more than the actions approved by its legislative assembly. It even aspired to redraw urban space, as demonstrated by the decision to demolish the Vendôme Column, considered a monument to barbarism and a reprehensible symbol of war, and to secularize certain places of worship by handing them over for use by the community. If the Commune managed to keep going, it was thanks to an extraordinary level of mass participation and a solid spirit of mutual assistance. In this spurning of authority, the revolutionary clubs that sprang up in nearly every *arrondissement* played a noteworthy role. There were at least 28 of them, representing one of the most eloquent examples of spontaneous mobilization.[10] Open every evening, they offered citizens the opportunity to meet after work to discuss freely the social and political situation, to check what their representatives had achieved, and to suggest alternative ways of solving day-to-day problems. They were horizontal associations, which favoured the formation and expression of popular sovereignty as well as the creation of genuine spaces of sisterhood and fraternity, where everyone could breathe the intoxicating air of control over their own destiny.

This emancipatory trajectory had no place for national discrimination. Citizenship of the Commune extended to all who strove for its development, and foreigners enjoyed the same social rights as French people. The principle of equality was evident in the prominent role played by the 3000 foreigners active in the Commune. Leo Frankel, a Hungarian member of

and Hollis Clayson, *Paris in Despair: Art and Everyday Life under Siege (1870–1871)* (Chicago: University of Chicago Press, 2002).

[10] For a list of the 28 clubs that existed at the time of the Paris Commune see Martin Philip Johnson, *The Paradise of Association: Political Culture and Popular Organizations in the Paris Commune of 1871* (Ann Arbor: University of Michigan Press, 1996), pp. 166–70.

the International Working Men's Association, was not only elected to the Council of the Commune but served as its 'minister' of labour—one of its key positions. Similarly, the Poles Jaroslaw Dombrowski and Walery Wroblewski were distinguished generals at the head of the National Guard.

Women, though still without the right to vote or to sit on the council of the Commune, played an essential role in the critique of the social order. In many cases, they transgressed the norms of bourgeois society and asserted a new identity in opposition to the values of the patriarchal family, moving beyond domestic privacy to engage with the public sphere. The Women's Union for the Defence of Paris and Care for the Wounded, whose origin owed a great deal to the tireless activity of the First International member Elisabeth Dmitrieff, was centrally involved in identifying strategic social battles. Women achieved the closure of licenced brothels, won parity for female and male teachers, coined the slogan 'equal pay for equal work', demanded equal rights within marriage and the recognition of free unions, and promoted exclusively female chambers in labour unions. When the military situation worsened in mid-May, with the Versailles at the gates of Paris, women took up arms and formed a battalion of their own. Many would breathe their last on the barricades. Bourgeois propaganda subjected them to the most vicious attacks, dubbing them *les pétroleuses* and accusing them of having set the city ablaze during the street battles.[11]

The genuine democracy that the Communards sought to establish was an ambitious and difficult project. Popular sovereignty required the participation of the greatest possible number of citizens. From late March on, Paris witnessed the mushrooming of central commissions, local subcommittees, revolutionary clubs and soldiers' battalions, which flanked the already complex duopoly of the Council of the Commune and the central committee of the National Guard. The latter had retained military control, often acting as a veritable counter-power to the Council. Although direct involvement of the population was a vital guarantee of democracy, the multiple authorities in play made the decision-making

[11] See Edith Thomas, *Les «Pétroleuses»* (Paris: Gallimard, 1963); and Alain Dalotel, 'La barricade des femmes, 1871', in: Alain Corbin and Jean-Marie Mayeur (eds.), *La barricade* (Paris: Éditions la Sorbonne, 1997), pp. 341–55.

process particularly difficult and meant that the implementation of decrees was a tortuous affair.[12]

The problem of the relationship between central authority and local bodies led to quite a few chaotic, at times paralyzing, situations. The delicate balance broke down altogether when, faced with the war emergency, indiscipline within the National Guard and the growing inefficacy of government, Jules Miot proposed the creation of a five-person Committee of Public Safety, along the lines of Maximilien Robespierre's dictatorial model in 1793. The measure was approved on the first of May, by a majority of 45 to 23. It proved to be a dramatic error, which marked the beginning of the end for a novel political experiment and split the Commune into two opposing blocs. The first of these, made up of neo-Jacobins and Blanquists, leaned towards the concentration of power and, in the end, to the primacy of the political over the social dimension. The second, including a majority of members of the International Working Men's Association, regarded the social sphere as more significant than the political. They thought that a separation of powers was necessary and insisted that the republic must never call political freedoms into question. Coordinated by Eugène Varlin, this latter bloc sharply rejected the authoritarian drift and did not take part in the elections to the Committee of Public Safety. In its view, the centralization of powers in the hands of a few individuals would flatly contradict the founding postulates of the Commune, since its elected representatives did not possess sovereignty—that belonged to the people—and had no right to cede it to a particular body. On 21 May, when the minority again took part in a session of the Council of the Commune, a new attempt was made to weave unity in its ranks. But it was already too late.

The Paris Commune was brutally crushed by the armies of Versailles. During the *Semaine sanglante*, the week of blood-letting between 21 and 28 May, a total of 17,000–25,000 citizens were slaughtered. The last hostilities took place along the walls of Père Lachaise cemetery. It was one of the bloodiest massacre in the history of France. Only 6000 managed to escape into exile in England, Belgium and Switzerland. The number of prisoners taken was 43,522. One hundred of these received death

[12] References on this topic include the classic study of Georges Bourgin, 'La Commune de Paris et le Comité central (1871)', *Revue historique*, vol. 1925, n. 150: 1–66; and the recent Pierre-Henri Zaidman, 'Le Comité central contre la Commune?', in: Cordillot, *La Commune de Paris 1871*, pp. 229–36.

sentences, following summary trials before courts martial, and another 13,500 were sent to prison or forced labour, or deported to remote areas such as New Caledonia.[13]

The spectre of the Commune intensified the anti-socialist repression all over Europe. Passing over the unprecedented violence of the Thiers state, the conservative and liberal press accused the Communards of the worst crimes and expressed great relief at the restoration of the 'natural order' and bourgeois legality, as well as satisfaction with the triumph of 'civilization' over anarchy. Those who had dared to violate the authority and attack the privileges of the ruling class were punished in exemplary fashion. Women were once again treated as inferior beings, and workers, with dirty, calloused hands who had brazenly presumed to govern, were driven back into positions for which they were deemed more suitable.

And yet, the insurrection in Paris gave strength to workers' struggles and pushed them in more radical directions.[14] The Commune had shown that the aim had to be one of building a society radically different from capitalism and embodied the idea of social-political change and its practical application. It became synonymous with the very concept of revolution, with an ontological experience of the working class.[15]

11.3 The International After the Paris Commune

Although Mikhail Bakunin had urged the workers to turn patriotic war into a revolutionary war,[16] the General Council of the International Working Men's Association in London initially opted for silence.[17] It charged Karl Marx with the task of writing a text in the name of the

[13] Some who went there solidarized with and shared the fate of the Algerian leaders of the anti-colonial Mokrani revolt, which had broken out at the same time as the Commune and also been drowned in blood by French troops.

[14] On the morrow of its defeat, Eugène Pottier wrote what was destined to become the most celebrated anthem of the workers' movement: 'Let us group together and tomorrow / The Internationale / Will be the human race!'.

[15] Cf. Henri Lefebvre, *La proclamation de la Commune, 26 mars 1871* (Paris: La fabrique éditions, 2018), p. 355.

[16] See Arthur Lehning, 'Introduction', in: Idem. (ed.), *Bakunin – Archiv*, vol. VI: *Michel Bakounine sur la Guerre Franco–Allemande et la Révolution Sociale en France (1870–1871)* (Leiden: Brill, 1977), p. xvi.

[17] See Marcello Musto, 'Introduction', in: Marcello Musto (ed.), *Workers Unite! The International 150 Years Later* (New York: Bloomsbury, 2014), pp. 30–6.

International, but he delayed its publication for complicated, deeply held reasons. Well aware of the real relationship of forces on the ground as well as the weaknesses of the Commune, he knew that it was doomed to defeat. He had even tried to warn the French working class back in September 1870, in his *Second Address on the Franco–Prussian War*:

> Any attempt at upsetting the new government in the present crisis, when the enemy is almost knocking at the doors of Paris, would be a desperate folly. The French workmen [...] must not allow themselves to be swayed by the national *souvenirs* of 1792 [...]. They have not to recapitulate the past, but to build up the future. Let them calmly and resolutely improve the opportunities of republican liberty, for the work of their own class organization. It will gift them with fresh herculean powers for the regeneration of France, and our common task – the emancipation of labour. Upon their energies and wisdom hinges the fate of the republic.[18]

A fervid declaration hailing the victory of the Commune would have risked creating false expectations among workers throughout Europe, eventually becoming a source of demoralization and distrust. Marx therefore decided to postpone delivery and stayed away from meetings of the General Council for several weeks. His grim forebodings soon proved all too well founded, and on 28 May, little more than two months after its proclamation, the Paris Commune was drowned in blood. Two days later, he reappeared at the General Council with a manuscript entitled *The Civil War in France*. It was read and unanimously approved, then published over the names of all the Council members. The document had a huge impact over the next few weeks, greater than any other document of the workers' movement in the nineteenth century. Three English editions in quick succession won acclaim among the workers and caused uproar in bourgeois circles. It was also translated fully or partly into a dozen other languages, appearing in newspapers, magazines and booklets in various European countries and the United States.

Despite Marx's passionate defence, and despite the claims both of reactionary opponents and of dogmatic Marxists eager to glorify the

[18] Karl Marx, *Second Address of the General Council of the International Working Men's Association on the Franco–Prussian War*, MECW, vol. 22, p. 269.

International,[19] it is out of the question that the General Council actually pushed for the Parisian insurrection. Marx himself pointed out that 'the majority of the Commune was in no sense socialist, nor could it have been'.[20]

After the defeat of the Paris Commune, the International was at the eye of the storm, held to blame for every act against the established order. 'When the great conflagration took place at Chicago', Marx mused with bitter irony, 'the telegraph round the world announced it as the infernal deed of the International; and it is really wonderful that to its demoniacal agency has not been attributed the hurricane ravaging the West Indies'.[21]

Marx had to spend whole days answering press slanders about the International and himself: 'at this moment', he wrote, [he was] 'the best calumniated and the most menaced man of London'.[22] Meanwhile, governments all over Europe sharpened their instruments of repression, fearing that other uprisings might follow the one in Paris. Thiers immediately outlawed the International and asked the British prime minister, William Ewart Gladstone, to follow his example; it was the first diplomatic exchange relating to a workers' organization. Pope Pius IX exerted similar pressure on the Swiss government, arguing that it would a serious mistake to continue tolerating 'that International sect which would like to treat the whole of Europe as it treated Paris. Those gentlemen [...] are to be feared, because they work on behalf of the eternal enemies of God and mankind'.[23] Giuseppe Mazzini—who for a time had looked to

[19] See Georges Haupt, *Aspect of International Socialism 1871–1914* (Cambridge: Cambridge University Press, 1986), who warned against 'the reshaping of the reality of the Commune in order to make it conform to an image transfigured by ideology', p. 25.

[20] Karl Marx to Domela Nieuwenhuis, 22 February 1881, MECW, vol. 46, p. 66.

[21] Karl Marx, *Report of the General Council to the Fifth Annual Congress of the International*, in: Institute of Marxism-Leninism of the C.C., C.P.S.U. (ed.), *The General Council of the First International 1871–1872: Minutes* (Moscow: Progress, 1986), p. 461.

[22] Karl Marx to Ludwig Kugelmann, 18 June 1871, MECW, vol. 44, p. 157.

[23] Institute of Marxism-Leninism (ed.), *The General Council of the First International 1871–1872*, p. 460.

the International with hope—had similar views and considered that principles of the International had become those of 'denial of God, [...] the fatherland, [...] and all individual property'.[24]

Criticism of the Paris Commune even spread to sections of the workers' movement. Following the publication of *The Civil War in France*, both the trade union leader George Odger and the old Chartist Benjamin Lucraft resigned from the International, bending under the pressure of the hostile press campaign. However, no trade union withdrew its support for the organization—which suggests once again that the failure of the International to grow in Britain was due mainly to political apathy in the working class.[25]

Despite the bloody denouement in Paris and the wave of calumny and government repression elsewhere in Europe, the International grew stronger and more widely known in the wake of the Commune. For the capitalists and the middle classes it represented a threat to the established order, but for the workers it fuelled hopes in a world without exploitation and injustice.[26] Insurrectionary Paris fortified the workers' movement, impelling it to adopt more radical positions and to intensify its militancy. The experience showed that revolution was possible, that the goal could and should be to build a society utterly different from the capitalist order, but also that, in order to achieve this, the workers would have to create durable and well-organized forms of political association.[27]

This enormous vitality was apparent everywhere. Newspapers linked to the International—such as *L'Égalité* in Geneva, *Der Volksstaat* in Leipzig, *La Emancipación* in Madrid, *Il Gazzettino Rosa* in Milan, *Socialisten* in Copenhagen, and *La Réforme Sociale* in Rouen—increased in both number and overall sales. Finally, and most significantly, the International continued to expand in Belgium and Spain—where the level of workers' involvement had already been considerable before the Paris Commune—, opened new sections in Portugal and Denmark, and experienced a real breakthrough in Italy. Many Mazzinians, disappointed with

[24] Giuseppe Mazzini, *L'Internazionale*, in: Gian Mario Bravo (ed.), *La Prima Internazionale: Storia documentaria*, vol. II (Roma: Editori Riuniti, 1978), pp. 499–501.

[25] Henry Collins and Chimen Abramsky, *Karl Marx and the British Labour Movement* (London: MacMillan, 1965), p. 222.

[26] See Georges Haupt, *L'Internazionale socialista dalla Comune a Lenin* (Torino: Einaudi, 1978), p. 28.

[27] Ibid., pp. 93–5.

the positions taken by their erstwhile leader, joined forces with the organization and Giuseppe Garibaldi, although he had only a vague idea of the International,[28] declared: 'The International is the sun of the future!'.[29]

11.4 *The Civil War in France* and Marx's Reflections on Communism

In a letter to Wilhelm Liebknecht, Marx complained of 'too great honesty' of the Parisian revolutionaries. In trying to avoid 'the appearance of having usurped power', they had 'lost precious moments' by organizing the election of the Commune. Their 'folly' had been 'not wanting to start a civil war – as if Thiers had not already started it by his attempt at forcibly disarming Paris'.[30] He made similar points to his friend Ludwig Kugelmann a week later: 'The right moment was missed because of conscientious scruples [...] Second mistake: The Central Committee surrendered power too soon, to make way for the Commune. Again from a too honourable scrupulousness'.

At any event, alongside critical observations on the course of events in France, Marx never failed to highlight the exceptional combative spirit and political ability of the Communards. He continued:

> What resilience, what historical initiative, what a capacity for sacrifice in these Parisians! After six months of hunger and ruin, caused rather by internal treachery than by the external enemy, they rise, beneath Prussian bayonets, as if there had never been a war between France and Germany and the enemy were not still at the gates of Paris! History has no like example of a like greatness.

Marx understood that whatever the outcome of the revolution, the Commune had opened a new chapter in the history of the workers' movement:

[28] See Nello Rosselli, *Mazzini e Bakunin* (Torino: Einaudi, 1927), pp. 323–4.

[29] Giuseppe Garibaldi to Giorgio Pallavicino, 14 November 1871, in: Enrico Emilio Ximenes, *Epistolario di Giuseppe Garibaldi*, vol. I (Milano: Brigola 1885), p. 350.

[30] Karl Marx to Wilhelm Liebknecht, 6 April 1871, MECW, vol. 44, p. 193.

> The present rising in Paris – even if it be crushed by the wolves, swine and vile curs of the old society – is the most glorious deed of our Party since the June Insurrection in Paris.[31] Compare these Parisians, storming the heavens, with the slaves to heaven of the German-Prussian Holy Roman Empire, with its posthumous masquerades reeking of the barracks, the Church, the cabbage Junkers and above all, of the philistines.[32]

Marx continued these reflections a few days later in another letter to Kugelmann. Whereas his close friend had wrongly compared the fighting in Paris to 'petty-bourgeois demonstrations' like those of 13 June 1849 in Paris, Marx again exalted the courage of the Communards: 'World history', he wrote, 'would indeed be very easy to make if the struggle were taken up only on condition of infallibly favourable chances'. His thinking here shows just how remote he was from the kind of fatalist determinism that his critics attributed to him:

> [History] would, on the other hand, be of a very mystical nature if 'accidents' played no part. These accidents themselves fall naturally into the general course of development and are compensated again by other accidents. But acceleration and delay are very dependent upon such 'accidents', which include the 'accident' of the character of those who first stand at the head of the movement.[33]

The circumstance that worked against the Commune was the presence of the Prussians on French soil, allied with the 'bourgeois riff-raff of Versailles'. Bolstered by their understanding with the Germans,[34] the Versailles 'presented the Parisians with the alternative of taking up the

[31] Marx is referring to the workers' uprising of June 1848, which was drowned in blood by a conservative republican government.

[32] Karl Marx to Ludwig Kugelmann, 12 April 1871, MECW, vol. 44, pp. 131–2.

[33] Karl Marx to Ludwig Kugelmann, 17 April 1871, MECW, vol. 44, pp. 136–7.

[34] See Karl Marx to Léo Frankel and Louis-Eugène Varlin (draft), 13 May 1871, MECW, vol. 44, p. 149: 'The Prussians won't hand over the forts to the Versailles people, but after the definitive conclusion of peace (26 May), they will allow the government to invest Paris with its gendarmes. [...] Thiers & Co. had [...] asked Bismarck to delay payment of the first instalment until the occupation of Paris. Bismarck accepted this condition. Prussia, being herself in urgent need of that money, will therefore provide the Versailles people with every possible facility to hasten the occupation of Paris. So be on your guard!'.

fight or succumbing without a struggle'. In the latter case, 'the demoralization of the working class would have been a far greater misfortune than the fall of any number of "leaders"'. Marx concluded: 'The struggle of the working class against the capitalist class and its state has entered upon a new phase with the struggle in Paris. Whatever the immediate results may be, a new point of departure of world-historic importance has been gained'.[35]

A fervid declaration hailing the victory of the Paris Commune would have risked creating false expectations among workers throughout Europe, eventually becoming a source of demoralization and distrust. Marx therefore decided to postpone delivery and stayed away from meetings of the General Council for several weeks. His grim forebodings soon proved all too well founded, and on 28 May, little more than two months after its proclamation, the Paris Commune was drowned in blood. Two days later, he reappeared at the General Council with a manuscript entitled *The Civil War in France*. It was read and unanimously approved, then published over the names of all the Council members.[36]

The document had a huge impact over the next few weeks, greater than any other document of the workers' movement in the nineteenth century.[37] Speaking of the Paris Commune, Marx wrote:

> The few but important functions which would still remain for a central government were not to be suppressed, as has been intentionally misstated, but were to be discharged by Communal and thereafter responsible agents. The unity of the nation was not to be broken, but, on the contrary, to be organized by Communal Constitution, and to become a reality by the destruction of the state power which claimed to be the embodiment of that unity independent of, and superior to, the nation itself, from which it was but a parasitic excresence. While the merely repressive organs of the old governmental power were to be amputated, its legitimate functions

[35] Karl Marx to Ludwig Kugelmann, 17 April 1871, MECW, vol. 44, p. 137.

[36] See Marcello Musto, *Another Marx: Early Manuscripts to the International* (London: Bloomsbury, 2018), pp. 199–220.

[37] Three English editions of *The Civil War in France* in quick succession won acclaim among the workers and caused uproar in bourgeois circles. It was also translated fully or partly into a dozen other languages, appearing in newspapers, magazines and booklets in various European countries and the United States.

> were to be wrested from an authority usurping pre-eminence over society itself, and restored to the responsible agents of society.[38]

The Paris Commune had been an altogether novel political experiment:

> It was essentially a working-class government, the product of the struggle of the producing against the appropriating class, the political form at last discovered under which to work out the economical emancipation of labour. Except on this last condition, the Communal Constitution would have been an impossibility and a delusion. The political rule of the producer cannot coexist with the perpetuation of his social slavery. The Commune was therefore to serve as a lever for uprooting the economical foundation upon which rests the existence of classes, and therefore of class rule. With labour emancipated, every man becomes a working man, and productive labour ceases to be a class attribute.[39]

For Marx, the new phase of class struggle that opened with the Paris Commune could be successful—and therefore produce radical changes—only through the realization of a clearly anti-capitalist programme:

> the Commune intended to abolish [...] class property which makes the labour of the many the wealth of the few. It aimed at the expropriation of the expropriators. It wanted to make individual property a truth by transforming the means of production, land, and capital, now chiefly the means of enslaving and exploiting labour, into mere instruments of free and associated labour. [...] If co-operative production is not to remain a sham and a snare; if it is to supersede the capitalist system; if united co-operative societies are to regulate national production upon common plan, thus taking it under their own control, and putting an end to the constant anarchy and periodical convulsions which are the fatality of capitalist production – what else, gentlemen, would it be but communism, 'possible' communism? The working class did not expect miracles from the Commune. They have no ready-made utopias to introduce by decree of the people. They know that in order to work out their own emancipation, and along with it that higher form to which present society is irresistibly tending by its own economical

[38] Karl Marx, 'On the Paris Commune', in: Musto (ed.), *Workers Unite!*, pp. 215–6.
[39] Ibid., pp. 217–8.

> agencies, they will have to pass through long struggles, through a series of historic processes, transforming circumstances and men. They have no ideals to realize, but to set free the elements of the new society with which old collapsing bourgeois society itself is pregnant.[40]

In communist society, along with transformative changes in the economy, the role of the state and the function of politics would also have to be redefined. In *The Civil War in France*, Marx was at pains to explain that, after the conquest of power, the working class would have to fight to 'uproot the economical foundations upon which rests the existence of classes, and therefore of class rule'. Once 'labour was emancipated, every man would become a working man, and productive labour [would] cease to be a class attribute'.[41] The well-known statement that 'the working class cannot simply lay hold of the ready-made state machinery and wield it for its own purposes' was meant to signify, as Marx and Engels clarified in the booklet *Fictitious Splits in the International*, that 'the functions of government [should] become simple administrative functions'.[42] And in a concise formulation in his *Conspectus on Bakunin's Statism and Anarchy*, Marx insisted that 'the distribution of general functions [should] become a routine matter which entails no domination'.[43] This would, as far as possible, avoid the danger that the exercise of political duties generated new dynamics of domination and subjugation.

Marx believed that, with the development of modern society, 'state power [had] assumed more and more the character of the national power of capital over labour, of a public force organized for social enslavement, of an engine of class despotism'.[44] In communism, by contrast, the workers would have to prevent the state from becoming an obstacle to full emancipation. It would be necessary to 'amputate' 'the merely repressive organs of the old governmental power, [to wrest] its legitimate functions from an authority usurping pre-eminence over society itself, and restore [them] to the responsible agents of society'.[45] In the *Critique of the Gotha*

[40] Ibid., pp. 218–9.

[41] Karl Marx, *The Civil War in France*, MECW, vol. 22, pp. 334–5.

[42] Karl Marx and Friedrich Engels, 'Fictitious Splits in the International', MECW, vol. 23, p. 121.

[43] Marx, 'Notes on Bakunin's Book *Statehood and Anarchy*', MECW, vol. 24, p. 519.

[44] Marx, *The Civil War in France*, p. 329.

[45] Ibid., pp. 332–3.

Programme, Marx observed that 'freedom consists in converting the state from an organ superimposed upon society into one completely subordinate to it', and shrewdly added that 'forms of state are more free or less free to the extent that they restrict the "freedom of the state"'.[46]

In the same text, Marx underlined the demand that, in communist society, public policies should prioritize the 'collective satisfaction of needs'. Spending on schools, healthcare and other common goods would 'grow considerably in comparison with present-day society and grow in proportion as the new society develop[ed]'.[47] Education would assume front-rank importance and—as he had pointed out in *The Civil War in France*, referring to the model adopted by the Communards in 1871—'all the educational institutions [would be] opened to the people gratuitously and [...] cleared of all interference of Church and State'. Only in this way would culture be 'made accessible to all' and 'science itself freed from the fetters which class prejudice and governmental force had imposed upon it'.[48]

Unlike liberal society, where 'equal right' leaves existing inequalities intact, in communist society 'right would have to be unequal rather than equal'. A change in this direction would recognize, and protect, individuals on the basis of their specific needs and the greater or lesser hardship of their conditions, since 'they would not be different individuals if they were not unequal'. Furthermore, it would be possible to determine each person's fair share of services and the available wealth. The society that aimed to follow the principle 'From each according to their abilities, to each according to their needs'[49] had before it this intricate road fraught with difficulties. However, the final outcome was not guaranteed by some 'magnificent progressive destiny' (in the words of Leopardi), nor was it irreversible.

Marx attached a fundamental value to individual freedom, and his communism was radically different from the levelling of classes envisaged

[46] Marx, *Critique of the Gotha Programme*, MECW, vol. 24, p. 94.

[47] Ibid., p. 85.

[48] Marx, *The Civil War in France*, p. 332.

[49] Marx, *Critique of the Gotha Programme*, p. 87.

by his various predecessors or pursued by many of his epigones.[50] In the *Urtext*, however, he pointed to the 'folly of those socialists (especially French socialists)' who, considering 'socialism to be the realization of [bourgeois] ideas, [...] purport[ed] to demonstrate that exchange and exchange-value, etc., were originally [...] a system of the freedom and equality of all, but [later] perverted by money [and] capital'.[51] In the *Grundrisse*, he labelled it an 'absurdity' to regard 'free competition as the ultimate development of human freedom'; it was tantamount to a belief that 'the rule of the bourgeoisie is the terminal point of world history', which he mockingly described as 'an agreeable thought for the parvenus of the day before yesterday'.[52]

In the same way, Marx contested the liberal ideology according to which 'the negation of free competition [was] equivalent to the negation of individual freedom and of social production based upon individual freedom'. In bourgeois society, the only possible 'free development' was 'on the limited basis of the domination of capital'. But that 'type of individual freedom' was, at the same time, 'the most sweeping abolition of all individual freedom and the complete subjugation of individuality to social conditions which assume the form of objective powers, indeed of overpowering objects [...] independent of the individuals relating to one another'.[53]

The alternative to capitalist alienation was achievable only if the subaltern classes became aware of their condition as new slaves and embarked on a struggle to radically transform the world in which they were exploited. Their mobilization and active participation in this process could not stop, however, on the day after the conquest of power. The Paris Commune had been a remarkable revolutionary example to follow. Social mobilization would have to continue after the revolution, in order to avert any drift towards the kind of state socialism that Marx always opposed with the utmost tenacity and conviction.

[50] See Marcello Musto, 'Communism', in: Marcello Musto (ed.), *The Marx Revival: Key Concepts and New Interpretations* (Cambridge: Cambridge University Press, 2020), pp. 24–50.

[51] Karl Marx, *Economic Manuscripts of 1857–58*, MECW, vol. 28, p. 180.

[52] Karl Marx, 'Outlines of the Critique of Political Economy (Rough Draft of 1857–58) [Second Instalment]', MECW, vol. 29, p. 40.

[53] Ibid.

In 1868, in a significant letter to the president of the General Association of German Workers, Marx explained that in Germany, 'where the worker is regulated bureaucratically from childhood onwards, where he believes in authority, in those set over him, the main thing is to teach him to walk by himself'.[54] He never changed this conviction throughout his life and it is not by chance that the first point of his draught of the Statutes of the International Working Men's Association states: 'The emancipation of the working classes must be conquered by the working classes themselves'. And they add immediately afterwards that the struggle for working-class emancipation 'means not a struggle for class privileges and monopolies, but for equal rights and duties'.[55]

References

Bourgin, Georges (1925), 'La Commune de Paris et le Comité central (1871)', *Revue historique*, vol. 1925, n. 150: 1–66.

Choury, Maurice (1960), *Les origenes de la Commune*, Paris: Éditions sociales.

Clayson, Hollis (2002), *Paris in Despair: Art and Everyday Life under Siege (1870–1871)*, Chicago: University of Chicago Press.

Collins, Henry, and Abramsky, Chimen (1965), *Karl Marx and the British Labour Movement*, London: MacMillan.

The Commune of Paris (1999), 'Declaration to the French People', in: Robert Tombs, *The Paris Commune 1871*, London: Longman, pp. 217–19.

Dalotel, Alain (1997), 'La barricade des femmes, 1871', in: Alain Corbin and Jean-Marie Mayeur (eds.), *La barricade*, Paris: Éditions la Sorbonne, pp. 341–55.

Dalotel, Alain, Faure, Alain, and Freiermuth, Jean-Claude (1980), *Aux origines de la Commune. Le movement des reunions publiques à Paris, 1868–1870*, Paris: Maspero.

Haupt, Georges (1978), *L'Internazionale socialista dalla Comune a Lenin*, Torino: Einaudi.

———. (1986), *Aspect of International Socialism 1871–1914*, Cambridge: Cambridge University Press.

Hugo, Victor (2004), 'Viro Major', in: Nic Maclellan (ed.), *Louise Michel*, New York: Ocean Press, pp. 24–5.

Institute of Marxism-Leninism of the C.C., C.P.S.U. (ed.) (1968), *The General Council of the First International 1871–1872: Minutes*, Moscow: Progress.

[54] Karl Marx to J. B. von Schweitzer, 13 October 1868, MECW, vol. 43, p. 134.

[55] Karl Marx, 'Provisional Rules of the Association', MECW, vol. 20, p. 14.

Johnson, Martin Philip (1996), *The Paradise of Association: Political Culture and Popular Organizations in the Paris Commune of 1871*, Ann Arbor: University of Michigan Press.

Latta, Claude (2021), 'Minorité et majorité au sein de la Commune (avril-mai 1871)', in: Michel Cordillot (ed.), *La Commune de Paris 1871. Les acteurs, l'événement, les lieux*, Ivry-sur-Seine: Les Éditions de l'Atelier/Éditions Ouvrières, pp. 941–4.

Lefebvre, Henri (2018), *La proclamation de la Commune, 26 mars 1871*, Paris: La fabrique éditions.

Lehning, Arthur (1977), 'Introduction', in: Idem. (ed.), *Bakunin – Archiv*, vol. VI: *Michel Bakounine sur la Guerre Franco–Allemande et la Révolution Sociale en France (1870–1871)*, Leiden: Brill, pp. xi–cxvii.

Lenoir, Hugues (2021), 'La Commune de Paris et l'éducation', in: Michel Cordillot (ed.), *La Commune de Paris 1871. Les acteurs, l'événement, les lieux*, Ivry-sur-Seine: Les Éditions de l'Atelier/Éditions Ouvrières, pp. 495–8.

Marx, Karl (1985), 'Provisional Rules of the Association', MECW, vol. 20, pp. 14–6.

———. (1986), *The Civil War in France*, MECW, vol. 22, pp. 307–59.

———. (1986), *Economic Manuscripts of 1857–58*, MECW, vol. 28.

———. (1986), *Second Address of the General Council of the International Working Men's Association on the Franco–Prussian War*, MECW, vol. 22, pp. 263–70.

———. (1987), 'Outlines of the Critique of Political Economy (Rough Draft of 1857–58) [Second Instalment]', MECW, vol. 29, pp. 5–417.

———. (1989), *Critique of the Gotha Programme*, MECW, vol. 24, pp. 75–99.

———. (1989), 'Notes on Bakunin's Book *Statehood and Anarchy*', MECW, vol. 24, pp. 485–526.

———. (2014), 'On the Paris Commune', in: Marcello Musto (ed.), *Workers Unite! The International 150 Years Later*, New York: Bloomsbury, pp. 211–44.

Marx, Karl, and Engels, Friedrich (1988), 'Fictitious Splits in the International', MECW, vol. 23, pp. 79–123.

———. (1988), *Letters 1868–70*, MECW, vol. 43.

———. (1989), *Letters 1870–73*, MECW, vol. 44.

———. (1992), *Letters 1880–83*, MECW, vol. 46.

Mazzini, Giuseppe (1978), *L'Internazionale*, in: Gian Mario Bravo (ed.), *La Prima Internazionale: Storia documentaria*, vol. II, Roma: Editori Riuniti, pp. 499–501.

Milza, Pierre (2009), *L'année terrible. I: La guerre franco–prussienne (septembre 1870–mars 1871)*, Paris: Perrin.

———. (2009), *L'année terrible. II: La Commune*, Paris: Perrin.

Musto, Marcello (2014), 'Introduction', in: Marcello Musto (ed.), *Workers Unite! The International 150 Years Later*, New York: Bloomsbury, pp. 1–68.

———. (2018), *Another Marx: Early Manuscripts to the International*, London: Bloomsbury.

———. (2020), 'Communism', in: Marcello Musto (ed.), *The Marx Revival: Key Concepts and New Interpretations*, Cambridge: Cambridge University Press, pp. 24–50.

Rosselli, Nello (1927), *Mazzini e Bakunin*, Torino: Einaudi.

Rougerie, Jacques (1988), *La Commune de 1871*, Paris: Presses Universitaires de France.

———. (1971), *Paris libre 1871*, Paris: Seuil.

Sanchez, Gonzalo J. (1997), *Organizing Independence: The Artists Federation of the Paris Commune and Its Legacy, 1871–1889*, Lincoln: University of Nebraska Press.

Thomas, Edith (1963), *Les «Pétroleuses»*, Paris: Gallimard.

Ximenes, Enrico Emilio (ed.) (1885), *Epistolario di Giuseppe Garibaldi*, vol. I, Milano: Brigola.

Zaidman, Pierre-Henri (2021), 'Le Comité central contre la Commune?', in: Michel Cordillot (ed.), *La Commune de Paris 1871. Les acteurs, l'événement, les lieux*, Ivry-sur-Seine: Les Éditions de l'Atelier/Éditions Ouvrières, pp. 229–36.

CHAPTER 12

Communism as Probability and Contingency

Álvaro García Linera

12.1 Probability and Contingency

What is communism? Regardless of the names used, communism, post-capitalism, libertarian socialism, commons or common goods, communism is one possible answer to the question, what is the future of humanity? It is one way of designating a probable and future organization of human life, different from the current capitalist organization, one that will be able to overcome the injustices and contradictions that capitalism itself is undergoing. In these cases, we refer to something likely and, in addition, something that concerns the future; something that does not yet exist but that could emerge over time.

Why should we speak of something that does not exist? Because society today generates considerable human suffering, considerable injustice and the domination of a few over others, hence, it is only to be expected that

Translated by Josefa Salmon with the collaboration of Bruno Bosteels and Mariela Padilla.

Á. García Linera (✉)
Rosa Luxemburg Foundation, Berlin, Germany

M. Musto (ed.), *Rethinking Alternatives with Marx*, Marx, Engels, and Marxisms, https://doi.org/10.1007/978-3-030-81764-0_12

people think and yearn for the existence of another type of society without suffering and injustice.

There is a logical problem here: Why something that does not exists, should exist? Why does not accept what exists as something that always will and what doesn't, as something that never will? Why not rule out from the infinite space of future probabilities something like communism, which has not happened yet? Because in order to discard the possibility of an existing future, of a social organization different from capitalism, one has to assume that capitalism is irreplaceable, that it is a supreme and definitive social order attained by humanity and, in that sense, history has reached its pinnacle, so that we would only have to worry about managing this last final goal reached by humanity.

The argumentative force of this response lies in its reliance on the legitimization of common sense by naturalizing the dominant social order, always inclined to show that what exists is the only possible existence. But we are dealing with a mystic and teleological view of human history. There are not reasons but beliefs that sustain the unmovable naturalization of the dominant order and its injustices; what we know of the course of human history, in an objective and convincing way, is a contingency, an aleatory articulation of circumstances that gave way to different modes of social and economic organization.

The course of mankind, over the past sixty thousand years, is a product of contingent human actions by humans themselves and it is not the fulfilment of previously elaborated paths outlined by mysterious forces hovering over humanity. To reject this historical contingency is to start debating the presence of supernatural or supra-earthly forces like gods, and if so, there is nothing further to discuss. Leaving aside the debate about the existence of superhuman forces as the great organizing entities of history, since, in that case, this would imply that there would no longer be social history but divine providence, what is clear is that religious mystification can play an effective role in legitimizing the existing relationships of domination.

Today, a more solid way of denying the possibility of communism as a designation of an alternative to capitalism is to claim that communism already existed and failed in the former Soviet Union. It is argued that it was there, in the Soviet Union that communism established itself, flourished for seventy years, generated other type of injustices and finally gave way to the democratic and technological impetus of capitalism.

Though this argument to invalidate communism historically rests, again, on the premise that a non-human hand is interfering to direct the trajectory of society and thereby justify the belief that a new and different experience of communism could not ever be possible, clearly, to acknowledge the collapse of the USSR is a stronger argument framed within a commonsense discourse. In fact, negating a likely communist future, based on the collapse of the Soviet Union, has led to the subsequent resignation of an entire generation of militants in the late twentieth century, most of whom descended regretfully into neoliberal greed, the testimonial resistance of micro-autonomies and rampant globalization or opted for the margins of an academic teaching post. In the past thirty years, the communist alternative, from a one-time horizon of hope in the people's struggle has become into a term of shame safeguarded by a loyal minority of semi-clandestine adherents.

Today, after the procession of a generation in mourning went by, the concept of communism, common goods, the commons, democratic socialism, postcapitalism is voiced again in different parts of the world, not only as a *chic* emblem of academic rebellion, but as a practical option, as a necessity in order to overcome the growing list of grievances that workers the world-over now face. There are reasons for it: the religious philosophy of the 'end of history' has exhausted its power for convincing and concealment; government and labour conflicts explode everywhere; even in wealthy Europe, working classes take to the streets to demand recognition and their rights; and the old inequalities that were supposed to have disappeared under the sway of globalization and free market, have returned to the outrageous levels seen in the early twentieth century.

Globalization, as an ideology of tolerance and compromise with the capitalist order, collapses in the face of Brexit, US tariffs and Angela Merkel's talk of 'continental security' towards China. Yesterday's representatives of free trade are today protectionists; the globalists have become nationalists and with this, the celebratory world discourse dominant since 1989 has exploded in a thousand pieces nowadays, causing a vacuum in the meaning of history, planetary turmoil and uncertainty. One could say that in the last decade, history has once again assumed its contingent character, unfinished character, driven by new social basis, new concepts, new victimized groups and new needs to be resolved: it is the inescapable debate of postcapitalism.

When it comes to building a better world today, the failure of capitalism to solve social injustice, the bonds of domination, climate change, universal usufruct of important technological developments is as powerful as was the failure of the Soviet Union in the last century. And thus, communism rises again under different circumstances, in different languages, as *a possible epochal horizon*.

12.2 Communism as an Idea and as Real Movement

> The Communists disdain to conceal their views and aims. They openly declare that their ends can be attained only by the forcible overthrow of all existing social conditions.[1]

Is communism an idea? How do we justify a different future from a capitalist one based on an idea? Speaking of something that does not exist but that could eventually exist at least has the merit of clearing away the superhuman explanation of the course of history and leaving open the contingency and uncertainty of social history. It is there where lies the logical consistency of communism as an idea, as a hypothesis, as a concept.[2] Nonetheless, its explanatory power becomes diluted because it is just one of one hundred, one thousand or one million ideas that exist concerning a better future for humanity.

Throughout history, thousands of people have imagined or conceptually configured diverse options of envisioning a different future than the prevailing one and none of those ideas have been achieved. Even, ideas with collective support and with the capacity to produce social behaviour, such as religions that offer means of salvation, have not been achieved, and in all likelihood they never will. Then, why would the communist idea have a different fate compared to the thousands of ideas, hypotheses and proposals for the future that have not been implemented?

If communism were only an idea, a logical hypothesis, its probability of becoming realized would have the same minimal range of probability for

[1] Karl Marx and Friedrich Engels, *Manifesto of the Communist Party*, MECW, vol. 6, p. 519.

[2] See Slavoj Žižek (ed.), *La idea de comunismo, The New York Conference (2011)* (Madrid: Akal, 2014); Alex Taek-Gwang Lee and Slavoj Žižek (eds.), *La idea de comunismo: The Seoul Conference (2013)* (Madrid: Akal, 2018); Alain Badiou, *Circonstances 5: L'hypothèse communiste* (París: Nouvelles Éditions Lignes, 2009); and Bruno Bosteels, *The Actuality of Communism* (London: Verso, 2011).

a better world future as the abundant political, religious or spiritual speculative hypotheses. Instead, the idea of communism, as a way of surpassing capitalism, has a higher probability of realization because, procedurally, it is a performative idea, it is an idea in-movement. It is not just an idea with the capacity to spread movement, which is already a major advantage over other futuristic ideas, but rather, it is the result of a real objective movement, a characteristic that asserts its performative capacity to actualize what it posits at the same time.

Marx and Engels wrote in *The German Ideology*: 'Communism is for us not a state of affairs which is to be established, an ideal to which reality [will] have to adjust itself. We call communism the real movement which abolishes the present state of things. The conditions of this movement result from the now existing premise'.[3] In the few generally encrypted references made by Marx in allusion to communism, one central assertion is that it is not an idea invented by some world reformer, but rather, it is an idea that *expresses*, that *emerges,* that is the result of a historical movement. In fact, in his research on the critique of political economy, in the chapter on machines in *Grundrisse*,[4] in *Capital*,[5] in the resolutions of the International Working Men's Association[6] and others, Marx insists that the material conditions within capitalism generate within themselves the 'material conditions', the material basis that opens up the real possibility for communism as a mode of production resulting from 'the old one'.[7]

This marks a decisive point of emphasis. The material and moral superiority of the communist hypothesis over any other idea of future lies in the fact that it is rooted in the real conditions of the present, in the economic and social relations which, though born within capitalism, used by capitalism, at the service of it, surpass capitalism itself. These conditions have a potential for realization beyond capital's own framework. What are these

[3] Karl Marx and Friedrich Engels, *The German Ideology*, MECW, vol. 5, p. 49.

[4] Karl Marx, *Elementos fundamentales para la crítica de la economía política (Grundrisse) 1857–1858*, vol. 2 (Mexico: Siglo XXI, 1983), pp. 216–35.

[5] Karl Marx, *El capital, Tomo III*, vol. 7 (Mexico: Siglo XXI, 1981), pp. 564–9. See also Karl Marx, 'Chapter XV: Machinery and Modern Industry', in: Karl Marx, *Capital, Volume I*, MECW, vol. 35, pp. 374–508.

[6] See Marcello Musto (ed.), *Workers Unite! The International 150 Years Later* (New York: Bloomsbury, 2014), in particular pp. 90, 92, 97–8, and 103–4.

[7] Marx, *Capital, Volume I*, pp. 504–5.

real conditions produced by capitalism that are more likely to expand beyond the capitalist logic?

They are, first of all, the planetary interconnection and interdependence of goods and human skills. Absolutely all forms of production before capitalism were local, regional. They consisted of individual family production; individual, family and communal labour production for the community; there was individual, familial and communal production for nearby communities or specific ones that asked for a specific production. Instead, with capitalism, production is be geared towards any buyer from any place in the region, country or the world, as long as its exchange-value and connected profit is realized in the process; and doing so while using as much labour from as many producers from around the world as is necessary in order to realize exchange-value and, with it, profit. Capitalism is the only mode of production whose objective is not to satisfy always restricted needs, but rather to satisfy unlimited profit by unlimited goods, unlimited consumption, with providers from everywhere and consumers from wherever possible. The only physical limitation is the world and only for the moment. In that sense, it is the first planetary-universal mode of production.

When Marx composes, draught after draught, the chapter on commodities,[8] what he is trying to find is the guiding principle of this universalizing quality of capitalism that allows it to interconnect the production and consumption of a region, then of a country, of many countries and of the entire world, and with this, the ability to connect the productiveness, inventiveness, the needs and resources of each person on the planet. The genetic code of this society in motion lays in the subordination of use-value to exchange-value within the process itself for the material production of commodities. When exchange-value subsumes use- value and becomes the aim of production, it opens up, ad infinitum, the options of use-value that will serve the goal of realizing the supreme objective of exchange-value. And when the doors open up to endless use-values (in both quantity and quality) in which exchange-value or profit will try to realize itself, there occurs a double process of universalization:

[8] Karl Marx, 'Chapter I: Commodities', in: *Capital, Volume I*, pp. 45–94. See also Karl Marx, 'The Production Process of Capital', in: Karl Marx, *Economic Manuscript of 1861–63*, MECW, vol. 30, pp. 9–171. Translated into Spanish as Karl Marx, 'El proceso de producción del capital', in: Karl Marx, *Comunidad, nacionalismos y capital: Textos inéditos* (La Paz: Vicepresidencia del Estado Plurinacional de Bolivia, 2018), pp. 243–353.

on the one hand, selling and buying spread throughout the world in order to reach higher profits. On the other hand, the impulse and subordination of humanity's infinite inventive capacity all over the world to produce new use-values that will bring about the desired profit and exchange-value. The world market at the service of capitalism is the visible and tangible form of this process of formal and real subsumption of production and consumption under capitalist profit-making. But the innermost process that puts in motion and overruns this capitalist limit of private pettiness is, on the one hand, the interconnection, the universal-social interdependence of human production and consumption; and, on the other, the universal-social interconnection and interdependence of the infinite creative and cognitive capabilities of human beings.

Capitalism, with its thirst for profit, subjects all the peoples of the world to create markets and seize knowledge. And in doing so, it broadens the process of valorization and the process of expanded capital accumulation but at the same time, it unintentionally triggers universal-social forces of production, global interdependence of production and knowledge that makes it possible to realize, materialize and organize another mode of production. A mode of production that has as its starting point this universalization of human capabilities and needs, but without the enslavement and mutilation entailed by private profit.

The same thing can be said about the 'general intellect'.[9] The commodity-form under capitalism or the domination of exchange-value over use-value splits into two the quality to satisfy human needs through the self-objectification of human labour; so that what counts as the main goal of production is no longer the *material content of wealth* (use value), reduced to a contingent packaging, but rather, what counts is the *magnitude of value*, the quantity of abstract human labour deposited in the object (exchange-value) in order to appropriate unpaid labour, that is profit. The obsessive goal of every new scientific and technological development will be the materialization of exchange-value, and with it, profit, with the help of all use-value forms including social technologies that allow the increase of unpaid labour time in each country, each region and each individual's factory. In this way, as new technologies arise that increase production by reducing the *necessary labour* time for the maintenance of the worker and by increasing the *surplus labour*

[9] Karl Marx, 'Outlines of the Critique of Political Economy (Rough Draft of 1857–58) [Second Instalment]', MECW, vol. 29, p. 92.

time appropriated by the capitalist, these will be incorporated immediately as a productive force for the development of capitalism. And so, new means invented in the most distant places of the world, new forms of knowledge generated in all parts of the globe will gradually be integrated into the production cycle in an effort to keep increasing more and more the surplus labour time appropriated by the capitalists. And for each new productive cycle, new means of production resulting from an articulation of planetary capabilities will be set in motion within each labour process, particularly decreasing the amount of necessary labour.

As the repercussion this will have is one of spreading into the other labour processes in the country and the world, therefore, in the long run, the living labour or total labour time needed to produce a certain commodity will also have been shortened, expanding the quantity of past labour transferred through those means of production and the technology produced worldwide. Following a kind of Moore's commercial law, that is, not applied to already integrated networks but to past labour time transferred to each commodity; every year, due to the new means of production, each commodity unit will incorporate a transferred past labour time that is greater than the living labour time integrated by the direct worker. This means that the composition of past labour and living labour comprised in the production of each commodity will tend to expand the past labour time and reduce the living labour to infinitesimal proportions close to zero.

In this way, as capitalism promotes a deployment of technical and scientific skills to shorten the necessary labour time in order to increase surplus labour time without wishing or seeking to do so, it unifies the creative and cognitive abilities of human beings in a type of abstract 'general intellect' and equally important, it tends to turn living labour, the direct labour of the wage-earner, into a mere overseeing or regulator activity overlooking the huge worldwide technical and cognitive production forces. Capitalism lives off unpaid living labour but tends to make it irrelevant within the production process. In all this, there is an awakened universal-social potential that is the universality of technology and knowledge, though it is continually severed and constrained in yielding to the interest and private greed of a few. Likewise, there is a potential to turn direct human labour into a mere managing activity of a giant world organism of technical and objectified knowledge, but capitalism once again subsumes this force under the petty interest of extracting unpaid living labour.

The world market interconnecting planetary production,[10] the 'general intellect' that places the individual as mere 'overseer'[11] of the social labour process in the world, the same cooperative factories 'as transitional forms from the capitalist mode of production' to one based on association,[12] etc., are what Marx already in the nineteenth century identified as the '*real* movement' which articulates a possible future with a material reality already in existence.[13]

To be clear, this is not a communist future that already exists within capitalism, it is a future whose actualization and real conditions of possibility are rooted in the present and, for this reason, it is a future-oriented movement, a process. Thus, communism names a possible future, but one whose movement arises from the present. It is not the present, but its conditions of existence lie in the present. The present 'is pregnant'[14] with the future, but that possible future will not come spontaneously or automatically. Its real conditions of possibility have to be generated 'separate and free from their antithetical capitalist character'[15] so as to enable the communist future.

Communism does not exist today, but the material conditions for its existence are being produced currently. Therefore, it is a future in motion, or better, a movement towards a communist future. For this reason, the idea of communism, the communist hypothesis is much more than a formal idea or a logical concept from which to speculate about the future. It is an idea that already manifests its communist intent, from the moment

[10] Karl Marx, 'Outlines of the Critique of Political Economy (Rough Draft of 1857–58) [First Instalment]', MECW, vol. 28, pp. 97–8, 465. See also Karl Marx, *Grundrisse*, vol. 2; Karl Marx, *El capital, Tomo III*, vol. 6 (Mexico: Siglo XXI, 1981), p. 341.

[11] Marx, 'Outlines of the Critique of Political Economy (Rough Draft of 1857–58) [Second Instalment]', p. 91.

[12] Karl Marx, *Capital, Volume III*, MECW, vol. 37, p. 438.

[13] Ibid., 'Hence' Marx says, 'the credit system accelerates the material development of the productive forces and the establishment of the world market. It is the historical mission of the capitalist mode of production to raise these material foundations of the new form of production to a certain degree of perfection', p. 439.

[14] Karl Marx, *Civil War in France*, MECW, vol. 22, 'The working class [...] have no ideals to realize, but to set free elements of the new society with which old collapsing bourgeois society itself is pregnant', p. 335.

[15] Marx, *Capital, Volume III*, p. 385.

it is enunciated, because it means struggle, effort, revolution for the liberation of something already present, trapped, distorted within reality in order to make it a real future. Marx insists that:

> To convert social production into one large and harmonious system of free and co-operative labour, *general social changes* are wanted, *changes of the general conditions of society*, never to be realised save by the transfer of the organised forces of society, viz., the state power, from capitalists and landlords to the producers themselves.[16]

Communism is an enunciation which allows for the creation of an idea for a future with practical intentionality to be distinct from capitalism because it represents that intentionality as something that exists trapped within capitalism itself. Or citing Austin[17] and Searle,[18] it is a performative enunciation with the objective of changing our current reality so that the future communist reality will coincide with the content of the speech act regarding the communist future. In other words, to speak of communism means also to start carrying it out, and this power of the word communism, of the communist idea, of producing things, real events towards communism, does not lie in a discursive quality of the enunciated future, but rather in the represented content of the present that strives to become future and that transforms the communist idea into a potential force for realization.

Communism is a performative enunciation, but communism's performativity does not reside in the word itself; its performativity lies in the fact that it articulates a reality in motion, and then, the word can enable the enunciated reality to emerge since there is a reality that is acting internally to be able to coincide with the word. In general, the performativity of words, their capacity to produce the reality they enunciate is not an ability that lies on the word or in the idea itself, but in how these words or ideas are inscribed in a network of socially shared representations and in what kind of realities are enabled by the possible course of action of this reality

[16] Karl Marx, 'Instructions for the Delegates of the Provisional General Council: The Different Questions', MECW, vol. 20, p. 190.

[17] John Austin, *How to Do Things with Words* (Cambridge: Harvard University Press, 1962).

[18] John Searle, *Making the Social World the Structure of Human Civilization* (Oxford: Oxford University Press, 2010).

itself. For this reason, the communist hypothesis is inseparable from the real movement towards communism in its double connotation; as generalized collective action and as material reality unfolding within capitalism. This constitutes the performativity of the communist enunciation.

The communist hypothesis would only be a pious desire in the midst of a million desires or a formal category in the midst of a million formal categories if it were not precisely for its representation of a real process that actualizes it in order to create the reality that it enunciates. For that reason, communism is an *idea-force*, that is, an idea that compromises the one who pronounces it, and with time, when it becomes a socially shared common sense, it will be able to challenge the political power in favour of the social producers themselves, it will help create the reality represented by the idea.

The communist idea, the communist hypothesis for a future, is nothing without the real process towards communism present in reality. Only the real movement seizes it from anonymity in which the thousands of impotent ideas about the future dwell by giving it consistency and increasing the probability of the realization of the communist future at the same ratio as the number of people increases who believe in and commit to the communist idea and fight for it politically. It is at that moment that the communist idea-process becomes a *communist horizon*.

That is why the communist process-idea is born, dies and is born again, it's destroyed again, reborn, falls and is reborn because the real conditions of its future existence are present and will remain present while capitalism prevails. In fact, capitalism needs to permanently kill the communist idea, debase it, banish it time after time in order to reproduce its own existence; the death of communism is, thus, a productive force of capitalism.

But at the same time, '*real* movement' on its own remains a tendency, a larval potential in a subsumed condition, but capable of going along indefinitely while the expanded reproduction of capitalism advances. So, in order to materialize, to arise, the real movement towards a communist future needs the idea-force latent in performative words that propels workers to collective action. Only the idea-force, the performative idea spreads the possible courses of action of communism itself. The articulation between the idea of communism and real movement that carries the potentiality for the materialization of communism is the idea-force, the effective collective action by subalterns; and, at the same time, it is that same universalizing collective action which unites the idea and the moving matter with a communist future. The unity of this relationship between idea, collective action, materiality, movement and future is what we call *communist horizon*.

For all these reasons, the communist idea today needs and is inseparable from real movement in contemporary society, and real movement is inseparable from the communist idea in order to be actualized, but as an idea-force, as a mobilizing idea capable of materializing that liberating potential for a new society. In other words, hope can only come about if there are material conditions to make it possible and these material conditions for a new future would arise only if the collective force of subjects is there to fight for them because, ultimately, just as today there is no communism, also there are no individuals nor social classes capable of leading it. For communism to be a force of a possible becoming, it requires that subjects be able to liberate that potential in the present; and this social, collectivity of subjects arises only from the struggle itself to liberate that real social potential. That collective subject who refuses to be capital's labour force and constitutes him/herself as an emancipating subject is part of that '*real* movement' that 'abolishes the present state of things'.[19]

Hypothesis, practical collective compromise and '*real* movement' in the present form an indivisible trilogy for communism to have historic viability. The communist idea without the other two components can only be a beautiful and impotent academic thought about the future, as are the many hundreds of sophisticated theoretical speculations. Practical commitment without orientation or real support can only be a passing exciting activism. And objective movement without collective action aimed at a horizon is nothing but a productive force belonging to the advancement of capitalism's own expanded reproduction. Only the idea transformed into collective action aimed at an emancipating horizon can liberate the existing real conditions of the enunciated horizon. The idea can be materialized through practical action, if and only if, that idea reflects the material movement itself. This is the *algorithm* of communist contingency.

[19] Marx, *Elementos fundamentales para la crítica de la economía política (Grundrisse) 1857–1858*, vol. 2.

12.3 Four Basic Components of the Communist Movement–Idea

Since communism does not exist yet, any specific experience to rule it out or to justify it will always be partial and limited; but in so far as it is a real movement and there were failed previous attempts in the last one hundred and fifty years, there are general tendencies that can be discerned as to what can be foreseen or what can no longer be possible to undertake. This should be the only intellectual and moral connection with failed, defeated, or uncompleted past revolutionary experiences of the last century, that is, there should be an awareness of practical experiences that do not lead to communism and of the courses of action that do help to strengthen the tendencies for a communist future.

(a) Individual–Social Property

> The alien property of the capitalist in this labour can only be abolished by converting his property into the property of the non-individual in its independent singularity, hence of the associated, social individual.[20]

One of the great issues in the struggle for communism in the past century was to think that the way out of capitalism, with its logic of private ownership of the means of production and ample private appropriation of social wealth, was through State ownership of society's main means of production. All twentieth century revolutions asserted that this was the way, a transient stage, in order to eliminate one of the conditions for the exploitation of labour of subaltern classes. The *Communist Manifesto* of 1848 and the communist debate during the first years of the Soviet and Chinese Revolution tend to justify State control as the first step of every triumphant revolution. Certainly, nationalization centralizes the ownership of the means of production in the hands of the State debilitating the economic power of the former dominant upper classes and also weakens the political power held by this economic power.

Temporarily, this would allow subaltern classes to better organize within the framework of centralized political power, to take advantage of economic resources for the improvement of the working-class' social rights, to encourage mechanisms for increased economic equality and

[20] Karl Marx, *Economic Manuscript of 1861–63*, MECW, vol. 34, p. 109.

to reduce the possibility of effective boycotts by large property-owners. However, this does not produce or lead to the formation of a new relationship of social production; it only shifts the legal jurisdiction of property relations, from appropriation and domination in private hands, to a public institution, the State, but this change of hands is still different and separated from that of the direct workers themselves.

In its classic form, capitalist private property unifies three things: (a) the legal property of the means of production, (b) the appropriation of economic surplus and (c) the direct and indirect control of the means of production, its use and consumption.

Nationalization withholds private property, now in the hands of the State, which set limits on the discretionary legal power of the means of production, but maintains ownership of economic surplus and control over the labour process which is disconnected from the workers and gradually clashes with the workers themselves. The appropriation of surplus is now a decision of State bureaucrats who have limitations on its discretionary use and disposal. This surplus is under the social controls of public goods but, just like the control of the production process, it remains separated and differentiated from the workers themselves, thus reproducing again what lies at the heart of commodity-form and capitalism: the objective conditions of labour alienation, automation and the control of the means of production, of the production process, over the worker.

The well-directed and socially regulated nationalization of the major means of production creates social conditions of life more favourable for subaltern classes, but it does not get rid of the rule of exchange-value and therefore, sooner or later, the material conditions of capitalism will reproduce themselves, this time, coming from the State itself. Historically no revolution in the last one hundred and fifty years has managed to overcome the real material conditions of exchange-value, or commodity-form, as the organizing nucleus of production and circulation of wealth at the local, national or global level.[21] For this reason, once the 'catharsis'[22]

[21] Regarding Lenin's debates and distress after concluding that the so-called 'war communism' (1917–1921), with the takeover of factories, the suppression of currencies and monetary exchange, outlawing inheritance, standardization of wages, etc., had not created a new economic system different from capitalism, see Álvaro García Linera, *¿Qué es una revolución?* (La Paz: Vicepresidencia del Estado Plurinacional de Bolivia, 2018).

[22] Antonio Gramsci, *Cuadernos de la cárcel*, vol. 4 (Mexico: Ediciones Era, 1986), p. 146.

of the revolutionary process has passed allowing for control and dispute of State surplus and of the instruments of labour themselves, it is inevitable that tendencies that promote gradual public privatization processes for the use of economic surplus by the State increases; thus, legal privatization would only be a matter of time.

Nationalization of the major means of production, aside from encouraging temporary processes of social equality that could help in the advancement of social alternatives to capitalism, can only buy time for insurgent subaltern classes at the national level, hoping that the political uprising of other working classes in different regions and in other countries could together create real change in the world economic system and in particular in the relations of production of material wealth at the supranational, at the continental and then at the global level.

A new form of property that would surpass capitalist private property and transform the capitalist production process has to, necessarily, go beyond the State as a unifying force of social affairs; it has to go beyond the national class struggle; it has to have an impact on the internal logic of the direct labour process itself allowing for the restitution of direct control of the worker's over production conditions as in ancient agrarian communities, except that now it is, at a social, planetary and global scale; in addition to modifying the relationship of labour processes at the national, regional and global level, as the only planetary workforce. Marx calls this individual-social production, 'free and co-operative labor',[23] etc. The base of his thought lies, on the one hand, in a universal-social characteristic being adopted by the process of labour and means of labour within capitalism, enabling real possibilities for the existence of universal-social forms of property. And on the other hand, on how these universal-social means of production become alien powers that subject the worker, ('alienation of labour',[24] 'commodity fetishism'[25]), therefore, the overcoming of that 'highly mysterious' quality of capitalist relations undergoes a direct and 'transparent' connection with those means of production, such as individual property, but when it belongs to all workers at a global scale, it becomes 'individual-social property'.

[23] Austin, *How to Do Things with Words*.

[24] Karl Marx, 'Estranged Labour', in: Karl Marx, *Economic and Philosophic Manuscripts of 1844*, MECW, vol. 3, pp. 270–82.

[25] Karl Marx, 'Section 4: The Fetishism of Commodities and the Secret Thereof', in: *Capital, Volume I*, pp. 81–94.

Of course, every day that goes by in capitalism, labour tools, knowledge and technology emerge as a social-universal product where all of humanity has contributed with something in its production, but the control of those socially constituted means of production, the control in the use of that socially constructed knowledge is private as is the use of its generated wealth. Therefore, it is reasonable to think that the private packaging will appear as a miserable and asphyxiating measure against its social potential, and so, a task for the movement towards communism is to break this private constraint and to liberate its universal human potential.

How might those concrete emancipating forms of production be? We don't know, only experience will show. What is clear is that the attempt to liberate these social potentialities via State ownership was a failure. Then, we need to awaken other means of action towards emancipating that universal potential; in that sense, communism is also a real movement of this pursuit and of this collective-historic experimentation.

(b) Use-Value over Exchange-Value

> Within the collective society based on common ownership of the means of production, the producers do not exchange their products; just as little does the labour employed on the products appear here as the value of these products, as a material quality possessed by them, since now, in contrast to capitalist society, individual labour no longer exists in an indirect fashion but directly as a component part of the total labour.[26]

In the enlightening Chapter 1, Volume I of *Capital*, Marx demonstrates that the determination of abstract labour time as a measure for the universal inter-exchangeability of the fruits of human labour constitutes the foundational core of the capitalist order of production and of modern social life. This commodification of human relations, value form, commodity-form are not the result of the market nor of peoples' hateful consumerist attitudes susceptible to dismiss by massaging their conscience or by sending chains of WhatsApp messages. They are the immediate result of people relationship with the social production conditions.

[26] Karl Marx, *Critique of the Gotha Programme*, MECW, vol. 24, p. 85.

Commodity fetishism—objects exerting power over humans and labour power standing before workers as an external and abusive force—is the result of the concurrence form of work activity, wherein isolated producers are submitted to labour forces which appear as forces that are alien to the workers themselves. Exchange value form, commodity-form, blocks the breathing space of a society and its origin is the colonization of labour process by that *value form* of concurrence and consumption of the means of labour.

How can we overcome exchange-value, value form as the measure of exchange of human products? Marx writes about 'free and co-operative labour',[27] 'free and equal producers, carrying on the social business on a common and rational plan'.[28] How would these concrete forms of association work? We do not know. What we do know by unsuccessful experience is that State property leaves value form in the production process untouched and that free and cooperative labour cannot be the bureaucratic decision of any State.

To overcome commodity-form, exchange-value form, would have to be a process created by the direct producers themselves coming from the immediate productive processes themselves that generate new ways for the population to access universal labour products. Labour centres would have to create their own patterns of self-organization capable of overcoming the imminent 'collective privatization' that the workers themselves of every labour centre could make use of the surplus generated by that common-universal effort. But at the same time, there would have to be forms of associated labour that must be able to interconnect among themselves directly at the national, then regional and global scales in order to monitor products from common-universal labour.

There would have to be sovereignty and direct worker control of the labour process or within worker's environment, plus general interconnectedness of the different labour processes and transparent social appropriation of the national and global product by the entire society. Ultimately, it is about bringing about plural and direct forms of transforming private production, private means, private surplus and private

[27] Marx, 'Instructions for the Delegates of the Provisional General Council: The Different Questions', p. 190.

[28] Karl Marx, 'The Nationalisation of the Land', MECW, vol. 23, p. 136.

control of production into the control, production and social surplus of associated producers themselves in partnership with the rest of society.

(c) Social Freedom

> But as soon as the immediate character of living labour is transcended, i.e., its character as merely individual, or as only internally or only externally general, with the positing of the activity of individuals as immediately general or social activity, this form of alienation is stripped from the reified moments of production. Then they are posited as [social] property, as the organic social body in which the individuals reproduce themselves as individuals, but as social individuals.[29]

The renewed struggle for communism finds its moral justification in the search for a real solution to injustices and inequalities, including colonization, racism and patriarchy which are continuously produced by capitalism. Thus, absolute equality and justice are necessarily communist touchstones.

Similarly, the struggle against capitalist exploitation, which is the driving force behind the injustice of inequality, is a radical communist tenet. However, communism, in the last hundred years has not embraced the cause of freedom and it must. By and large, we, communists, have surrendered the torch to liberal currents that have constrained and crippled the concept of freedom to mere commercial freedom, private enrichment or the oppression of some by others; nevertheless, there is an absolute freedom expressed as equality which Marx calls *social freedom*, where the free development of each individual has to contribute to the social freedom of the rest, where the potentials of every human being serve to empower free association with the rest of humanity.

Free development of individuality is neither situated in nor safeguarded by the State, corporations or market; it is the mutual free association of individuals that enables the free development of their individual potential. Under these conditions of free association of individuals, the cumulative civil and political liberties developed since the eighteenth century represent no more than a small chapter of infinite freedoms and potentials required for communism to be actualized. In fact, communism or

[29] Marx, 'Outlines of the Critique of Political Economy (Rough Draft of 1857–58) [Second Instalment]', p. 210.

communisms—one must speak in the plural—are unthinkable without this array of inherited civil liberties and more recent associative liberties both of which form the legacy of common action. Labour and political freedom of association, freedom of expression, freedom of communication, free will in one's life choices, in family life, are only a prelude to other more important freedoms to be achieved in the future; for example, the freedom over one's body, denied to women today, or the freedom over production in one's work place, denied to workers today, or the freedom to manage our own common resources, which today is denied to citizens in every country in the world.

This is not an innocent statement. It's not a creative play on words; it has implications for Leftist tradition and I mention two of them: the first one is that the different forms for social democratization, starting with associationism, parliamentarism, direct democracy, communal democracy, intercultural democracy and any other type of direct and associated participation of peoples that have common issues, form part of a flexible concentric circle geared towards actively broadening individual-social participation in decision-making over all aspects of social life, whether it in politics, economics or production, or in terms of family life, control over one's body, etc. In this sense, communism could be understood as a radical democratizing process spreading into all aspects of life, starting with the production of wealth to guarantee real equality among people. In this way, as social freedom produces real equality among peoples, we can talk about the construction of communism.

The second implication is that there is not just one organizational means in the struggle towards communism. The party, unions, soviets, communes, networks, associations, autonomous collectives, social movements are all contingent and are local forms of a single movement towards a universal community. No organizational structure is more valid than another, and in practice, wherever collective actions by subaltern classes arise, these classes are always able to create and to innovate different forms of organization capable of channelling their social force.

Experience shows that social classes viewed as pure conglomerates that are defined by territory, quantified by demographics and characterized sociologically are found only in books and statistical data. Real social classes are hybrid, overlapping, motley and they only become defined and materialized through a process of struggle through elective affinities, cultural similarities and impelling discourse. It is through this contingent action that social boundaries are established, leadership is construed, more effective courses of action are tested, mobilizing calls for action are issued, mobilizing narrative discourses are tested, expectations as well as symbolic referents are constructed and alliances (long lasting or sporadic) are forged, thereby bringing about a multi-layered process of self-construction by mobilized, leading and hegemonic social classes. Because of this, efficient organizational forms are always an uncertainty that is resolved at the heart of the movement's development and it can never be an anticipated certainty previous to collective action. Previous organizational forms in the past, emanating from other circumstances of struggle, achieving other experiences (like unions, parties, etc.) can facilitate the rise of the movement, help reinforce it, propel the expansion and national articulation of these new associative democratizing modes that arise from the social movement. But these previous organizational forms can never impose themselves or serve as a substitute.

(d) **Rational Metabolism Between Humans and Nature**

> Freedom in this field can only consist in socialised man, the associated producers, rationally regulating their interchange with Nature, bringing it under their common control, instead of being ruled by it as by the blind forces of Nature.[30]

Capitalism's alienated labour process has been instrumental in the separation of man, of human activity from nature. While in previous societies, such as agrarian communities, nature and the forces of nature were treated as living subjects, as an organic part of individuals,[31] in capitalism, nature becomes an object, something lifeless and therefore something subjected to corporate profit.

[30] Karl Marx, 'Chapter XLVIII: The Trinity Formula', in: Karl Marx, *Capital, Volume III*, p. 807.

[31] Karl Marx, 'Formas que preceden a la producción capitalista. Acerca del proceso que precede a la formación de la relación de capital o a la acumulación originaria', in: Karl Marx, *Elementos fundamentales para la crítica de la economía política (Grundrisse) 1857–1858*, vol. 1 (Mexico: Siglo XXI, 1971), pp. 433–79.

The antinomy human being/nature is a contradiction belonging to capitalism itself. It allows for the utilization of nature as one more source from which to obtain private profit. Just like the worker, under capitalism, is one more thing to dominate and from whom to obtain unpaid labour, so is nature a thing from which to extract its vital energy for the accumulation of wealth. Science itself, as an understanding of nature's inner workings, is developed to immediately be curtailed so that the remaining knowledge can be manipulated to serve corporate profit. Even 'green capitalism' endorsed by many countries and companies is not the result of a remorseful and unhappy consciousness in view of the catastrophe caused by capitalist production itself; rather it is the refinement of corporative mechanisms of accumulation to have lucrative gains from the effects of environmental catastrophes and to impose a type of environmental surplus-value to Third World countries where forests and biological diversity exists. We are dealing with a structural blindness, impossible to remedy, which is taking humans and terrestrial life to an abysmal destruction of no return. And if this continues, it is certain that without fail, there will be capitalists competing to sell the last coffin even in humanity's last hour.

Only communism can free scientific production, the 'general intellect', the most refined form of universal-social production, from subjection to private profit in order to put them at the disposal of an amplified reproduction of biodiversity and to re-establish a mutually vital metabolic relationship between humans and nature. Just like the universal community of free individuals requires the free development of an individual's liberty, so does the community respectful between humans and nature, which allows the propagation of life in all its forms, including human life, needs to reconstruct its relationship as a living part of its own social body, now at a universal, not only at the local-communal scale.

To paraphrase the young Marx, the humanized respectful and sustainable relationship with nature can only be possible by naturalizing humanity.[32] And it is this junction that overcomes the catastrophic rift between man and nature, which is also a name for communism.

[32] Marx, *Economic and Philosophic Manuscripts of 1844*, 'This communism, as fully developed naturalism, equals humanism, and as fully developed humanism equals naturalism; it is the *genuine* resolution of the conflict between man and nature [...] Thus *society* is the complete unity of man with nature –the true resurrection of nature – the accomplished naturalism of man and the accomplished humanism of nature', pp. 296, 298.

Finally, and definitely, communism is a contingency for a different future from capitalism, a future that grows as the collective will towards communism finds support in the growing material possibilities created by this desired communism.

References

Austin, John (1962), *How to Do Things with Words*, Cambridge: Harvard University Press.

Badiou, Alain (2009), *Circonstances 5: L'hypothèse communiste*, París: Nouvelles Éditions Lignes.

Bosteels, Bruno (2011), *The Actuality of Communism*, London: Verso.

García Linera, Álvaro (2018), *¿Qué es una revolución?*, La Paz: Vicepresidencia del Estado Plurinacional de Bolivia.

Gramsci, Antonio (1986), *Cuadernos de la cárcel*, vol. 4, Mexico: Ediciones Era.

Marx, Karl (1971), *Elementos fundamentales para la crítica de la economía política (Grundrisse) 1857–1858*, vol. 1, Mexico: Siglo XXI.

———. (1971), 'Formas que preceden a la producción capitalista. Acerca del proceso que precede a la formación de la relación de capital o a la acumulación originaria', in: Karl Marx, *Elementos fundamentales para la crítica de la economía política (Grundrisse) 1857–1858*, vol. 1, Mexico: Siglo XXI, pp. 433–79.

———. (1975), *Economic and Philosophic Manuscripts of 1844*, MECW, vol. 3, pp. 229–348.

———. (1975), 'Estranged Labour', in: Karl Marx, *Economic and Philosophic Manuscripts of 1844*, MECW, vol. 3, pp. 270–82.

———. (1981), *El capital, Tomo III*, vol. 6, Mexico: Siglo XXI.

———. (1981), *El capital, Tomo III*, vol. 7, Mexico: Siglo XXI.

———. (1983), *Elementos fundamentales para la crítica de la economía política (Grundrisse) 1857–1858*, vol. 2, Mexico: Siglo XXI.

———. (1985), 'Instructions for the Delegates of the Provisional General Council: The Different Questions', MECW, vol. 20, pp. 185–94.

———. (1986), *Civil War in France*, MECW, vol. 22, pp. 307–59.

———. (1986), 'Outlines of the Critique of Political Economy (Rough Draft of 1857–58) [First Instalment]', MECW, vol. 28, pp. 49–540.

———. (1986), 'Outlines of the Critique of Political Economy (Rough Draft of 1857–58) [Second Instalment]', MECW, vol. 29, pp. 5–417.

———. (1988), 'The Nationalisation of the Land', MECW, vol. 23, pp. 131–6.

———. (1988), 'The Production Process of Capital', in: Karl Marx, *Economic Manuscript of 1861–63*, MECW, vol. 30, pp. 9–171.

———. (1989), *Critique of the Gotha Programme*, MECW, vol. 24, pp. 75–99.

———. (1994), *Economic Manuscript of 1861–63*, MECW, vol. 34.

———. (1996), *Capital, Volume I*, MECW, vol. 35.

———. (1996), 'Chapter I: Commodities', in: Karl Marx, *Capital, Volume I*, MECW, vol. 35, pp. 45–94.

———. (1996), 'Chapter XV: Machinery and Modern Industry', in: *Capital, Volume I*, MECW, vol. 35, pp. 374–508.

———. (1996), 'Section 4: The Fetishism of Commodities and the Secret Thereof', in: Karl Marx, *Capital, Volume I*, MECW, vol. 35, pp. 81–94.

———. (1998), *Capital, Volume III*, MECW, vol. 37.

———. (1998), 'Chapter XLVIII: The Trinity Formula', in: Karl Marx, *Capital, Volume III*, MECW, vol. 37, pp. 801–17.

———. (2018), 'El proceso de producción del capital', in: Karl Marx, *Comunidad, nacionalismos y capital: Textos inéditos*, La Paz: Vicepresidencia del Estado Plurinacional de Bolivia, pp. 243–353.

Marx, Karl, and Engels, Friedrich (1976), *The German Ideology*, MECW, vol. 5, pp. 19–539.

———. (1976), *Manifesto of the Communist Party*, MECW, vol. 6, pp. 477–517.

Musto, Marcello (ed.) (2014), *Workers Unite! The International 150 Years Later*, New York: Bloomsbury.

Searle, John (2010), *Making the Social World the Structure of Human Civilization*, Oxford: Oxford University Press.

Taek-Gwang Lee, Alex, and Žižek, Slavoj (eds.) (2018), *La idea de comunismo: The Seoul Conference (2013)*, Madrid: Akal.

Žižek, Slavoj (ed.) (2014), *La idea de comunismo: The New York Conference (2011)*, Madrid: Akal.

CHAPTER 13

Uniting Communism and Liberalism: An Unsolvable Task or a Most Urgent Necessity?

Michael Brie

13.1 The Great Socialist Transformation of the Twentieth Century That Never Was

For the first time in history, humanity finds itself confronted with the task of consciously, deliberately and very rapidly revolutionizing its metabolic process and social relationship with nature. The end of the Cold War in 1989 presented an opportunity to pursue this task, but this opportunity was wasted—Gorbachev's 'new thinking'[1] was not implemented, and the global ecological revolution proclaimed by the Club of Rome in 1991[2] failed to materialize. Decades on, the Earth Summit has remained almost without consequence. Instead, the window of opportunity of

[1] Mikhail S. Gorbachev, *Perestroika: New Thinking for Our Country and the World* (New York: Harper & Row, 1988).

[2] Alexander King and Bertrand Schneider, *The First Global Revolution: A Report to the Club of Rome* (New York: Pantheon Books, 1991).

M. Brie (✉)
Rosa Luxemburg Foundation, Berlin, Germany

M. Musto (ed.), *Rethinking Alternatives with Marx*, Marx, Engels, and Marxisms, https://doi.org/10.1007/978-3-030-81764-0_13

1989 was exploited to globalize neoliberal financialized capitalism and construct a permanent unilateral US hegemony. The result of this is evident: a pincer crisis (Zangenkrise) of the accelerated capitalist privatization of the world on the one side, and of the exceedance of ecological planetary boundaries on the other.[3] The pressure from both sides has subjected societies to an ever-greater amount of stress that finds expression in populist, authoritarian and even fascist tendencies.[4] The instability of both the international order and of national orders is increasing exponentially. Never before has it been so urgent to gain social control over the dynamics inherent in complex societies, and to reorient these dynamics without oppressing or eradicating the freedom of individual and collective actors in economy, politics and culture. This is why socialism yet again finds itself on the world-historical agenda.

As far back as the end of the First World War, attempts have been made to escape from capitalism—that is, from the economic and social order dominated by capital accumulation—through a socialisttransformation. The first strand of such attempts consisted of the great experiment of communist reformation controlled by one party, as undertaken first in the Soviet Union and then in the People's Republic of China, Cuba and other states; of the kibbutz movement in Palestine and Israel; by Nyerere's African socialism and by other socialist projects. Aiming to collaboratively organize both production and life, be it on a centralized or local basis, these attempts subjected complex modern societies to an immediate communist reorganization. However, as the German sociologist Ferdinand Tönnies had already predicted in the concluding chapter of his 1887 work *Community and Civil Society*, 'all attempts to impose centralized control on business and on labour itself through the mechanism of the state [...], if they were to succeed, would put an end to the whole of competitive market society and its civilisation'.[5] The communist experiments experienced early successes buoyed by enthusiasm, state

[3] Anders Wijkman and Johan Rockström, *Bankrupting Nature: Denying Our Planetary Boundaries* (New York: Routledge, 2012).

[4] On the concept of the pincer crisis (*Zangenkrise*), see: Klaus Dörre, 'Risiko Kapitalismus. Landnahme, Zangenkrise, Nachhaltigkeitsrevolution', in: Klaus Dörre, Hartmut Rosa, Karina Becker, Sophie Bose, and Benjamin Seyd (eds.), *Große Transformation? Zur Zukunft moderner Gesellschaften* (Wiesbaden: Springer VS, 2019), pp. 3–34.

[5] Ferdinand Tönnies, *Community and Civil Society* (Cambridge: Cambridge University Press, 2001), p. 290.

mobilization and resource extraction, yet they eventually stagnated and failed to withstand the market capitalist societies of the West.[6] They were either abandoned or radically reformed, as was the case in China.

The second strand of post First World War attempts to overcome capitalism and build a socialist society was formed within the framework of Social Democratic projects. In addition to democratizing politics and expanding and universalizing social rights, some Social Democrats sought to go a step further and bring the economy under the control of society and the wage-dependent majority. From the 1920s to the 1970s, Sweden was the most prominent example of this strategy, which was based on the concept of a *functional socialism.*[7] According to this concept, particular instances of private property should be socialized while others remain private:

> The key to the new strategy was the use of public power, founded in organizational resources and exercised through the government, to encroach upon the power of capital. Through economic policies the *business* cycles would be *evened out*. The level of employment, of crucial importance for the welfare of the working class, would be kept high through political means, and thereby partly withdrawn from the control of capital.[8]

Erik Olin Wright further developed this concept of a functional socialism founded upon the control of civil society over economic resources as both opposed to capitalism, in which the owners of private equity control economic resources, and to statism, in which the state holds this power in its hands.[9]

[6] Michael Brie, 'Der Sowjetische Staatsparteisozialismus im Lichte der Marxschen Theorie "Progressiver Epochen der ökonomischen Gesellschaftsformation"', in: Rosa-Luxemburg-Stiftung Sachen (ed.), *Aufstieg und Fall des osteuropäischen Staatssozialismus: Ursachen und Wirkungen* (Leipzig: Rosa-Luxemburg-Stiftung Sachsen, 2004), pp. 197–233.

[7] Erik Gurgsdies, 'Schweden: Zivilgesellschaft im universalistischen Sozialstaat', in: Thomas Meyer (ed.), *Praxis der Sozialen Demokratie* (Wiesbaden: VS Verlag für Sozialwissenschaften, 2006), pp. 47–129.

[8] Quoted in Hans-Michael Trautwein, *Arbeitnehmerfonds in Schweden – Der Dritte Weg? Entwicklung und Kritik eines aktuellen Modells zur Demokratisierung der Wirtschaft* (Frankfurt am Main: Lang, 1986), p. 44.

[9] Erik Olin Wright, *Envisioning Real Utopias* (London: Verso, 2010), pp. 110–49.

The success of this Social Democratic strategy in Sweden until the late 1960s resulted in a series of unintended consequences that undermined its very preconditions. First, it led to the fracturing of the workforce. Higher-ranking employees in the public sector such as those in higher wage groups no longer wanted to be bound to the course of relative income equalization that benefitted less qualified workers. This divided the electorate of Social Democracy, whose share of the vote fell below 50%. Meanwhile, outside of the electoral realm, wildcat strikes were becoming increasingly frequent. Second, politics became oriented around providing support for especially efficient companies, which themselves were becoming more oriented towards export markets and less dependent on domestic demand. Entry to the European Union also meant market deregulation, which increased the power of large corporations while weakening the agency of wage labourers and their trade unions. Economic development was concentrated in southern Sweden, with other regions becoming relatively pauperised as the cost of living in urban centres exploded. When the national budget was no longer able to make up for these imbalances, a regime of austerity was implemented under conditions of already high unemployment. As politically weakened employees were becoming more divided among themselves, they found themselves confronted by an increasingly cohesive and strengthened capital front eager to free itself from the shackles of the Swedish model.

It became clear that under capitalist conditions, in which private entrepreneurial actors make the essential investment decisions, the Swedish model of simultaneously strengthening Social Democracy and increasing the efficiency of a capitalist economy could not be maintained. The strategy of implementing a functional socialism resulted in dysfunctionality in the relationship between (capitalist-dominated) economy and Social Democratic politics. In this situation, the German émigré labour economist Rudolf Meidner proposed gradually transferring Sweden's most important capital assets into employee investment funds (called wage earner funds) as a strategy for overcoming the dominance of capital valourization. According to this plan, a specific portion of company profits would be used to purchase shares for employee investment funds, while a mixture of national, regional and company-specific arrangements would

pursue with regards to the expansion of worker participation in decision-making across various fields.[10] Yet neither the trade unions nor the Social Democratic Workers' Party of Sweden decisively backed this proposal. It was eventually stripped of its transformative potential and ultimately abandoned all together years later.[11]

The failure of party-Communist and Social Democratic projects of socialisttransformation in the twentieth century came about in the context of a neoliberal offensive that intensified the subjugation of economy and society to the imperative of capital valourization while promising new freedoms beyond class, race, gender and state paternalism.[12] Unfettered capitalism was conflated with freedom. The multifaceted crisis of globalized capitalism that emerged from neoliberalism[13] has both shown the limits of this neoliberal offensive and yielded the reversal of this promise, giving way to open racism, neo-patriarchism, new wars, growing inequality, numerous failed states and the degeneration of liberal democracy under pressure from the crises and from accelerating ecological destruction.[14]

The pincer crisis caused by neoliberal capitalism poses the question of whether socialisttransformation will again be on the agenda in the twenty-first century, or whether the field of alternatives will be entirely abandoned to nationalist and proto-fascist projects. On the one hand, the twentieth century showed that a perpetual and systematic elimination of liberal economic, political and social rights will ultimately strangle collective freedoms and lead to stagnation and regression, which in turn give way to major crises. On the other, it also made clear that the tremendous forces unleashed by liberal-capitalist modernity led to extraordinarily

[10] Erik Åsard, 'Employee Participation in Sweden 1971–1979: The Issue of Economic Democracy', *Economic and Industrial Democracy: An International Journal*, vol. 1 (1980), n. 3: 371–93.

[11] Stefan Sjöberg, 'Kollektive Vermögensbildung in Arbeitnehmerhand', *Utopie Kreativ*, vol. 2006, n. 186: 311–22.

[12] Luc Boltanski and Eve Chiapello, *The New Spirit of Capitalism* (London: Verso, 2005).

[13] Mario Candeias, 'Interregnum. Molekulare Verdichtung Und Organische Krise', in: Alex Demirović, et al. (eds.), *Vielfachkrise. Im finanzmarktdominierten Kapitalismus* (Hamburg: VSA, 2011), pp. 45–61.

[14] Nancy Fraser, 'Feminism, Capitalism, and the Cunning of History', in: Nancy Fraser, *Fortunes of Feminism: From State-Managed Capitalism to Neoliberal Crisis* (London: Verso, 2013), pp. 209–26.

dangerous crises absent the social control and protection of the most important common goods (education, healthcare, security, law, finance, transportation, ecosystems, etc.). These goods are the communist basis of complex societies.[15] New attempts to overcome capitalism through a socialisttransformation must take both experiences seriously—that of the indispensability of both liberal and communist institutions for the development of modern societies.

In 1918, Soviet Russia's apparent transition to an open dictatorship with the oppression of elementary freedoms by leadership of the Bolsheviks prompted Rosa Luxemburg to engage with the problem of the relationship between liberalism and communism. As she formulated against the backdrop of the experiences of the day,

> We have always distinguished the social kernel from the political form of *bourgeois* democracy; we have always revealed the hard kernel of social inequality and lack of freedom hidden under the sweet shell of formal equality and freedom – not in order to reject the latter but to spur the working class into not being satisfied with the shell, but rather, by conquering political power, to create a socialist democracy to replace bourgeois democracy – not to eliminate democracy altogether.[16]

In the end, all socialist-oriented transformation strategies of the twentieth century failed because of their inability to do justice to the double demand of preserving the liberal heritage and implementing solidary, communist objectives.

The pincer crisis of unfettered neoliberal capital valorization and ecological destruction has both increased the probability of reaching irreversible tipping points in our relationship with nature and strengthened tendencies towards the fascist restructuring of liberal-democratic states. As leading representatives of Fridays for Future with the support of numerous scientists have written to global elites, 'We understand and know very well that the world is complicated and that what we are asking for may not be easy. The changes necessary to safeguard humanity may seem very unrealistic. But it is much more unrealistic to believe that our

[15] Michael Brie, *Wie der Sozialismus praktisch wurde. Robert Owen – Reformer, Visionär, Experimentator* (Berlin: Helle Panke, 2015), p. 25.

[16] Rosa Luxemburg, *The Russian Revolution*, in: Peter Hudis and Kevin B. Anderson (eds.), *The Rosa Luxemburg Reader* (New York: Monthly Review Press, 2004), p. 308.

society would be able to survive the global heating we're heading for, as well as other disastrous ecological consequences of today's business as usual'.[17] The interventions needed to halt or at least significantly blunt the approaching catastrophes are enormous. As the necessary transformation has been continuously delayed following 1989, these interventions must indeed now occur with 'wartime speed'[18] and at warlike dimensions. They will require decades-long expenditures of ten or even 15% of gross domestic product. Changes such as these will demand massive political action be taken in the economy, in society and in the mode of production and living in order to achieve transformative ends, ***and yet***, such action will only be possible if individual and collective civil rights and liberties are preserved. While the defence and expansion of the communist foundations of modern societies calls for a tremendous additional effort, and indeed must be placed at the heart of politics, it can only succeed by harnessing the powers of individuals, collectives, enterprises and organizations. Individual interest and initiative are essential conditions for a successful Great Transformation. The 'volonté Générale' and the 'volonté de tous'—that is, the unifying general insights and a planning and governance based upon them on the one hand, and the knowledge of the great diversity of actors with their own interests on the other—must complement each other.

13.2 Marx's Attempts at a Communist Solution of the Fundamental Contradiction of Complex Societies

It was the German philosopher Hegel who first attempted to unite individual freedomand the rational ordering of society as a whole within one system suited to the complexity of modern societies. In the introduction to his 1820 work *Outlines of the Philosophy of Right*, Hegel argued that in modern society, '*negative* freedom, or freedom as the understanding

[17] Luisa Neubauer, Greta Thunberg, Anuna de Wever van der Heyden, and Adélaïde Charlier, 'Open Letter and Demands to World Leaders', 16 July 2020, https://climateemergencyeu.org.

[18] Lester R. Brown, *PLAN B 3.0: Mobilizing to Save Civilization* (New York: W. W. Norton & Co., 2008), p. xi.

conceives it',[19] passes through alienated relations under the direction of 'alien authority'[20] into a higher freedom: 'The human being is *in himself* [or implicitly] rational, but he must also become so *for himself* [or explicitly] by working to create himself, not only by going outside himself but also by developing himself internally'.[21]

Here, the central normative claim of Hegelian philosophy becomes clear: by simultaneously appreciating bourgeois society and working through the contradictions of bourgeois social forms, Hegel sought to lay the foundations of a free society. He wanted to demonstrate that a society whose constitutive element was the private interests of the many and the purely external relationships of these interests to each other could maintain itself as a free, moral and rational whole. In the introduction to the *Outlines*, Hegel attempted to define how 'negative freedom' could lead to 'individuality [...] filled with its free universality',[22] or in other words, how '*the free* [...] *wills the free will*'.[23] According to his argument, the modern condition of the negative freedom of the individual enabled a rational universality to be realized: 'Morality, ethical life, the interest of the state'—'each one of them is a specific determination and existence of freedom',[24] and 'one is subordinated to the other'.[25] Ultimately, the state stands at the apex of social institutions: 'The right of the state [...] stands above the preceding stages; it is freedom in its most concrete shape and as such is subordinate to one thing alone—the supreme absolute truth of the world-spirit'.[26]

Hegel's task was to prove—at least in philosophy—that the state embodies 'freedom in its most concrete shape'. However, his claim that a (relative) unity of reason and reality existed in Prussia became increasingly suspect as a period of European restoration drew to a close with the French Revolutionof 1830 and the British Great Reform Act of 1832. In

[19] G. W. F. Hegel, *Outlines of the Philosophy of Right* (Oxford: Oxford University Press, 2008), p. 29.

[20] Ibid., p. 46.

[21] Ibid., p. 35.

[22] Ibid., p. 36.

[23] Ibid., p. 46.

[24] Ibid., p. 47.

[25] Ibid., p. 48.

[26] Ibid., p. 52.

Prussia, the situation came to a head with the royal succession of 1840. At that time, Karl Marx belonged to a group of German intellectuals who used Hegelian philosophy to criticize the reality of Prusso-Germany, and his position as editor-in-chief of the *Rheinische Zeitung* newspaper provided him with a platform for doing precisely this. This position also brought Marx into a relationship with communism. Already on his first day as editor-in-chief, he composed an article titled *Communism and the Augsburg Allgemeine Zeitung*. Speaking on behalf of the rest of the editors (except for Moses Hess, who already held firm communist views at the time), he wrote therein that 'The *Rheinische Zeitung*, which does not admit that communist ideas in their present form possess even *theoretical reality,* and therefore can still less desire their *practical realization,* or even consider it possible, will subject these ideas to thoroughgoing criticism'.[27] At the same time, Marx also warned of the idea of communism:

> We are firmly convinced that the real *danger* lies not in *practical attempts,* but in the *theoretical elaboration* of communist ideas, for practical attempts, even *mass attempts,* can be answered by *cannon* as soon as they become dangerous, whereas *ideas,* which have conquered our intellect and taken possession of our minds, ideas to which reason has fettered our conscience, are chains from which one cannot free oneself without a broken heart; they are demons which human beings can vanquish only by submitting to them.[28]

The backdrop of Marx's continued engagement with communism was formed by the practical experiences he gained during his work as editor-in-chief of the Rheinische Zeitung, which revealed the basic assumptions of Hegelian social philosophy to directly contradict the reality of both the Prussian state and of society based on private property more generally. Standing at the centre of *A Contribution to the Critique of Hegel's Philosophy of Law*, a critique of Hegel issued by Marx in 1843 after having left the *Rheinische Zeitung*, is nothing other than a position of Hegel's that Marx viewed as fundamental to the entirety of Hegelian social philosophy: namely, the 'identity (as an ought, a dual identity) of the system of particular interest (the family and civil society) with the system of general

[27] Karl Marx, 'Communism and the Augsburg Allgemeine Zeitung', MECW, vol. 1, p. 220.

[28] Ibid., pp. 220–1.

interest (the state)'.[29] With regards to this position, Marx made three methodological decisions. The first of these came about in an article published in the *Rheinische Zeitung* in December 1842. Taking bourgeois society as essentially consisting of the relations between the owners of private property, Marx wrote in this article with the utmost clarity and poignancy that 'the particular in its isolated activity is always the enemy'.[30] This is a radical rejection of liberalism, for which the well-being of all ultimately depends above all on the autonomous decisions of private individuals. The second methodological decision occurred at the very beginning of Marx's *A Contribution to the Critique of Hegel's Philosophy of Law* in the observation that 'the state issues from the multitude in their existence as members of families and as members of civil society', a 'fact' of which Marx would be convinced henceforth.[31] This assumption allowed him to derive the state from the socio-economic interests of the actors of bourgeois society.[32] Marx's third methodological decision, the groundwork for which had been laid by his *Rheinische Zeitung* articles and Ludwig Feuerbach's materialist turn, was also introduced in *A Contribution to the Critique of Hegel's Philosophy of Law*. It was the decision to no longer identify the driving forces of society within ideas, but rather within real-life individuals who had been shaped by actual social relations. However, if the liberal relations of bourgeois society stood *opposed* to the rational whole when they determined the state and minted society's dynamic by shaping real individuals, then the Hegelian system could no longer be maintained. For this reason, Marx's three methodological decisions are inseparably bound with the search for a new normative vision, with a radically transformed horizon of emancipation for a free society as elaborated against Hegel.

Marx took Hegel's aspiration radically seriously. Hegel as well was concerned with 'the prodigious unification of self-subsistent individuality

[29] Karl Marx, *Contribution to the Critique of Hegel's Philosophy of Law*, MECW, vol. 3, p. 5.

[30] Karl Marx, 'The Supplement to Nos. 335 and 336 of the Augsburg Allgemeine Zeitung on the Commissions of the Estates in Prussia', MECW, vol. 1, p. 305.

[31] Marx, *Contribution to the Critique of Hegel's Philosophy of Law*, p. 9.

[32] Karl Marx, *A Contribution to the Critique of Political Economy. Preface*, MECW, vol. 29, p. 263.

with universal substantiality'.[33] In this regard, Marx remained committed to the legacy of Rousseau and Hegel until the end of his life. However, his experiences from 1841 to 1843, especially as the editor of the Rheinische Zeitung, led him to break with the Hegelian solution to this problem and with Hegel's idealization of bureaucracy as a general power. For Marx, bureaucracy was merely an expression of the impossibility of unifying the particular and the general on the basis of private property and bourgeois relations, which he now saw as the formative forces of modern societies. As he wrote, 'The abolition of the bureaucracy is only possible by the general interest *actually*—and not, as with Hegel, merely in thought, in *abstraction*—becoming the particular interest, which in turn is only possible as a result of the *particular* actually becoming the *general* interest'.[34] With this, Marx had named *the central problem* he believed needed to be solved if society were to be ordered in accordance with reason: namely, the problem of *how the particular interest can become general in a way so that the general interest can at the same time actually become the particular interest*. It was his attempt to answer this question that led him to opt for communism.

At this point, Marx took up the separation of bourgeois society and state, which he had recognized as a constitutive principle of Hegel's philosophy of state and law, and intensified his critique of it. This entailed comprehensive studies of the history of the French Revolution, of the constitutional debate in the United States, of the history of a series of European states (England, Poland, Sweden) as well as a re-reading of Rousseau's *Social Contract* and of Montesquieu and Machiavelli. In *On the Jewish Question*, Marx identified a hard antinomy between 'the perfect political state' and 'material life': whereas the former, a state in which political emancipation is achieved, represents 'its *universality* only in opposition to [the] elements of its being',[35] the latter amounts to an egoistic life. In the political sphere, the human being is a '*communal being*', whereas in 'life in *civil society*, […] he acts as a *private individual*, regards other men as a means, degrades himself into a means, and becomes the plaything of alien powers'.[36] For Marx, bourgeois society

[33] Hegel, *Outlines of the Philosophy of Right*, p. 70.

[34] Marx, *Contribution to the Critique of Hegel's Philosophy of Law*, p. 48.

[35] Karl Marx, 'On the Jewish Question', MECW, vol. 3, p. 153.

[36] Ibid., p. 154.

was the 'sphere of egoism, of *bellum omnium contra omnes*', an 'expression of man's *separation* from his *community*, from himself and from other men'.[37] In view of this, he adopted the Hegelian terminology of truth and essence, of existence and reality. Claiming that the human being was divided into 'a *public man* and a *private man*',[38] into '*bourgeois*' and 'citoyen',[39] Marx saw the untrue reality of the relationships between egoistic private individuals at war with each other as contrasting with the true unreality of the political community, the abstract world of individuals opposed to each other as contrasting with the equally abstract world of the communal-general. 'None of the so-called rights of man, therefore, go beyond egoistic man, beyond man as a member of civil society, that is, an individual withdrawn into himself, into the confines of his private interests and private caprice, and separated from the community',[40] he argued, before adding that 'the *citoyen* is declared to be the servant of egoistic *homme*'.[41] This line of argumentation from 'On the Jewish Question' can be summed up as follows: ***human emancipation must align the reality of the vital activities of individuals with their truth as social beings.***

In order to grasp this immediate unity of the vital activities of individuals with their social essence as an historical possibility, Marx invoked Rousseau's *Social Contract* in a further step in *On the Jewish Question*. In this text from 1762, Rousseau had highlighted the difficulty of finding 'a form of association which will defend and protect, with the whole of its joint strength, the person and property of each associate, and under which each of them, uniting himself to all, will obey himself alone, and remain as free as before'. According to him, this constituted 'the fundamental problem to which the social contract gives the answer'.[42] Elaborating on this solution, Rousseau wrote as follows:

> Whoever dares undertake to establish a people's institutions must feel himself capable of changing, as it were, human *nature*, of transforming

[37] Ibid., p. 155.

[38] Ibid.

[39] Ibid., p. 154.

[40] Ibid., p. 164.

[41] Ibid.

[42] Jean-Jacques Rousseau, 'The Social Contract', in: Jean-Jacques Rousseau, *Discourse on Political Economy and The Social Contract* (Oxford: Oxford University Press, 1994), pp. 55–6.

> each individual, who by himself is a complete and solitary whole, into a *part* of a larger whole, from which, in a sense, the individual receives his life and his being, of substituting a *limited* and *mental existence* for the physical and independent existence. He has to take from *man his own powers*, and give him in exchange alien powers which he cannot employ without the help of other men.[43]

After citing this passage in *On the Jewish Question*, Marx then commented on it with the famous claim that 'All emancipation is a *reduction* of the human world and relationships to *man himself*'.[44]

However, by reduction to the human being, Marx did not mean reduction 'to an *egoistic, independent* individual' or 'to a *citizen*, a juridical person',[45] but to the human being as an immediately social being. According to the Marxian understanding, emancipation is a mandate to shape society, a mandate that can only be realized through an all-encompassing process of transformation. The reversal of alienation was conceived of by Marx as a dual process of transforming individuals' modes of labour and activity as well as the social organization of the power of individuals:

> Only when the real, individual man re-absorbs in himself the abstract citizen, and as an individual human being has become a *species-being* in his everyday life, in his particular work, and in his particular situation, only when man has recognised and organized his "*forces propres*" as *social* forces, and consequently no longer separates social power from himself in the shape of *political* power, only then will human emancipation have been accomplished.[46]

These sentences conclude the main part of Marx's article *On the Jewish Question.*

Marx's solution to the 'fundamental problem' posed by Rousseau drew on the socialists of the early nineteenth century. Together with Charles Fourier and many other French socialists, Marx insisted that the labour of individuals and their individual relationships formed the immediate basis

[43] Marx, 'On the Jewish Question', pp. 167–8.

[44] Ibid., p. 168.

[45] Ibid.

[46] Ibid.

for the development of their species-power and for the modes of creative self-realization that directly contributed to the universal development of all. Labour should no longer be mechanical and abstract; the human being should no longer be forced to lead a partial existence. A revolution of the entire mode of production and living, of how people lived, worked and communicated, of intercourse and enjoyment, had already been envisioned by the early French socialists, whom Marx had studied at the time. At the same time, Marx also drew on contemporary communist positions: his demand for the social organization of social forces was the demand for the transfer of the means of production to social ownership and for the common social administration of labour, production and collective life. In this way, the activity of individuals was to become immediately social. The goal of this socialist-communist solution of the problem of complex societies was to achieve 'the prodigious unification of self-subsistent individuality with universal substantiality' demanded by Hegel. It can also be said that Marx wanted to establish an *emancipatory solution of the fundamental problem of complex modern societies—the problem of the relationship between individual and social development—upon a socialist-communist foundation*. This foundation was supposed to make possible the unmediated, contradiction-free identity of the human being as an individual and as a social being, an identity between the reality of individuals' vital activity and their truth as social beings. Marx's decision for socialism and communism in 'On the Jewish Question' was a *philosophically* justified decision.[47]

Over the forty years of his life that followed *On the Jewish Question*, Marx stuck to his decision for socialism-communism while further developing and refining it in collaboration with Friedrich Engels. Ultimately, he left behind a clear vision: that of a social revolution giving way to a dictatorship of the proletariat that would establish common ownership of the means of production, consequently employing the power of the state to transform the entirety of the mode of production and living until having created the conditions under which the free development of individuals and the solidary development of all are immediately interdependent. In this vision, the immediate sociality of individuals' vital activity and their free self-realization come together upon the foundation

[47] Michael Löwy, *The Theory of Revolution in the Young Marx* (Chicago: Haymarket Books, 2005), p. 53.

of communism. Meanwhile, the contradiction between social and individual interests and the necessity of markets, law and the state die out upon this same foundation.

From 1844 on, communism meant to Marx a society founded upon the common ownership of the entirety of the means of production. The producers of this society's wealth and relations would act according to a predetermined plan, and individuals within this society would only be able to become proprietors on the basis of social ownership.[48] By revolutionizing the mode of production, social ownership would become individual property in the sense that it would enable society's wealth to be freely appropriated by individuals for the sake of their own solidary self-realization. Labour would come to mean the free development of individuals and to be viewed as the primary necessity of life.[49]

With the publication of the first volume of *Capital* in 1867, Marx articulated this understanding of communism when describing a society whose wealth would be produced by free individuals'carrying on their work with means of production in common, in which the labour-power of all the different individuals is consciously applied as the combined labour-power of the community'.[50] In this society, the labour of each and every individual would become immediately social, while labour would become manifest as the immediate self-realization of individuals. Here, society is

[48] Invoking the perspective of a communist society in Karl Marx, *Capital, Volume I*, MECW, vol. 35. Marx wrote: 'The capitalist production begets, with the inexorability of a law of Nature, its own negation. It is the negation of negation. This does not re-establish private property for the producer, but gives him individual property based on the acquisitions of the capitalist era: i.e., on co-operation and the possession in common of the land and of the means of production', ibid., p. 751.

[49] In the *German Ideology* this is summarized as follows: 'Within communist society, the only society in which the genuine and free development of individuals ceases to be a mere phrase, this development is determined precisely by the connection of individuals, a connection which consists partly in the economic prerequisites and partly in the necessary solidarity of the free development of all, and, finally, in the universal character of the activity of individuals on the basis of the existing productive forces', Karl Marx and Friedrich Engels, *The German Ideology*, MECW, vol. 5, p. 439.

[50] Marx, *Capital, Volume I*, p. 89.

understood as a communist monosubject consisting of individuals realizing themselves in a completely free manner.[51] In this model, interests of all and of each and every individual *immediately* coincide.

In their 1848 *Manifesto of the Communist Party*, Marx and Engels outlined the vision of 'an association, in which the free development of each is the condition for the free development of all'.[52] Marx later summarized conditions for the emergence of such an association in his 1875 text *Critique of the Gotha Programme*. Following the social revolution, a dictatorship of the proletariat would establish a 'collective society based on common ownership of the means of production',[53] initiating a long-term process of transformation. Marx described the goal of this process thusly: 'In a higher phase of communist society, after the enslaving subordination of the individual to the division of labour, and thereby also the antithesis between mental and physical labour, has vanished; after labour has become not only a means of life but life's prime want; after the productive forces have also increased with the all-round development of the individual, and all the springs of common wealth flow more y then can the narrow horizon of bourgeois right be crossed in its entirety and society inscribe on its banners: From each according to his abilities, to each according to his needs!'.[54]

Faced with the fundamental contradiction of complex societies, namely, the contradiction between the freedom of individuals and the sociality of their conditions of life, Marx seemed to come up with an elegant solution. Yet as elegant as this solution may appear, so too does it resemble Alexander the Great's 'solution' to the Gordian knot by simply eliminating the problem. In a first step, a demand is issued for the *complete* subordination of individuals to the socially determined plan, which in a second step is said to lead to the *highest* freedom by turning labour

[51] On the relationship between Marx's work on *Capital* and his understanding of communism, see W. S. Wygodski, *Das Werden der ökonomischen Theorie von Marx und der wissenschaftliche Kommunismus* (Berlin: Karl Dietz, 1978).

[52] Karl Marx and Friedrich Engels, *Manifesto of the Communist Party*, MECW, vol. 6, p. 506.

[53] Karl Marx, *Critique of the Gotha Programme*, MECW, vol. 24, p. 85.

[54] Ibid., p. 87.

into 'the all-round development of the individual'. Yet as labour becomes both more individual and collective, and as the development of both individuals and of the collective becomes more creative, so too do the differences grow between the knowledge, skills and interests of individuals, of the collective and of society as a whole. Although one can remove the exploitative, antagonistic character of these differences, organizing relations on the basis of solidarity, these differences will still constitute a contradiction. Contrary to Marx's assumption in the first volume of *Capital*, under no circumstances are the relations of a complex society 'perfectly simple and intelligible'.[55] He was wrong to assume that they would be so in a society of associated labour: 'All the characteristics of Robinson's labour are here repeated, but with this difference, that they are social, instead of individual'.[56] If the Marxian solution failed with the party-Communist projects of the twentieth century, then the question remains as to whether there is another way in which individual freedomand social control might be socialistically unified as a complex society develops so that human civilisation might be able to escape from the pincer crisis of unfettered capitalism and ecological destruction.

13.3 The Strengths and Limits of Capitalism

Orthodox conceptions of capitalism, such as prevailed in the Second International at the end of the nineteenth century, were characterized by a central assumption which August Bebel expressed in *Woman and Socialism* in this way:

> All social evils, without exception, spring from the present social order, which, as has been shown, is founded on capitalism, on the capitalistic method of production. This method of production enables the capitalist class the owners of all the means of production, the ground, mines, raw materials, tools, machines, means of transportation to exploit and oppress the masses, which leads to insecurity of existence and to the degradation of the exploited classes.[57]

[55] Marx, *Capital, Volume I*, p. 90.

[56] Ibid., p. 89.

[57] August Bebel, *Woman and Socialism* (New York: Socialist Literature Co., 1910), p. 366.

The conclusion that was drawn from this was unambiguous:

> Accordingly, the shortest and quickest step would be to transform this capitalist property into social property (cooperative property) through a general expropriation. Commodity production would be transformed into socialist production, that is production carried out for and by society. The large firms and the continuously growing production capacity of social labour, until now a source of misery and oppression for the exploited classes, will become a source of the greatest welfare and harmonious education of all.[58]

This orthodox-Marxist understanding of socialism cannot explain why the ability of the capitalist mode of production to 'constantly revolutioniz[e] the instruments of production, and thereby the regulations of production, and with them the whole relations of society'[59] did not persist under the conditions of state-social ownership in the Soviet Union, and why the Soviet Union never managed to intensively expand the capacity of its economy, even though its leaders viewed this as a matter of life and death at latest from the 1960s onward. An understanding of capitalism that sees its essence in the capitalist ownership of the means of production misses what is specifically 'capitalist' about this kind of property, and does not permit the question of how a postcapitalist social order would look that would not regress behind capitalism's developmental capacity. In the words of Wolfgang Fritz Haug,

> Today an epoch-making emptiness yawns where there used to be a historically fundamental faith [in socialism and its productive potential]. It forms the negative core of the post-communist situation. An anti-capitalism that does not go beyond the "anti" in respect to capitalism to arrive at a "pro", a "pro" that attempts to liberate that kind of productivity from the competitive logic of profit and in so doing from its destructiveness, cannot dispute capitalism's right to exist.[60]

[58] Ibid., pp. 366–7.

[59] Marx and Engels, *Manifesto of the Communist Party*, p. 487.

[60] Wolfgang Fritz Haug, 'Zur Dialektik des Antikapitalismus', *Das Argument*, vol. 269 (2007): 20.

The productivity of the capitalist mode of production is inseparably bound with what Marx referred to in the first volume of *Capital: A Critique of Political Economy* as the general formula of capital: M-C-M′—the transformation of money (M) into more money (M′) by way of commodity exchange (C). The claim to property rights embodied in money is given on credit in the expectation of getting back a higher claim (money with interest: surplus value) in the future.[61] Capitalist economy is a credit economy. It aims at the 'self-valorisation of value'. Capitalist property is a relation of permanent and dynamic self-renewal. The precondition of this formula is that the labour forceand the means of production are transformed into commodities and used as such. The universalization of the commodity-form of society's wealth characterizes the capitalist social order. The general formula of capital can only become the defining form of a particular historical-social formation if it subjects production to itself and uses commodities as a means of its own valorisation. In his article 'Capitalism', Michael R. Krätke summarizes this as follows: 'the most accurate formula for modern capitalism would not be "production of commodities by means of commodities", but rather "production of commodities as the product of capital by means of commodities as the product of capital"'.[62] The movement of self-valorisation of value is *tied to the future*. It is a matter of speculation or betting on a 'richer' future. Capitalism is therefore growth oriented. From the point of view of the development of the last century's gross social product, this bet on the future has paid off. Before 1750, the worldwide increase of per-capita gross domestic product was no more than 0.08% (less than one thousandth per year). This doubled in the next hundred years until 1850, quintupled in the period between 1850 and 1950 (0.88%), reached more than 2.2% between 1950 and 1990 and came out to between 2.5 and 3.25% in the last decade.

It is undisputed that the capitalist mode of production is what initially enabled a larger part of the global population to leave behind a life in poverty. However, the question stands as to why capitalism has so far been unable to complete this process. What follows will demonstrate that this inability is caused by capitalism itself: although capitalism creates the most

[61] Marx, *Capital, Volume I*, pp. 157ff.

[62] Michael R. Krätke, 'Capitalism', in: Marcello Musto (ed.), *The Marx Revival: Key Concepts and New Interpretations* (Cambridge: Cambridge University Press, 2020), p. 7.

important technological, institutional and cultural *conditions* for the free and solidary development of all, it transforms these conditions into the means of subordinating all to the constraints of its own valorisation and to the antagonistic accumulation of power by a small, oligarchic minority. Capitalism is a realm of material necessity based on the abundance of extremely unequally disturbed material wealth. In themselves, the conditions for a realm of freedom have long existed, but they are systematically transformed into means of subjecting individuals to reified conditions. And given that capitalism is not in a position to solve this contradiction, but indeed is constituted by it, it keeps putting socialism on the agenda of history. Yet to be able to answer the question of *which* form of socialism would be able to solve the problem posed by capitalism while also potentially completing the transition into the realm of freedom, the strengths and systematic limits of capitalism must first be understood.

Capitalism only takes hold of the whole of society when capitalist enterprises can freely dispose of the necessary factors of production after these have been torn out of their embeddedness in traditional contexts. This applies in the same way to land, raw materials, instruments of production and above all to labour-power. Capitalism can only spread when the traditional connection between means of production and labour-power is broken (a process Marx referred to in *Capital* as the 'primitive accumulation of capital') and when these factors of production, transport, services, communication can be newly combined by the enterprises on their own risk and responsibility. The access to these factors is mediated via markets (capital markets, labour marketsand markets for means of production) on the basis of credit. Securing this process requires important elements of a liberal 'open access order'.[63] Only then will there be a constant recombination of production factors—a phenomenon both enabled by the credit system, the labour marketsand other production factors, and forced by competition between enterprises. In this sense, capitalism is marked by both destructive creation and by 'creative destruction'.[64]

Capitalism's creative possibility is realized when enterprises have to compete for credit, that is, when lenders can choose among competing offers. This then institutionalizes both the compulsion to grow (for

[63] Douglass C. North, John Joseph Wallis, and Barry R. Weingast, *Violence and Social Orders: A Conceptual Framework for Interpreting Recorded Human History* (Cambridge: Cambridge University Press, 2009), pp. 21–5.

[64] Joseph A. Schumpeter, *Capitalism, Socialism, and Democracy* (New York: Routledge, 2003), pp. 81–6.

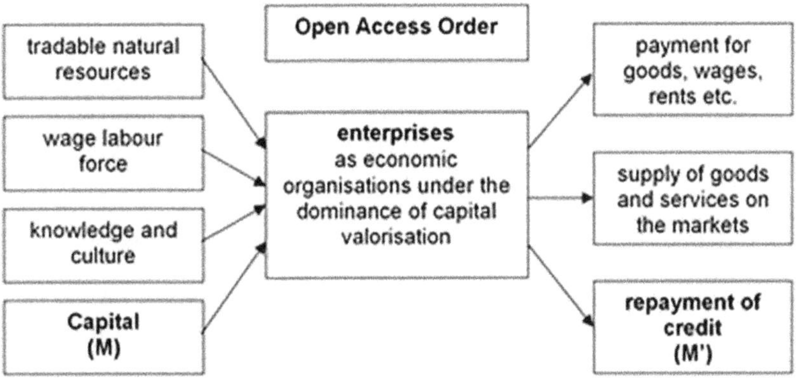

Fig. 13.1 The elementary form of the capitalist mode of production

the sake of their own survival, enterprises must produce surpluses) as well as the compulsion towards renewal (enterprises can generate higher yields especially through innovative combination of the factors of production). The capitalist mode of production is an economy dominated by the self-valorization of capital (see Fig. 13.1). It is organized as a capital valorisation economy.[65] Because of this, however, it is destructively creative. As Karl Polanyi made clear in *The Great Transformation*, the main cause of this destruction lies in the fact that the market-mediated combination of production factors is only possible when goods that are *not commodities* by nature assume the 'commodity-form':

> The crucial point is this: labor, land, and money are essential elements of industry; they also must be organized in markets; in fact, these markets form an absolutely vital part of the economic system. But labor, land, and money are obviously *not* commodities; the postulate that anything that is bought and sold must have been produced for sale is emphatically untrue in regard to them. In other words, according to the empirical definition of a commodity they are not commodities. Labor is only another name for a human activity which goes with life itself, which in its turn is not produced for sale but for entirely different reasons, nor can that activity be

[65] Rainer Land, *Ökokapital. Bedingungen der Möglichkeit eines neuen Regimes wirtschaftlicher Entwicklung. Ein systemtheoretischer Bauplan* (Düsseldorf: Forschungsinstitut für gesellschaftliche Weiterentwicklung, 2018), pp. 63–5.

> detached from the rest of life, be stored or mobilized; land is only another name for nature, which is not produced by man; actual money, finally, is merely a token of purchasing power which, as a rule, is not produced at all, but comes into being through the mechanism of banking or state finance. None of them is produced for sale. The commodity description of labor, land, and money is entirely fictitious.[66]

As culture and knowledge are used by capitalist enterprises, they must be transformed into fictitious commodities as well.

The four factors of production identified above in Fig. 13.1—natural resources, labour-power, capital, and knowledge—are produced and reproduced in spheres that are an immediate component of capital accumulation only to a limited extent. This is doubtless true of the earth's ecosystem and of what is also referred to as the gaiasphere—the thin layer of atmosphere over the surface of the earth and water, this surface itself and the seas and upper layers of rock. Yet it is also true of the lifeworlds of families, neighbourhoods and labour collectives as well as of the entire system of social institutions, of which the financial system is an inseparable part—the system that makes lending possible, establishes legal certainty and creates institutional confidence. It also applies to the sphere of the public-cultural. The capital valorization economy is embedded in these four spheres, from which it draws its resources and to which it returns its products. The dominance of capital accumulation over the total dynamic of the reproduction of all four spheres results from the particular role that the capital valorisation economy occupies in societies shaped by capitalism.[67] If this dominance were to take full effect, the gaiasphere would be transformed into a mere source of raw materials and site of waste disposal, the lifeworld would be nothing more than wage labour and consumption, a capitalist oligarchy would dominate the sphere of social institutions and culture would be reduced to valorisable knowledge and the entertainment industry (Fig. 13.2). As Marx wrote in the first volume of *Capital: A Critique of Political Economy*, 'Capitalist production [...] only develops the techniques and the degree of combination of the social

[66] Karl Polanyi, *The Great Transformation: The Political and Economic Origins of Our Time* (Boston: Beacon Press, 2001), pp. 75–6.

[67] See in detail: ibid., pp. 157–79.

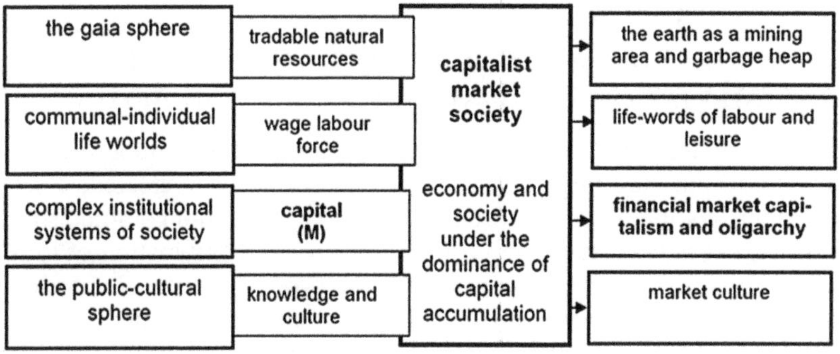

Fig. 13.2 The market society

process of production by simultaneously undermining the original sources of all wealth – the soil and the worker'.[68]

Proceeding from these limits, one can also draw the following conclusion: the capitalist mode of production strives to universalise itself yet can never fully do so.[69] It can only exist as a particular mode of the economy alongside others, or it destroys society. At the moment in which the economy of a society is completely penetrated by capitalism and this economy determines society, precisely the phenomena arise that are always enumerated by the critics of capitalism. *It therefore makes sense to distinguish from capitalism itself the capitalist mode of economy as a particular sector of modern society. Capitalismis the dominance of the tendencies peculiar to the capitalist sector of economy over the whole economy and the subordination of the whole society to this economy.* This raises the question of how this dominance can be broken without destroying the developmental capacity and productive potential that characterize the capitalist mode of production. For one thing is doubtless true: whoever is not prepared to talk about the strengths of capitalism should also remain silent about its alternatives and about socialism.

[68] Marx, *Capital, Volume I*, p. 638.

[69] Rosa Luxemburg, *The Accumulation of Capital: A Contribution to the Economic Theory of Imperialism*, in: Peter Hudis (ed.), *The Complete Works of Rosa Luxemburg, Volume I: Economic Writings 2* (London: Verso, 2015), p. 341.

13.4 The Communist Foundations, the Liberal Elements and the Socialist Mediation Forms of Sustainable Societies

In order to accurately state the problem of socialism that abolishes capitalism without negating the developmental capacity it created, a fatal misunderstanding must first be cleared up: socialism is not communism,[70] it is not a society of common property, but of the combination of forms of common property and forms of separate property at the autonomous disposal of productive assets by individuals or collective economic actors. The analytical distinction in Ferdinand Tönnies's *Community and Civil Society* between communism as a system of communal relations and society as a (liberal) system of contract relations is an indelible part of modernity. Both elements *always* exist in actual relations, but they do respectively follow their own logic. Both are needed: the safeguarding of the common foundations of a good and rich life—of the gaiasphere, the communal-individual lifeworlds, the institutional systems of society, of science and culture—*and* the economic, political and cultural freedom of the person. Whereas communism as an ideological tendency of modernity has made one pole absolute, modern liberalism has done so to the other. When attempts are made to realize such utopian projects to subdue complex societies totally under one or the other principle, they bring complex societies to the edge of the abyss.

Firstly, modern societies have communist foundations, without whose preservation the sustainable reproduction of these societies cannot be ensured. These are the four aforementioned spheres from which the capital valorisation economy derives its factors of production. One could also refer to them as common pool resource systems.[71] They exist in the immediate lifeworld of families all the way up to the global community. It is the preservation, development and enrichment of these foundations that secures everything built upon them. Marx was entirely correct when he wrote in the third volume of *Capital: A Critique of Political Economy* that 'Even a whole society, a nation, or even all simultaneously existing societies taken together, are not the owners of the globe. They are only

[70] Peter Ruben, 'Die Kommunistische Antwort auf die soziale Frage', *Berliner Debatte Initial*, vol. 9 (1998), n. 1: 5–18.

[71] Elinor Ostrom, *Governing the Commons: The Evolution of Institutions for Collective Action* (Cambridge: Cambridge University Press, 1990), p. 30.

its possessors, its usufructuaries, and, like *boni patres familias*, they must hand it down to succeeding generations in an improved condition'.[72] These communist foundations are therefore not property to be disposed of arbitrarily, but rather belong in the trusteeship of organizations that should take on the task outlined by Marx of ensuring their preservation and enrichment,[73] representing the 'volonté Générale' and leading major transformations in the process. This is also the rational kernel of what Marx and Engels referred to as the dictatorship of the proletariat.

However, trusteeship over society's communist foundations must not give way to the immediate common control of all means of production and labour, which would destroy the particular developmental capacity of modern societies and their potential for constant renewal. The relative individual and collective self-determination of actors over the conditions of their economic, political and cultural activity, the 'volonté de tous', is a second basic characteristic of modern societies. Complex societies require many different forms of ownership and political representation. They should not suppress the free development of individuals or of their collective forms of organization, but rather enhance the consciously solidary shaping of this development to transform it into the 'free development of all'. In neoliberal strategies, the freedom of the individual is made absolute, freedom identified with private property and state activity reduced to the enforcement of the institutional conditions of private property. All this is done in pursuit of the stark utopia of a market society. In *The Great Transformation*, Polanyi blamed 'utopian endeavour of economic liberalism to set up a self-regulating market system'[74] as directly responsible for the rise of fascism in the 1920s and 1930s. On the basis of his triple experience of capitalism, fascism and Soviet socialism, Ernst Bloch formulated the task of a socialist translation thusly:

> Happiness and dignity, the concerns emphasized on the one hand by social utopias and on the other by doctrines of natural law, for so long marched separately and sadly never stuck together with the priority of human care and support, and the *primat* of human dignity: It is more than ever necessary that along with the concrete heritage of social utopian thought, an

[72] Karl Marx, *Capital, Volume III*, MECW, vol. 37, p. 763.

[73] Peter Barnes, *Capitalism 3.0: A Guide to Reclaiming the Commons* (San Francisco: Berrett-Koehler, 2006), pp. 79–100.

[74] Polanyi, *The Great Transformation*, p. 31.

> equally concrete program of the *citoyen* be recognized. It is more necessary than ever before that even the differences in the intentional fields finally be recognized as functionally related and practically surmounted. This thanks to the certainty that there can be no human dignity without the end of misery and need, but also no human happiness without the end of old and new forms of servitude.[75]

There is a dangerous infantile ideological disorder endemic to socialism that repeats itself in almost every new movement and generation: the longing for a world beyond the contradictions of modernity. This longing identifies the overcoming of the capitalist, statist or fascist form of these contradictions with their elimination as such. It too is a false utopia that leads to catastrophes, be they small or great in scale, and stands in the way of a genuine socialisttransformation. One of the tasks of real, transformative movements is to not flee from the contradictions of complex societies, but rather to discover them, to face them and to reshape them with passion and vigour. Free communist sociality in the spirit of Karl Marx and communally responsible liberal freedomin the spirit of John Stuart Mill[76] form the major poles of opposition in modern societies, whose complexity stems from the mediation of these opposites. The latter can stand under the domination of capital valorisation, or of a statist or of fundamentalist project.

The normative point of reference for modern societies was formulated in the Great French Revolution: the unity of freedom and equality on the basis of a solidary mediation of society's contradictions. If the aforementioned four spheres form the social foundations of modernity, its earthly foundation that must be preserved, then equaliberty[77] in a solidary community forms modernity's sky. Socialism understood as the real movement that abolishes modern society's various forms of subordination to capital valorisation, to statism or ideological fundamentalism is a socialism that searches for the concrete forms in which communist sociality and

[75] Ernst Bloch, *Natural Law and Human Dignity* (Cambridge: MIT Press, 1987), p. 208.

[76] John Stuart Mill, 'On Liberty', in: John Stuart Mill, *On Liberty, Utilitarianism and Other Essays* (Oxford: Oxford University Press, 2015), pp. 1–112.

[77] Etienne Balibar, *Equaliberty: Political Essays* (Durham: Duke University Press, 2014), pp. 35–7.

liberal freedomcan be mediated in a solidary manner. Such socialism must protect and develop the foundations of the communist earth while orienting itself according to the fixed star of equaliberty. Between this heaven and earth, its task is to face the plurality of mixed communist and liberal forms of regulating the complex relations of a multiplicity of actors, and to shape these forms in accordance with solidarity.

References

Åsard, Erik (1980), 'Employee Participation in Sweden 1971–1979: The Issue of Economic Democracy', *Economic and Industrial Democracy: An International Journal*, vol. 1, n. 3: 371–93.

Balibar, Etienne (2014), *Equaliberty: Political Essays*, Durham: Duke University Press.

Barnes, Peter (2006), *Capitalism 3.0: A Guide to Reclaiming the Commons*, San Francisco: Berrett-Koehler.

Bebel, August (1910), *Woman and Socialism*, New York: Socialist Literature Co.

Bloch, Ernst (1987), *Natural Law and Human Dignity*, Cambridge: MIT Press.

Boltanski, Luc, and Chiapello, Eve (2005), *The New Spirit of Capitalism*, London: Verso.

Brie, Michael (2004), 'Der Sowjetische Staatsparteisozialismus im Lichte der Marxschen Theorie "Progressiver Epochen der ökonomischen Gesellschaftsformation"', in: Rosa-Luxemburg-Stiftung Sachsen (ed.), *Aufstieg und Fall des osteuropäischen Staatssozialismus: Ursachen und Wirkungen*, Leipzig: Rosa-Luxemburg-Stiftung Sachsen, pp. 197–233.

———. (2015),*Wie der Sozialismus praktisch wurde. Robert Owen – Reformer, Visionär, Experimentator*, Berlin: Helle Panke.

Brown, Lester R. (2008), *PLAN B 3.0: Mobilizing to Save Civilization*, New York: W. W. Norton & Co.

Candeias, Mario (2011), 'Interregnum. Molekulare Verdichtung und organische Krise', in: Alex Demirović, Julia Dück, Florian Becker, and Pauline Bader, *Vielfachkrise. Im Finanzmarktdominierten Kapitalismus*, Hamburg: VSA, pp. 45–61.

Dörre, Klaus (2019), 'Risiko Kapitalismus. Landnahme, Zangenkrise, Nachhaltigkeitsrevolution', in: Klaus Dörre, Hartmut Rosa, Karina Becker, Sophie Bose, and Benjamin Seyd (eds.), *Große Transformation? Zur Zukunft moderner Gesellschaften. Sonderband des Berliner Journals für Soziologie*, Wiesbaden: Springer VS, pp. 3–34.

Fraser, Nancy (2013), 'Feminism, Capitalism, and the Cunning of History', in: Nancy Fraser, *Fortunes of Feminism: From State-Managed Capitalism to Neoliberal Crisis*, London: Verso, pp. 209–26.

Gorbachev, Mikhail S. (1988), *Perestroika: New Thinking for Our Country and the World*, New York: Harper & Row.

Gurgsdies, Erik (2006), 'Schweden: Zivilgesellschaft im universalistischen Sozialstaat', in: Thomas Meyer (ed.), *Praxis der Sozialen Demokratie*, Wiesbaden: VS Verlag für Sozialwissenschaften, pp. 47–129.

Hegel, G. W. F. (2008), *Outlines of the Philosophy of Right*, Oxford: Oxford University Press.

Haug, Wolfgang Fritz (2007), 'Zur Dialektik des Antikapitalismus', *Das Argument*, vol. 269: 11–34.

Jessop, Bob (2008), 'Zur Relevanz von Luhmanns Systemtheorie und von Laclau und Mouffes Diskursanalyse für die Weiterentwicklung der Marxistischen Staatstheorie', in: Joachim Hirsch, John Kannankulam, and Jens Wissel (eds.), *Der Staat der Bürgerlichen Gesellschaft. Zum Staatsverständnis von Karl Marx*, Baden-Baden: Nomos, pp. 157–79.

King, Alexander, and Schneider, Bertrand (1991), *The First Global Revolution: A Report*, New York: Pantheon Books.

Krätke, Michael R. (2020), 'Capitalism', in: Marcello Musto (ed.), *The Marx Revival: Key Concepts and New Interpretations*, Cambridge: Cambridge University Press, pp. 1–23.

Land, Rainer (2018), *Ökokapital. Bedingungen der Möglichkeit eines neuen Regimes wirtschaftlicher Entwicklung. Ein systemtheoretischer Bauplan*, Düsseldorf: Forschungsinstitut für gesellschaftliche Weiterentwicklung.

Löwy, Michael (2005), *The Theory of Revolution in the Young Marx*, Chicago: Haymarket Books.

Luxemburg, Rosa (2004), *The Russian Revolution*, in: Peter Hudis and Kevin B. Anderson (eds.), *The Rosa Luxemburg Reader*, New York: Monthly Review Press, pp. 281–310.

———. (2015), *The Accumulation of Capital: A Contribution to the Economic Theory of Imperialism*, in: Peter Hudis (ed.), *The Complete Works of Rosa Luxemburg, Volume I: Economic Writings 2*, London: Verso, pp. 1–342.

Marx, Karl (1975), 'Communism and the Augsburg Allgemeine Zeitung', MECW, vol. 1, pp. 215–21.

———. (1975), 'The Supplement to Nos. 335 and 336 of the Augsburg Allgemeine Zeitung on the Commissions of the Estates in Prussia', MECW, vol. 1, pp. 292–306.

———. (1975), *Contribution to the Critique of Hegel's Philosophy of Law*, MECW, vol. 3, pp. 3–129.

———. (1975), 'On the Jewish Question', *MECW*, vol. 3, pp. 146–74.

———. (1987), *A Contribution to the Critique of Political Economy. Preface*, MECW, vol. 29, pp. 261–5.

———. (1989), *Critique of the Gotha Programme*, MECW, vol. 24, pp. 75–99.

———. (1996), *Capital, Volume I*, MECW, vol. 35.

———. (1998), *Capital, Volume III*, MECW, vol. 37.

Marx, Karl, and Engels, Friedrich (1976), *Manifesto of the Communist Party*, MECW, vol. 6, pp. 477–519.

———. (1976), *The German Ideology*, MECW, vol. 5, pp. 19–539.

Mill, John Stuart (2015), 'On Liberty', in: John Stuart Mill, *On Liberty, Utilitarianism and Other Essays*, Oxford: Oxford University Press, pp. 1–112.

Neubauer, Luisa, Thunberg, Greta, van der Heyden, Anuna de Wever, and Charlier, Adélaïde (2020), 'Open Letter and Demands to World Leaders', *Climate Emergency EU*, 16 July, https://climateemergencyeu.org.

North, Douglass C., Wallis, John Joseph, and Weingast, Barry R. (2009), *Violence and Social Orders: A Conceptual Framework for Interpreting Recorded Human History*, Cambridge: Cambridge University Press.

Ostrom, Elinor (1990), *Governing the Commons: The Evolution of Institutions for Collective Action*, Cambridge: Cambridge University Press.

Polanyi, Karl (2001), *The Great Transformation: The Political and Economic Origins of Our Time*, Boston: Beacon Press.

Rousseau, Jean-Jacques (1994), 'The Social Contract', in: Jean-Jacques Rousseau, *Discourse on Political Economy and The Social Contract*, Oxford: Oxford University Press, pp. 43–175.

Ruben, Peter (1998), 'Die Kommunistische Antwort Auf Die Soziale Frage', *Berliner Debatte Initial*, vol. 9, n. 1: 5–18.

Schumpeter, Joseph A. (2003), *Capitalism, Socialism, and Democracy*, New York: Routledge.

Sjöberg, Stefan (2006), 'Kollektive Vermögensbildung in Arbeitnehmerhand', *Utopie Kreativ*, n. 186: 311–22.

Tönnies, Ferdinand (2001), *Community and Civil Society*, Cambridge: Cambridge University Press.

Trautwein, Hans-Michael (1986), *Arbeitnehmerfonds in Schweden – Der Dritte Weg? Entwicklung und Kritik eines aktuellen Modells zur Demokratisierung der Wirtschaft*, Frankfurt am Main: Lang.

Wijkman, Anders, and Rockström, Johan (2012), *Bankrupting Nature: Denying Our Planetary Boundaries*, New York: Routledge.

Wright, Erik Olin (2010), *Envisioning Real Utopias*, London: Verso.

Wygodski, W. S. (1978), *Das Werden der ökonomischen Theorie von Marx und der Wissenschaftliche Kommunismus*, Berlin: Karl Dietz.

Index

M. Musto (ed.), *Rethinking Alternatives with Marx*, Marx, Engels, and Marxisms, https://doi.org/10.1007/978-3-030-81764-0

T

U

V

Ingram Content Group UK Ltd.
Milton Keynes UK
UKHW010224150623
423483UK00002B/18

9 783030 817633